Routing Protocols
Lab Manual

Cisco Networking Academy

Cisco Press
800 East 96th Street
Indianapolis, Indiana 46240

Routing Protocols Lab Manual

Cisco Networking Academy

First Printing October 2013

Library of Congress Control Number: 2013948299

ISBN-13: 978-1-58713-322-0

ISBN-10: 1-58713-322-9

Warning and Disclaimer

This book is designed to provide information about Routing Protocols. Every effort has been made to make this book as complete and as accurate as possible, but no warranty or fitness is implied.

The information is provided on an "as is" basis. The authors, Cisco Press, and Cisco Systems, Inc. shall have neither liability nor responsibility to any person or entity with respect to any loss or damages arising from the information contained in this book or from the use of the discs or programs that may accompany it.

The opinions expressed in this book belong to the author and are not necessarily those of Cisco Systems, Inc.

Trademark Acknowledgments

All terms mentioned in this book that are known to be trademarks or service marks have been appropriately capitalized. Cisco Press or Cisco Systems, Inc., cannot attest to the accuracy of this information. Use of a term in this book should not be regarded as affecting the validity of any trademark or service mark.

Feedback Information

At Cisco Press, our goal is to create in-depth technical books of the highest quality and value. Each book is crafted with care and precision, undergoing rigorous development that involves the unique expertise of members from the professional technical community.

Readers' feedback is a natural continuation of this process. If you have any comments regarding how we could improve the quality of this book, or otherwise alter it to better suit your needs, you can contact us through email at feedback@ciscopress.com. Please make sure to include the book title and ISBN in your message.

We greatly appreciate your assistance.

Publisher	**Paul Boger**
Associate Publisher	**Dave Dusthimer**
Business Operations Manager, Cisco Press	**Jan Cornelssen**
Executive Editor	**Mary Beth Ray**
Managing Editor	**Sandra Schroeder**
Project Editor	**Seth Kerney**
Editorial Assistant	**Vanessa Evans**
Cover Designer	**Mark Shirar**
Compositor	**TnT Design, Inc.**

Americas Headquarters	**Asia Pacific Headquarters**	**Europe Headquarters**
Cisco Systems, Inc.	Cisco Systems (USA) Pte. Ltd.	Cisco Systems International BV
San Jose, CA	Singapore	Amsterdam, The Netherlands

Cisco has more than 200 offices worldwide. Addresses, phone numbers, and fax numbers are listed on the Cisco Website at **www.cisco.com/go/offices.**

Contents

About This Lab Manual

Routing Protocols Lab Manual contains all the labs and class activities from the Cisco Networking Academy course of the same name. It is meant to be used within this program of study.

More Practice

If you would like more practice activities, combine your Lab Manual with the new *CCENT Practice and Study Guide* ISBN: 9781587133459

Other Related Titles

CCNA Routing and Switching Portable Command Guide ISBN: 9781587204302 (or eBook ISBN: 9780133381368)

Routing Protocols Companion Guide ISBN: 9781587133237 (or eBook ISBN: 9780133476323)

Routing Protocols Course Booklet ISBN: 9781587133213

Command Syntax Conventions

The conventions used to present command syntax in this book are the same conventions used in the IOS Command Reference. The Command Reference describes these conventions as follows:

- **Boldface** indicates commands and keywords that are entered literally as shown. In actual configuration examples and output (not general command syntax), boldface indicates commands that are manually input by the user (such as a **show** command).

- *Italic* indicates arguments for which you supply actual values.

- Vertical bars (|) separate alternative, mutually exclusive elements.

- Square brackets ([ ]) indicate an optional element.

- Braces ({ }) indicate a required choice.

- Braces within brackets ([{ }]) indicate a required choice within an optional element.

Chapter 1 — Routing Concepts

1.0.1.2 Class Activity– Do We Really Need a Map?

Objectives

Describe the primary functions and features of a router.

Scenario

Using the Internet and Google Maps, located at http://maps.google.com, find a route between the capital city of your country and some other distant town, or between two places within your own city. Pay close attention to the driving or walking directions Google Maps suggests.

Notice that in many cases, Google Maps suggests more than one route between the two locations you chose. It also allows you to put additional constraints on the route, such as avoiding highways or tolls.

- Copy at least two route instructions supplied by Google Maps for this activity. Place your copies into a word processing document and save it for to use with the next step.

- Open the .pdf accompanying this modeling activity and complete it with a fellow student. Discuss the reflection questions listed on the .pdf and record your answers.

Be prepared to present your answers to the class.

Resources

- Internet connection
- Web browser
- Google Maps, http://maps.google.com/

Reflection

1. What do the individual driving, or walking based on your criteria you input, and non-highway directions look like? What exact information do they contain? How do they relate to IP routing?

2. If Google Maps offered a set of different routes, what makes this route different from the first? Why would you choose one route over another?

3. What criteria can be used to evaluate the usefulness of a route?

4. Is it sensible to expect that a single route can be "the best one", i.e. meeting all various requirements? Justify your answer.

5. As a network administrator or developer, how could you use a network map, or routing table, in your daily network activities?

1.1.1.9 Lab – Mapping the Internet

Objectives

Part 1: Determine Network Connectivity to a Destination Host

Part 2: Trace a Route to a Remote Server Using Tracert

Background / Scenario

Route tracing computer software lists the networks that data traverses from the user's originating end device to a distant destination device.

This network tool is typically executed at the command line as:

```
tracert <destination network name or end device address>
```

(Microsoft Windows systems)

or

```
traceroute <destination network name or end device address>
```

(UNIX, Linux systems, and Cisco devices, such as switches and routers)

Both **tracert** and **traceroute** determine the route taken by packets across an IP network.

The **tracert** (or **traceroute**) tool is often used for network troubleshooting. By showing a list of routers traversed, the user can identify the path taken to reach a particular destination on the network or across internetworks. Each router represents a point where one network connects to another network and through which the data packet was forwarded. The number of routers is known as the number of hops the data traveled from source to destination.

The displayed list can help identify data flow problems when trying to access a service such as a website. It can also be useful when performing tasks, such as downloading data. If there are multiple websites (mirrors) available for the same data file, one can trace each mirror to get a good idea of which mirror would be the fastest to use.

Command-line based route tracing tools are usually embedded with the operating system of the end device. This activity should be performed on a computer that has Internet access and access to a command line.

Required Resources

PC with Internet access

Part 1:   Determine Network Connectivity to a Destination Host

To trace the route to a distant network, the PC used must have a working connection to the Internet. Use the **ping** command to test whether a host is reachable. Packets of information are sent to the remote host with instructions to reply. Your local PC measures whether a response is received to each packet, and how long it takes for those packets to cross the network.

a. At the command-line prompt, type **ping www.cisco.com** to determine if it is reachable.

```
C:\>ping www.cisco.com

Pinging e144.dscb.akamaiedge.net [23.1.48.170] with 32 bytes of data:
Reply from 23.1.48.170: bytes=32 time=56ms TTL=57
Reply from 23.1.48.170: bytes=32 time=55ms TTL=57
Reply from 23.1.48.170: bytes=32 time=54ms TTL=57
Reply from 23.1.48.170: bytes=32 time=54ms TTL=57

Ping statistics for 23.1.48.170:
    Packets: Sent = 4, Received = 4, Lost = 0 (0% loss),
Approximate round trip times in milli-seconds:
    Minimum = 54ms, Maximum = 56ms, Average = 54ms
```

b. Now ping one of the Regional Internet Registry (RIR) websites located in different parts of the world to determine if it is reachable:

Africa: **www.afrinic.net**

Australia: **www.apnic.net**

South America: **www.lacnic.net**

North America: **www.arin.net**

Note: At the time of writing, the European RIR www.ripe.net does not reply to ICMP echo requests.

The website you selected will be used in Part 2 for use with the **tracert** command.

Part 2:   Trace a Route to a Remote Server Using Tracert

After you determine if your chosen websites are reachable by using **ping**, you will use **tracert** to determine the path to reach the remote server. It is helpful to look more closely at each network segment that is crossed.

Each hop in the **tracert** results displays the routes that the packets take when traveling to the final destination. The PC sends three ICMP echo request packets to the remote host. Each router in the path decrements the time to live (TTL) value by 1 before passing it onto the next system. When the decremented TTL value reaches 0, the router sends an ICMP Time Exceeded message back to the source with its IP address and the current time. When the final destination is reached, an ICMP echo reply is sent to the source host.

For example, the source host sends three ICMP echo request packets to the first hop (192.168.1.1) with the TTL value of 1. When the router 192.168.1.1 receives the echo request packets, it decrements the TTL value to 0. The router sends an ICMP Time Exceeded message back to the source. This process continues until the source hosts sends the last three ICMP echo request packets with TTL values of 8 (hop number 8 in the output below), which is the final destination. After the ICMP echo request packets arrive at the final destination, the router responds to the source with ICMP echo replies.

For hops 2 and 3, these IP addresses are private addresses. These routers are the typical setup for point-of-presence (POP) of ISP. The POP devices connect users to an ISP network.

A web-based whois tool is found at http://whois.domaintools.com/. It is used to determine the domains traveled from the source to destination.

a. At the command-line prompt, trace the route to www.cisco.com. Save the **tracert** output in a text file. Alternatively, you can redirect the output to a text file by using **>** or **>>**.

```
C:\Users\User1> tracert www.cisco.com
```

or

```
C:\Users\User1> tracert www.cisco.com > tracert-cisco.txt


Tracing route to e144.dscb.akamaiedge.net [23.67.208.170]

over a maximum of 30 hops:


  1      1 ms     <1 ms     <1 ms   192.168.1.1

  2     14 ms      7 ms      7 ms   10.39.0.1

  3     10 ms      8 ms      7 ms   172.21.0.118

  4     11 ms     11 ms     11 ms   70.169.73.196

  5     10 ms      9 ms     11 ms   70.169.75.157

  6     60 ms     49 ms      *      68.1.2.109

  7     43 ms     39 ms     38 ms   Equinix-DFW2.netarch.akamai.com [206.223.118.102]

  8     33 ms     35 ms     33 ms   a23-67-208-170.deploy.akamaitechnologies.com
[23.67.208.170]


Trace complete.
```

b. The web-based tool at http://whois.domaintools.com/ can be used to determine the owners of both the resulting IP address and domain names shown in the tracert tools output. Now perform a **tracert** to one of RIR web sites from Part 1 and save the results.

Africa: **www.afrinic.net**

Australia: **www.apnic.net**

Europe: **www.ripe.net**

South America: **www.lacnic.net**

North America: **www.arin.net**

List the domains below from your tracert results using the web-based whois tool.

____

____

c. Compare the lists of domains crossed to reach the final destinations.

Reflection

What can affect **tracert** results?

____

____

1.1.4.6 Lab – Configuring Basic Router Settings with IOS CLI

Topology

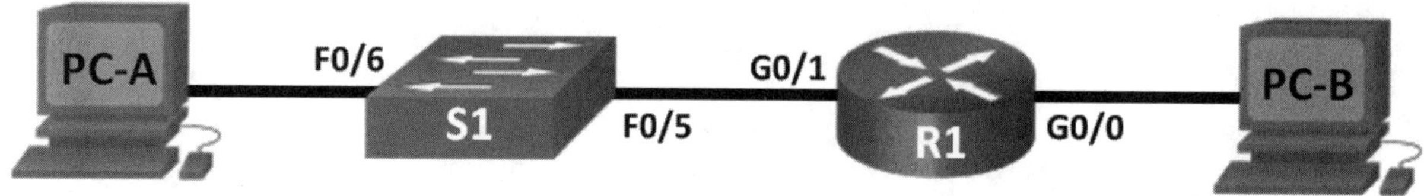

Addressing Table

Device	Interface	IP Address	Subnet Mask	Default Gateway
R1	G0/0	192.168.0.1	255.255.255.0	N/A
	G0/1	192.168.1.1	255.255.255.0	N/A
PC-A	NIC	192.168.1.3	255.255.255.0	192.168.1.1
PC-B	NIC	192.168.0.3	255.255.255.0	192.168.0.1

Objectives

Part 1: Set Up the Topology and Initialize Devices

- Cable equipment to match the network topology.
- Initialize and restart the router and switch.

Part 2: Configure Devices and Verify Connectivity

- Assign static IPv4 information to the PC interfaces.
- Configure basic router settings.
- Verify network connectivity.
- Configure the router for SSH.

Part 3: Display Router Information

- Retrieve hardware and software information from the router.
- Interpret the output from the startup configuration.
- Interpret the output from the routing table.
- Verify the status of the interfaces.

Part 4: Configure IPv6 and Verify Connectivity

Background / Scenario

This is a comprehensive lab to review previously covered IOS router commands. In Parts 1 and 2, you will cable the equipment and complete basic configurations and IPv4 interface settings on the router.

In Part 3, you will use SSH to connect to the router remotely and utilize IOS commands to retrieve information from the device to answer questions about the router. In Part 4, you will configure IPv6 on the router so that PC-B can acquire an IP address and then verify connectivity.

For review purposes, this lab provides the commands necessary for specific router configurations.

Note: The routers used with CCNA hands-on labs are Cisco 1941 Integrated Services Routers (ISRs) with Cisco IOS Release 15.2(4)M3 (universalk9 image). The switches used are Cisco Catalyst 2960 with Cisco IOS Release 15.0(2) (lanbasek9 image). Other routers, switches, and Cisco IOS versions can be used. Depending on the model and Cisco IOS version, the commands available and output produced might vary from what is shown in the labs. Refer to the Router Interface Summary Table at the end of this lab for the correct interface identifiers.

Note: Make sure that the router and switch have been erased and have no startup configurations. Refer to Appendix A for the procedures to initialize and reload devices.

Required Resources

- 1 Router (Cisco 1941 with Cisco IOS Release 15.2(4)M3 universal image or comparable)
- 1 Switch (Cisco 2960 with Cisco IOS Release 15.0(2) lanbasek9 image or comparable)
- 2 PCs (Windows 7, Vista, or XP with terminal emulation program, such as Tera Term)
- Console cables to configure the Cisco IOS devices via the console ports
- Ethernet cables as shown in the topology

Note: The Gigabit Ethernet interfaces on Cisco 1941 ISRs are autosensing and an Ethernet straight-through cable can be used between the router and PC-B. If using another model Cisco router, it may be necessary to use an Ethernet crossover cable.

Part 1: Set Up the Topology and Initialize Devices

Step 1: Cable the network as shown in the topology.

a. Attach the devices as shown in the topology diagram, and cable as necessary.

b. Power on all the devices in the topology.

Step 2: Initialize and reload the router and switch.

Note: Appendix A details the steps to initialize and reload the devices.

Part 2: Configure Devices and Verify Connectivity

Step 1: Configure the PC interfaces.

a. Configure the IP address, subnet mask, and default gateway settings on PC-A.

b. Configure the IP address, subnet mask, and default gateway settings on PC-B.

Step 2: Configure the router.

a. Console into the router and enable privileged EXEC mode.

```
Router> enable
Router#
```

b. Enter into global configuration mode.

```
Router# config terminal
Router(config)#
```

c. Assign a device name to the router.

```
Router(config)# hostname R1
```

d. Disable DNS lookup to prevent the router from attempting to translate incorrectly entered commands as though they were hostnames.

```
R1(config)# no ip domain-lookup
```

e. Require that a minimum of 10 characters be used for all passwords.

```
R1(config)# security passwords min-length 10
```

Besides setting a minimum length, list other ways to strengthen passwords.

____

f. Assign **cisco12345** as the privileged EXEC encrypted password.

```
R1(config)# enable secret cisco12345
```

g. Assign **ciscoconpass** as the console password, establish a timeout, enable login, and add the **logging synchronous** command. The **logging synchronous** command synchronizes debug and Cisco IOS software output and prevents these messages from interrupting your keyboard input.

```
R1(config)# line con 0
R1(config-line)# password ciscoconpass
R1(config-line)# exec-timeout 5 0
R1(config-line)# login
R1(config-line)# logging synchronous
R1(config-line)# exit
R1(config)#
```

For the **exec-timeout** command, what do the **5** and **0** represent?

____

h. Assign **ciscovtypass** as the vty password, establish a timeout, enable login, and add the **logging synchronous** command.

```
R1(config)# line vty 0 4
R1(config-line)# password ciscovtypass
R1(config-line)# exec-timeout 5 0
R1(config-line)# login
R1(config-line)# logging synchronous
R1(config-line)# exit
R1(config)#
```

i. Encrypt the clear text passwords.

```
R1(config)# service password-encryption
```

j. Create a banner that warns anyone accessing the device that unauthorized access is prohibited.

```
R1(config)# banner motd #Unauthorized access prohibited!#
```

k. Configure an IP address and interface description. Activate both interfaces on the router.

```
R1(config)# int g0/0
R1(config-if)# description Connection to PC-B
R1(config-if)# ip address 192.168.0.1 255.255.255.0
R1(config-if)# no shutdown
R1(config-if)# int g0/1
R1(config-if)# description Connection to S1
R1(config-if)# ip address 192.168.1.1 255.255.255.0
R1(config-if)# no shutdown
R1(config-if)# exit
R1(config)# exit
R1#
```

l. Set the clock on the router; for example:

```
R1# clock set 17:00:00 18 Feb 2013
```

m. Save the running configuration to the startup configuration file.

```
R1# copy running-config startup-config
Destination filename [startup-config]?
Building configuration...
[OK]
R1#
```

What would be the result of reloading the router prior to completing the **copy running-config startup-config** command?

____

Step 3:   **Verify network connectivity.**

a. Ping PC-B from a command prompt on PC-A.

Note: It may be necessary to disable the PCs firewall.

Were the pings successful? _____

After completing this series of commands, what type of remote access could be used to access R1?

____

b. Remotely access R1 from PC-A using the Tera Term Telnet client.

Open Tera Term and enter the G0/1 interface IP address of R1 in the Host: field of the Tera Term: New Connection window. Ensure that the **Telnet** radio button is selected and then click **OK** to connect to the router.

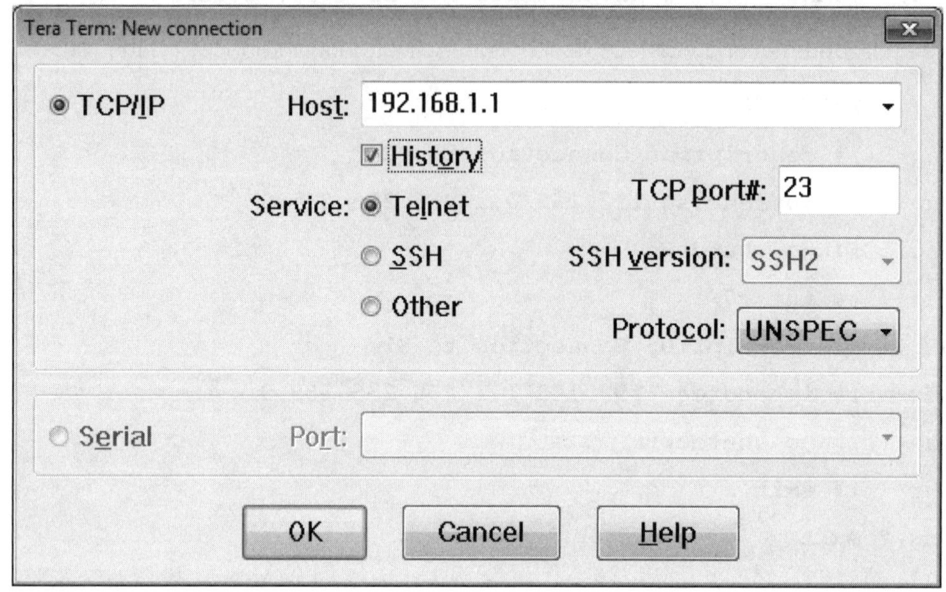

Was remote access successful? _____

Why is the Telnet protocol considered to be a security risk?

____

Step 4:   Configure the router for SSH access.

a. Enable SSH connections and create a user in the local database of the router.

```
R1# configure terminal
R1(config)# ip domain-name CCNA-lab.com
R1(config)# username admin privilege 15 secret adminpass1
R1(config)# line vty 0 4
R1(config-line)# transport input ssh
R1(config-line)# login local
R1(config-line)# exit
R1(config)# crypto key generate rsa modulus 1024
R1(config)# exit
```

b. Remotely access R1 from PC-A using the Tera Term SSH client.

Open Tera Term and enter the G0/1 interface IP address of R1 in the Host: field of the Tera Term: New Connection window. Ensure that the **SSH** radio button is selected and then click **OK** to connect to the router.

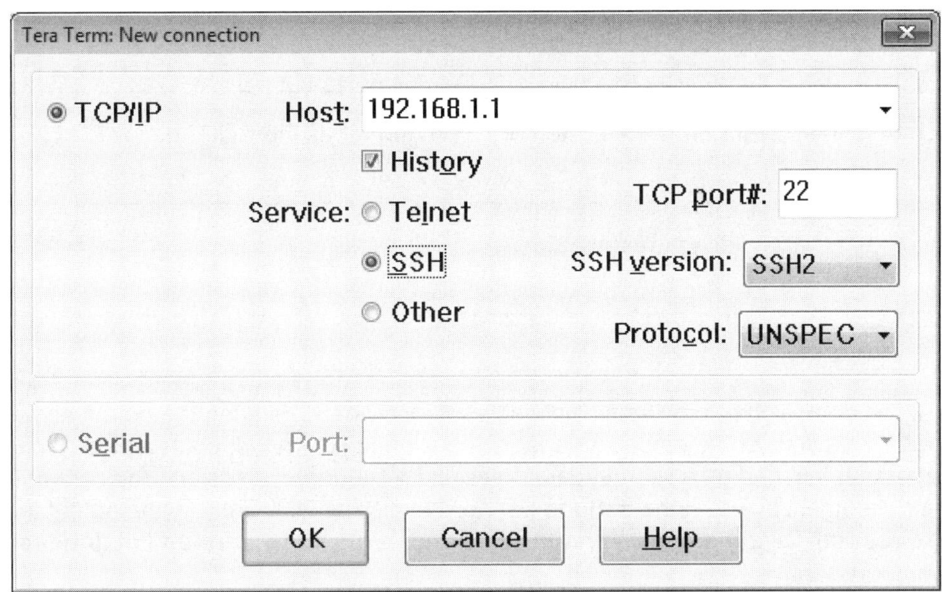

Was remote access successful? _____

Part 3: Display Router Information

In Part 3, you will use **show** commands from an SSH session to retrieve information from the router.

Step 1: Establish an SSH session to R1.

Using Tera Term on PC-B, open an SSH session to R1 at IP address 192.168.0.1 and log in as **admin** with the password **adminpass1**.

Step 2: Retrieve important hardware and software information.

a. Use the **show version** command to answer questions about the router.

What is the name of the IOS image that the router is running?

How much non-volatile random-access memory (NVRAM) does the router have?

How much Flash memory does the router have?

b. The **show** commands often provide multiple screens of outputs. Filtering the output allows a user to display certain sections of the output. To enable the filtering command, enter a pipe (|) character after a **show** command, followed by a filtering parameter and a filtering expression. You can match the output to the filtering statement by using the **include** keyword to display all lines from the output that contain the filtering expression. Filter the **show version** command, using **show version | include register** to answer the following question.

What is the boot process for the router on the next reload?

Step 3:   **Display the startup configuration.**

Use the **show startup-config** command on the router to answer the following questions.

How are passwords presented in the output?

____

____

____

Use the **show startup-config | begin vty** command.

What is the result of using this command?

____

____

Step 4:   **Display the routing table on the router.**

Use the **show ip route** command on the router to answer the following questions.

What code is used in the routing table to indicate a directly connected network?

How many route entries are coded with a C code in the routing table? ______

Step 5: **Display a summary list of the interfaces on the router.**

Use the **show ip interface brief** command on the router to answer the following question.

What command changed the status of the Gigabit Ethernet ports from administratively down to up?

Part 4: Configure IPv6 and Verify Connectivity

Step 1: **Assign IPv6 addresses to R1 G0/0 and enable IPv6 routing.**

Note: Assigning an IPv6 address in addition to an IPv4 address on an interface is known as dual stacking, because both the IPv4 and IPv6 protocol stacks are active. By enabling IPv6 unicast routing on R1, PC-B receives the R1 G0/0 IPv6 network prefix and can autoconfigure its IPv6 address and its default gateway.

a. Assign an IPv6 global unicast address to interface G0/0, assign the link-local address in addition to the unicast address on the interface, and enable IPv6 routing.

```
R1# configure terminal
R1(config)# interface g0/0
R1(config-if)# ipv6 address 2001:db8:acad:a::1/64
R1(config-if)# ipv6 address fe80::1 link-local
R1(config-if)# no shutdown
R1(config-if)# exit
R1(config)# ipv6 unicast-routing
R1(config)# exit
```

b.   Use the **show ipv6 int brief** command to verify IPv6 settings on R1.

If no IPv6 address is assigned to G0/1, why is it listed as [up/up]?

____

____

c.   Issue the **ipconfig** command on PC-B to examine the IPv6 configuration.

What is the IPv6 address assigned to PC-B?

____

What is the default gateway assigned to PC-B? ______________

Issue a ping from PC-B to the R1 default gateway link local address. Was it successful? ________

Issue a ping from PC-B to the R1 IPv6 unicast address 2001:db8:acad:a::1. Was it successful? ________

Reflection

1.   In researching a network connectivity issue, a technician suspects that an interface was not enabled. What **show** command could the technician use to troubleshoot this issue?

____

2.   In researching a network connectivity issue, a technician suspects that an interface was assigned an incorrect subnet mask. What **show** command could the technician use to troubleshoot this issue?

____

3.   After configuring IPv6 on the R1 G0/0 PC-B LAN, if you were to ping from PC-A to the PC-B IPv6 address, would the ping succeed? Why or why not?

____

Router Interface Summary Table

Router Interface Summary				
Router Model	**Ethernet Interface #1**	**Ethernet Interface #2**	**Serial Interface #1**	**Serial Interface #2**
1800	Fast Ethernet 0/0 (F0/0)	Fast Ethernet 0/1 (F0/1)	Serial 0/0/0 (S0/0/0)	Serial 0/0/1 (S0/0/1)
1900	Gigabit Ethernet 0/0 (G0/0)	Gigabit Ethernet 0/1 (G0/1)	Serial 0/0/0 (S0/0/0)	Serial 0/0/1 (S0/0/1)
2801	Fast Ethernet 0/0 (F0/0)	Fast Ethernet 0/1 (F0/1)	Serial 0/1/0 (S0/1/0)	Serial 0/1/1 (S0/1/1)
2811	Fast Ethernet 0/0 (F0/0)	Fast Ethernet 0/1 (F0/1)	Serial 0/0/0 (S0/0/0)	Serial 0/0/1 (S0/0/1)
2900	Gigabit Ethernet 0/0 (G0/0)	Gigabit Ethernet 0/1 (G0/1)	Serial 0/0/0 (S0/0/0)	Serial 0/0/1 (S0/0/1)

Note: To find out how the router is configured, look at the interfaces to identify the type of router and how many interfaces the router has. There is no way to effectively list all the combinations of configurations for each router class. This table includes identifiers for the possible combinations of Ethernet and Serial interfaces in the device. The table does not include any other type of interface, even though a specific router may contain one. An example of this might be an ISDN BRI interface. The string in parenthesis is the legal abbreviation that can be used in Cisco IOS commands to represent the interface.

Appendix A: Initializing and Reloading a Router and Switch

Step 1:   Initialize and reload the router.

    a.   Console into the router and enable privileged EXEC mode.

```
Router> enable
Router#
```

    b.   Type the **erase startup-config** command to remove the startup configuration from NVRAM.

```
Router# erase startup-config
Erasing the nvram filesystem will remove all configuration files! Continue? [confirm]
[OK]
Erase of nvram: complete
Router#
```

    c.   Issue the **reload** command to remove an old configuration from memory. When prompted to **Proceed with reload**, press Enter to confirm the reload. (Pressing any other key aborts the reload.)

```
Router# reload
Proceed with reload? [confirm]
*Nov 29 18:28:09.923: %SYS-5-RELOAD: Reload requested by console. Reload Reason:
Reload Command.
```

    Note: You may be prompted to save the running configuration prior to reloading the router. Type **no** and press Enter.

```
System configuration has been modified. Save? [yes/no]: no
```

d. After the router reloads, you are prompted to enter the initial configuration dialog. Enter **no** and press Enter.

```
Would you like to enter the initial configuration dialog? [yes/no]: no
```

e. You are prompted to terminate autoinstall. Type **yes** and then press Enter.

```
Would you like to terminate autoinstall? [yes]: yes
```

Step 2:   Initialize and reload the switch.

a. Console into the switch and enter privileged EXEC mode.

```
Switch> enable
Switch#
```

b. Use the **show flash** command to determine if any VLANs have been created on the switch.

```
Switch# show flash

Directory of flash:/

    2  -rwx        1919    Mar 1 1993 00:06:33 +00:00  private-config.text
    3  -rwx        1632    Mar 1 1993 00:06:33 +00:00  config.text
    4  -rwx       13336    Mar 1 1993 00:06:33 +00:00  multiple-fs
    5  -rwx    11607161    Mar 1 1993 02:37:06 +00:00  c2960-lanbasek9-mz.150-2.SE.bin
    6  -rwx         616    Mar 1 1993 00:07:13 +00:00  vlan.dat

32514048 bytes total (20886528 bytes free)
Switch#
```

c. If the **vlan.dat** file was found in flash, then delete this file.

```
Switch# delete vlan.dat
Delete filename [vlan.dat]?
```

d. You are prompted to verify the filename. At this point, you can change the filename or just press Enter if you have entered the name correctly.

e. You are prompted to confirm deleting this file. Press Enter to confirm deletion. (Pressing any other key aborts the deletion.)

```
Delete flash:/vlan.dat? [confirm]
Switch#
```

f. Use the **erase startup-config** command to erase the startup configuration file from NVRAM. You are prompted to confirm removing the configuration file. Press Enter to confirm to erase this file. (Pressing any other key aborts the operation.)

```
Switch# erase startup-config
Erasing the nvram filesystem will remove all configuration files! Continue? [confirm]
[OK]
Erase of nvram: complete
Switch#
```

g. Reload the switch to remove any old configuration information from memory. You are prompted to confirm reloading the switch. Press Enter to proceed with the reload. (Pressing any other key aborts the reload.)

```
Switch# reload

Proceed with reload? [confirm]
```

Note: You may be prompted to save the running configuration prior to reloading the switch. Type **no** and press Enter.

```
System configuration has been modified. Save? [yes/no]: no
```

h. After the switch reloads, you should be prompted to enter the initial configuration dialog. Type **no** and press Enter.

```
Would you like to enter the initial configuration dialog? [yes/no]: no

Switch>
```

1.1.4.7 Lab – Configuring Basic Router Settings with CCP

Topology

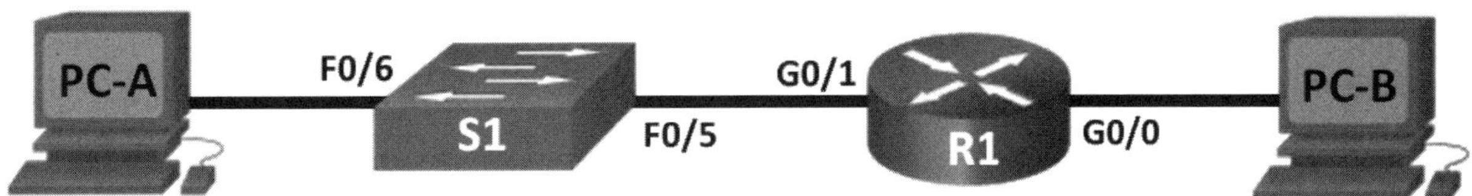

Addressing Table

Device	Interface	IP Address	Subnet Mask	Default Gateway
R1	G0/0	192.168.0.1	255.255.255.0	N/A
	G0/1	192.168.1.1	255.255.255.0	N/A
S1	VLAN 1	N/A	N/A	N/A
PC-A	NIC	192.168.1.3	255.255.255.0	192.168.1.1
PC-B	NIC	192.168.0.3	255.255.255.0	192.168.0.1

Objectives

Part 1: Set Up the Topology and Initialize Devices

Part 2: Configure Devices and Verify Connectivity

Part 3: Configure Router to Allow CCP Access

Part 4: (Optional) Install and Set Up CCP on PC-A

Part 5: Configure R1 Settings Using CCP

Part 6: Use CCP Utilities

Background / Scenario

Cisco Configuration Professional (CCP) is a PC-based application that provides GUI-based device management for Integrated Services Routers (ISRs). It simplifies the configuration of routing, firewall, VPN, WAN, LAN, and other settings through menus and easy-to-use wizards.

In this lab, you will configure the router settings using the configuration from the previous lab in this chapter. Layer 3 connectivity must be established between the PC running CCP (PC-A) and R1 before CCP can establish a connection. In addition, HTTP access and authentication must be configured on R1.

You will download and install CCP on the PC and then use it to monitor R1's interface status, configure an interface, set the date and time, add a user to the local database, and edit vty settings. You will also use some of the utilities included in CCP.

Note: Router configurations performed using CCP generate IOS CLI commands. CCP can be very useful for configuring more complex router features because it does not require specific knowledge of the Cisco IOS command syntax.

Note: The routers used with CCNA hands-on labs are Cisco 1941 Integrated Services Routers (ISRs) with Cisco IOS Release 15.2(4)M3 (universalk9 image). The switches used are Cisco Catalyst 2960s with Cisco IOS Release 15.0(2) (lanbasek9 image). Other routers, switches, and Cisco IOS versions can be used. Depending on the model and Cisco IOS version, the commands available and output produced might vary from what is shown in the labs. Refer to the Router Interface Summary Table at the end of this lab for the correct interface identifiers.

Note: Make sure that the router and switch have been erased and have no startup configurations. If you are unsure, contact your instructor.

Required Resources

- 1 Router (Cisco 1941 with Cisco IOS Release 15.2(4)M3 universal image or comparable)
- 1 Switch (Cisco 2960 with Cisco IOS Release 15.0(2) lanbasek9 image or comparable)
- 2 PCs (Windows 7, Vista, or XP with terminal emulation program, such as Tera Term)
- Console cables to configure the Cisco IOS devices via the console ports
- Ethernet cables as shown in the topology

Note: PC system requirements for CCP version 2.6 are:

- 2 GHz processor or faster
- 1 GB DRAM minimum; 2 GB recommended
- 400 MB of available hard disk space
- Internet Explorer 6.0 or above
- Screen resolution of 1024x768 or higher
- Java Runtime Environment (JRE) version 1.6.0_11 or later.
- Adobe Flash Player version 10.0 or later, with Debug set to No

Note: The Gigabit Ethernet interfaces on Cisco 1941 ISRs are autosensing and an Ethernet straight-through cable may be used between the router and PC-B. If using another model Cisco router, it may be necessary to use an Ethernet crossover cable.

Part 1:   Set Up the Topology and Initialize Devices

Step 1:   Cable the network as shown in the topology.

a.   Attach the devices shown in the topology diagram, and cable as necessary.

b.   Power on all the devices in the topology.

Step 2:   Initialize and reload the router and switch.

Part 2:   Configure Devices and Verify Connectivity

In Part 2, you will configure basic settings, such as the interface IP addresses (G0/1 only), secure device access, and passwords. Refer to the Topology and Addressing Table for device names and address information.

Step 1: Configure the PC interfaces.

   a. Configure the IP address, subnet mask, and default gateway settings on PC-A.

   b. Configure the IP address, subnet mask, and default gateway settings on PC-B.

Step 2: Configure the router.

   Note: Do NOT configure interface G0/0 at this time. You will configure this interface using CCP later in the lab.

   a. Console into the router and enable privileged EXEC mode.

   b. Enter into global configuration mode.

   c. Disable DNS lookup.

   d. Assign a device name to the router.

   e. Require that a minimum of 10 characters be used for all passwords.

   f. Assign **cisco12345** as the privileged EXEC encrypted password.

   g. Assign **ciscoconpass** as the console password and enable login.

   h. Assign **ciscovtypass** as the vty password and enable login,

   i. Configure **logging synchronous** on the console and vty lines.

   j. Encrypt the clear text passwords.

   k. Create a banner that warns anyone accessing the device that unauthorized access is prohibited.

   l. Configure the IP addresses, an interface description, and activate G0/1 interface on the router.

   m. Save the running configuration to the startup configuration file.

Step 3: Verify network connectivity.

   Verify that you can ping R1 G0/1 from PC-A.

Part 3: Configure the Router to Allow CCP Access

   In Part 3, you will set up the router to allow CCP access by enabling HTTP and HTTPS server services. You will also enable HTTP authentication to use the local database.

Step 1: Enable HTTP and HTTPS server services on the router.

```
R1(config)# ip http server
R1(config)# ip http secure-server
```

Step 2: Enable HTTP authentication to use the local database on the router.

```
R1(config)# ip http authentication local
```

Step 3:   Configure the router for CCP access.

Assign a user in the router local database for accessing CCP using username **admin** and password **admin-pass1**.

```
R1(config)# username admin privilege 15 secret adminpass1
```

Part 4:   (Optional) Install and Set Up CCP on PC-A

Step 1:   Install CCP.

Note: This step can be skipped if CCP is already installed on PC-A.

a.   Download CCP 2.6 from Cisco's website:

http://software.cisco.com/download/release.html?mdfid=281795035&softwareid=282159854&release=2.6&rellifecycle=&relind=AVAILABLE&reltype=all

b.   Choose the **cisco-config-pro-k9-pkg-2_6-en.zip** file.

Note: Verify that you select the correct CCP file and not CCP Express. If there is a more current release of CCP, you may choose to download it; however, this lab is based on CCP 2.6.

c.   Agree to the terms and conditions, and download and save the file to the desired location.

d.   Open the zip file and run the CCP executable.

e.   Follow the on-screen instructions to install CCP 2.6 on your PC.

Step 2:   Change settings to run as the administrator.

CCP may fail to launch correctly if it is not run as an administrator. You can change the launch settings so that it automatically runs in administrator mode.

a.   Right-click the **CCP** desktop icon (or click the **Start** button) and then right-click **Cisco Configuration Professional**. In the drop-down list, select **Properties**.

b.   In the Properties dialog box, select the **Compatibility** tab. In the Privilege Level section, click the **Run this program as an administrator** checkbox, and then click **OK**.

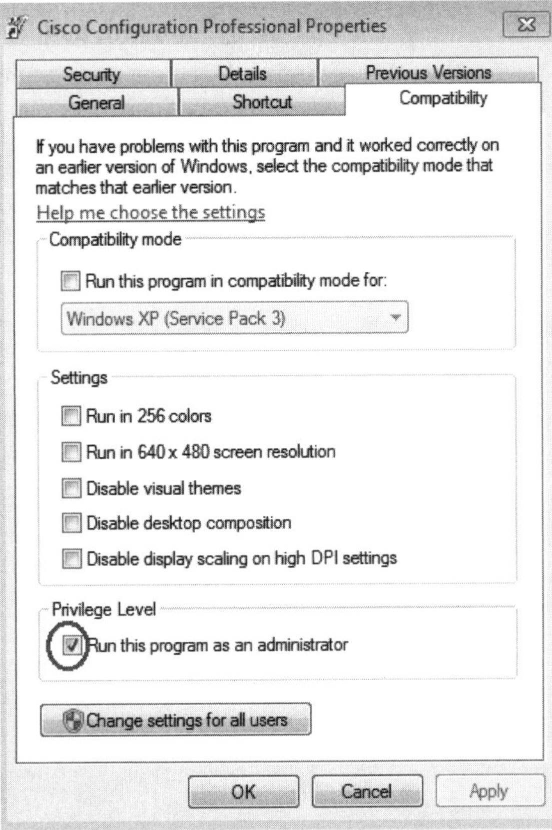

Step 3: **Create or manage communities.**

a. On PC-A, start CCP. (Double-click the CCP desktop icon or click **Start** > **Cisco Configuration Professional**.)

b. If you receive a security warning message prompting to allow the CiscoCP.exe program to make changes to the computer, click **Yes**.

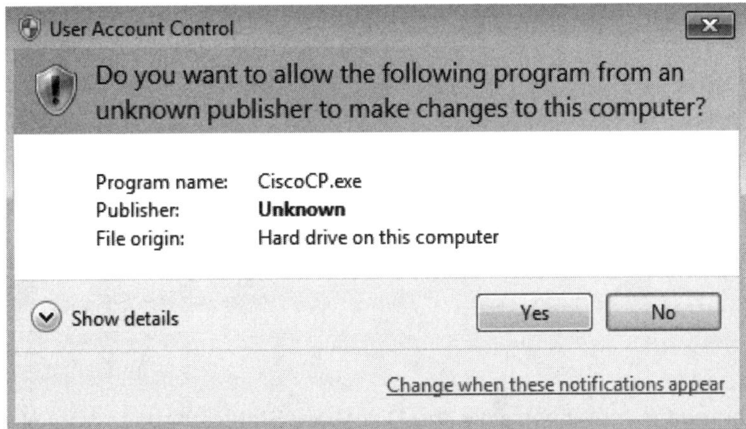

c. When CCP starts, the **Select / Mange Community** dialog box displays. Enter the IP address for R1 G0/1, and the username **admin** and password **adminpass1** that you added to the local database during the router configuration in Part 2. Click **OK**.

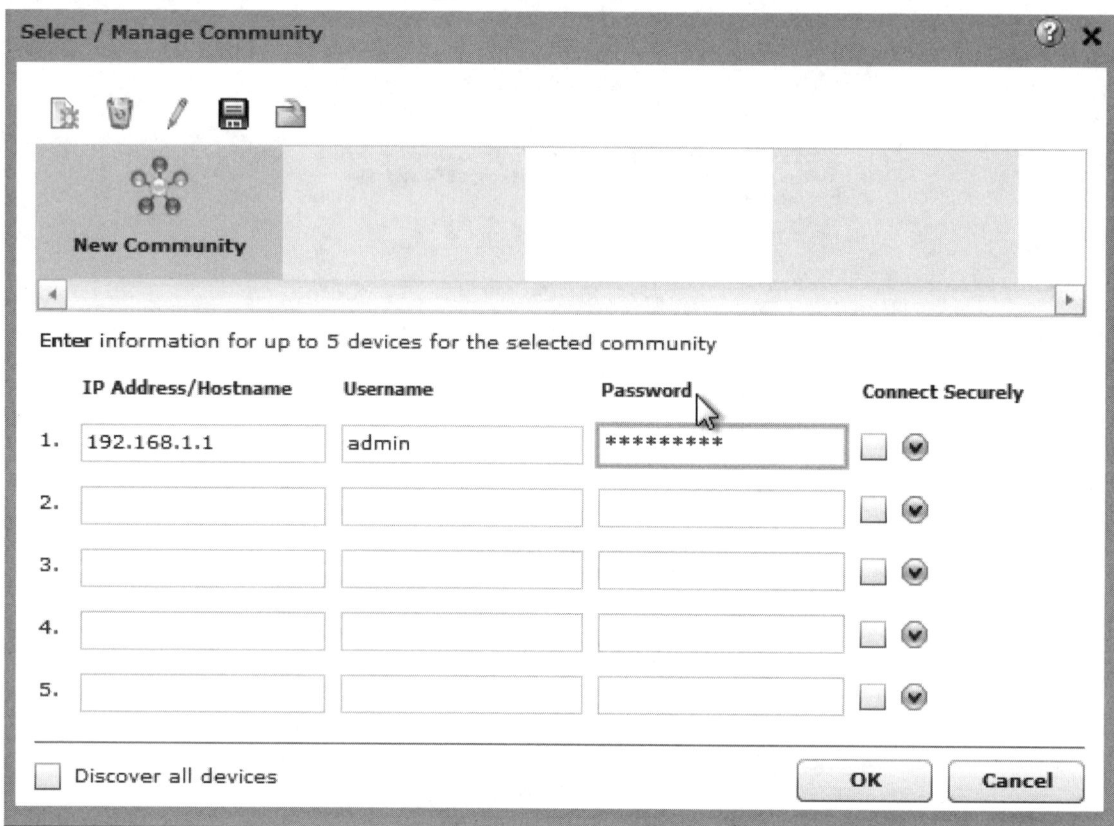

d. In the Community Information window, click **Discover**.

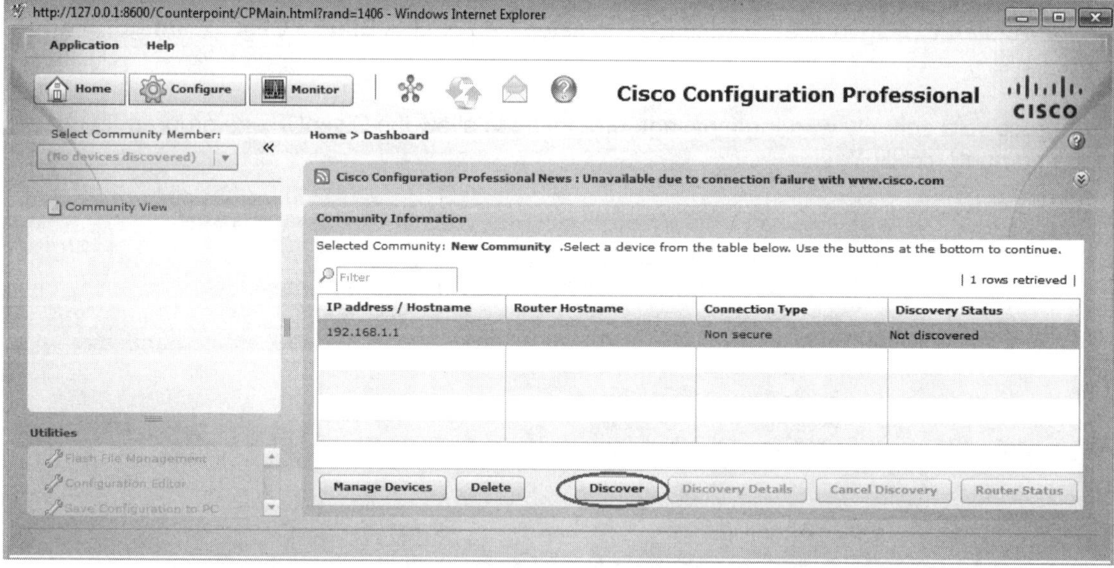

If you have configured the router correctly, the Discovery Status changes from **Not discovered** to **Discovered**, and R1 appears in the Router Hostname column.

Note: If there is a problem with your configuration, you will see a "Discovery failed" status. Click **Discovery Details** to determine why the discovery process failed and then troubleshoot the problem.

Part 5: Configure R1 Settings Using CCP

In Part 5, you will use CCP to display information about R1, configure interface G0/0, set the date and time, add a user to the local database, and change your vty settings.

Step 1: **View the status of the interfaces on R1.**

a. On the CCP toolbar, click **Monitor**.

b. In the left navigation pane, click **Router** > **Overview** to display the Monitor Overview screen in the right content pane.

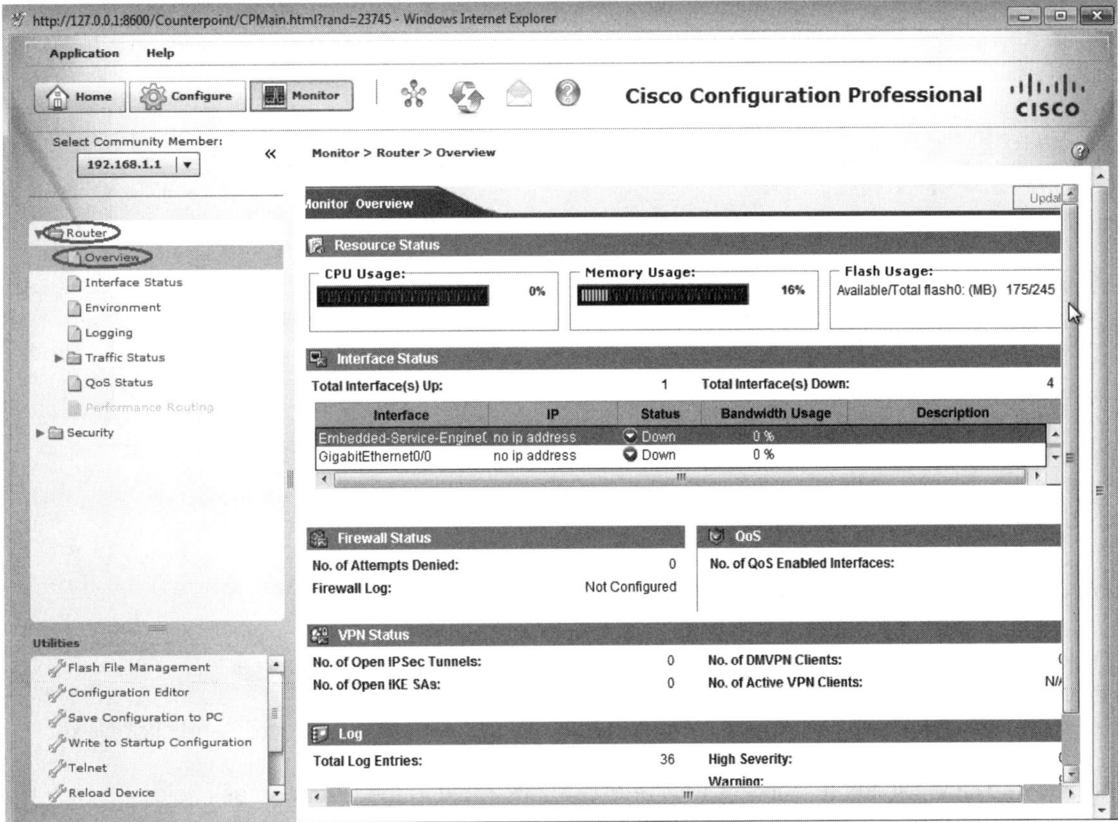

c. Use the up and down arrows to the right of the interface list to scroll through the list of interfaces for the router.

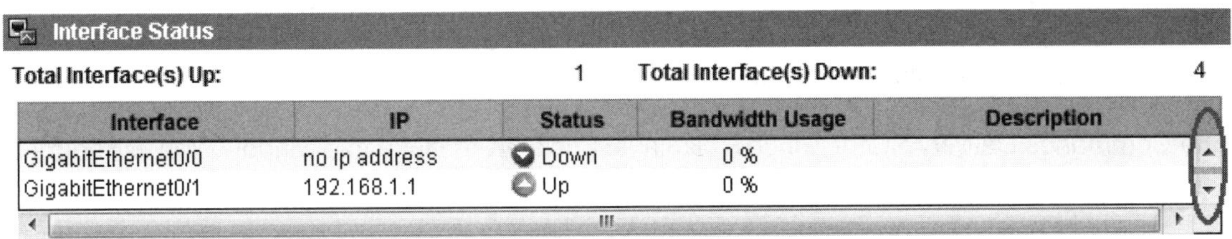

Step 2:   **Use the Ethernet LAN wizard to configure interface G0/0.**

a.   On the CCP toolbar, click **Configure**.

b.   In the left navigation pane, click **Interface Management** > **Interface and Connections** to display the Interfaces and Connections screen in the right content pane.

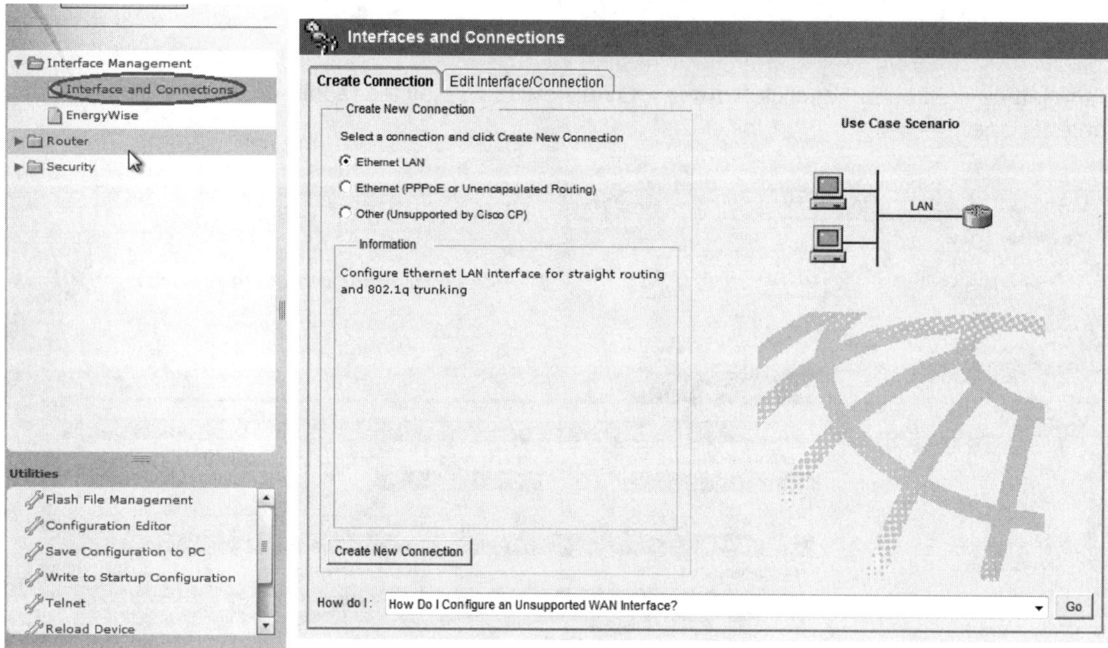

c.   Click **Create New Connection** to start the Ethernet LAN wizard.

d.   When you are prompted to enable AAA on the router, click **No**.

e.   Click **Next** to be guided through the Layer 3 Ethernet interface creation process.

f.   Keep the **Configure this interface for straight routing** radio button selected and click **Next**.

g.   Enter **192.168.0.1** in the IP address field and **255.255.255.0** in the Subnet mask field and click **Next**.

h.   Keep the **No** radio button selected on the DHCP server screen and click **Next**.

i.   Review the summary screen and click **Finish**.

j.   Click the **Save running config to device's startup config** check box, and then click **Deliver**. This adds the commands shown in the preview window to the running configuration, and then saves the running configuration to the startup configuration on the router.

k.   The Commands Delivery Status window displays. Click **OK** to close this window. You will be routed back to the Interfaces and Connections screen; G0/0 should have turned green and displayed as Up in the Status column.

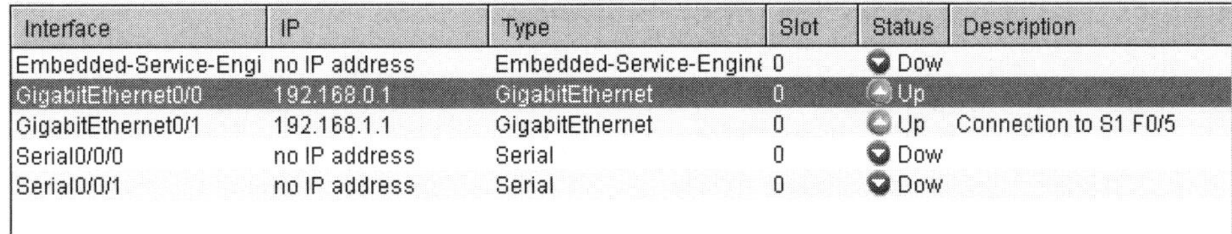

Interface	IP	Type	Slot	Status	Description
Embedded-Service-Engi	no IP address	Embedded-Service-Engine	0	Dow	
GigabitEthernet0/0	192.168.0.1	GigabitEthernet	0	Up	
GigabitEthernet0/1	192.168.1.1	GigabitEthernet	0	Up	Connection to S1 F0/5
Serial0/0/0	no IP address	Serial	0	Dow	
Serial0/0/1	no IP address	Serial	0	Dow	

Step 3: **Set the date and time on the router.**

a. In the left navigation pane, select **Router** > **Time** > **Date and Time** to display the Additional Tasks > Date/ Time screen in the right content pane. Click **Change Settings….**

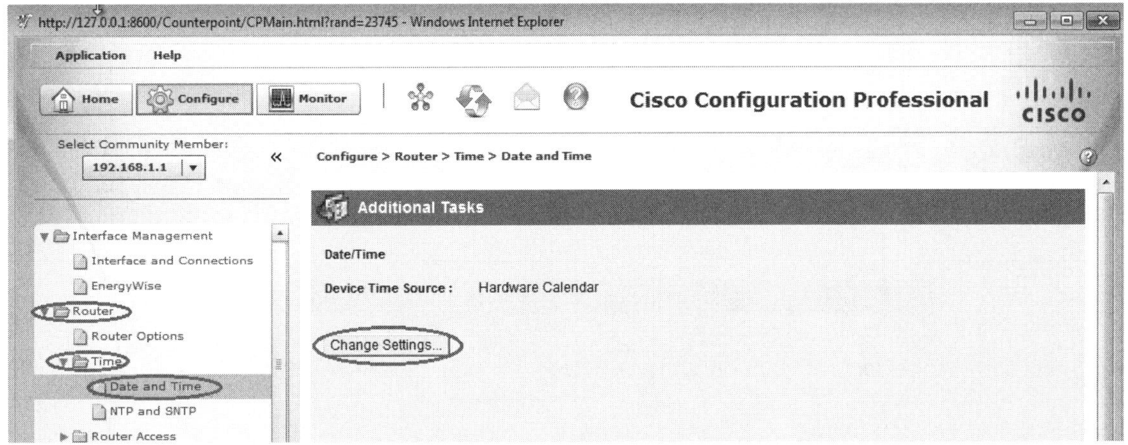

b. In the Date and Time Properties window, edit the Date, Time, and Time Zone. Click **Apply.**

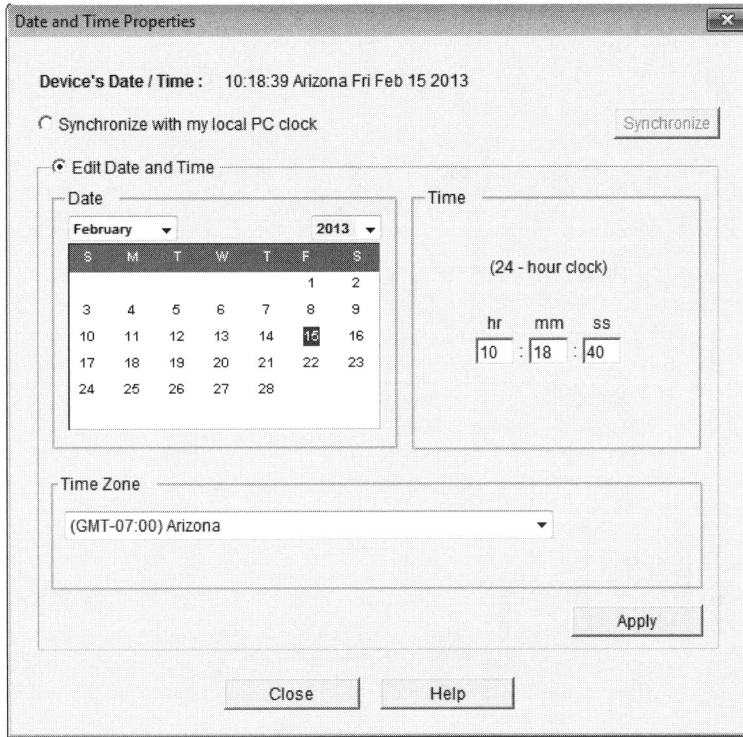

c. In the Router's clock configured window, click **OK**. In the Date and Time Properties window, click **Close**.

Step 4:   **Add a new user account to the local database.**

a.   In the left navigation pane, select **Router** > **Router Access** > **User Accounts/View** to display the Additional Tasks > User Accounts/View screen in the content pane on the right. Click the **Add...** button.

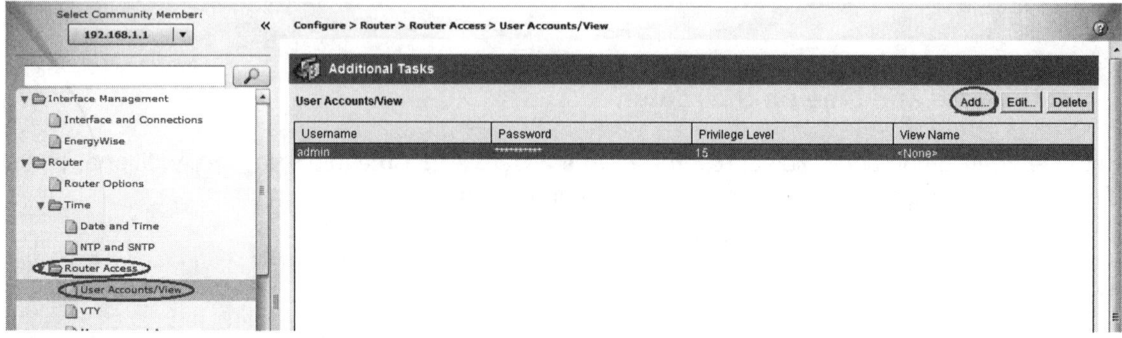

b.   Enter **ccpadmin** in the Username: field. Enter **ciscoccppass** in the New Password: and Confirm New Password: fields. Select **15** in the Privilege Level: drop-down list. Click **OK** to add this user to the local database.

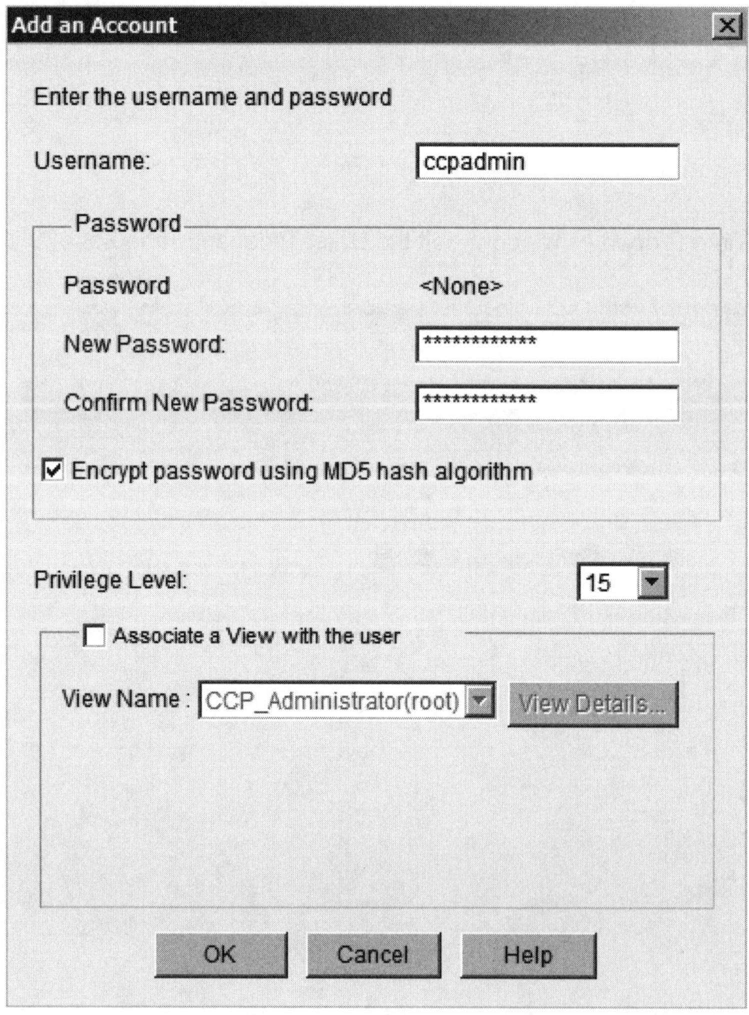

c.   In the Deliver Configuration to Device window, click the **Save running config to device's startup config** check box, and then click **Deliver**.

d. Review the information in the Commands Delivery Status window, and click **OK**. The new user account should now appear in the content pane on the right.

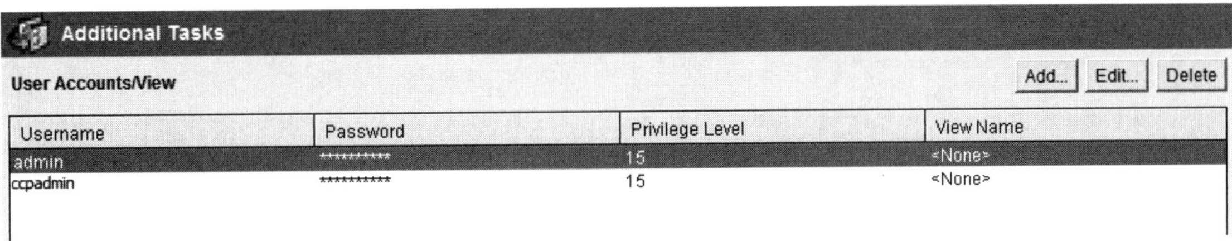

Step 5: **Edit vty line settings.**

a. In the left navigation pane, select **Router Access** > **VTY** to display the Additional Tasks > VTYs screen in the content pane on the right. Click **Edit…**.

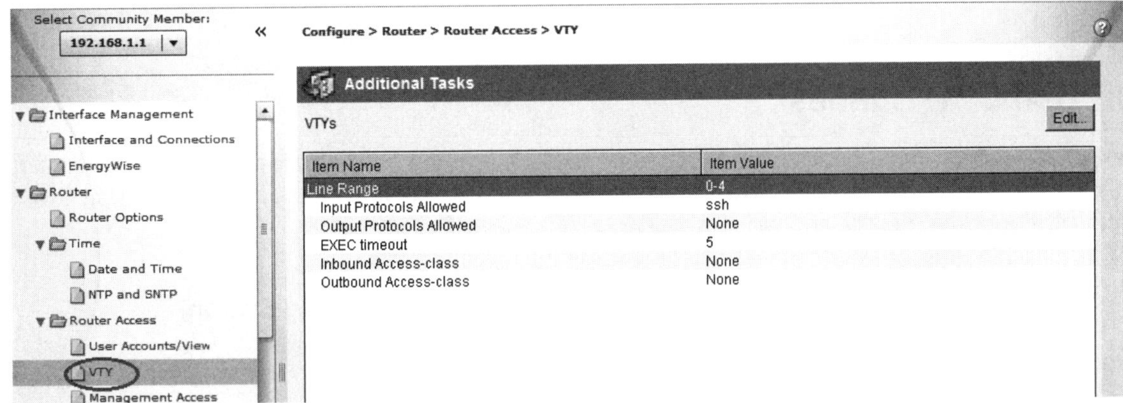

b. In the Edit VTY Lines window, change the Time out: field to **15** minutes. Click the **Input Protocol** > **Telne**t check box. Review the other options available. Also select the **SSH** checkbox. Then click **OK**.

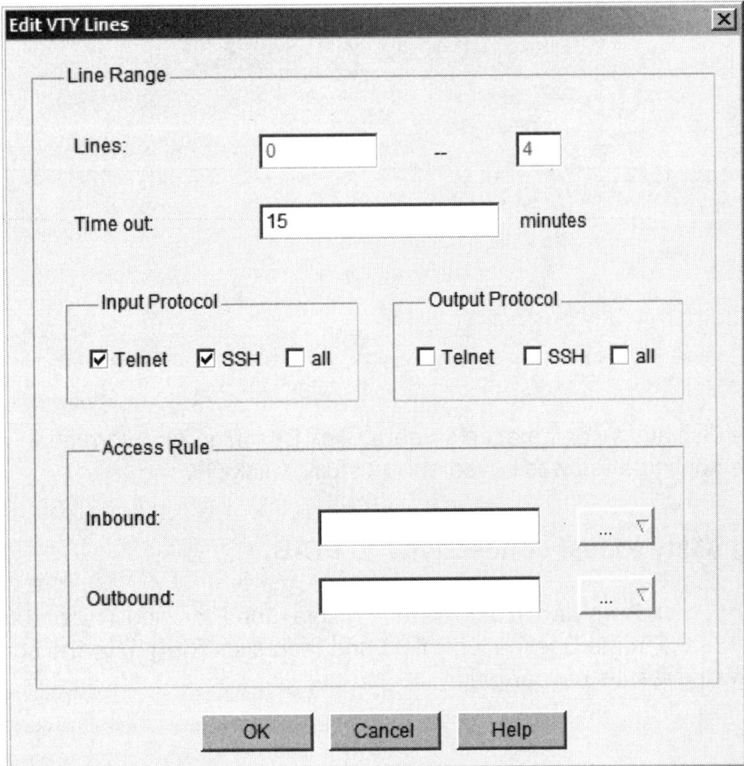

c. Review the commands that will be delivered to the running configuration on the Deliver Configuration to Device screen and click **Deliver**. In the Commands Delivery Status window, click **OK**. The content pane on the right should reflect the changes to the EXEC timeout value.

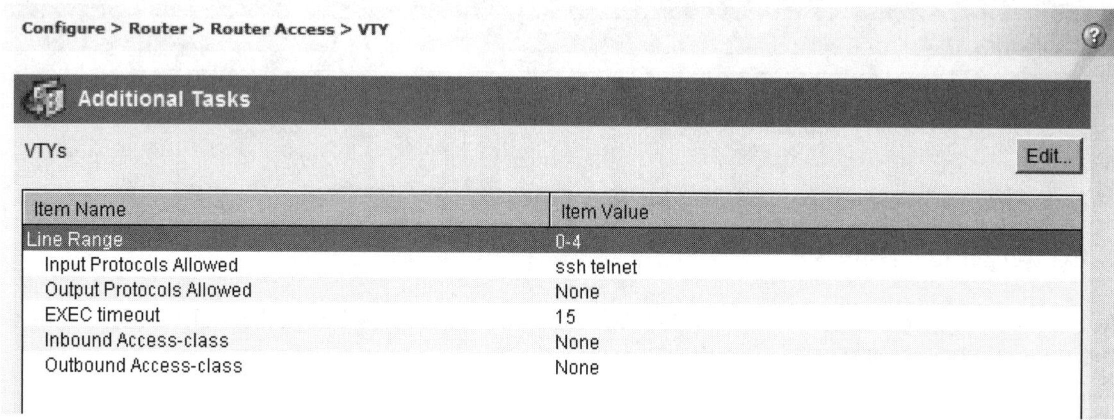

Part 6: Use CCP Utilities

In Part 6, you will use the Utilities pane to save the router's running configuration to the startup configuration. The Ping utility will be used to test network connectivity, and the View utility will be used to show the router's running configuration. Finally, you will close CCP.

Step 1: **Save the router's running configuration to the startup configuration.**

a. At the bottom of the left navigation pane, locate the Utilities pane. Click **Write to Startup Configuration**.

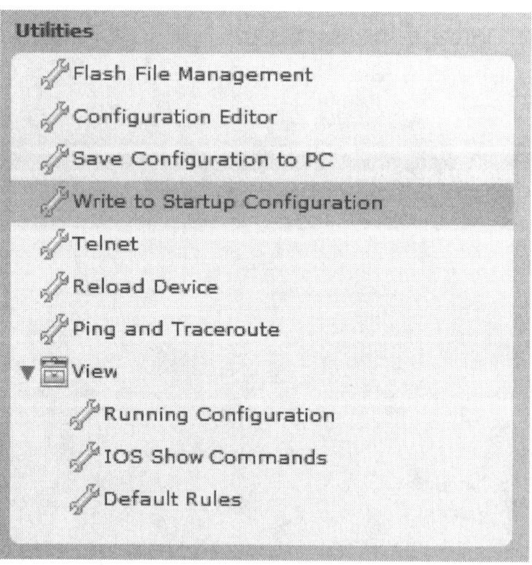

b. The content pane displays a confirmation screen. Click **Confirm**. An Information window displays, letting you know that the configuration was saved successfully. Click **OK**.

Step 2: **Use the Ping utility to test connectivity to PC-B.**

a. In the Utilities pane, click **Ping and Traceroute** to display the Ping and Traceroute screen in the content pane. Enter **192.168.0.3** in the Destination*: field and then click **Ping**. Use the scrollbar to the right of the results box to view the results of your ping.

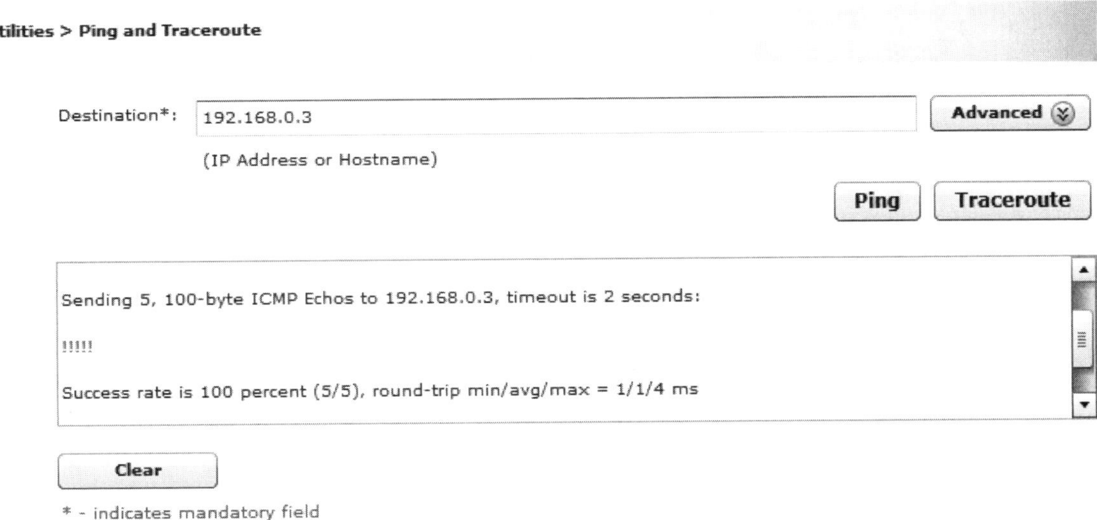

Step 3:   Use the View utility to show the running configuration for the router.

a. In the Utilities pane, click **View > IOS Show Commands** to display the IOS Show Commands screen in the content pane.

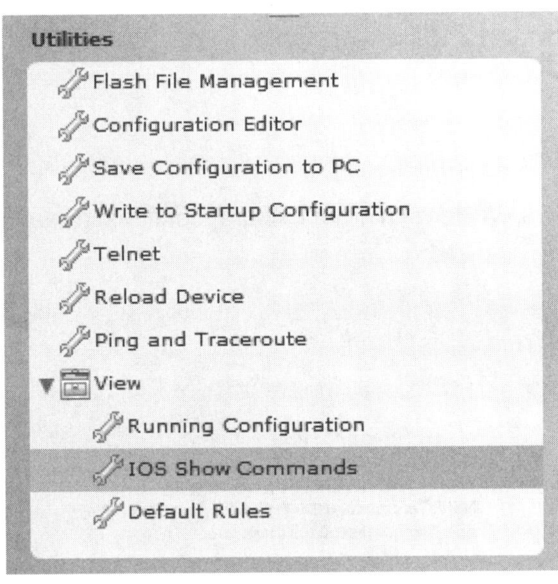

b. Select **show run** from the drop-down list and click **Show**. The router's running configuration is displayed in the content pane.

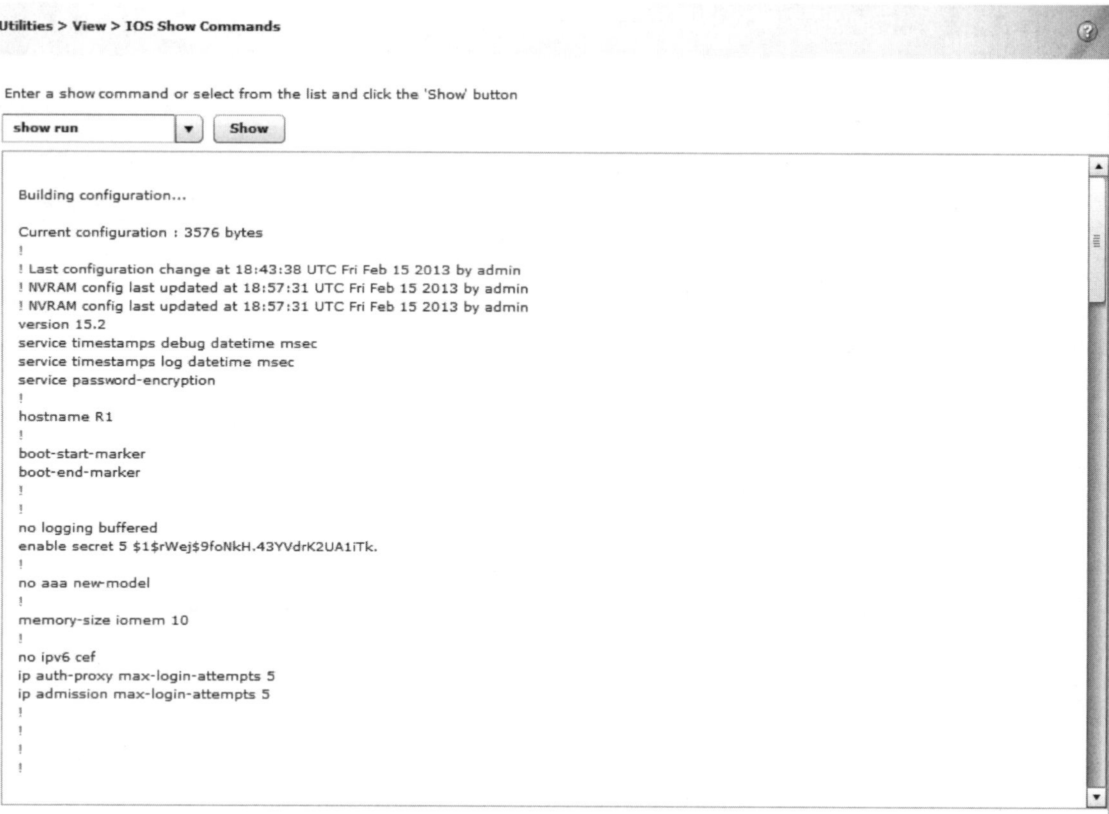

Step 4:   **Close CCP.**

Close the CCP window. When a Windows Internet Explorer confirmation window displays, click **Leave this page**.

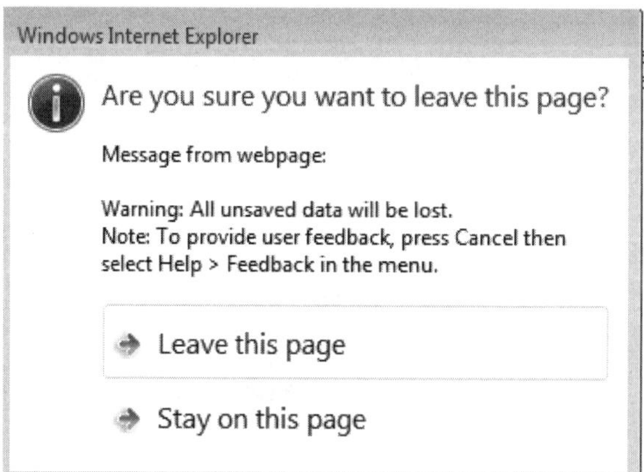

Reflection

1.   What transport protocol does CCP use to access the router and what commands are used to allow access?

2. What router command tells CCP to use the local database to authenticate?

3. What other **show** commands are available in the Utilities pane of CCP?

4. Why would you want to use CCP instead of the IOS CLI?

Router Interface Summary Table

Router Interface Summary				
Router Model	**Ethernet Interface #1**	**Ethernet Interface #2**	**Serial Interface #1**	**Serial Interface #2**
1800	Fast Ethernet 0/0 (F0/0)	Fast Ethernet 0/1 (F0/1)	Serial 0/0/0 (S0/0/0)	Serial 0/0/1 (S0/0/1)
1900	Gigabit Ethernet 0/0 (G0/0)	Gigabit Ethernet 0/1 (G0/1)	Serial 0/0/0 (S0/0/0)	Serial 0/0/1 (S0/0/1)
2801	Fast Ethernet 0/0 (F0/0)	Fast Ethernet 0/1 (F0/1)	Serial 0/1/0 (S0/1/0)	Serial 0/1/1 (S0/1/1)
2811	Fast Ethernet 0/0 (F0/0)	Fast Ethernet 0/1 (F0/1)	Serial 0/0/0 (S0/0/0)	Serial 0/0/1 (S0/0/1)
2900	Gigabit Ethernet 0/0 (G0/0)	Gigabit Ethernet 0/1 (G0/1)	Serial 0/0/0 (S0/0/0)	Serial 0/0/1 (S0/0/1)

Note: To find out how the router is configured, look at the interfaces to identify the type of router and how many interfaces the router has. There is no way to effectively list all the combinations of configurations for each router class. This table includes identifiers for the possible combinations of Ethernet and Serial interfaces in the device. The table does not include any other type of interface, even though a specific router may contain one. An example of this might be an ISDN BRI interface. The string in parenthesis is the legal abbreviation that can be used in Cisco IOS commands to represent the interface.

1.4.1.1 Class Activity – We Really Could Use a Map!

Objectives

Describe the three types of routes that are populated in a routing table (to include: directly-connected, static, and dynamic).

Scenario

Use the Ashland and Richmond routing tables shown below. With the help of a classmate, draw a network topology using the information from the tables. To assist you with this activity, follow these guidelines:

- Start with the Ashland router - use its routing table to identify ports and IP addresses/networks.
- Add the Richmond router - use its routing table to identify ports and IP addresses/networks.
- Add any other intermediary and end devices, as specified by the tables.

In addition, record answers from your group to the reflection questions provided with this activity.

Be prepared to share your work with another group or the class.

Resources

```
Ashland> show ip route

Codes: L - local, C - connected, S - static, R - RIP, M - mobile, B - BGP

D - EIGRP, EX - EIGRP external, O - OSPF, IA - OSPF inter area

N1 - OSPF NSSA external type 1, N2 - OSPF NSSA external type 2

E1 - OSPF external type 1, E2 - OSPF external type 2, E - EGP

i - IS-IS, L1 - IS-IS level-1, L2 - IS-IS level-2, ia - IS-IS inter area

* - candidate default, U - per-user static route, o - ODR

P - periodic downloaded static route


Gateway of last resort is not set


      192.168.1.0/24 is variably subnetted, 2 subnets, 2 masks

C     192.168.1.0/24 is directly connected, GigabitEthernet0/1

L     192.168.1.1/32 is directly connected, GigabitEthernet0/1

      192.168.2.0/24 is variably subnetted, 2 subnets, 2 masks

C     192.168.2.0/24 is directly connected, Serial0/0/0

L     192.168.2.1/32 is directly connected, Serial0/0/0

D     192.168.3.0/24 [90/2170368] via 192.168.4.2, 01:53:50, GigabitEthernet0/0

      192.168.4.0/24 is variably subnetted, 2 subnets, 2 masks

C     192.168.4.0/24 is directly connected, GigabitEthernet0/0

L     192.168.4.1/32 is directly connected, GigabitEthernet0/0

D     192.168.5.0/24 [90/3072] via 192.168.4.2, 01:59:14, GigabitEthernet0/0

S     192.168.6.0/24 [1/0] via 192.168.2.2

Ashland>
```

```
Richmond> show ip route

Codes: L - local, C - connected, S - static, R - RIP, M - mobile, B - BGP

D - EIGRP, EX - EIGRP external, O - OSPF, IA - OSPF inter area

N1 - OSPF NSSA external type 1, N2 - OSPF NSSA external type 2

E1 - OSPF external type 1, E2 - OSPF external type 2, E - EGP

i - IS-IS, L1 - IS-IS level-1, L2 - IS-IS level-2, ia - IS-IS inter area

* - candidate default, U - per-user static route, o - ODR

P - periodic downloaded static route


Gateway of last resort is not set


S 192.168.1.0/24 [1/0] via 192.168.3.1

D 192.168.2.0/24 [90/2170368] via 192.168.5.2, 01:55:09, GigabitEthernet0/1

192.168.3.0/24 is variably subnetted, 2 subnets, 2 masks

C 192.168.3.0/24 is directly connected, Serial0/0/0

L 192.168.3.2/32 is directly connected, Serial0/0/0

D 192.168.4.0/24 [90/3072] via 192.168.5.2, 01:55:09, GigabitEthernet0/1

192.168.5.0/24 is variably subnetted, 2 subnets, 2 masks

C 192.168.5.0/24 is directly connected, GigabitEthernet0/1

L 192.168.5.1/32 is directly connected, GigabitEthernet0/1

192.168.6.0/24 is variably subnetted, 2 subnets, 2 masks

C 192.168.6.0/24 is directly connected, GigabitEthernet0/0

L 192.168.6.1/32 is directly connected, GigabitEthernet0/0

Richmond>
```

Reflection

1. How many directly connected routes are listed on the Ashland router? What letter represents a direct connection to a network on a routing table?

____

2. Find the route to the 192.168.6.0/24 network. What kind of route is this? Was it dynamically discovered by the Ashland router or manually configured by a network administrator on the Ashland router?

____

3. If you were configuring a default (static route) to any network from the Ashland router and wanted to send all data to 192.168.2.2 (the next hop) for routing purposes, how would you write it?

____

4. If you were configuring a default (static route) to any network from the Ashland router and wanted to send all data through your exit interface, how would you write it?

____

5. When would you choose to use static routing, instead of letting dynamic routing take care of the routing paths for you?

6. What is the significance of the L on the left side of the routing table?

Chapter 2 — Static Routing

2.0.1.2 Class Activity – Which Way Should We Go?

Objectives

Explain the benefits of using static routes.

Scenario

A huge sporting event is about to take place in your city. To attend the event, you make concise plans to arrive at the sports arena on time to see the entire game.

There are two routes you can take to drive to the event:

- Highway route - It is easy to follow and fast driving speeds are allowed.

- Alternative, direct route - You found this route using a city map. Depending on conditions, such as the amount of traffic or congestion, this just may be the way to get to the arena on time!

With a partner, discuss these options. Choose a preferred route to arrive at the arena in time to see every second of the huge sporting event.

Compare your optional preferences to network traffic, which route would you choose to deliver data communications for your small- to medium-sized business? Would it be the fastest, easiest route or the alternative, direct route? Justify your choice.

Complete the modeling activity .pdf and be prepared to justify your answers to the class or with another group.

Required Resources

None

Reflection

1. Which route did you choose as your first preference? On what criteria did you base your decision?

2. If traffic congestion were to occur on either route, would this change the path you would take to the arena? Explain your answer.

3. A popular phrase that can be argued is "the shortest distance between two points is a straight line." Is this always true with delivery of network data? How do you compare your answer to this modeling activity scenario?

2.2.2.5 Lab – Configuring IPv4 Static and Default Routes

Topology

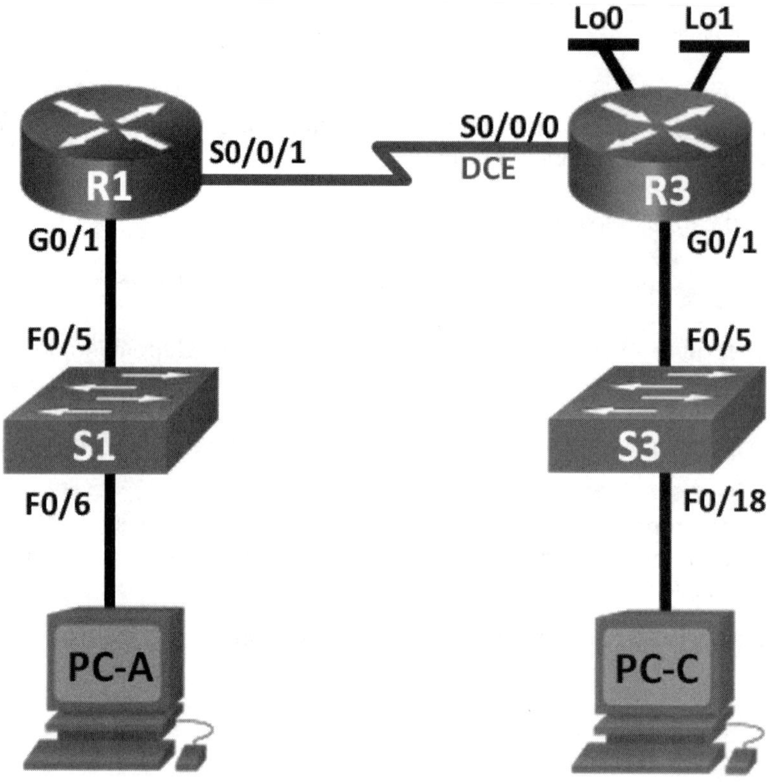

Addressing Table

Device	Interface	IP Address	Subnet Mask	Default Gateway
R1	G0/1	192.168.0.1	255.255.255.0	N/A
	S0/0/1	10.1.1.1	255.255.255.252	N/A
R3	G0/1	192.168.1.1	255.255.255.0	N/A
	S0/0/0 (DCE)	10.1.1.2	255.255.255.252	N/A
	Lo0	209.165.200.225	255.255.255.224	N/A
	Lo1	198.133.219.1	255.255.255.0	N/A
PC-A	NIC	192.168.0.10	255.255.255.0	192.168.0.1
PC-C	NIC	192.168.1.10	255.255.255.0	192.168.1.1

Objectives

Part 1: Set Up the Topology and Initialize Devices

Part 2: Configure Basic Device Settings and Verify Connectivity

Part 3: Configure Static Routes

- Configure a recursive static route.
- Configure a directly connected static route.
- Configure and remove static routes.

Part 4: Configure and Verify a Default Route

Background / Scenario

A router uses a routing table to determine where to send packets. The routing table contains a set of routes that describe which gateway or interface the router uses to reach a specified network. Initially, the routing table contains only directly connected networks. To communicate with distant networks, routes must be specified and added to the routing table.

In this lab, you will manually configure a static route to a specified distant network based on a next-hop IP address or exit interface. You will also configure a static default route. A default route is a type of static route that specifies a gateway to use when the routing table does not contain a path for the destination network.

Note: This lab provides minimal assistance with the actual commands necessary to configure static routing. However, the required commands are provided in Appendix A. Test your knowledge by trying to configure the devices without referring to the appendix.

Note: The routers used with CCNA hands-on labs are Cisco 1941 Integrated Services Routers (ISRs) with Cisco IOS Release 15.2(4)M3 (universalk9 image). The switches used are Cisco Catalyst 2960s with Cisco IOS Release 15.0(2) (lanbasek9 image). Other routers, switches, and Cisco IOS versions can be used. Depending on the model and Cisco IOS version, the commands available and output produced might vary from what is shown in the labs. Refer to the Router Interface Summary Table at the end of this lab for the correct interface identifiers.

Note: Make sure that the routers and switches have been erased and have no startup configurations. If you are unsure, contact your instructor.

Required Resources

- 2 Routers (Cisco 1941 with Cisco IOS Release 15.2(4)M3 universal image or comparable)
- 2 Switches (Cisco 2960 with Cisco IOS Release 15.0(2) lanbasek9 image or comparable)
- 2 PCs (Windows 7, Vista, or XP with terminal emulation program, such as Tera Term)
- Console cables to configure the Cisco IOS devices via the console ports
- Ethernet and serial cables as shown in the topology

Part 1: Set Up the Topology and Initialize Devices

Step 1: Cable the network as shown in the topology.

Step 2: Initialize and reload the router and switch.

Part 2: Configure Basic Device Settings and Verify Connectivity

In Part 2, you will configure basic settings, such as the interface IP addresses, device access, and passwords. You will verify LAN connectivity and identify routes listed in the routing tables for R1 and R3.

Step 1:   **Configure the PC interfaces.**

Step 2:   **Configure basic settings on the routers.**

    a.   Configure device names, as shown in the Topology and Addressing Table. _____

    b.   Disable DNS lookup.

    c.   Assign **class** as the enable password and assign **cisco** as the console and vty password.

    d.   Save the running configuration to the startup configuration file.

Step 3:   **Configure IP settings on the routers.**

    a.   Configure the R1 and R3 interfaces with IP addresses according to the Addressing Table.

    b.   The S0/0/0 connection is the DCE connection and requires the **clock rate** command. The R3 S0/0/0 configuration is displayed below.

```
R3(config)# interface s0/0/0
R3(config-if)# ip address 10.1.1.2 255.255.255.252
R3(config-if)# clock rate 128000
R3(config-if)# no shutdown
```

Step 4:   **Verify connectivity of the LANs.**

    a.   Test connectivity by pinging from each PC to the default gateway that has been configured for that host.

       From PC-A, is it possible to ping the default gateway? ___________

       From PC-C, is it possible to ping the default gateway? ___________

    b.   Test connectivity by pinging between the directly connected routers.

       From R1, is it possible to ping the S0/0/0 interface of R3? ___________

       If the answer is **no** to any of these questions, troubleshoot the configurations and correct the error.

    c.   Test connectivity between devices that are not directly connected.

       From PC-A, is it possible to ping PC-C? ___________

       From PC-A, is it possible to ping Lo0? ___________

       From PC-A, is it possible to ping Lo1? ___________

       Were these pings successful? Why or why not?

       ____

       ____

       Note: It may be necessary to disable the PC firewall to ping between PCs.

Step 5:   Gather information.

a.   Check the status of the interfaces on R1 with the **show ip Interface brief** command.

How many interfaces are activated on R1? ___________

b.   Check the status of the interfaces on R3.

How many interfaces are activated on R3? ___________

c.   View the routing table information for R1 using the **show ip route** command.

What networks are present in the Addressing Table of this lab, but not in the routing table for R1?

____

d.   View the routing table information for R3.

What networks are present in the Addressing Table in this lab, but not in the routing table for R3?

Why are all the networks not in the routing tables for each of the routers?

Part 3:   **Configure Static Routes**

In Part 3, you will employ multiple ways to implement static and default routes, you will confirm that the routes have been added to the routing tables of R1 and R3, and you will verify connectivity based on the introduced routes.

Note: This lab provides minimal assistance with the actual commands necessary to configure static routing. However, the required commands are provided in Appendix A. Test your knowledge by trying to configure the devices without referring to the appendix.

Step 1:   **Configure a recursive static route.**

With a recursive static route, the next-hop IP address is specified. Because only the next-hop IP is specified, the router must perform multiple lookups in the routing table before forwarding packets. To configure recursive static routes, use the following syntax:

```
Router(config)# ip route network-address subnet-mask ip-address
```

a.   On the R1 router, configure a static route to the 192.168.1.0 network using the IP address of the Serial 0/0/0 interface of R3 as the next-hop address. Write the command you used in the space provided.

b.   View the routing table to verify the new static route entry.

How is this new route listed in the routing table?

From host PC-A, is it possible to ping the host PC-C? ___________

These pings should fail. If the recursive static route is correctly configured, the ping arrives at PC-C. PC-C sends a ping reply back to PC-A. However, the ping reply is discarded at R3 because R3 does not have a return route to the 192.168.0.0 network in the routing table.

Step 2: Configure a directly connected static route.

With a directly connected static route, the *exit-interface* parameter is specified, which allows the router to resolve a forwarding decision in one lookup. A directly connected static route is typically used with a point-to-point serial interface. To configure directly connected static routes with an exit interface specified, use the following syntax:

```
Router(config)# ip route network-address subnet-mask exit-intf
```

a. On the R3 router, configure a static route to the 192.168.0.0 network using S0/0/0 as the exit interface. Write the command you used in the space provided.

b. View the routing table to verify the new static route entry.

How is this new route listed in the routing table?

____

c.   From host PC-A, is it possible to ping the host PC-C? ___________

This ping should be successful.

Note: It may be necessary to disable the PC firewall to ping between PCs.

Step 3:   Configure a static route.

a.   On the R1 router, configure a static route to the 198.133.219.0 network using one of the static route configuration options from the previous steps. Write the command you used in the space provided.

____

b.   On the R1 router, configure a static route to the 209.165.200.224 network on R3 using the other static route configuration option from the previous steps. Write the command you used in the space provided.

____

c.   View the routing table to verify the new static route entry.

How is this new route listed in the routing table?

____

d. From host PC-A, is it possible to ping the R1 address 198.133.219.1? ____________

This ping should be successful.

Step 4:   Remove static routes for loopback addresses.

a. On R1, use the **no** command to remove the static routes for the two loopback addresses from the routing table. Write the commands you used in the space provided.

____

b. View the routing table to verify the routes have been removed.

How many network routes are listed in the routing table on R1? ____________

Is the Gateway of last resort set? ____________

Part 4:   Configure and Verify a Default Route

In Part 4, you will implement a default route, confirm that the route has been added to the routing table, and verify connectivity based on the introduced route.

A default route identifies the gateway to which the router sends all IP packets for which it does not have a learned or static route. A default static route is a static route with 0.0.0.0 as the destination IP address and subnet mask. This is commonly referred to as a "quad zero" route.

In a default route, either the next-hop IP address or exit interface can be specified. To configure a default static route, use the following syntax:

```
Router(config)# ip route 0.0.0.0 0.0.0.0 {ip-address or exit-intf}
```

a.   Configure the R1 router with a default route using the exit interface of S0/0/1. Write the command you used in the space provided.

____

b.   View the routing table to verify the new static route entry.

How is this new route listed in the routing table?

____

What is the Gateway of last resort?

____

c.   From host PC-A, is it possible to ping the 209.165.200.225? ____________

d.   From host PC-A, is it possible to ping the 198.133.219.1? ____________

These pings should be successful.

Reflection

1. A new network 192.168.3.0/24 is connected to interface G0/0 on R1. What commands could be used to configure a static route to that network from R3?

2. Is there a benefit to configuring a directly connected static route instead of a recursive static route?

3. Why is it important to configure a default route on a router?

Router Interface Summary Table

Router Interface Summary				
Router Model	**Ethernet Interface #1**	**Ethernet Interface #2**	**Serial Interface #1**	**Serial Interface #2**
1800	Fast Ethernet 0/0 (F0/0)	Fast Ethernet 0/1 (F0/1)	Serial 0/0/0 (S0/0/0)	Serial 0/0/1 (S0/0/1)
1900	Gigabit Ethernet 0/0 (G0/0)	Gigabit Ethernet 0/1 (G0/1)	Serial 0/0/0 (S0/0/0)	Serial 0/0/1 (S0/0/1)
2801	Fast Ethernet 0/0 (F0/0)	Fast Ethernet 0/1 (F0/1)	Serial 0/1/0 (S0/1/0)	Serial 0/1/1 (S0/1/1)
2811	Fast Ethernet 0/0 (F0/0)	Fast Ethernet 0/1 (F0/1)	Serial 0/0/0 (S0/0/0)	Serial 0/0/1 (S0/0/1)
2900	Gigabit Ethernet 0/0 (G0/0)	Gigabit Ethernet 0/1 (G0/1)	Serial 0/0/0 (S0/0/0)	Serial 0/0/1 (S0/0/1)

Note: To find out how the router is configured, look at the interfaces to identify the type of router and how many interfaces the router has. There is no way to effectively list all the combinations of configurations for each router class. This table includes identifiers for the possible combinations of Ethernet and Serial interfaces in the device. The table does not include any other type of interface, even though a specific router may contain one. An example of this might be an ISDN BRI interface. The string in parenthesis is the legal abbreviation that can be used in Cisco IOS commands to represent the interface.

Appendix A: Configuration Commands for Parts 2, 3, and 4

The commands listed in Appendix A are for reference only. This Appendix does not include all the specific commands necessary to complete this lab.

Basic Device Settings

Configure IP settings on the router.

```
R3(config)# interface s0/0/0
R3(config-if)# ip address 10.1.1.2 255.255.255.252
R3(config-if)# clock rate 128000
R3(config-if)# no shutdown
```

Static Route Configurations

Configure a recursive static route.

```
R1(config)# ip route 192.168.1.0 255.255.255.0 10.1.1.2
```

Configure a directly connected static route.

```
R3(config)# ip route 192.168.0.0 255.255.255.0 s0/0/0
```

Remove static routes.

```
R1(config)# no ip route 209.165.200.224 255.255.255.224 serial0/0/1
```

or

```
R1(config)# no ip route 209.165.200.224 255.255.255.224 10.1.1.2
```

or

```
R1(config)# no ip route 209.165.200.224 255.255.255.224
```

Default Route Configuration

```
R1(config)# ip route 0.0.0.0 0.0.0.0 s0/0/1
```

2.2.4.5 Lab – Configuring IPv6 Static and Default Routes

Topology

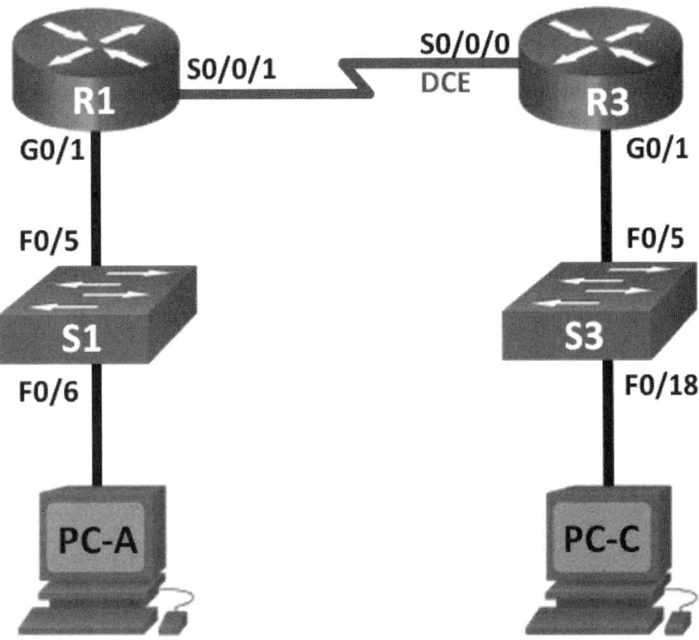

Addressing Table

Device	Interface	IPv6 Address / Prefix Length	Default Gateway
R1	G0/1	2001:DB8:ACAD:A::/64 eui-64	N/A
	S0/0/1	FC00::1/64	N/A
R3	G0/1	2001:DB8:ACAD:B::/64 eui-64	N/A
	S0/0/0	FC00::2/64	N/A
PC-A	NIC	SLAAC	SLAAC
PC-C	NIC	SLAAC	SLAAC

Objectives

Part 1: Build the Network and Configure Basic Device Settings

- Enable IPv6 unicast routing and configure IPv6 addressing on the routers.
- Disable IPv4 addressing and enable IPv6 SLAAC for the PC network interfaces.
- Use **ipconfig** and **ping** to verify LAN connectivity.
- Use **show** commands to verify IPv6 settings.

Part 2: Configure IPv6 Static and Default Routes

- Configure a directly attached IPv6 static route.
- Configure a recursive IPv6 static route.
- Configure a default IPv6 static route.

Background / Scenario

In this lab, you will configure the entire network to communicate using only IPv6 addressing, including configuring the routers and PCs. You will use stateless address auto-configuration (SLAAC) for configuring the IPv6 addresses for the hosts. You will also configure IPv6 static and default routes on the routers to enable communication to remote networks that are not directly connected.

Note: The routers used with CCNA hands-on labs are Cisco 1941 Integrated Services Routers (ISRs) with Cisco IOS Release 15.2(4)M3 (universalk9 image). The switches used are Cisco Catalyst 2960s with Cisco IOS Release 15.0(2) (lanbasek9 image). Other routers, switches, and Cisco IOS versions can be used. Depending on the model and Cisco IOS version, the commands available and output produced might vary from what is shown in the labs. Refer to the Router Interface Summary Table at the end of this lab for the correct interface identifiers.

Note: Make sure that the routers and switches have been erased and have no startup configurations. If you are unsure, contact your instructor.

Required Resources

- 2 Routers (Cisco 1941 with Cisco IOS Release 15.2(4)M3 universal image or comparable)
- 2 Switches (Cisco 2960 with Cisco IOS Release 15.0(2) lanbasek9 image or comparable)
- 2 PCs (Windows 7, Vista, or XP with terminal emulation program, such as Tera Term)
- Console cables to configure the Cisco IOS devices via the console ports
- Ethernet and serial cables as shown in the topology

Part 1: Build the Network and Configure Basic Device Settings

In Part 1, you will cable and configure the network to communicate using IPv6 addressing.

Step 1: Cable the network as shown in the topology diagram.

Step 2: Initialize and reload the routers and switches.

Step 3: Enable IPv6 unicast routing and configure IPv6 addressing on the routers.

a. Using Tera Term, console into the router labeled R1 in the topology diagram and assign the router the name R1.

b. Within global configuration mode, enable IPv6 routing on R1.

```
R1(config)# ipv6 unicast-routing
```

c. Configure the network interfaces on R1 with IPv6 addresses. Notice that IPv6 is enabled on each interface. The G0/1 interface has a globally routable unicast address and EUI-64 is used to create the interface identifier portion of the address. The S0/0/1 interface has a privately routable, unique-local address, which is recommended for point-to-point serial connections.

```
R1(config)# interface g0/1
R1(config-if)# ipv6 address 2001:DB8:ACAD:A::/64 eui-64
R1(config-if)# no shutdown
R1(config-if)# interface serial 0/0/1
R1(config-if)# ipv6 address FC00::1/64
R1(config-if)# no shutdown
R1(config-if)# exit
```

d.   Assign a device name to router R3.

e.   Within global configuration mode, enable IPv6 routing on R3.

```
R3(config)# ipv6 unicast-routing
```

f.   Configure the network interfaces on R3 with IPv6 addresses. Notice that IPv6 is enabled on each interface. The G0/1 interface has a globally routable unicast address and EUI-64 is used to create the interface identifier portion of the address. The S0/0/0 interface has a privately routable, unique-local address, which is recommended for point-to-point serial connections. The clock rate is set because it is the DCE end of the serial cable.

```
R3(config)# interface gigabit 0/1

R3(config-if)# ipv6 address 2001:DB8:ACAD:B::/64 eui-64

R3(config-if)# no shutdown

R3(config-if)# interface serial 0/0/0

R3(config-if)# ipv6 address FC00::2/64

R3(config-if)# clock rate 128000

R3(config-if)# no shutdown

R3(config-if)# exit
```

Step 4:   Disable IPv4 addressing and enable IPv6 SLAAC for the PC network interfaces.

a.   On both PC-A and PC-C, navigate to the **Start** menu > **Control Panel**. Click the **Network and Sharing Center** link while viewing with icons. In the Network and Sharing Center window, click the **Change adapter settings** link on the left side of the window to open the Network Connections window.

b.   In the Network Connections window, you see the icons for your network interface adapters. Double-click the Local Area Connection icon for the PC network interface that is connected to the switch. Click the **Properties** to open the Local Area Connection Properties dialogue window.

c.   With the Local Area Connection Properties window open, scroll down through the items and uncheck the item **Internet Protocol Version 4 (TCP/IPv4)** check box to disable the IPv4 protocol on the network interface.

d.   With the Local Area Connection Properties window still open, click the **Internet Protocol Version 6 (TCP/IPv6)** check box, and then click **Properties**.

e.   With the Internet Protocol Version 6 (TCP/IPv6) Properties window open, check to see if the radio buttons for **Obtain an IPv6 address automatically** and **Obtain DNS server address automatically** are selected. If not, select them.

f.   With the PCs configured to obtain an IPv6 address automatically, they will contact the routers to obtain the network subnet and gateway information, and auto-configure their IPv6 address information. In the next step, you will verify the settings.

Step 5:   Use ipconfig and ping to verify LAN connectivity.

a.   From PC-A, open a command prompt, type **ipconfig /all** and press Enter. The output should look similar to that shown below. In the output, you should see that the PC now has an IPv6 global unicast address, a link-local IPv6 address, and a link-local IPv6 default gateway address. You may also see a temporary IPv6 address and under the DNS server addresses, three site-local addresses that start with FEC0. Site-local addresses are private addresses that were meant to be backwards compatible with NAT. However, they are not supported in IPv6 and are replaced by unique-local addresses.

```
C:\Users\User1> ipconfig /all

Windows IP Configuration


<Output omitted>


Ethernet adapter Local Area Connection:


    Connection-specific DNS Suffix. . . :
    Description . . . . . . . . . . . : Intel(R) 82577LC Gigabit Network Connection
    Physical Address. . . . . . . . . : 1C-C1-DE-91-C3-5D
    DHCP Enabled. . . . . . . . . . . : No
    Autoconfiguration Enabled. . . . . : Yes
    IPv6 Address. . . . . . . . . . . : 2001:db8:acad:a:7c0c:7493:218d:2f6c(Preferred)
    Temporary IPv6 Address. . . . . . : 2001:db8:acad:a:bc40:133a:54e7:d497(Preferred)
    Link-local IPv6 Address . . . . . : fe80::7c0c:7493:218d:2f6c%13(Preferred)
    Default Gateway . . . . . . . . . : fe80::6273:5cff:fe0d:1a61%13
    DNS Servers . . . . . . . . . . . : fec0:0:0:ffff::1%1
                                        fec0:0:0:ffff::2%1
                                        fec0:0:0:ffff::3%1
    NetBIOS over Tcpip. . . . . . . . : Disabled
```

Based on your network implementation and the output of the **ipconfig /all** command, did PC-A receive IPv6 addressing information from R1?

____

____

____

b. What is the PC-A global unicast IPv6 address?

____

c. What is the PC-A link-local IPv6 address?

____

d. What is the PC-A default gateway IPv6 address?

____

e. From PC-A, use the **ping -6** command to issue an IPv6 ping to the link-local default gateway address. You should see replies from the R1 router.

```
C:\Users\User1> ping -6 <default-gateway-address>
```

Did PC-A receive replies to the ping from PC-A to R1?

____

f. Repeat Step 5a from PC-C.

Did PC-C receive IPv6 addressing information from R3?

____

g. What is the PC-C global unicast IPv6 address?

____

h. What is the PC-C link-local IPv6 address?

____

i. What is the PC-C default gateway IPv6 address?

____

j. From PC-C, use the **ping -6** command to ping the PC-C default gateway.

Did PC-C receive replies to the pings from PC-C to R3?

____

k.   Attempt an IPv6 **ping -6** from PC-A to the PC-C IPv6 address.

```
C:\Users\User1> ping -6 PC-C-IPv6-address
```

Was the ping successful? Why or why not?

____

____

____

____

Step 6:   **Use show commands to verify IPv6 settings.**

a.   Check the status of the interfaces on R1 with the **show ipv6 interface brief** command.

What are the two IPv6 addresses for the G0/1 interface and what kind of IPv6 addresses are they?

____

What are the two IPv6 addresses for the S0/0/1 interface and what kind of IPv6 addresses are they?

____

b.   To see more detailed information on the IPv6 interfaces, type a **show ipv6 interface** command on R1 and press Enter.

What are the multicast group addresses for the Gigabit Ethernet 0/1 interface?

What are the multicast group addresses for the S0/0/1 interface?

What is an FF02::1 multicast address used for?

What is an FF02::2 multicast address used for?

What kind of multicast addresses are FF02::1:FF00:1 and FF02::1:FF0D:1A60, and what are they used for?

c. View the IPv6 routing table information for R1 using the **show ipv6 route** command. The IPv6 routing table should have two connected routes, one for each interface, and three local routes, one for each interface and one for multicast traffic to a Null0 interface.

In what way does the routing table output of R1 reveal why you were unable to ping PC-C from PC-A?

____

____

Part 2: Configure IPv6 Static and Default Routes

In Part 2, you will configure IPv6 static and default routes three different ways. You will confirm that the routes have been added to the routing tables, and you will verify successful connectivity between PC-A and PC-C.

You will configure three types of IPv6 static routes:

- **Directly Connected IPv6 Static Route** – A directly connected static route is created when specifying the outgoing interface.

- **Recursive IPv6 Static Route** – A recursive static route is created when specifying the next-hop IP address. This method requires the router to execute a recursive lookup in the routing table in order to identify the outgoing interface.

- **Default IPv6 Static Route** – Similar to a quad zero IPv4 route, a default IPv6 static route is created by making the destination IPv6 prefix and prefix length all zeros, ::/0.

Step 1: Configure a directly connected IPv6 static route.

In a directly connected IPv6 static route, the route entry specifies the router outgoing interface. A directly connected static route is typically used with a point-to-point serial interface. To configure a directly attached IPv6 static route, use the following command format:

```
Router(config)# ipv6 route <ipv6-prefix/prefix-length> <outgoing-interface-type>
<outgoing-interface-number>
```

a. On router R1, configure an IPv6 static route to the 2001:DB8:ACAD:B::/64 network on R3, using the R1 outgoing S0/0/1 interface.

```
R1(config)# ipv6 route 2001:DB8:ACAD:B::/64 serial 0/0/1

R1(config)#
```

b. View the IPv6 routing table to verify the new static route entry.

What is the code letter and routing table entry for the newly added route in the routing table?

c.   Now that the static route has been configured on R1, is it now possible to ping the host PC-C from PC-A?

These pings should fail. If the recursive static route is correctly configured, the ping arrives at PC-C. PC-C sends a ping reply back to PC-A. However, the ping reply is discarded at R3 because R3 does not have a return route to the 2001:DB8:ACAD:A::/64 network in the routing table. To successfully ping across the network, you must also create a static route on R3.

d.   On router R3, configure an IPv6 static route to the 2001:DB8:ACAD:A::/64 network, using the R3 outgoing S0/0/0 interface.

```
R3(config)# ipv6 route 2001:DB8:ACAD:A::/64 serial 0/0/0
R3(config)#
```

e.   Now that both routers have static routes, attempt an IPv6 **ping -6** from PC-A to the PC-C global unicast IPv6 address.

Was the ping successful? Why?

Step 2:   Configure a recursive IPv6 static route.

In a recursive IPv6 static route, the route entry has the next-hop router IPv6 address. To configure a recursive IPv6 static route, use the following command format:

```
Router(config)# ipv6 route <ipv6-prefix/prefix-length> <next-hop-ipv6-address>
```

a. On router R1, delete the directly attached static route and add a recursive static route.

```
R1(config)# no ipv6 route 2001:DB8:ACAD:B::/64 serial 0/0/1
R1(config)# ipv6 route 2001:DB8:ACAD:B::/64 FC00::2
R1(config)# exit
```

b. On router R3, delete the directly attached static route and add a recursive static route.

```
R3(config)# no ipv6 route 2001:DB8:ACAD:A::/64 serial 0/0/0
R3(config)# ipv6 route 2001:DB8:ACAD:A::/64 FC00::1
R3(config)# exit
```

c. View the IPv6 routing table on R1 to verify the new static route entry.

What is the code letter and routing table entry for the newly added route in the routing table?

____

d. Verify connectivity by issuing a **ping -6** command from PC-A to PC-C.

Was the ping successful? ____________________

Note: It may be necessary to disable the PC firewall to ping between PCs.

Step 3:   Configure a default IPv6 static route.

In a default static route, the destination IPv6 prefix and prefix length are all zeros.

```
Router(config)# ipv6 route ::/0 <outgoing-interface-type> <outgoing-interface-
number> {and/or} <next-hop-ipv6-address>
```

a. On router R1, delete the recursive static route and add a default static route.

```
R1(config)# no ipv6 route 2001:DB8:ACAD:B::/64 FC00::2
R1(config)# ipv6 route ::/0 serial 0/0/1
R1(config)#
```

b. Delete the recursive static route and add a default static route on R3.

c. View the IPv6 routing table on R1 to verify the new static route entry.

What is the code letter and routing table entry for the newly added default route in the routing table?

____

d. Verify connectivity by issuing a **ping -6** command from PC-A to PC-C.

Was the ping successful? ____________________

Note: It may be necessary to disable the PC firewall to ping between PCs.

Reflection

1. This lab focuses on configuring IPv6 static and default routes. Can you think of a situation where you would need to configure both IPv6 and IPv4 static and default routes on a router?

____

____

____

2. In practice, configuring an IPv6 static and default route is very similar to configuring an IPv4 static and default route. Aside from the obvious differences between the IPv6 and IPv4 addressing, what are some other differences when configuring and verifying an IPv6 static route as compared to an IPv4 static route?

____

____

____

Router Interface Summary Table

Router Interface Summary				
Router Model	**Ethernet Interface #1**	**Ethernet Interface #2**	**Serial Interface #1**	**Serial Interface #2**
1800	Fast Ethernet 0/0 (F0/0)	Fast Ethernet 0/1 (F0/1)	Serial 0/0/0 (S0/0/0)	Serial 0/0/1 (S0/0/1)
1900	Gigabit Ethernet 0/0 (G0/0)	Gigabit Ethernet 0/1 (G0/1)	Serial 0/0/0 (S0/0/0)	Serial 0/0/1 (S0/0/1)
2801	Fast Ethernet 0/0 (F0/0)	Fast Ethernet 0/1 (F0/1)	Serial 0/1/0 (S0/1/0)	Serial 0/1/1 (S0/1/1)
2811	Fast Ethernet 0/0 (F0/0)	Fast Ethernet 0/1 (F0/1)	Serial 0/0/0 (S0/0/0)	Serial 0/0/1 (S0/0/1)
2900	Gigabit Ethernet 0/0 (G0/0)	Gigabit Ethernet 0/1 (G0/1)	Serial 0/0/0 (S0/0/0)	Serial 0/0/1 (S0/0/1)

Note: To find out how the router is configured, look at the interfaces to identify the type of router and how many interfaces the router has. There is no way to effectively list all the combinations of configurations for each router class. This table includes identifiers for the possible combinations of Ethernet and Serial interfaces in the device. The table does not include any other type of interface, even though a specific router may contain one. An example of this might be an ISDN BRI interface. The string in parenthesis is the legal abbreviation that can be used in Cisco IOS commands to represent the interface.

2.3.3.7 Lab – Designing and Implementing IPv4 Addressing with VLSM

Topology

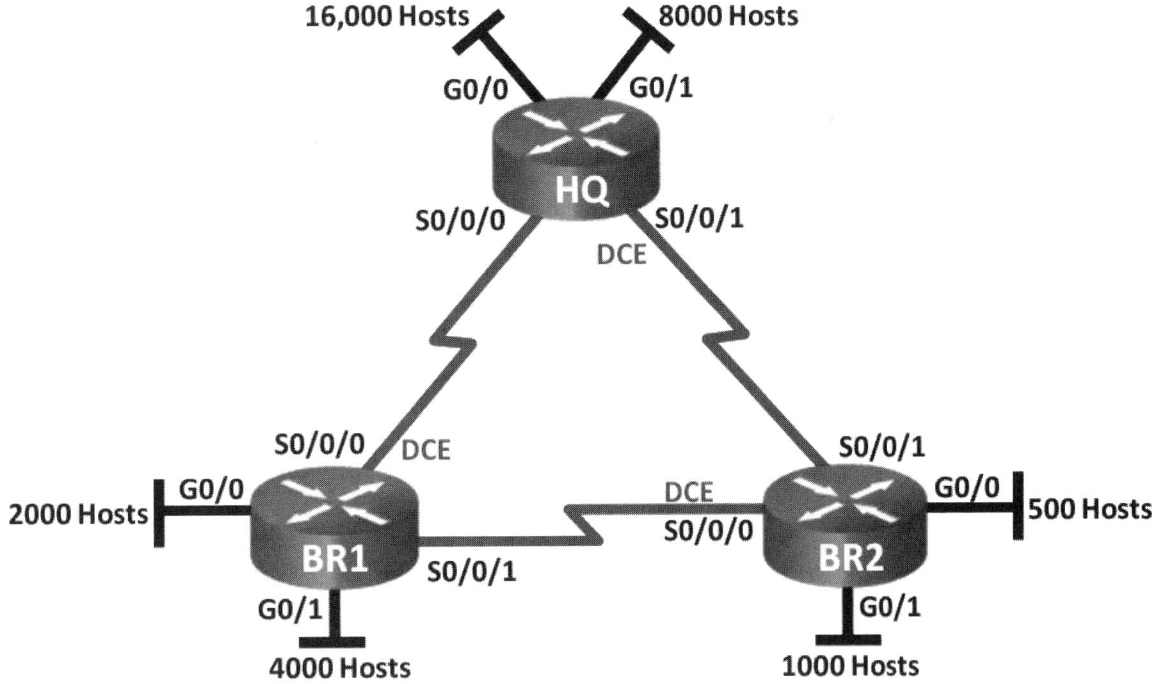

Objectives

Part 1: Examine the Network Requirements

Part 2: Design the VLSM Address Scheme

Part 3: Cable and Configure the IPv4 Network

Background / Scenario

The Variable Length Subnet Mask (VLSM) was designed to help conserve IP addresses. With VLSM, a network is subnetted and then subnetted again. This process can be repeated multiple times to create subnets of various sizes based on the number of hosts required in each subnet. Effective use of VLSM requires address planning.

In this lab, you are given the network address 172.16.128.0/17 to develop an address scheme for the network shown in the Topology diagram. VLSM will be used so that the addressing requirements can be met. After you have designed the VLSM address scheme, you will configure the interfaces on the routers with the appropriate IP address information.

Note: The routers used with CCNA hands-on labs are Cisco 1941 Integrated Services Routers (ISRs) with Cisco IOS Release 15.2(4)M3 (universalk9 image). Other routers and Cisco IOS versions can be used. Depending on the model and Cisco IOS version, the commands available and output produced might vary from what is shown in the labs. Refer to the Router Interface Summary Table at the end of this lab for the correct interface identifiers.

Note: Make sure that the routers have been erased and have no startup configurations. If you are unsure, contact your instructor.

Required Resources

- 3 Routers (Cisco 1941 with Cisco IOS Release 15.2(4)M3 universal image or comparable)
- 1 PC (with terminal emulation program, such as Tera Term, to configure routers)
- Console cable to configure the Cisco IOS devices via the console ports
- Ethernet (optional) and serial cables as shown in the topology
- Windows Calculator (optional)

Part 1:   Examine the Network Requirements

In Part 1, you will examine the network requirements to develop a VLSM address scheme for the network shown in the Topology diagram using the network address of 172.16.128.0/17.

Note: You may use the Windows Calculator application and the www.ipcalc.org IP subnet calculator to help with your calculations.

Step 1:   Determine how many host addresses are available and how many subnets are needed.

How many host addresses are available in a /17 network? _________

What is the total number of host addresses needed in the topology diagram? _________

How many subnets are needed in the network topology? _______

Step 2:   Determine the largest subnet needed.

Subnet description (e.g. BR1 G0/1 LAN or BR1-HQ WAN link) ____________________

How many IP addresses are needed in the largest subnet? ___________

What is the smallest subnet that supports that many addresses?

____

How many host addresses does that subnet support? __________

Can the 172.16.128.0/17 network be subnetted to support this subnet? ______

What are the two network addresses that would result from this subnetting?

____

____

Use the first network address for this subnet.

Step 3:   Determine the second largest subnet needed.

Subnet description ______________________________

How many IP addresses are needed for the second largest subnet? _______

What is the smallest subnet that supports that many hosts?

____

How many host addresses does that subnet support? _____________

Can the remaining subnet be subnetted again and still support this subnet? _______

What are the two network addresses that would result from this subnetting?

____

____

Use the first network address for this subnet.

Step 4:   **Determine the next largest subnet needed.**

Subnet description ____

How many IP addresses are needed for the next largest subnet? _______

What is the smallest subnet that supports that many hosts?

____

How many host addresses does that subnet support? _____________

Can the remaining subnet be subnetted again and still support this subnet? _______

What are the two network addresses that would result from this subnetting?

____

____

Use the first network address for this subnet.

Step 5:   **Determine the next largest subnet needed.**

Subnet description ____

How many IP addresses are needed for the next largest subnet? _______

What is the smallest subnet that supports that many hosts?

____

How many host addresses does that subnet support? _____________

Can the remaining subnet be subnetted again and still support this subnet? _______

What are the two network addresses that would result from this subnetting?

____

____

Use the first network address for this subnet.

Step 6:   Determine the next largest subnet needed.

Subnet description ______________________________

How many IP addresses are needed for the next largest subnet? ______

What is the smallest subnet that supports that many hosts?

____

How many host addresses does that subnet support? __________

Can the remaining subnet be subnetted again and still support this subnet? ______

What are the two network addresses that would result from this subnetting?

____

____

Use the first network address for this subnet.

Step 7:   Determine the next largest subnet needed.

Subnet description ______________________________

How many IP addresses are needed for the next largest subnet? ______

What is the smallest subnet that supports that many hosts?

____

How many host addresses does that subnet support? __________

Can the remaining subnet be subnetted again and still support this subnet? ______

What are the two network addresses that would result from this subnetting?

____

____

Use the first network address for this subnet.

Step 8:   **Determine the subnets needed to support the serial links.**

How many host addresses are needed for each serial subnet link? _______

What is the smallest subnet that supports that many host addresses?

____

a.   Subnet the remaining subnet and write the network addresses that result from this subnetting below.

____

____

b.   Continue subnetting the first subnet of each new subnet until you have four /30 subnets. Write the first three network addresses of these /30 subnets below.

____

____

____

c.   Enter the subnet descriptions for these three subnets below.

____

____

____

Part 2:   Design the VLSM Address Scheme

Step 1:   **Calculate the subnet information.**

Use the information that you obtained in Part 1 to fill in the table below.

Subnet Description	Number of Hosts Needed	Network Address /CIDR	First Host Address	Broadcast Address
HQ G0/0	16,000			
HQ G0/1	8,000			
BR1 G0/1	4,000			
BR1 G0/0	2,000			
BR2 G0/1	1,000			
BR2 G0/0	500			
HQ S0/0/0 – BR1 S0/0/0	2			
HQ S0/0/1 – BR2 S0/0/1	2			
BR1 S0/0/1 – BR2 S0/0/0	2			

Step 2:   **Complete the device interface address table.**

Assign the first host address in the subnet to the Ethernet interfaces. HQ should be given the first host address on the serial links to BR1 and BR2. BR1 should be given the first host address for the serial link to BR2.

Device	Interface	IP Address	Subnet Mask	Device Interface
HQ	G0/0			16,000 Host LAN
	G0/1			8,000 Host LAN
	S0/0/0			BR1 S0/0/0
	S0/0/1			BR2 S0/0/1
BR1	G0/0			2,000 Host LAN
	G0/1			4,000 Host LAN
	S0/0/0			HQ S0/0/0
	S0/0/1			BR2 S0/0/0
BR2	G0/0			500 Host LAN
	G0/1			1,000 Host LAN
	S0/0/0			BR1 S0/0/1
	S0/0/1			HQ S0/0/1

Part 3: Cable and Configure the IPv4 Network

In Part 3, you will cable the network topology and configure the three routers using the VLSM address scheme that you developed in Part 2.

Step 1: Cable the network as shown in the topology.

Step 2: Configure basic settings on each router.

a.   Assign the device name to the router.

b.   Disable DNS lookup to prevent the router from attempting to translate incorrectly entered commands as though they were hostnames.

c.   Assign **class** as the privileged EXEC encrypted password.

d.   Assign **cisco** as the console password and enable login.

e.   Assign **cisco** as the vty password and enable login.

f.   Encrypt the clear text passwords.

g.   Create a banner that warns anyone accessing the device that unauthorized access is prohibited.

Step 3: Configure the interfaces on each router.

a.   Assign an IP address and subnet mask to each interface using the table that you completed in Part 2.

b.   Configure an interface description for each interface.

c.   Set the clocking rate on all DCE serial interfaces to 128000.

```
HQ(config-if)# clock rate 128000
```

d.   Activate the interfaces.

Step 4: Save the configuration on all devices.

Step 5: **Test Connectivity.**

a. From HQ, ping BR1's S0/0/0 interface address.

b. From HQ, ping BR2's S0/0/1 interface address.

c. From BR1, ping BR2's S0/0/0 interface address.

d. Troubleshoot connectivity issues if pings were not successful.

Note: Pings to the GigabitEthernet interfaces on other routers are unsuccessful. The LANs defined for the GigabitEthernet interfaces are simulated. Because no devices are attached to these LANs, they are in a down/down state. A routing protocol must be in place for other devices to be aware of those subnets. The GigabitEthernet interfaces must also be in an up/up state before a routing protocol can add the subnets to the routing table. These interfaces remain in a down/down state until a device is connected to the other end of the Ethernet interface cable. The focus of this lab is on VLSM and configuring the interfaces.

Reflection

Can you think of a shortcut for calculating the network addresses of consecutive /30 subnets?

____

____

____

____

Router Interface Summary Table

Router Interface Summary				
Router Model	**Ethernet Interface #1**	**Ethernet Interface #2**	**Serial Interface #1**	**Serial Interface #2**
1800	Fast Ethernet 0/0 (F0/0)	Fast Ethernet 0/1 (F0/1)	Serial 0/0/0 (S0/0/0)	Serial 0/0/1 (S0/0/1)
1900	Gigabit Ethernet 0/0 (G0/0)	Gigabit Ethernet 0/1 (G0/1)	Serial 0/0/0 (S0/0/0)	Serial 0/0/1 (S0/0/1)
2801	Fast Ethernet 0/0 (F0/0)	Fast Ethernet 0/1 (F0/1)	Serial 0/1/0 (S0/1/0)	Serial 0/1/1 (S0/1/1)
2811	Fast Ethernet 0/0 (F0/0)	Fast Ethernet 0/1 (F0/1)	Serial 0/0/0 (S0/0/0)	Serial 0/0/1 (S0/0/1)
2900	Gigabit Ethernet 0/0 (G0/0)	Gigabit Ethernet 0/1 (G0/1)	Serial 0/0/0 (S0/0/0)	Serial 0/0/1 (S0/0/1)

Note: To find out how the router is configured, look at the interfaces to identify the type of router and how many interfaces the router has. There is no way to effectively list all the combinations of configurations for each router class. This table includes identifiers for the possible combinations of Ethernet and Serial interfaces in the device. The table does not include any other type of interface, even though a specific router may contain one. An example of this might be an ISDN BRI interface. The string in parenthesis is the legal abbreviation that can be used in Cisco IOS commands to represent the interface.

2.4.2.5 Lab – Calculating Summary Routes with IPv4 and IPv6

Topology

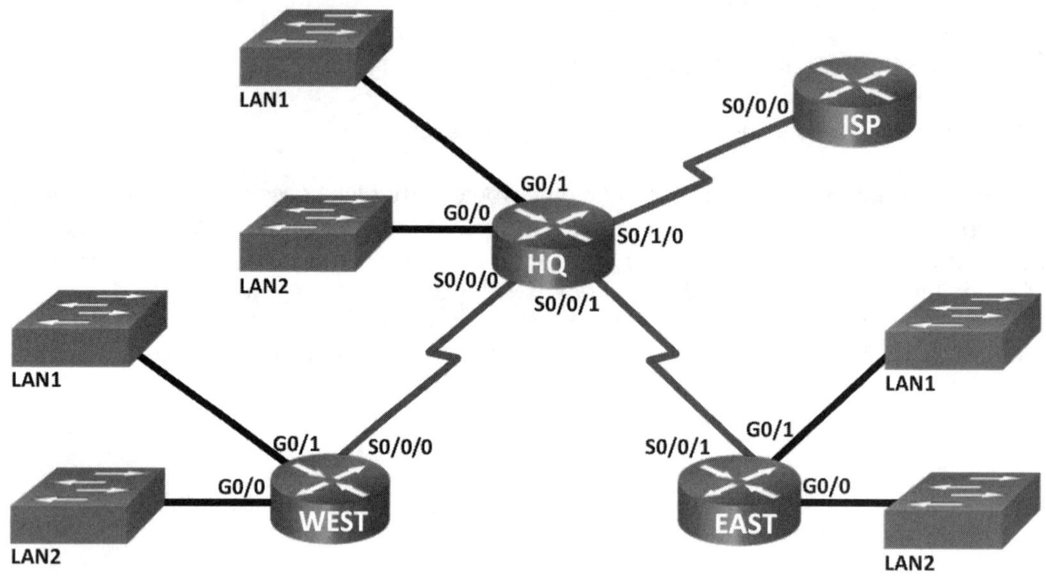

Addressing Table

Subnet	IPv4 Address	IPv6 Address
HQ LAN1	192.168.64.0/23	2001:DB8:ACAD:E::/64
HQ LAN2	192.168.66.0/23	2001:DB8:ACAD:F::/64
EAST LAN1	192.168.68.0/24	2001:DB8:ACAD:1::/64
EAST LAN2	192.168.69.0/24	2001:DB8:ACAD:2::/64
WEST LAN1	192.168.70.0/25	2001:DB8:ACAD:9::/64
WEST LAN2	192.168.70.128/25	2001:DB8:ACAD:A::/64
Link from HQ to EAST	192.168.71.4/30	2001:DB8:ACAD:1000::/64
Link from HQ to WEST	192.168.71.0/30	2001:DB8:ACAD:2000::/64
Link from HQ to ISP	209.165.201.0/30	2001:DB8:CC1E:1::/64

Objectives

Part 1: Calculate IPv4 Summary Routes

- Determine the summary route for the HQ LANs.
- Determine the summary route for the EAST LANs.
- Determine the summary route for the WEST LANs.
- Determine the summary route for the HQ, EAST, and WEST LANs.

Part 2: Calculate IPv6 Summary Routes

- Determine the summary route for the HQ LANs.
- Determine the summary route for the EAST LANs.
- Determine the summary route for the WEST LANs.
- Determine the summary route for the HQ, EAST, and WEST LANs.

Background / Scenario

Summary routes reduce the number of entries in routing tables and make the routing table lookup process more efficient. This process also reduces the memory requirements for the router. A single static route can be used to represent a few routes or thousands of routes.

In this lab, you will determine the summary routes for different subnets of a network. You will then determine the summary route for the entire network. Summary routes will be determined for both IPv4 and IPv6 addresses. Because IPv6 uses hexadecimal (hex) values, you will be required to convert hex to binary.

Required Resources

- 1 PC (Windows 7, Vista, or XP with Internet access)
- Optional: calculator for converting hex and decimal to binary

Part 1:   Calculate IPv4 Summary Routes

In Part 1, you will determine summarized routes that can be used to reduce the size of routing tables. Fill in the tables, after each set of steps, with the appropriate IPv4 addressing information.

Step 1:   List the HQ LAN1 and HQ LAN2 IP subnet mask in decimal form.

Step 2:   List the HQ LAN1 and HQ LAN2 IP address in binary form.

Step 3:   Count the number of far left matching bits to determine the subnet mask for the summary route.

a.   How many far left matching bits are present in the two networks? _______________

b.   List the subnet mask for the summary route in decimal form.

Step 4:   Copy the matching binary bits and then add all zeros to determine the summarized network address.

a.   List the matching binary bits for HQ LAN1 and HQ LAN2 subnets.

b.   Add zeros to comprise the remainder of the network address in binary form.

c.   List the summarized network address in decimal form.

Subnet	IPv4 Address	Subnet Mask	Subnet IP Address in Binary Form
HQ LAN1	192.168.64.0		
HQ LAN2	192.168.66.0		
HQ LANs Summary Address			

Step 5:   List the EAST LAN1 and EAST LAN2 IP subnet mask in decimal form.

Step 6:   **List the EAST LAN1 and EAST LAN2 IP address in binary form.**

Step 7:   **Count the number of far left matching bits to determine the subnet mask for the summary route.**

    a.   How many far left matching bits are present in the two networks? _______________

    b.   List the subnet mask for the summary route in decimal form.

Step 8:   **Copy the matching binary bits and then add all zeros to determine the summarized network address.**

    a.   List the matching binary bits for EAST LAN1 and EAST LAN2 subnets.

    b.   Add zeros to comprise the remainder of the network address in binary form.

    c.   List the summarized network address in decimal form.

Subnet	IPv4 Address	Subnet Mask	Subnet Address in Binary Form
EAST LAN1	192.168.68.0		
EAST LAN2	192.168.69.0		
EAST LANs Summary Address			

Step 9:   **List the WEST LAN1 and WEST LAN2 IP subnet mask in decimal form.**

Step 10:   **List the WEST LAN1 and WEST LAN2 IP address in binary form.**

Step 11:   **Count the number of far left matching bits to determine the subnet mask for the summary route.**

    a.   How many far left matching bits are present in the two networks? _______________

    b.   List the subnet mask for the summary route in decimal form.

Step 12:   **Copy the matching binary bits and then add all zeros to determine the summarized network address.**

    a.   List the matching binary bits for WEST LAN1 and WEST LAN2 subnets.

    b.   Add zeros to comprise the remainder of the network address in binary form.

    c.   List the summarized network address in decimal form.

Subnet	IPv4 Address	Subnet Mask	Subnet IP Address in Binary Form
WEST LAN1	192.168.70.0		
WEST LAN2	192.168.70.128		
WEST LANs Summary Address			

Step 13: List the HQ, EAST, and WEST summary route IP address and subnet mask in decimal form.

Step 14: List the HQ, EAST, and WEST summary route IP address in binary form.

Step 15: Count the number of far left matching bits to determine the subnet mask for the summary route.

a.   How many far left matching bits are present in the three networks? _______________

b.   List the subnet mask for the summary route in decimal form.

Step 16: Copy the matching binary bits and then add all zeros to determine the summarized network address.

a.   List the matching binary bits for HQ, EAST, and WEST subnets.

b.   Add zeros to comprise the remainder of the network address in binary form.

c.   List the summarized network address in decimal form.

Subnet	IPv4 Address	Subnet Mask	Subnet IP Address in Binary Form
HQ			
EAST			
WEST			
Network Address Summary Route			

Part 2:   Calculate IPv6 Summary Routes

In Part 2, you will determine summarized routes that can be used to reduce the size of routing tables. Complete the tables after each set of steps, with the appropriate IPv6 addressing information.

Topology

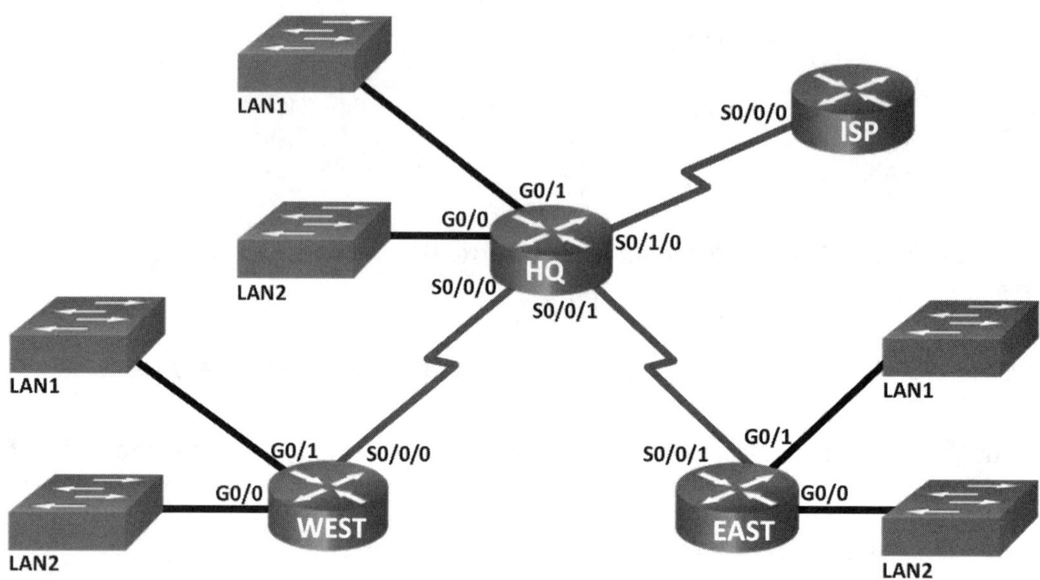

Addressing Table

Subnet	IPv6 Address
HQ LAN1	2001:DB8:ACAD:E::/64
HQ LAN2	2001:DB8:ACAD:F::/64
EAST LAN1	2001:DB8:ACAD:1::/64
EAST LAN2	2001:DB8:ACAD:2::/64
WEST LAN1	2001:DB8:ACAD:9::/64
WEST LAN2	2001:DB8:ACAD:A::/64
Link from HQ to EAST	2001:DB8:ACAD:1000::/64
Link from HQ to WEST	2001:DB8:ACAD:2000::/64
Link from HQ to ISP	2001:DB8:CC1E:1::/64

Step 1:   List the first 64 bits of the HQ LAN1 and HQ LAN2 IP subnet mask in hexadecimal form.

Step 2:   List the HQ LAN1 and HQ LAN2 subnet ID (bits 48-64) in binary form.

Step 3:   Count the number of far left matching bits to determine the subnet mask for the summary route.

a.   How many far left matching bits are present in the two subnet IDs? ________________

b.   List the subnet mask for the first 64 bits of the summary route in decimal form.

Step 4:   Copy the matching binary bits and then add all zeros to determine the summarized network address.

a.   List the matching subnet ID binary bits for HQ LAN1 and HQ LAN2 subnets.

b. Add zeros to comprise the remainder of the subnet ID address in binary form.

c. List the summarized network address in decimal form.

Subnet	IPv6 Address	Subnet Mask for First 64 bits	Subnet ID in Binary Form
HQ LAN1	2001:DB8:ACAD:E::/64		
HQ LAN2	2001:DB8:ACAD:F::/64		
HQ LANs Summary Address			

Step 5:   **List the first 64 bits of the EAST LAN1 and EAST LAN2 IP subnet mask in hexadecimal form.**

Step 6:   **List the EAST LAN1 and EAST LAN2 subnet ID (bits 48-64) in binary form.**

Step 7:   **Count the number of far left matching bits to determine the subnet mask for the summary route.**

a. How many far left matching bits are present in the two subnet IDs? _______________

b. List the subnet mask for the first 64 bits of the summary route in decimal form.

Step 8:   **Copy the matching binary bits and then add all zeros to determine the summarized network address.**

a. List the matching binary bits for EAST LAN1 and EAST LAN2 subnets.

b. Add zeros to comprise the remainder of the subnet ID address in binary form.

c. List the summarized network address in decimal form.

Subnet	IPv6 Address	Subnet Mask for First 64 bits	Subnet ID in Binary Form
EAST LAN1	2001:DB8:ACAD:1::/64		
EAST LAN2	2001:DB8:ACAD:2::/64		
EAST LANs Summary Address			

Step 9:   **List the first 64 bits of the WEST LAN1 and WEST LAN2 IP subnet mask in decimal form.**

Step 10: **List the WEST LAN1 and WEST LAN2 subnet ID (bits 48-64) in binary form.**

Step 11: **Count the number of far left matching bits to determine the subnet mask for the summary route.**

a. How many far left matching bits are present in the two subnet IDs? _______________

b. List the subnet mask for the first 64 bits of the summary route in decimal form.

Step 12: Copy the matching binary bits and then add all zeros to determine the summarized network address.

    a.   List the matching binary bits for WEST LAN1 and WEST LAN2 subnets.

    b.   Add zeros to comprise the remainder of the subnet ID address in binary form.

    c.   List the summarized network address in decimal form.

Subnet	IPv6 Address	Subnet Mask for First 64 bits	Subnet ID in Binary Form
WEST LAN1	2001:DB8:ACAD:9::/64		
WEST LAN2	2001:DB8:ACAD:A::/64		
WEST LANs Summary Address			

Step 13: List the HQ, EAST, and WEST summary route IP address and the first 64 bits of the subnet mask in decimal form.

Step 14: List the HQ, EAST, and WEST summary route subnet ID in binary form.

Step 15: Count the number of far left matching bits to determine the subnet mask for the summary route.

    a.   How many far left matching bits are present in the three subnet IDs? _______________

    b.   List the subnet mask for the first 64 bits of the summary route in decimal form.

Step 16: Copy the matching binary bits and then add all zeros to determine the summarized network address.

    a.   List the matching binary bits for HQ, EAST, and WEST subnets.

    b.   Add zeros to comprise the remainder of the subnet ID address in binary form.

    c.   List the summarized network address in decimal form.

Subnet	IPv6 Address	Subnet Mask for first 64 bits	Subnet ID in Binary Form
HQ			
EAST			
WEST			
Network Address Summary Route			

Reflection

1. How is determining the summary route for IPv4 different from IPv6?

2. Why are summary routes beneficial to a network?

2.5.2.5 Lab – Troubleshooting IPv4 and IPv6 Static Routes

Topology

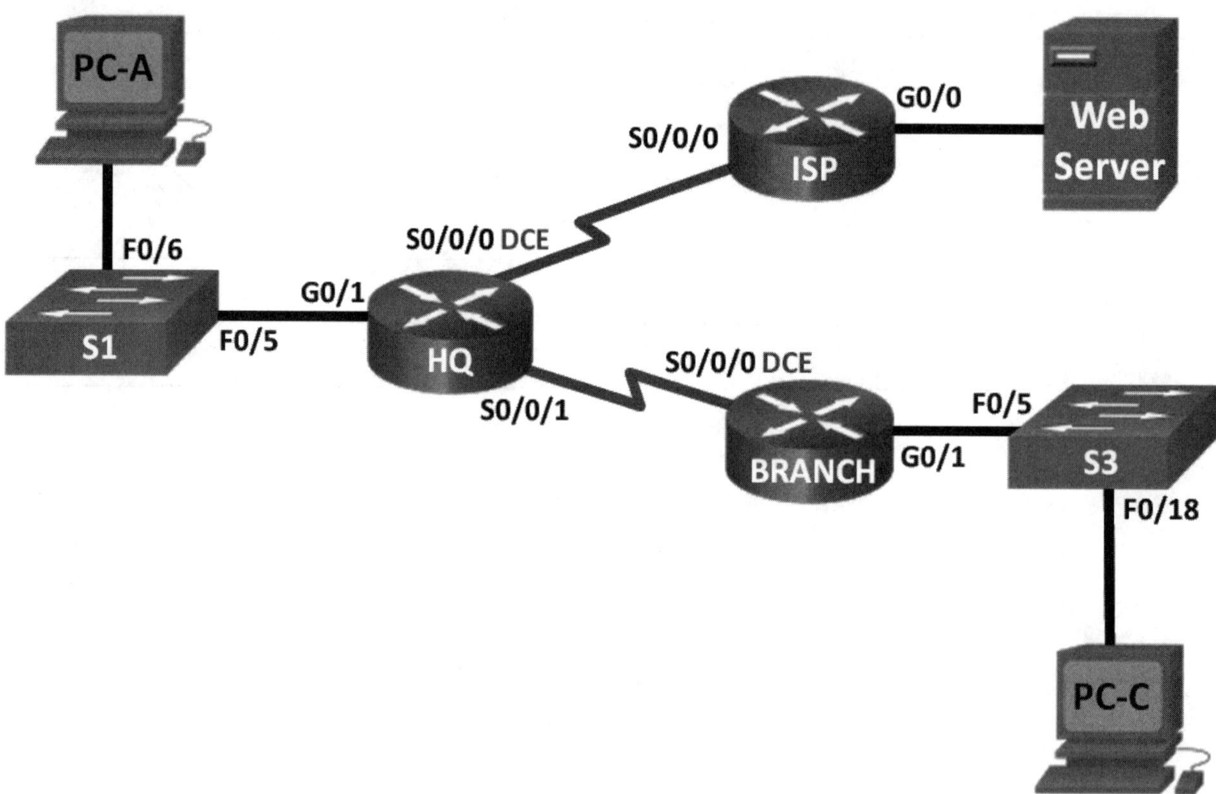

Addressing Table

Device	Interface	IP Address	Default Gateway
HQ	G0/1	192.168.0.1/25 2001:DB8:ACAD::1/64 FE80::1 link-local	N/A
	S0/0/0 (DCE)	10.1.1.2/30 2001:DB8:ACAD::20:2/64	N/A
	S0/0/1	192.168.0.253/30 2001:DB8:ACAD:2::1/30	N/A
ISP	G0/0	172.16.3.1/24 2001:DB8:ACAD:30::1/64 FE80::1 link-local	N/A
	S0/0/0	10.1.1.1/30 2001:DB8:ACAD:20::/64	N/A
BRANCH	G0/1	192.168.1.1/24 2001:DB8:ACAD:1::1/64 FE80::1 link-local	N/A
	S0/0/0 (DCE)	192.168.0.254/30 2001:DB8:ACAD:2::2/64	N/A
S1	VLAN 1	N/A	N/A
S3	VLAN 1	N/A	N/A
PC-A	NIC	192.168.0.3/25 2001:DB8:ACAD::3/64	192.168.0.1 FE80::1
Web Server	NIC	172.16.3.3/24 2001:DB8:ACAD:30::3/64	172.16.3.1 FE80::1
PC-C	NIC	192.168.1.3/24 2001:DB8:ACAD:1::3/64	192.168.1.1 FE80::1

Objectives

Part 1: Build the Network and Configure Basic Device Settings

Part 2: Troubleshoot Static Routes in an IPv4 Network

Part 3: Troubleshoot Static Routes in an IPv6 Network

Background / Scenario

As a network administrator, you must be able to configure routing of traffic using static routes. Understanding how to configure and troubleshoot static routing is a requirement. Static routes are commonly used for stub networks and default routes. Your company's ISP has hired you to troubleshoot connectivity issues on the network. You will have access to the HQ, BRANCH, and the ISP routers.

In this lab, you will begin by loading configuration scripts on each of the routers. These scripts contain errors that will prevent end-to-end communication across the network. You will need to troubleshoot each router to determine the configuration errors, and then use the appropriate commands to correct the configurations.

When you have corrected all of the configuration errors, the hosts on the network should be able to communicate with each other.

Note: The routers used with CCNA hands-on labs are Cisco 1941 Integrated Services Routers (ISRs) with Cisco IOS Release 15.2(4)M3 (universalk9 image). The switches used are Cisco Catalyst 2960s with Cisco IOS Release 15.0(2) (lanbasek9 image). Other routers, switches, and Cisco IOS versions can be used. Depending on the model and Cisco IOS version, the commands available and output produced might vary from what is shown in the labs. Refer to the Router Interface Summary Table at the end of this lab for the correct interface identifiers.

Note: Make sure that the routers and switches have been erased and have no startup configurations. If you are unsure, contact your instructor.

Required Resources

- 3 Routers (Cisco 1941 with Cisco IOS Release 15.2(4)M3 universal image or comparable)
- 2 Switches (Cisco 2960 with Cisco IOS Release 15.0(2) lanbasek9 image or comparable)
- 3 PCs (Windows 7, Vista, or XP with terminal emulation program, such as Tera Term)
- Console cables to configure the Cisco IOS devices via the console ports
- Ethernet and serial cables as shown in the topology

Part 1:   Build the Network and Configure Basic Device Settings

In Part 1, you will set up the network topology and configure the routers and switches with some basic settings, such as passwords and IP addresses. Preset configurations are also provided for you for the initial router configurations. You will also configure the IP settings for the PCs in the topology.

Step 1:   Cable the network as shown in the topology.

Attach the devices as shown in the topology diagram and cable, as necessary.

Step 2:   Initialize and reload the routers and switches.

Step 3:   Configure basic settings for each router.

a.   Disable DNS lookup.

b.   Configure device name as shown in the topology.

c.   Assign **class** as the privileged EXEC mode password.

d.   Assign **cisco** as the console and vty passwords.

e.   Configure **logging synchronous** to prevent console messages from interrupting command entry.

Step 4:   Configure hosts and Web Server.

a.   Configure IP addresses for IPv4 and IPv6.

b.   Configure IPv4 default gateway.

Step 5: **Load router configurations.**

Router HQ

```
hostname HQ
ipv6 unicast-routing
interface GigabitEthernet0/1
 ipv6 address 2001:DB8:ACAD::1/64
 ip address 192.168.0.1 255.255.255.128
 ipv6 address FE80::1 link-local

interface Serial0/0/0
 ipv6 address 2001:DB8:ACAD:20::2/64
 ip address 10.1.1.2 255.255.255.252
 clock rate 800000
 no shutdown
interface Serial0/0/1
 ipv6 address 2001:DB8:ACAD:2::3/64

 ip address 192.168.0.253 255.255.255.252
 no shutdown
ip route 172.16.3.0 255.255.255.0 10.1.1.1
ip route 192.168.1.0 255.255.255.0 192.16.0.254

ipv6 route 2001:DB8:ACAD:1::/64 2001:DB8:ACAD:2::2
ipv6 route 2001:DB8:ACAD:30::/64 2001:DB8:ACAD::20:1
```

Router ISP

```
hostname ISP
ipv6 unicast-routing
interface GigabitEthernet0/0
 ipv6 address 2001:DB8:ACAD:30::1/64
 ip address 172.16.3.11 255.255.255.0

 ipv6 address FE80::1 link-local
 no shutdown
interface Serial0/0/0
 ipv6 address 2001:DB8::ACAD:20:1/64

 ip address 10.1.1.1 255.255.255.252
 no shutdown
```

```
ip route 192.168.1.0 255.255.255.0 10.1.1.2


ipv6 route 2001:DB8:ACAD::/62 2001:DB8:ACAD:20::2
```

Router BRANCH

```
hostname BRANCH

ipv6 unicast-routing

interface GigabitEthernet0/1

 ipv6 address 2001:DB8:ACAD:1::1/64

 ip address 192.168.1.1 255.255.255.0

 ipv6 address FE80::1 link-local

 no shutdown

interface Serial0/0/0

 ipv6 address 2001:DB8:ACAD:2::2/64

 clock rate 128000

 ip address 192.168.0.249 255.255.255.252


 clock rate 128000

 no shutdown

ip route 0.0.0.0 0.0.0.0 10.1.1.2



ipv6 route ::/0 2001:DB8:ACAD::1
```

Part 2:   Troubleshoot Static Routes in an IPv4 Network

IPv4 Addressing Table

Device	Interface	IP Address	Subnet Mask	Default Gateway
HQ	G0/1	192.168.0.1	255.255.255.0	N/A
	S0/0/0 (DCE)	10.1.1.2	255.255.255.252	N/A
	S0/0/1	192.168.0.253	255.255.255.252	N/A
ISP	G0/0	172.16.3.1	255.255.255.0	N/A
	S0/0/0	10.1.1.1	255.255.255.252	N/A
BRANCH	G0/1	192.168.1.1	255.255.255.0	N/A
	S0/0/0 (DCE)	192.168.0.254	255.255.255.252	N/A
S1	VLAN 1	192.168.0.11	255.255.255.128	192.168.0.1
S3	VLAN 1	192.168.1.11	255.255.255.0	192.168.1.1
PC-A	NIC	192.168.0.3	255.255.255.128	192.168.0.1
Web Server	NIC	172.16.3.3	255.255.255.0	172.16.3.1
PC-C	NIC	192.168.1.3	255.255.255.0	192.168.1.1

Step 1:   Troubleshoot the HQ router.

The HQ router is the link between the ISP router and the BRANCH router. The ISP router represents the outside network while the BRANCH router represents the corporate network. The HQ router is configured with static routes to ISP and BRANCH networks.

a.   Display the status of the interfaces on HQ. Enter **show ip interface brief**. Record and resolve any issues as necessary.

---

b.   Ping from HQ router to BRANCH router (192.168.0.254). Were the pings successful? _________

c.   Ping from HQ router to ISP router (10.1.1.1). Were the pings successful? _________

d.   Ping from PC-A to the default gateway. Were the pings successful? _________

e.   Ping from PC-A to PC-C. Were the pings successful? _________

f.   Ping from PC-A to Web Server. Were the pings successful? _________

g.   Display the routing table on HQ. What non-directly connected routes are shown in the routing table?

---

h.   Based on the results of the pings, routing table output, and static routes in the running configuration, what can you conclude about network connectivity?

---

i.   What commands (if any) need to be entered to resolve routing issues? Record the command(s).

---

j.   Repeat any of the steps from b to f to verify whether the problems have been resolved. Record your observations and possible next steps in troubleshooting connectivity.

____

____

____

Step 2:   **Troubleshoot the ISP router.**

For the ISP router, there should be a route to HQ and BRANCH routers. One static route is configured on ISP router to reach the 192.168.1.0/24, 192.168.0.0/25, and 192.168.0.252/30 networks.

a.   Display the status of interfaces on ISP. Enter **show ip interface brief**. Record and resolve any issues as necessary.

____

____

____

b.   Ping from the ISP router to the HQ router (10.1.1.2). Were the pings successful? _________

c.   Ping from Web Server to the default gateway. Were the pings successful? _________

d.   Ping from Web Server to PC-A. Were the pings successful? _________

e.   Ping from Web Server to PC-C. Were the pings successful? _________

f.   Display the routing table on ISP. What non-directly connected routes are shown in the routing table?

____

____

g.   Based on the results of the pings, routing table output, and static routes in the running configuration, what can you conclude about network connectivity?

____

____

____

h.   What commands (if any) need to be entered to resolve routing issues? Record the command(s).

(Hint: ISP only requires one summarized route to the company's networks 192.168.1.0/24, 192.168.0.0/25, and 192.168.0.252/32.)

i.   Repeat any of the steps from b to e to verify whether the problems have been resolved. Record your observations and possible next steps in troubleshooting connectivity.

Step 3:   Troubleshoot the BRANCH router.

For the BRANCH router, a default route is set to reach the rest of the network and ISP.

a.   Display the status of the interfaces on BRANCH. Enter **show ip interface brief**. Record and resolve any issues, as necessary.

b.   Ping from the BRANCH router to the HQ router (192.168.0.253). Were the pings successful? _________

c.   Ping from PC-C to the default gateway. Were the pings successful? _________

d.   Ping from PC-C to PC-A. Were the pings successful? _________

e.   Ping from PC-C to Web Server. Were the pings successful? _________

f.   Display the routing table on BRANCH. What non-directly connected routes are shown in the routing table?

g. Based on the results of the pings, routing table output, and static routes in the running configuration, what can you conclude about network connectivity?

____

____

____

h. What commands (if any) need to be entered to resolve routing issues? Record the command(s).

____

____

____

i. Repeat any of the steps from b to e to verify whether the problems have been resolved. Record your observations and possible next steps in troubleshooting connectivity.

____

____

____

Part 3:   Troubleshoot Static Routes in an IPv6 Network

Device	Interface	IPv6 Address	Prefix Length	Default Gateway
HQ	G0/1	2001:DB8:ACAD::1	64	N/A
	S0/0/0 (DCE)	2001:DB8:ACAD::20:2	64	N/A
	S0/0/1	2001:DB8:ACAD:2::1	64	N/A
ISP	G0/0	2001:DB8:ACAD:30::1	64	N/A
	S0/0/0	2001:DB8:ACAD:20::1	64	N/A
BRANCH	G0/1	2001:DB8:ACAD:1::1	64	N/A
	S0/0/0 (DCE)	2001:DB8:ACAD:2::2	64	N/A
PC-A	NIC	2001:DB8:ACAD::3	64	FE80::1
Web Server	NIC	2001:DB8:ACAD:30::3	64	FE80::1
PC-C	NIC	2001:DB8:ACAD:1::3	64	FE80::1

Step 1:   Troubleshoot the HQ router.

The HQ router is the link between the ISP router and the BRANCH router. The ISP router represents the outside network while the BRANCH router represents the corporate network. The HQ router is configured with static routes to both the ISP and the BRANCH networks.

a. Display the status of the interfaces on HQ. Enter **show ipv6 interface brief**. Record and resolve any issues, as necessary.

____

____

b. Ping from the HQ router to the BRANCH router (2001:DB8:ACAD:2::2). Were the pings successful?

____

c. Ping from the HQ router to the ISP router (2001:DB8:ACAD:20::1). Were the pings successful? _______________

d. Ping from PC-A to the default gateway. Were the pings successful? _______________

e. Ping from PC-A to Web Server. Were the pings successful? _______________

f. Ping from PC-A to PC-C. Were the pings successful? _______________

g. Display the routing table by issuing a **show ipv6 route** command. What non-directly connected routes are shown in the routing table?

____

____

____

h. Based on the results of the pings, routing table output, and static routes in the running configuration, what can you conclude about network connectivity?

____

____

____

i. What commands (if any) need to be entered to resolve routing issues? Record the command(s).

____

____

j.   Repeat any of the steps from b to f to verify whether the problems have been resolved. Record your observations and possible next steps in troubleshooting connectivity.

____

____

____

Step 2:   Troubleshoot the ISP router.

On the ISP router, one static route is configured to reach all the networks on HQ and BRANCH routers.

a.   Display the status of the interfaces on ISP. Enter **show ipv6 interface brief**. Record and resolve any issues, as necessary.

____

____

b.   Ping from the ISP router to the HQ router (2001:DB8:ACAD:20::2). Were the pings successful? _________

c.   Ping from Web Server to the default gateway. Were the pings successful? _________

d.   Ping from Web Server to PC-A. Were the pings successful? _________

e.   Ping from Web Server to PC-C. Were the pings successful? _________

f.   Display the routing table. What non-directly connected routes are shown in the routing table?

____

____

g.   Based on the results of the pings, routing table output, and static routes in the running configuration, what can you conclude about network connectivity?

____

____

____

h. What commands (if any) need to be entered to resolve routing issues? Record the command(s).

____

____

i. Repeat any of the steps from b to e to verify whether the problems have been resolved. Record your observations and possible next steps in troubleshooting connectivity.

____

____

____

Step 3: **Troubleshoot the BRANCH router.**

For the BRANCH routers, there is a default route to the HQ router. This default route allows the BRANCH network to the ISP router and Web Server.

a. Display the status of the interfaces on BRANCH. Enter **show ipv6 interface brief**. Record and resolve any issues, as necessary.

____

____

b. Ping from the BRANCH router to the HQ router (2001:DB8:ACAD:2::1). Were the pings successful?
____

c. Ping from the BRANCH router to the ISP router (2001:DB8:ACAD:20::1). Were the pings successful?
____

d. Ping from PC-C to the default gateway. Were the pings successful? ________

e. Ping from PC-C to PC-A. Were the pings successful? ________

f. Ping from PC-C to Web Server. Were the pings successful? ________

g. Display the routing table. What non-directly connected routes are shown in the routing table?

____

____

h. Based on the results of the pings, routing table output, and static routes in the running configuration, what can you conclude about network connectivity?

____

____

____

i. What commands (if any) need to be entered to resolve routing issues? Record the command(s).

____

____

j. Repeat any of the steps from b to f to verify whether the problems have been resolved. Record your observations and possible next steps in troubleshooting connectivity.

____

____

____

Router Interface Summary Table

Router Interface Summary				
Router Model	**Ethernet Interface #1**	**Ethernet Interface #2**	**Serial Interface #1**	**Serial Interface #2**
1800	Fast Ethernet 0/0 (F0/0)	Fast Ethernet 0/1 (F0/1)	Serial 0/0/0 (S0/0/0)	Serial 0/0/1 (S0/0/1)
1900	Gigabit Ethernet 0/0 (G0/0)	Gigabit Ethernet 0/1 (G0/1)	Serial 0/0/0 (S0/0/0)	Serial 0/0/1 (S0/0/1)
2801	Fast Ethernet 0/0 (F0/0)	Fast Ethernet 0/1 (F0/1)	Serial 0/1/0 (S0/1/0)	Serial 0/1/1 (S0/1/1)
2811	Fast Ethernet 0/0 (F0/0)	Fast Ethernet 0/1 (F0/1)	Serial 0/0/0 (S0/0/0)	Serial 0/0/1 (S0/0/1)
2900	Gigabit Ethernet 0/0 (G0/0)	Gigabit Ethernet 0/1 (G0/1)	Serial 0/0/0 (S0/0/0)	Serial 0/0/1 (S0/0/1)

Note: To find out how the router is configured, look at the interfaces to identify the type of router and how many interfaces the router has. There is no way to effectively list all the combinations of configurations for each router class. This table includes identifiers for the possible combinations of Ethernet and Serial interfaces in the device. The table does not include any other type of interface, even though a specific router may contain one. An example of this might be an ISDN BRI interface. The string in parenthesis is the legal abbreviation that can be used in Cisco IOS commands to represent the interface.

2.6.1.1 Class Activity – Make It Static!

Objectives

Configure a static route.

As the use of IPv6 addressing becomes more prevalent, it is important for network administrators to be able to direct network traffic between routers.

To prove that you are able to direct IPv6 traffic correctly and review the IPv6 default static route curriculum concepts, use the topology as shown in the .pdf file provided, specifically for this activity. Work with a partner to write an IPv6 statement for each of the three scenarios. Try to write the route statements without the assistance of completed labs, Packet Tracer files, etc.

- **Scenario 1**

  IPv6 default static route from R2 directing all data through your S0/0/0 interface to the next hop address on R1.

- **Scenario 2**

  IPv6 default static route from R3 directing all data through your S0/0/1 interface to the next hop address on R2.

- **Scenario 3**

  IPv6 default static route from R2 directing all data through your S0/0/1 interface to the next hop address on R3.

When complete, get together with another group and compare your written answers. Discuss any differences found in your comparisons.

Resources

Topology Diagram

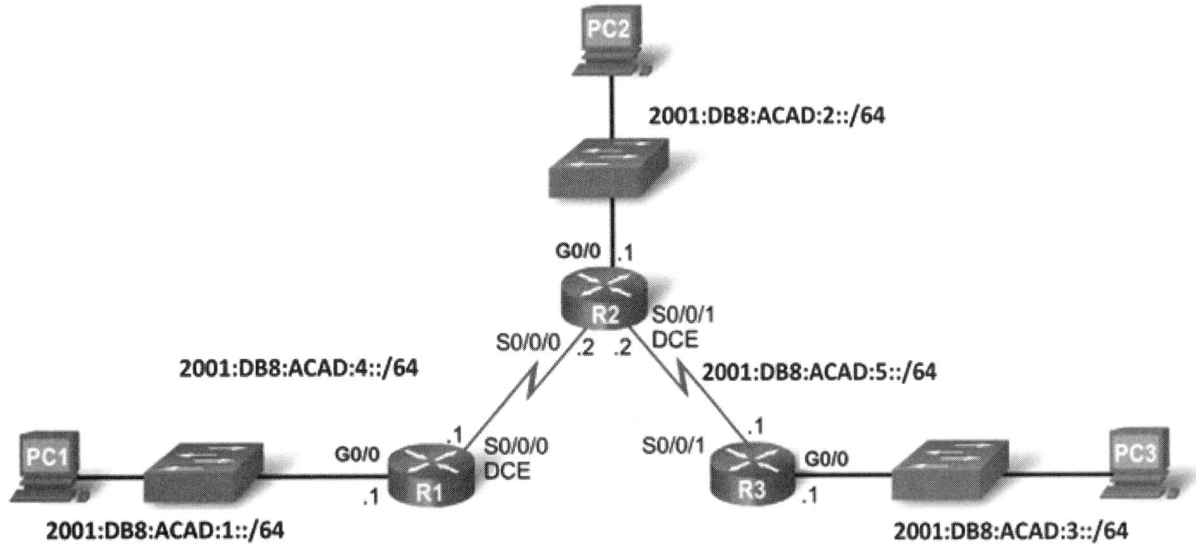

- **Scenario 1**

  IPv6 default static route from R2 directing all data to the next hop address on R1.

Configuration Command	IPv6 Network to Route	Next Hop IPv6 Address
R2(config)# **ipv6 route**		

- **Scenario 2**

  IPv6 default static route from R3 directing all data to the next hop address on R2.

Configuration Command	IPv6 Network to Route	Next Hop IPv6 Address
R3(config)# **ipv6 route**		

- **Scenario 3**

  IPv6 default static route from R2 directing all data to the next hop address on R3.

Configuration Command	IPv6 Network to Route	Next Hop IPv6 Address
R2(config)# **ipv6 route**		

Chapter 3 — Routing Dynamically

3.0.1.2 Class Activity – How Much Does This Cost?

Objectives

Explain the operation of dynamic routing protocols.

Scenario

This modeling activity illustrates the network concept of routing cost.

You will be a member of a team of five students who travel routes to complete the activity scenarios. One digital camera or bring your own device (BYOD) with camera, a stopwatch, and the student file for this activity will be required per group. One person will function as the photographer and event recorder, as selected by each group. The remaining four team members will actively participate in the scenarios below.

A school or university classroom, hallway, outdoor track area, school parking lot, or any other location can serve as the venue for these activities.

Activity 1

The tallest person in the group establishes a start and finish line by marking 15 steps from start to finish, indicating the distance of the team route. Each student will take 15 steps from the start line toward the finish line and then stop on the 15th step—no further steps are allowed.

Note: Not all of the students may reach the same distance from the start line due to their height and stride differences. The photographer will take a group picture of the entire team's final location after taking the 15 steps required.

Activity 2

A new start and finish line will be established; however, this time, a longer distance for the route will be established than the distance specified in Activity 1. No maximum steps are to be used as a basis for creating this particular route. One at a time, students will "walk the new route from beginning to end twice".

Each team member will count the steps taken to complete the route. The recorder will time each student and at the end of each team member's route, record the time that it took to complete the full route and how many steps were taken, as recounted by each team member and recorded on the team's student file.

Once both activities have been completed, teams will use the digital picture taken for Activity 1 and their recorded data from Activity 2 file to answer the reflection questions.

Group answers can be discussed as a class, time permitting.

Required Resources

- Digital or BYOD camera to record Activity 1's team results. Activity 2's data is based solely upon number of steps taken and the time it took to complete the route and no camera is necessary for Activity 2.

- Stopwatch

- Student file accompanying this modeling activity so that Activity 2 results can be recorded as each student finishes the route.

Scenario – Part 2 Recording Matrix

Student Team Member Name	Time Used to Finish the Route	Number of Steps Taken to Finish the Route

Reflection Questions

1. The photographer took a picture of the team's progress after taking 15 steps for Activity 1. Most likely, some team members did not reach the finish line on their 15th step due to height and stride differences. What do you think would happen if network data did not reach the finish line, or destination, in the allowed number of hops or steps?

2. What could be done to help team members reach the finish line if they did not reach it in Activity 1?

3. Which person would best be selected to deliver data using the network route completed in Activity 2? Justify your answer.

4. Using the data recorded in Activity 2 and a limit of 255 steps, or hops, did all members of the team take more than 255 steps to finish their route? What would happen if they had to stop on the 254th step, or hop?

5. Use the data that was recorded in Activity 2. Would you say the parameters for the route were enough to finish it successfully if all team members reached the finish line with 255 or less steps, or hops? Justify your answer.

6. In network routing, different parameters are set for routing protocols. Use the data recorded for Activity 2. Would you select time, or number of steps, or hops, or a combination of both as your preferred routing type? List at least three reasons for your answers.

3.3.2.4 Lab – Configuring Basic RIPv2 and RIPng

Topology

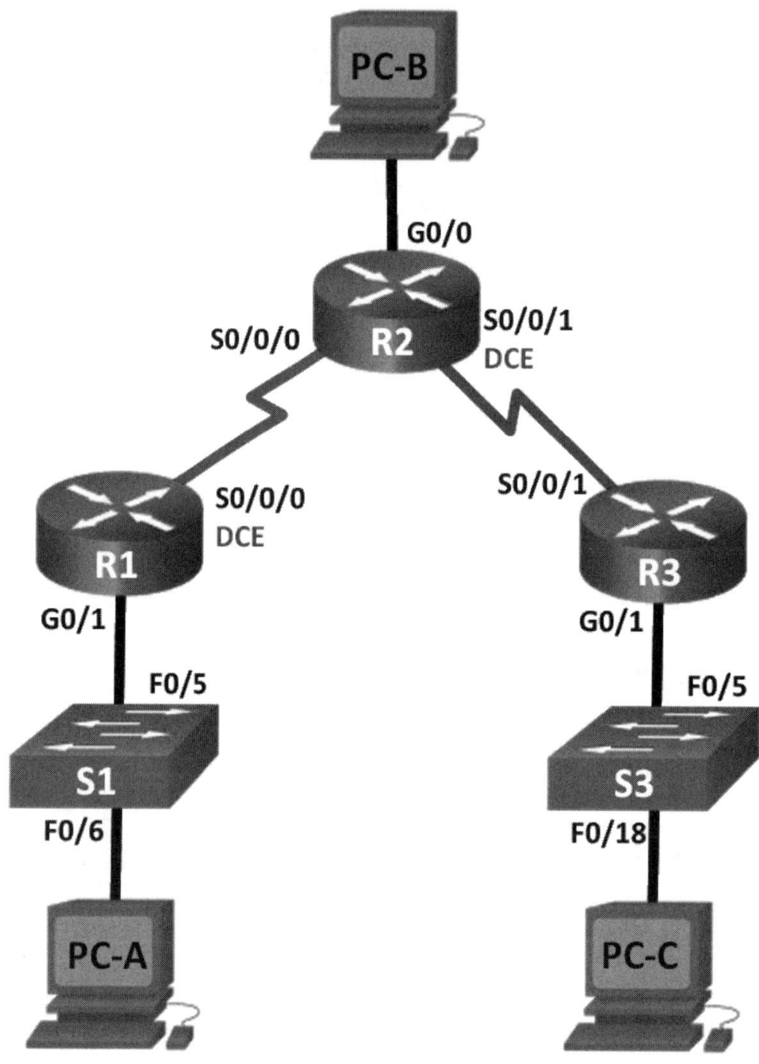

Addressing Table

Device	Interface	IP Address	Subnet Mask	Default Gateway
R1	G0/1	172.30.10.1	255.255.255.0	N/A
	S0/0/0 (DCE)	10.1.1.1	255.255.255.252	N/A
R2	G0/0	209.165.201.1	255.255.255.0	N/A
	S0/0/0	10.1.1.2	255.255.255.252	N/A
	S0/0/1 (DCE)	10.2.2.2	255.255.255.252	N/A
R3	G0/1	172.30.30.1	255.255.255.0	N/A
	S0/0/1	10.2.2.1	255.255.255.252	N/A
S1	N/A	VLAN 1	N/A	N/A
S3	N/A	VLAN 1	N/A	N/A
PC-A	NIC	172.30.10.3	255.255.255.0	172.30.10.1
PC-B	NIC	209.165.201.2	255.255.255.0	209.165.201.1
PC-C	NIC	172.30.30.3	255.255.255.0	172.30.30.1

Objectives

Part 1: Build the Network and Configure Basic Device Settings

Part 2: Configure and Verify RIPv2 Routing

- Configure and verify RIPv2 is running on routers.
- Configure a passive interface.
- Examine routing tables.
- Disable automatic summarization.
- Configure a default route.
- Verify end-to-end connectivity.

Part 3: Configure IPv6 on Devices

Part 4: Configure and Verify RIPng Routing

- Configure and verify RIPng is running on routers.
- Examine routing tables.
- Configure a default route.
- Verify end-to-end connectivity.

Background / Scenario

RIP version 2 (RIPv2) is used for routing of IPv4 addresses in small networks. RIPv2 is a classless, distance-vector routing protocol, as defined by RFC 1723. Because RIPv2 is a classless routing protocol, subnet masks are included in the routing updates. By default, RIPv2 automatically summarizes networks at major network boundaries. When automatic summarization has been disabled, RIPv2 no longer summarizes networks to their classful address at boundary routers.

RIPng (RIP Next Generation) is a distance-vector routing protocol for routing IPv6 addresses, as defined by RFC 2080. RIPng is based on RIPv2 and has the same administrative distance and 15-hop limitation.

In this lab, you will configure the network topology with RIPv2 routing, disable automatic summarization, propagate a default route, and use CLI commands to display and verify RIP routing information. You will then configure the network topology with IPv6 addresses, configure RIPng, propagate a default route, and use CLI commands to display and verify RIPng routing information.

Note: The routers used with CCNA hands-on labs are Cisco 1941 Integrated Services Routers (ISRs) with Cisco IOS Release 15.2(4)M3 (universalk9 image). The switches used are Cisco Catalyst 2960s with Cisco IOS Release 15.0(2) (lanbasek9 image). Other routers, switches, and Cisco IOS versions can be used. Depending on the model and Cisco IOS version, the commands available and output produced might vary from what is shown in the labs. Refer to the Router Interface Summary Table at the end of the lab for the correct interface identifiers.

Note: Make sure that the routers and switches have been erased and have no startup configurations. If you are unsure, contact your instructor.

Required Resources

- 3 Routers (Cisco 1941 with Cisco IOS Release 15.2(4)M3 universal image or comparable)
- 2 Switches (Cisco 2960 with Cisco IOS Release 15.0(2) lanbasek9 image or comparable)
- 3 PCs (Windows 7, Vista, or XP with terminal emulation program, such as Tera Term)
- Console cables to configure the Cisco IOS devices via the console ports
- Ethernet and Serial cables as shown in the topology

Part 1:   Build the Network and Configure Basic Device Settings

In Part 1, you will set up the network topology and configure basic settings.

Step 1:   Cable the network as shown in the topology.

Step 2:   Initialize and reload the router and switch.

Step 3:   Configure basic settings for each router and switch.

a. Disable DNS lookup.

b. Configure device names as shown in the topology.

c. Configure password encryption.

d. Assign **class** as the privileged EXEC password.

e. Assign **cisco** as the console and vty passwords.

f. Configure a MOTD banner to warn users that unauthorized access is prohibited.

g. Configure **logging synchronous** for the console line.

h. Configure the IP address listed in the Addressing Table for all interfaces.

i. Configure a description to each interface with an IP address.

j. Configure the clock rate if applicable to the DCE serial interface.

k. Copy the running-configuration to the startup-configuration.

Step 4:   Configure PC hosts.

Refer to the Addressing Table for PC host address information.

Step 5:   Test connectivity.

At this point, the PCs are unable to ping each other.

a.   Each workstation should be able to ping the attached router. Verify and troubleshoot if necessary.

b.   The routers should be able to ping one another. Verify and troubleshoot if necessary.

Part 2:   Configure and Verify RIPv2 Routing

In Part 2, you will configure RIPv2 routing on all routers in the network and then verify that routing tables are updated correctly. After RIPv2 has been verified, you will disable automatic summarization, configure a default route, and verify end-to-end connectivity.

Step 1:   Configure RIPv2 routing.

a.   On R1, configure RIPv2 as the routing protocol and advertise the appropriate networks.

```
R1# config t
R1(config)# router rip
R1(config-router)# version 2
R1(config-router)# passive-interface g0/1
R1(config-router)# network 172.30.0.0
R1(config-router)# network 10.0.0.0
```

The **passive-interface** command stops routing updates out the specified interface. This process prevents unnecessary routing traffic on the LAN. However, the network that the specified interface belongs to is still advertised in routing updates that are sent out across other interfaces.

b.   Configure RIPv2 on R3 and use the **network** statement to add appropriate networks and prevent routing updates on the LAN interface.

c.   Configure RIPv2 on R2. Do not advertise the 209.165.201.0 network.

Note: It is not necessary to make the G0/0 interface passive on R2 because the network associated with this interface is not being advertised.

Step 2:   Examine current state of network.

a.   The status of the two serial links can quickly be verified using the **show ip interface brief** command on R2.

```
R2# show ip interface brief
Interface                      IP-Address      OK? Method Status                Protocol
Embedded-Service-Engine0/0 unassigned         YES unset  administratively down down
GigabitEthernet0/0             209.165.201.1   YES manual up                     up
GigabitEthernet0/1             unassigned      YES unset  administratively down down
Serial0/0/0                    10.1.1.2        YES manual up                     up
```

```
Serial0/0/1                    10.2.2.2            YES manual up                    up
```

b. Check connectivity between PCs.

From PC-A, is it possible to ping PC-B? __________ Why?

From PC-A, is it possible to ping PC-C? __________ Why?

From PC-C, is it possible to ping PC-B? __________ Why?

From PC-C, is it possible to ping PC-A? __________ Why?

c. Verify that RIPv2 is running on the routers.

You can use the **debug ip rip**, **show ip protocols**, and **show run** commands to confirm that RIPv2 is running. The **show ip protocols** command output for R1 is shown below.

```
R1# show ip protocols

Routing Protocol is "rip"

Outgoing update filter list for all interfaces is not set

Incoming update filter list for all interfaces is not set

Sending updates every 30 seconds, next due in 7 seconds

Invalid after 180 seconds, hold down 180, flushed after 240

Redistributing: rip

Default version control: send version 2, receive 2

  Interface              Send  Recv  Triggered RIP  Key-chain
  Serial0/0/0            2     2
Automatic network summarization is in effect

Maximum path: 4

Routing for Networks:

  10.0.0.0

  172.30.0.0

Passive Interface(s):

    GigabitEthernet0/1

Routing Information Sources:

  Gateway          Distance      Last Update
  10.1.1.2             120
Distance: (default is 120)
```

When issuing the **debug ip rip** command on R2, what information is provided that confirms RIPv2 is running?

When you are finished observing the debugging outputs, issue the **undebug all** command at the privileged EXEC prompt.

When issuing the **show run** command on R3, what information is provided that confirms RIPv2 is running?

____

____

d. Examine the automatic summarization of routes.

The LANs connected to R1 and R3 are composed of discontiguous networks. R2 displays two equal-cost paths to the 172.30.0.0/16 network in the routing table. R2 displays only the major classful network address of 172.30.0.0 and does not display any of the subnets for this network.

```
R2# show ip route
<Output omitted>
         10.0.0.0/8 is variably subnetted, 4 subnets, 2 masks
C           10.1.1.0/30 is directly connected, Serial0/0/0
L           10.1.1.2/32 is directly connected, Serial0/0/0
C           10.2.2.0/30 is directly connected, Serial0/0/1
L           10.2.2.2/32 is directly connected, Serial0/0/1
R        172.30.0.0/16 [120/1] via 10.2.2.1, 00:00:23, Serial0/0/1
                       [120/1] via 10.1.1.1, 00:00:09, Serial0/0/0
         209.165.201.0/24 is variably subnetted, 2 subnets, 2 masks
C           209.165.201.0/24 is directly connected, GigabitEthernet0/0
L           209.165.201.1/32 is directly connected, GigabitEthernet0/0
```

R1 displays only its own subnets for the 172.30.0.0 network. R1 does not have any routes for the 172.30.0.0 subnets on R3.

```
R1# show ip route
<Output omitted>
         10.0.0.0/8 is variably subnetted, 3 subnets, 2 masks
C           10.1.1.0/30 is directly connected, Serial0/0/0
L           10.1.1.1/32 is directly connected, Serial0/0/0
R           10.2.2.0/30 [120/1] via 10.1.1.2, 00:00:21, Serial0/0/0
         172.30.0.0/16 is variably subnetted, 2 subnets, 2 masks
C           172.30.10.0/24 is directly connected, GigabitEthernet0/1
L           172.30.10.1/32 is directly connected, GigabitEthernet0/1
```

R3 only displays its own subnets for the 172.30.0.0 network. R3 does not have any routes for the 172.30.0.0 subnets on R1.

```
R3# show ip route
<Output omitted>
         10.0.0.0/8 is variably subnetted, 3 subnets, 2 masks
C           10.2.2.0/30 is directly connected, Serial0/0/1
L           10.2.2.1/32 is directly connected, Serial0/0/1
R           10.1.1.0/30 [120/1] via 10.2.2.2, 00:00:23, Serial0/0/1
```

```
        172.30.0.0/16 is variably subnetted, 2 subnets, 2 masks
C          172.30.30.0/24 is directly connected, GigabitEthernet0/1
L          172.30.30.1/32 is directly connected, GigabitEthernet0/1
```

Use the **debug ip rip** command on R2 to determine the routes received in the RIP updates from R3 and list them here.

____

R3 is not sending any of the 172.30.0.0 subnets, only the summarized route of 172.30.0.0/16, including the subnet mask. Therefore, the routing tables on R1 and R2 do not display the 172.30.0.0 subnets on R3.

Step 3:   **Disable automatic summarization.**

a.   The **no auto-summary** command is used to turn off automatic summarization in RIPv2. Disable auto summarization on all routers. The routers will no longer summarize routes at major classful network boundaries. R1 is shown here as an example.

```
R1(config)# router rip

R1(config-router)# no auto-summary
```

b.   Issue the **clear ip route *** command to clear the routing table.

```
R1(config-router)# end

R1# clear ip route *
```

c.   Examine the routing tables. Remember will it take some time to converge the routing tables after clearing them.

The LAN subnets connected to R1 and R3 should now be included in all three routing tables.

```
R2# show ip route

<Output omitted>

Gateway of last resort is not set


        10.0.0.0/8 is variably subnetted, 4 subnets, 2 masks
C          10.1.1.0/30 is directly connected, Serial0/0/0
L          10.1.1.2/32 is directly connected, Serial0/0/0
C          10.2.2.0/30 is directly connected, Serial0/0/1
L          10.2.2.2/32 is directly connected, Serial0/0/1
        172.30.0.0/16 is variably subnetted, 3 subnets, 2 masks
R          172.30.0.0/16 [120/1] via 10.2.2.1, 00:01:01, Serial0/0/1
                         [120/1] via 10.1.1.1, 00:01:15, Serial0/0/0
R          172.30.10.0/24 [120/1] via 10.1.1.1, 00:00:21, Serial0/0/0
R          172.30.30.0/24 [120/1] via 10.2.2.1, 00:00:04, Serial0/0/1
        209.165.201.0/24 is variably subnetted, 2 subnets, 2 masks
C          209.165.201.0/24 is directly connected, GigabitEthernet0/0
L          209.165.201.1/32 is directly connected, GigabitEthernet0/0

R1# show ip route

<Output omitted>
```

```
Gateway of last resort is not set


        10.0.0.0/8 is variably subnetted, 3 subnets, 2 masks
C          10.1.1.0/30 is directly connected, Serial0/0/0
L          10.1.1.1/32 is directly connected, Serial0/0/0
R          10.2.2.0/30 [120/1] via 10.1.1.2, 00:00:12, Serial0/0/0
        172.30.0.0/16 is variably subnetted, 3 subnets, 2 masks
C          172.30.10.0/24 is directly connected, GigabitEthernet0/1
L          172.30.10.1/32 is directly connected, GigabitEthernet0/1
R          172.30.30.0/24 [120/2] via 10.1.1.2, 00:00:12, Serial0/0/0
```

R3# **show ip route**

```
<Output omitted>
        10.0.0.0/8 is variably subnetted, 3 subnets, 2 masks
C          10.2.2.0/30 is directly connected, Serial0/0/1
L          10.2.2.1/32 is directly connected, Serial0/0/1
R          10.1.1.0/30 [120/1] via 10.2.2.2, 00:00:23, Serial0/0/1
        172.30.0.0/16 is variably subnetted, 2 subnets, 2 masks
C          172.30.30.0/24 is directly connected, GigabitEthernet0/1
L          172.30.30.1/32 is directly connected, GigabitEthernet0/1
R          172.30.10.0 [120/2] via 10.2.2.2, 00:00:16, Serial0/0/1
```

d. Use the **debug ip rip** command on R2 to exam the RIP updates.

R2# **debug ip rip**

After 60 seconds, issue the **no debug ip rip** command.

What routes are in the RIP updates that are received from R3?

____

Are the subnet masks now included in the routing updates? __________

Step 4:   Configure and redistribute a default route for Internet access.

a. From R2, create a static route to network 0.0.0.0 0.0.0.0, using the **ip route** command. This forwards any unknown destination address traffic to the R2 G0/0 toward PC-B, simulating the Internet by setting a Gateway of Last Resort on the R2 router.

R2(config)# **ip route 0.0.0.0 0.0.0.0 209.165.201.2**

b. R2 will advertise a route to the other routers if the **default-information originate** command is added to its RIP configuration.

R2(config)# **router rip**

R2(config-router)# **default-information originate**

Step 5:   **Verify the routing configuration.**

a.   View the routing table on R1.

```
R1# show ip route
<Output omitted>
Gateway of last resort is 10.1.1.2 to network 0.0.0.0

R*      0.0.0.0/0 [120/1] via 10.1.1.2, 00:00:13, Serial0/0/0
        10.0.0.0/8 is variably subnetted, 3 subnets, 2 masks
C          10.1.1.0/30 is directly connected, Serial0/0/0
L          10.1.1.1/32 is directly connected, Serial0/0/0
R          10.2.2.0/30 [120/1] via 10.1.1.2, 00:00:13, Serial0/0/0
        172.30.0.0/16 is variably subnetted, 3 subnets, 2 masks
C          172.30.10.0/24 is directly connected, GigabitEthernet0/1
L          172.30.10.1/32 is directly connected, GigabitEthernet0/1
R          172.30.30.0/24 [120/2] via 10.1.1.2, 00:00:13, Serial0/0/0
```

How can you tell from the routing table that the subnetted network shared by R1 and R3 has a pathway
for Internet traffic?

____

____

b.   View the routing table on R2.

How is the pathway for Internet traffic provided in its routing table?

____

____

Step 6:   **Verify connectivity.**

a.   Simulate sending traffic to the Internet by pinging from PC-A and PC-C to 209.165.201.2.

Were the pings successful? _______

b.   Verify that hosts within the subnetted network can reach each other by pinging between PC-A and PC-C.

Were the pings successful? _______

Note: It may be necessary to disable the PCs firewall.

Part 3:   **Configure IPv6 on Devices**

In Part 3, you will configure all interfaces with IPv6 addresses and verify connectivity.

Addressing Table

Device	Interface	IPv6 Address / Prefix Length	Default Gateway
R1	G0/1	2001:DB8:ACAD:A::1/64 FE80::1 link-local	N/A
	S0/0/0	2001:DB8:ACAD:12::1/64 FE80::1 link-local	N/A
R2	G0/0	2001:DB8:ACAD:B::2/64 FE80::2 link-local	N/A
	S0/0/0	2001:DB8:ACAD:12::2/64 FE80::2 link-local	N/A
	S0/0/1	2001:DB8:ACAD:23::2/64 FE80::2 link-local	N/A
R3	G0/1	2001:DB8:ACAD:C::3/64 FE80::3 link-local	N/A
	S0/0/1	2001:DB8:ACAD:23::3/64 FE80::3 link-local	N/A
PC-A	NIC	2001:DB8:ACAD:A::A/64	FE80::1
PC-B	NIC	2001:DB8:ACAD:B::B/64	FE80::2
PC-C	NIC	2001:DB8:ACAD:C::C/64	FE80::3

Step 1:   **Configure PC hosts.**

Refer to the Addressing Table for PC host address information.

Step 2:   **Configure IPv6 on routers.**

Note: Assigning an IPv6 address in addition to an IPv4 address on an interface is known as dual stacking. This is because both IPv4 and IPv6 protocol stacks are active.

a.   For each router interface, assign the global and link local address from the Addressing Table.

b.   Enable IPv6 routing on each router.

c.   Enter the appropriate command to verify IPv6 addresses and link status. Write the command in the space below.

   d.   Each workstation should be able to ping the attached router. Verify and troubleshoot if necessary.

   e.   The routers should be able to ping one another. Verify and troubleshoot if necessary.

Part 4:   Configure and Verify RIPng Routing

In Part 4, you will configure RIPng routing on all routers, verify that routing tables are updated correctly, configure and distribute a default route, and verify end-to-end connectivity.

Step 1:   Configure RIPng routing.

With IPv6, it is common to have multiple IPv6 addresses configured on an interface. The network statement has been eliminated in RIPng. RIPng routing is enabled at the interface level instead, and is identified by a locally significant process name as multiple processes can be created with RIPng.

   a.   Issue the **ipv6 rip Test1 enable** command for each interface on R1 that is to participate in RIPng routing, where **Test1** is the locally significant process name.

```
R1(config)# interface g0/1
R1(config)# ipv6 rip Test1 enable
R1(config)# interface s0/0/0
R1(config)# ipv6 rip Test1 enable
```

   b.   Configure RIPng for the serial interfaces on R2 with **Test2** as the process name. Do not configure for the G0/0 interface.

   c.   Configure RIPng for each interface on R3 with **Test3** as the process name.

   d.   Verify that RIPng is running on the routers.

The **show ipv6 protocols, show run, show ipv6 rip database**, and **show ipv6 rip** *process name* commands can all be used to confirm that RIPng is running. On R1, issue the **show ipv6 protocols** command.

```
R1# show ipv6 protocols
IPv6 Routing Protocol is "connected"
IPv6 Routing Protocol is "ND"
IPv6 Routing Protocol is "rip Test1"
  Interfaces:
    Serial0/0/0
    GigabitEthernet0/1
  Redistribution:
    None
```

How is the RIPng listed in the output?

____

e. Issue the **show ipv6 rip Test1** command.

```
R1# show ipv6 rip Test1
RIP process "Test1", port 521, multicast-group FF02::9, pid 314
     Administrative distance is 120. Maximum paths is 16
     Updates every 30 seconds, expire after 180
     Holddown lasts 0 seconds, garbage collect after 120
     Split horizon is on; poison reverse is off
     Default routes are not generated
     Periodic updates 1, trigger updates 0
     Full Advertisement 0, Delayed Events 0
  Interfaces:
    GigabitEthernet0/1
    Serial0/0/0
  Redistribution:
    None
```

How are RIPv2 and RIPng similar?

____

____

f. Inspect the IPv6 routing table on each router. Write the appropriate command used to view the routing table in the space below.

____

On R1, how many routes have been learned by RIPng? __________

On R2, how many routes have been learned by RIPng? __________

On R3, how many routes have been learned by RIPng? __________

g. Check connectivity between PCs.

From PC-A, is it possible to ping PC-B? __________

From PC-A, is it possible to ping PC-C? __________

From PC-C, is it possible to ping PC-B? __________

From PC-C, is it possible to ping PC-A? __________

Why are some pings successful and others not?

____

Step 2: Configure and redistribute a default route.

a. From R2, create a static default route to network ::/64 using the **ipv6 route** command, and the IP address of exit interface G0/0. This forwards any unknown destination address traffic to the R2 G0/0 interface toward PC-Bs, simulating the Internet. Write the command used in the space below.

____

b. Static routes can be included in RIPng updates by using the **ipv6 rip** *process name* **default-information originate** command in interface configuration mode. Configure the serial links on R2 to send the default route in RIPng updates.

```
R2(config)# int s0/0/0

R2(config-rtr)# ipv6 rip Test2 default-information originate

R2(config)# int s0/0/1

R2(config-rtr)# ipv6 rip Test2 default-information originate
```

Step 3: Verify the routing configuration.

a. View the IPv6 routing table on R2.

```
R2# show ipv6 route

IPv6 Routing Table - 10 entries

Codes: C - Connected, L - Local, S - Static, R - RIP, B - BGP

       U - Per-user Static route, M - MIPv6

       I1 - ISIS L1, I2 - ISIS L2, IA - ISIS interarea, IS - ISIS summary

       O - OSPF intra, OI - OSPF inter, OE1 - OSPF ext 1, OE2 - OSPF ext 2

       ON1 - OSPF NSSA ext 1, ON2 - OSPF NSSA ext 2

       D - EIGRP, EX - EIGRP external

S    ::/64 [1/0]

       via

R    2001:DB8:ACAD:A::/64 [120/2]

       via FE80::1, Serial0/0/0
```

```
C    2001:DB8:ACAD:B::/64 [0/0]
        via ::, GigabitEthernet0/1
L    2001:DB8:ACAD:B::2/128 [0/0]
        via ::, GigabitEthernet0/1
R    2001:DB8:ACAD:C::/64 [120/2]
        via FE80::3, Serial0/0/1
C    2001:DB8:ACAD:12::/64 [0/0]
        via ::, Serial0/0/0
L    2001:DB8:ACAD:12::2/128 [0/0]
        via ::, Serial0/0/0
C    2001:DB8:ACAD:23::/64 [0/0]
        via ::, Serial0/0/1
L    2001:DB8:ACAD:23::2/128 [0/0]
        via ::, Serial0/0/1
L    FF00::/8 [0/0]
        via ::, Null0
```

How can you tell from the routing table that R2 has a pathway for Internet traffic?

____

b. View the routing tables on R1 and R3.

How is the pathway for Internet traffic provided in their routing tables?

____

Step 4: **Verify connectivity.**

Simulate sending traffic to the Internet by pinging from PC-A and PC-C to 2001:DB8:ACAD:B::B/64.

Were the pings successful? _______

Reflection

1. Why would you turn off automatic summarization for RIPv2?

2. In both scenarios, how did R1 and R3 learn the pathway to the Internet?

3. How are configuring RIPv2 and RIPng different?

Router Interface Summary Table

Router Interface Summary				
Router Model	**Ethernet Interface #1**	**Ethernet Interface #2**	**Serial Interface #1**	**Serial Interface #2**
1800	Fast Ethernet 0/0 (F0/0)	Fast Ethernet 0/1 (F0/1)	Serial 0/0/0 (S0/0/0)	Serial 0/0/1 (S0/0/1)
1900	Gigabit Ethernet 0/0 (G0/0)	Gigabit Ethernet 0/1 (G0/1)	Serial 0/0/0 (S0/0/0)	Serial 0/0/1 (S0/0/1)
2801	Fast Ethernet 0/0 (F0/0)	Fast Ethernet 0/1 (F0/1)	Serial 0/1/0 (S0/1/0)	Serial 0/1/1 (S0/1/1)
2811	Fast Ethernet 0/0 (F0/0)	Fast Ethernet 0/1 (F0/1)	Serial 0/0/0 (S0/0/0)	Serial 0/0/1 (S0/0/1)
2900	Gigabit Ethernet 0/0 (G0/0)	Gigabit Ethernet 0/1 (G0/1)	Serial 0/0/0 (S0/0/0)	Serial 0/0/1 (S0/0/1)

Note: To find out how the router is configured, look at the interfaces to identify the type of router and how many interfaces the router has. There is no way to effectively list all the combinations of configurations for each router class. This table includes identifiers for the possible combinations of Ethernet and Serial interfaces in the device. The table does not include any other type of interface, even though a specific router may contain one. An example of this might be an ISDN BRI interface. The string in parenthesis is the legal abbreviation that can be used in Cisco IOS commands to represent the interface.

3.6.1.1 Class Activity – IPv6 - Details, Details...

Objectives

Analyze a routing table to determine the route source, administrative distance, and metric for a given route to include IPv4/IPv6.

Scenario

After studying the concepts presented in this chapter concerning IPv6, you should be able to read a routing table easily and interpret the IPv6 routing information listed within it.

With a partner, use the IPv6 routing table diagram and the .pdf provided with this activity. Record your answers to the Reflection questions. Then compare your answers with, at least, one other group from the class.

Required Resources

- Routing Table Diagram (as shown below)
- Two PCs or bring your own devices (BYODs): one PC or BYOD will display the Routing Table Diagram for your group to access while recording answers to the Reflection questions on the other PC or BYOD.

Routing Table Diagram

```
R3# show ipv6 route
IPv6 Routing Table - default - 8 entries
Codes: C - Connected, L - Local, S - Static, U - Per-user Static route
       B - BGP, R - RIP, I1 - ISIS L1, I2 - ISIS L2
       IA - ISIS interarea, IS - ISIS summary, D - EIGRP, EX - EIGRP external
       ND - ND Default, NDp - ND Prefix, DCE - Destination, NDr - Redirect
       O - OSPF Intra, OI - OSPF Inter, OE1 - OSPF ext 1, OE2 - OSPF ext 2
       ON1 - OSPF NSSA ext 1, ON2 - OSPF NSSA ext 2
R    2001:DB8:CAFE:1::/64 [120/3]
      via FE80::FE99:47FF:FE71:78A0, Serial0/0/1
R    2001:DB8:CAFE:2::/64 [120/2]
      via FE80::FE99:47FF:FE71:78A0, Serial0/0/1
C    2001:DB8:CAFE:3::/64 [0/0]
      via GigabitEthernet0/0, directly connected
L    2001:DB8:CAFE:3::1/128 [0/0]
      via GigabitEthernet0/0, receive
(output omitted)
```

Reflection

1. How many different IPv6 networks are shown on the routing table diagram? List them in the table provided below.

Routing Table IPv6 Networks

2. The 2001:DB8:CAFE:3:: route is listed twice on the routing table, once with a /64 and once with a /128. What is the significance of this dual network entry?

3. How many routes in this table are RIP routes? What type of RIP routes are listed: RIP, RIPv2, or RIPng?

4. Use the first RIP route, as listed on the routing table, as a reference. What is the administrative distance of this route? What is the cost? What is the significance of these two values?

5. Use the second RIP route, as referenced by the routing table diagram. How many hops would it take to get to the 2001:DB8:CAFE:2::/64 network? What would happen to this routing table entry if the cost for this route exceeded 15 hops?

6. You are designing an IPv6 addressing scheme to add another router to your network's physical topology. Use the /64 prefix for this addressing scheme and an IPv6 network base of 2001:DB8:CAFF:2::/64,. What would be the next, numerical network assignment you could use if the first three hextets remained the same? Justify your answer.

Chapter 4 — EIGRP

4.0.1.2 Class Activity – Classless EIGRP

Objectives

Describe the basic features of EIGRP.

Scenario

EIGRP was introduced as a Distance-Vector routing protocol in 1992. It was originally designed to work as a proprietary protocol on Cisco devices only. In 2013, EIGRP became a multi-vendor routing protocol, meaning that it can be used by other device vendors in addition to Cisco devices.

View the *Fundamental Configuration and Verification of EIGRP* video located at http://www.cisco.com/E-Learning/ bulk/subscribed/tac/netbits/iprouting/eigrp/01_fundamental_eigrp/start.htm. In order to view the video you must have a cisco.com account. If you do not have a cisco.com account, please register to create one.

While viewing the video, pay close attention to the following concepts and terms:

- Subnet mask reporting to routing tables for classful and classless networks
- Auto-summarization of networks in routing tables
- Autonomous system numbers
- Wildcard masks
- Passive interfaces
- EIGRP configuration commands
- EIGRP verification commands

Complete the reflection questions which accompany the PDF file for this activity. Save your work and be prepared to share your answers with the class.

Resources

Internet access

Reflection

1. Explain classful routing protocols.

____

2. Explain classless routing protocols.

____

3. What is network auto-summarization?

____

4. What is an autonomous system number?

____

5.   What are wildcard masks?

6.   What is a passive interface?

7.   Is EIGRP considered a distance-vector or a link-state routing protocol?

4.2.2.5 Lab – Configuring Basic EIGRP for IPv4

Topology

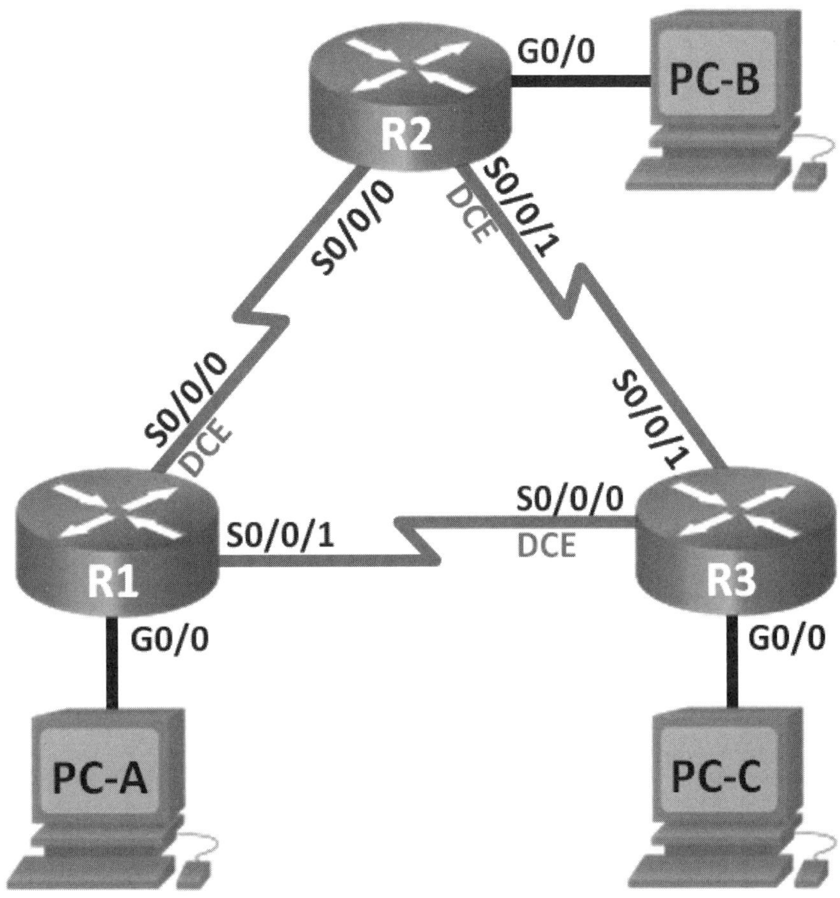

Addressing Table

Device	Interface	IP Address	Subnet Mask	Default Gateway
R1	G0/0	192.168.1.1	255.255.255.0	N/A
	S0/0/0 (DCE)	10.1.1.1	255.255.255.252	N/A
	S0/0/1	10.3.3.1	255.255.255.252	N/A
R2	G0/0	192.168.2.1	255.255.255.0	N/A
	S0/0/0	10.1.1.2	255.255.255.252	N/A
	S0/0/1 (DCE)	10.2.2.2	255.255.255.252	N/A
R3	G0/0	192.168.3.1	255.255.255.0	N/A
	S0/0/0 (DCE)	10.3.3.2	255.255.255.252	N/A
	S0/0/1	10.2.2.1	255.255.255.252	N/A
PC-A	NIC	192.168.1.3	255.255.255.0	192.168.1.1
PC-B	NIC	192.168.2.3	255.255.255.0	192.168.2.1
PC-C	NIC	192.168.3.3	255.255.255.0	192.168.3.1

Objectives

Part 1: Build the Network and Verify Connectivity

Part 2: Configure EIGRP Routing

Part 3: Verify EIGRP Routing

Part 4: Configure Bandwidth and Passive Interfaces

Background / Scenario

Enhanced Interior Gateway Routing Protocol (EIGRP) is a powerful distance vector routing protocol and is relatively easy to configure for basic networks.

In this lab, you will configure EIGRP for the topology and networks shown above. You will modify bandwidth and configure passive interfaces to allow EIGRP to function more efficiently.

Note: The routers used with CCNA hands-on labs are Cisco 1941 Integrated Services Routers (ISRs) with Cisco IOS Release 15.2(4)M3 (universalk9 image). Other routers and Cisco IOS versions can be used. Depending on the model and Cisco IOS version, the commands available and output produced might vary from what is shown in the labs. Refer to the Router Interface Summary Table at the end of this lab for the correct interface identifiers.

Note: Make sure that the routers have been erased and have no startup configurations. If you are unsure, contact your instructor.

Required Resources

- 3 Routers (Cisco 1941 with Cisco IOS Release 15.2(4)M3 universal image or comparable)
- 3 PCs (Windows 7, Vista, or XP with terminal emulation program, such as Tera Term)
- Console cables to configure the Cisco IOS devices via the console ports
- Ethernet and serial cables as shown in the topology

Part 1:   Build the Network and Verify Connectivity

In Part 1, you will set up the network topology and configure basic settings, such as the interface IP addresses, device access, and passwords.

Step 1:   Cable the network as shown in the topology.

Step 2:   Configure PC hosts.

Step 3:   Initialize and reload the routers as necessary.

Step 4:   Configure basic settings for each router.

a.   Disable DNS lookup.

b.   Configure IP addresses for the routers, as listed in the Addressing Table.

c.   Configure device name as shown in the topology.

d.   Assign **cisco** as the console and vty passwords.

e.   Assign **class** as the privileged EXEC password.

f.   Configure **logging synchronous** to prevent console and vty messages from interrupting command entry.

g.   Configure a message of the day.

h.   Copy the running configuration to the startup configuration.

Step 5:   **Verify connectivity.**

The routers should be able to ping one another, and each PC should be able to ping its default gateway. The PCs will not be able to ping other PCs until EIGRP routing is configured. Verify and troubleshoot if necessary.

Part 2:   **Configure EIGRP Routing**

Step 1:   **Enable EIGRP routing on R1. Use AS number 10.**

```
R1(config)# router eigrp 10
```

Step 2:   **Advertise the directly connected networks on R1 using the wildcard mask.**

```
R1(config-router)# network 10.1.1.0 0.0.0.3
R1(config-router)# network 192.168.1.0 0.0.0.255
R1(config-router)# network 10.3.3.0 0.0.0.3
```

Why is it a good practice to use wildcard masks when advertising networks? Could the mask have been omitted from any of the network statements above? If so, which one(s)?

____

____

____

Step 3:   **Enable EIGRP routing and advertise the directly connected networks on R2 and R3.**

You will see neighbor adjacency messages as interfaces are added to the EIGRP routing process. The messages on R2 are displayed as an example.

```
*Apr 14 15:24:59.543: %DUAL-5-NBRCHANGE: EIGRP-IPv4 10: Neighbor 10.1.1.1
(Serial0/0/0) is up: new adjacency
```

Step 4:   **Verify end-to-end connectivity.**

All devices should be able to ping each other if EIGRP is configured correctly.

Note: Depending on the operating system, it may be necessary to disable the firewall for the pings to the host PCs to be successful.

Part 3:   Verify EIGRP Routing

Step 1:   Examine the EIGRP neighbor table.

On R1, issue the **show ip eigrp neighbors** command to verify that the adjacency has been established with its neighboring routers.

```
R1# show ip eigrp neighbors
EIGRP-IPv4 Neighbors for AS(10)
H   Address                 Interface          Hold Uptime     SRTT    RTO  Q  Seq
                                               (sec)           (ms)       Cnt Num
1   10.3.3.2                Se0/0/1            13 00:24:58       8    100  0  17
0   10.1.1.2                Se0/0/0            13 00:29:23       7    100  0  23
```

Step 2:   Examine the IP EIGRP routing table.

```
R1# show ip route eigrp
Codes: L - local, C - connected, S - static, R - RIP, M - mobile, B - BGP
       D - EIGRP, EX - EIGRP external, O - OSPF, IA - OSPF inter area
       N1 - OSPF NSSA external type 1, N2 - OSPF NSSA external type 2
       E1 - OSPF external type 1, E2 - OSPF external type 2
       i - IS-IS, su - IS-IS summary, L1 - IS-IS level-1, L2 - IS-IS level-2
       ia - IS-IS inter area, * - candidate default, U - per-user static route
       o - ODR, P - periodic downloaded static route, H - NHRP, l - LISP
       + - replicated route, % - next hop override


Gateway of last resort is not set


      10.0.0.0/8 is variably subnetted, 5 subnets, 2 masks
D        10.2.2.0/30 [90/2681856] via 10.3.3.2, 00:29:01, Serial0/0/1
                     [90/2681856] via 10.1.1.2, 00:29:01, Serial0/0/0
D      192.168.2.0/24 [90/2172416] via 10.1.1.2, 00:29:01, Serial0/0/0
D      192.168.3.0/24 [90/2172416] via 10.3.3.2, 00:27:56, Serial0/0/1
```

Why does R1 have two paths to the 10.2.2.0/30 network?

____

Step 3:   Examine the EIGRP topology table.

```
R1# show ip eigrp topology
EIGRP-IPv4 Topology Table for AS(10)/ID(192.168.1.1)
Codes: P - Passive, A - Active, U - Update, Q - Query, R - Reply,
       r - reply Status, s - sia Status


P 192.168.3.0/24, 1 successors, FD is 2172416
        via 10.3.3.2 (2172416/28160), Serial0/0/1
```

```
P 192.168.2.0/24, 1 successors, FD is 2172416
        via 10.1.1.2 (2172416/28160), Serial0/0/0
P 10.2.2.0/30, 2 successors, FD is 2681856
        via 10.1.1.2 (2681856/2169856), Serial0/0/0
        via 10.3.3.2 (2681856/2169856), Serial0/0/1
P 10.3.3.0/30, 1 successors, FD is 2169856
        via Connected, Serial0/0/1
P 192.168.1.0/24, 1 successors, FD is 2816
        via Connected, GigabitEthernet0/0
P 10.1.1.0/30, 1 successors, FD is 2169856
        via Connected, Serial0/0/0
```

Why are there no feasible successors listed in the R1 topology table?

___

Step 4:   Verify the EIGRP routing parameters and networks advertised.

Issue the **show ip protocols** command to verify the EIGRP routing parameters used.

```
R1# show ip protocols
*** IP Routing is NSF aware ***

Routing Protocol is "eigrp 10"
  Outgoing update filter list for all interfaces is not set
  Incoming update filter list for all interfaces is not set
  Default networks flagged in outgoing updates
  Default networks accepted from incoming updates
  EIGRP-IPv4 Protocol for AS(10)
    Metric weight K1=1, K2=0, K3=1, K4=0, K5=0
    NSF-aware route hold timer is 240
    Router-ID: 192.168.1.1
    Topology : 0 (base)
      Active Timer: 3 min
      Distance: internal 90 external 170
      Maximum path: 4
      Maximum hopcount 100
      Maximum metric variance 1

  Automatic Summarization: disabled
  Maximum path: 4
  Routing for Networks:
    10.1.1.0/30
    10.3.3.0/30
```

```
    192.168.1.0
  Routing Information Sources:
    Gateway          Distance       Last Update
    10.3.3.2               90        02:38:34
    10.1.1.2               90        02:38:34
  Distance: internal 90 external 170
```

Based on the output of issuing the **show ip protocols** command, answer the following questions.

What AS number is used? _____

What networks are advertised?

\
\

What is the administrative distance for EIGRP? _____________________

How many equal cost paths does EIGRP use by default? _____

Part 4: Configure Bandwidth and Passive Interfaces

EIGRP uses a default bandwidth based on the type of interface in the router. In Part 4, you will modify the bandwidth so that the link between R1 and R3 has a lower bandwidth than the link between R1/R2 and R2/R3. In addition, you will set passive interfaces on each router.

Step 1: Observe the current routing settings.

a.   Issue the **show interface s0/0/0** command on R1.

```
R1# show interface s0/0/0
Serial0/0/0 is up, line protocol is up
  Hardware is WIC MBRD Serial
  Internet address is 10.1.1.1/30
  MTU 1500 bytes, BW 1544 Kbit/sec, DLY 20000 usec,
     reliability 255/255, txload 1/255, rxload 1/255
  Encapsulation HDLC, loopback not set
  Keepalive set (10 sec)
  Last input 00:00:01, output 00:00:02, output hang never
  Last clearing of "show interface" counters 03:43:45
  Input queue: 0/75/0/0 (size/max/drops/flushes); Total output drops: 0
  Queueing strategy: fifo
  Output queue: 0/40 (size/max)
  5 minute input rate 0 bits/sec, 0 packets/sec
  5 minute output rate 0 bits/sec, 0 packets/sec
     4050 packets input, 270294 bytes, 0 no buffer
     Received 1554 broadcasts (0 IP multicasts)
     0 runts, 0 giants, 0 throttles
     1 input errors, 0 CRC, 0 frame, 0 overrun, 0 ignored, 1 abort
```

```
4044 packets output, 271278 bytes, 0 underruns

0 output errors, 0 collisions, 5 interface resets

4 unknown protocol drops

0 output buffer failures, 0 output buffers swapped out

12 carrier transitions

DCD=up   DSR=up   DTR=up   RTS=up   CTS=up
```

What is the default bandwidth for this serial interface?

____

b. How many routes are listed in the routing table to reach the 10.2.2.0/30 network? _______________

Step 2: **Modify the bandwidth on the routers.**

a. Modify the bandwidth on R1 for the serial interfaces.

```
R1(config)# interface s0/0/0
R1(config-if)# bandwidth 2000
R1(config-if)# interface s0/0/1
R1(config-if)# bandwidth 64
```

Issue **show ip route** command on R1. Is there a difference in the routing table? If so, what is it?

```
Codes: L - local, C - connected, S - static, R - RIP, M - mobile, B - BGP
       D - EIGRP, EX - EIGRP external, O - OSPF, IA - OSPF inter area
       N1 - OSPF NSSA external type 1, N2 - OSPF NSSA external type 2
       E1 - OSPF external type 1, E2 - OSPF external type 2
       i - IS-IS, su - IS-IS summary, L1 - IS-IS level-1, L2 - IS-IS level-2
       ia - IS-IS inter area, * - candidate default, U - per-user static route
       o - ODR, P - periodic downloaded static route, H - NHRP, l - LISP
       + - replicated route, % - next hop override


Gateway of last resort is not set


      10.0.0.0/8 is variably subnetted, 5 subnets, 2 masks
C        10.1.1.0/30 is directly connected, Serial0/0/0
L        10.1.1.1/32 is directly connected, Serial0/0/0
D        10.2.2.0/30 [90/2681856] via 10.1.1.2, 00:03:09, Serial0/0/0
C        10.3.3.0/30 is directly connected, Serial0/0/1
L        10.3.3.1/32 is directly connected, Serial0/0/1
      192.168.1.0/24 is variably subnetted, 2 subnets, 2 masks
C        192.168.1.0/24 is directly connected, GigabitEthernet0/0
L        192.168.1.1/32 is directly connected, GigabitEthernet0/0
D      192.168.2.0/24 [90/1794560] via 10.1.1.2, 00:03:09, Serial0/0/0
D      192.168.3.0/24 [90/2684416] via 10.1.1.2, 00:03:08, Serial0/0/0
```

b. Modify the bandwidth on the R2 and R3 serial interfaces.

```
R2(config)# interface s0/0/0
R2(config-if)# bandwidth 2000
R2(config-if)# interface s0/0/1
R2(config-if)# bandwidth 2000


R3(config)# interface s0/0/0
R3(config-if)# bandwidth 64
R3(config-if)# interface s0/0/1
R3(config-if)# bandwidth 2000
```

Step 3:   **Verify the bandwidth modifications.**

a. Verify bandwidth modifications. Issue a **show interface serial 0/0/x** command, with x being the appropriate serial interface on all three routers to verify that bandwidth is set correctly. R1 is shown as an example.

```
R1# show interface s0/0/0
Serial0/0/0 is up, line protocol is up
  Hardware is WIC MBRD Serial
  Internet address is 10.1.1.1/30
  MTU 1500 bytes, BW 2000 Kbit/sec, DLY 20000 usec,
     reliability 255/255, txload 1/255, rxload 1/255
  Encapsulation HDLC, loopback not set
  Keepalive set (10 sec)
  Last input 00:00:01, output 00:00:02, output hang never
  Last clearing of "show interface" counters 04:06:06
  Input queue: 0/75/0/0 (size/max/drops/flushes); Total output drops: 0
  Queueing strategy: fifo
  Output queue: 0/40 (size/max)
  5 minute input rate 0 bits/sec, 0 packets/sec
  5 minute output rate 0 bits/sec, 0 packets/sec
     4767 packets input, 317155 bytes, 0 no buffer
     Received 1713 broadcasts (0 IP multicasts)
     0 runts, 0 giants, 0 throttles
     1 input errors, 0 CRC, 0 frame, 0 overrun, 0 ignored, 1 abort
     4825 packets output, 316451 bytes, 0 underruns
     0 output errors, 0 collisions, 5 interface resets
     4 unknown protocol drops
     0 output buffer failures, 0 output buffers swapped out
     12 carrier transitions
     DCD=up  DSR=up  DTR=up  RTS=up  CTS=up
```

Based on your bandwidth configuration, try and determine what the R2 and R3 routing tables will look like before you issue a **show ip route** command. Are their routing tables the same or different?

____

____

____

Step 4:   Configure G0/0 interface as passive on R1, R2, and R3.

A passive interface does not allow outgoing and incoming routing updates over the configured interface. The **passive-interface** _interface_ command causes the router to stop sending and receiving Hello packets over an interface; however, the network associated with the interface is still advertised to other routers through the non-passive interfaces. Router interfaces connected to LANs are typically configured as passive.

```
R1(config)# router eigrp 10
R1(config-router)# passive-interface g0/0


R2(config)# router eigrp 10
R2(config-router)# passive-interface g0/0


R3(config)# router eigrp 10
R3(config-router)# passive-interface g0/0
```

Step 5:   Verify the passive interface configuration.

Issue a **show ip protocols** command on R1, R2, and R3 and verify that G0/0 has been configured as passive.

```
R1# show ip protocols
*** IP Routing is NSF aware ***


Routing Protocol is "eigrp 10"
  Outgoing update filter list for all interfaces is not set
  Incoming update filter list for all interfaces is not set
  Default networks flagged in outgoing updates
  Default networks accepted from incoming updates
  EIGRP-IPv4 Protocol for AS(10)
    Metric weight K1=1, K2=0, K3=1, K4=0, K5=0
    NSF-aware route hold timer is 240
    Router-ID: 192.168.1.1
    Topology : 0 (base)
      Active Timer: 3 min
      Distance: internal 90 external 170
      Maximum path: 4
      Maximum hopcount 100
      Maximum metric variance 1
```

```
Automatic Summarization: disabled

Maximum path: 4

Routing for Networks:

   10.1.1.0/30

   10.3.3.0/30

   192.168.1.0

Passive Interface(s):

   GigabitEthernet0/0

Routing Information Sources:

   Gateway          Distance        Last Update

   10.3.3.2               90         00:48:09

   10.1.1.2               90         00:48:26

Distance: internal 90 external 170
```

Reflection

You could have used only static routing for this lab. What is an advantage of using EIGRP?

____

____

____

Router Interface Summary Table

Router Interface Summary				
Router Model	**Ethernet Interface #1**	**Ethernet Interface #2**	**Serial Interface #1**	**Serial Interface #2**
1800	Fast Ethernet 0/0 (F0/0)	Fast Ethernet 0/1 (F0/1)	Serial 0/0/0 (S0/0/0)	Serial 0/0/1 (S0/0/1)
1900	Gigabit Ethernet 0/0 (G0/0)	Gigabit Ethernet 0/1 (G0/1)	Serial 0/0/0 (S0/0/0)	Serial 0/0/1 (S0/0/1)
2801	Fast Ethernet 0/0 (F0/0)	Fast Ethernet 0/1 (F0/1)	Serial 0/1/0 (S0/1/0)	Serial 0/1/1 (S0/1/1)
2811	Fast Ethernet 0/0 (F0/0)	Fast Ethernet 0/1 (F0/1)	Serial 0/0/0 (S0/0/0)	Serial 0/0/1 (S0/0/1)
2900	Gigabit Ethernet 0/0 (G0/0)	Gigabit Ethernet 0/1 (G0/1)	Serial 0/0/0 (S0/0/0)	Serial 0/0/1 (S0/0/1)

Note: To find out how the router is configured, look at the interfaces to identify the type of router and how many interfaces the router has. There is no way to effectively list all the combinations of configurations for each router class. This table includes identifiers for the possible combinations of Ethernet and Serial interfaces in the device. The table does not include any other type of interface, even though a specific router may contain one. An example of this might be an ISDN BRI interface. The string in parenthesis is the legal abbreviation that can be used in Cisco IOS commands to represent the interface.

4.4.3.5 Lab – Configuring Basic EIGRP for IPv6

Topology

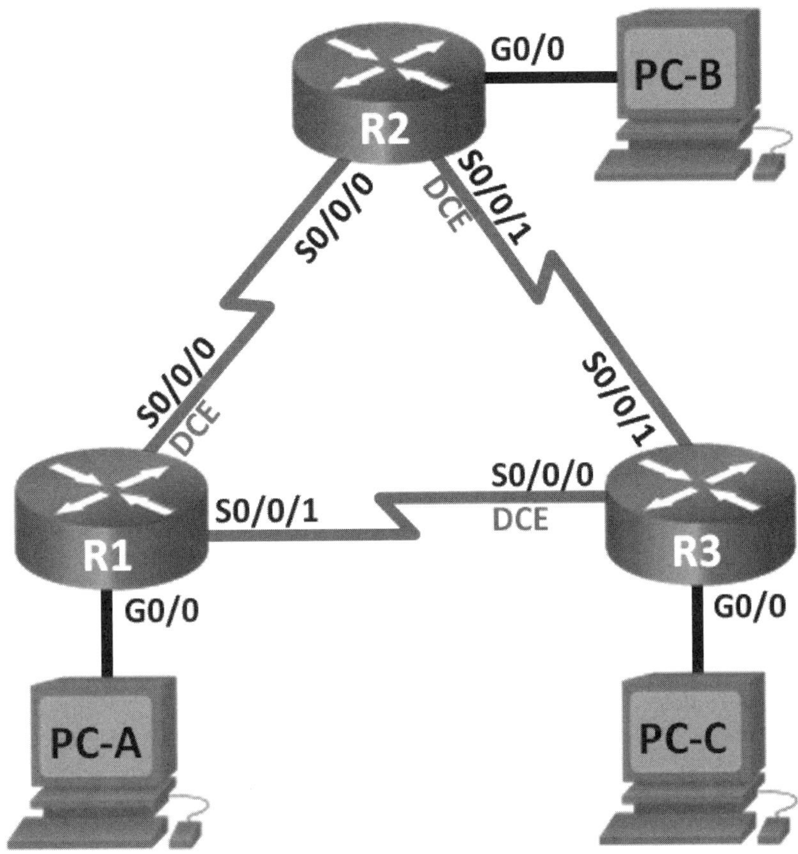

Addressing Table

Device	Interface	IP Address	Default Gateway
R1	G0/0	2001:DB8:ACAD:A::1/64 FE80::1 link-local	N/A
	S0/0/0 (DCE)	2001:DB8:ACAD:12::1/64 FE80::1 link-local	N/A
	S0/0/1	2001:DB8:ACAD:13::1/64 FE80::1 link-local	N/A
R2	G0/0	2001:DB8:ACAD:B::1/64 FE80::2 link-local	N/A
	S0/0/0	2001:DB8:ACAD:12::2/64 FE80::2 link-local	N/A
	S0/0/1 (DCE)	2001:DB8:ACAD:23::2/64 FE80::2 link-local	N/A
R3	G0/0	2001:DB8:ACAD:C::1/64 FE80::3 link-local	N/A
	S0/0/0 (DCE)	2001:DB8:ACAD:13::3/64 FE80::3 link-local	N/A
	S0/0/1	2001:DB8:ACAD:23::3/64 FE80::3 link-local	N/A
PC-A	NIC	2001:DB8:ACAD:A::3/64	FE80::1
PC-B	NIC	2001:DB8:ACAD:B::3/64	FE80::2
PC-C	NIC	2001:DB8:ACAD:C::3/64	FE80::3

Objectives

Part 1: Build the Network and Verify Connectivity

Part 2: Configure EIGRP for IPv6 Routing

Part 3: Verify EIGRP for IPv6 Routing

Part 4: Configure and Verify Passive Interfaces

Background / Scenario

EIGRP for IPv6 has the same overall operation and features as EIGRP for IPv4. However, there are a few major differences between them:

- EIGRP for IPv6 is configured directly on the router interfaces.
- With EIGRP for IPv6, a router ID is required on each router or the routing process does not start.
- The EIGRP for IPv6 routing process uses a shutdown feature.

In this lab, you will configure the network with EIGRP routing for IPv6. You will also assign router IDs, configure passive interfaces, verify the network is fully converged, and display routing information using CLI **show** commands.

Note: The routers used with CCNA hands-on labs are Cisco 1941 Integrated Services Routers (ISRs) with Cisco IOS Release 15.2(4)M3 (universalk9 image). Other routers and Cisco IOS versions can be used. Depending on the model and Cisco IOS version, the commands available and output produced might vary from what is shown in the labs. Refer to the Router Interface Summary Table at the end of this lab for the correct interface identifiers.

Note: Make sure that the routers have been erased and have no startup configurations. If you are unsure, contact your instructor.

Required Resources

- 3 Routers (Cisco 1941 with Cisco IOS Release 15.2(4)M3 universal image or comparable)
- 3 PCs (Windows 7, Vista, or XP with terminal emulation program, such as Tera Term)
- Console cables to configure the Cisco IOS devices via the console ports
- Ethernet and serial cables as shown in the topology

Part 1:   Build the Network and Verify Connectivity

In Part 1, you will set up the network topology and configure basic settings, such as the interface IP addresses, device access, and passwords.

Step 1:   Cable the network as shown in the topology.

Step 2:   Configure PC hosts.

Step 3:   Initialize and reload the routers as necessary.

Step 4:   Configure basic settings for each router.

a.   Disable DNS lookup.

b.   Configure IP addresses for the routers as listed in Addressing Table.

    Note: Configure the FE80::x link-local address and the unicast address for each router interface.

c.   Configure device name as shown in the topology.

d.   Assign **cisco** as the console and vty passwords.

e.   Assign **class** as the privileged EXEC password.

f.   Configure **logging synchronous** to prevent console and vty messages from interrupting command entry.

g.   Configure a message of the day.

h.   Copy the running configuration to the startup configuration.

Step 5:   Verify connectivity.

The routers should be able to ping one another, and each PC should be able to ping its default gateway. The PCs will not be able to ping other PCs until EIGRP routing is configured. Verify and troubleshoot if necessary.

Part 2: Configure EIGRP for IPv6 Routing

Step 1: Enable IPv6 routing on the routers.

```
R1(config)# ipv6 unicast-routing
```

Step 2: Assign a router ID to each router.

a. To begin the EIGRP for IPv6 routing configuration process, issue the **ipv6 router eigrp 1** command, where **1** is the AS number.

```
R1(config)# ipv6 router eigrp 1
```

b. EIGRP for IPv6 requires a 32-bit address for the router ID. Use the **router-id** command to configure the router ID in the router configuration mode.

```
R1(config)# ipv6 router eigrp 1
R1(config-rtr)# router-id 1.1.1.1


R2(config)# ipv6 router eigrp 1
R2(config-rtr)# router-id 2.2.2.2


R3(config)# ipv6 router eigrp 1
R3(config-rtr)# router-id 3.3.3.3
```

Step 3: Enable EIGRP for IPv6 routing on each router.

The IPv6 routing process is shut down by default. Issue the **no shutdown** command to enable EIGRP for IPv6 routing on all routers.

```
R1(config)# ipv6 router eigrp 1
R1(config-rtr)# no shutdown


R2(config)# ipv6 router eigrp 1
R2(config-rtr)# no shutdown


R3(config)# ipv6 router eigrp 1
R3(config-rtr)# no shutdown
```

Step 4: Configure EIGRP for IPv6 using AS 1 on the Serial and Gigabit Ethernet interfaces on the routers.

a. Issue the **ipv6 eigrp 1** command on the interfaces that participate in the EIGRP routing process. The AS number is 1 as assigned in Step 2. The configuration for R1 is displayed below as an example.

```
R1(config)# interface g0/0
R1(config-if)# ipv6 eigrp 1
R1(config-if)# interface s0/0/0
R1(config-if)# ipv6 eigrp 1
```

```
R1(config-if)# interface s0/0/1

R1(config-if)# ipv6 eigrp 1
```

b. Assign EIGRP participating interfaces on R2 and R3. You will see neighbor adjacency messages as interfaces are added to the EIGRP routing process. The messages on R1 are displayed below as an example.

```
R1(config-if)#

*Apr 12 00:25:49.183: %DUAL-5-NBRCHANGE: EIGRP-IPv6 1: Neighbor FE80::2 (Serial0/0/0)
is up: new adjacency

*Apr 12 00:26:15.583: %DUAL-5-NBRCHANGE: EIGRP-IPv6 1: Neighbor FE80::3 (Serial0/0/1)
is up: new adjacency
```

What address is used to indicate the neighbor in the adjacency messages? _______________________

Step 5: **Verify end-to-end connectivity.**

Part 3: **Verify EIGRP for IPv6 Routing**

Step 1: **Examine the neighbor adjacencies.**

On R1, issue the **show ipv6 eigrp neighbors** command to verify that the adjacency has been established with its neighboring routers. The link-local addresses of the neighboring routers are displayed in the adjacency table.

```
R1# show ipv6 eigrp neighbors

EIGRP-IPv6 Neighbors for AS(1)
H   Address                    Interface         Hold Uptime    SRTT    RTO  Q  Seq
                                                 (sec)          (ms)        Cnt Num
1   Link-local address:        Se0/0/1           13 00:02:42      1    100  0  7
    FE80::3
0   Link-local address:        Se0/0/0           13 00:03:09     12    100  0  9
    FE80::2
```

Step 2: **Examine the IPv6 EIGRP routing table.**

Use the **show ipv6 route eigrp** command to display IPv6 specific EIGRP routes on all the routers.

```
R1# show ipv6 route eigrp

IPv6 Routing Table - default - 10 entries
Codes: C - Connected, L - Local, S - Static, U - Per-user Static route
       B - BGP, R - RIP, I1 - ISIS L1, I2 - ISIS L2
       IA - ISIS interarea, IS - ISIS summary, D - EIGRP, EX - EIGRP external
       ND - ND Default, NDp - ND Prefix, DCE - Destination, NDr - Redirect
       O - OSPF Intra, OI - OSPF Inter, OE1 - OSPF ext 1, OE2 - OSPF ext 2
       ON1 - OSPF NSSA ext 1, ON2 - OSPF NSSA ext 2
D   2001:DB8:ACAD:B::/64 [90/2172416]
     via FE80::2, Serial0/0/0
D   2001:DB8:ACAD:C::/64 [90/2172416]
     via FE80::3, Serial0/0/1
```

```
D   2001:DB8:ACAD:23::/64 [90/2681856]
      via FE80::2, Serial0/0/0
      via FE80::3, Serial0/0/1
```

Step 3: Examine the EIGRP topology.

```
R1# show ipv6 eigrp topology
EIGRP-IPv6 Topology Table for AS(1)/ID(1.1.1.1)
Codes: P - Passive, A - Active, U - Update, Q - Query, R - Reply,
       r - reply Status, s - sia Status


P 2001:DB8:ACAD:A::/64, 1 successors, FD is 28160
        via Connected, GigabitEthernet0/0
P 2001:DB8:ACAD:C::/64, 1 successors, FD is 2172416
        via FE80::3 (2172416/28160), Serial0/0/1
P 2001:DB8:ACAD:12::/64, 1 successors, FD is 2169856
        via Connected, Serial0/0/0
P 2001:DB8:ACAD:B::/64, 1 successors, FD is 2172416
        via FE80::2 (2172416/28160), Serial0/0/0
P 2001:DB8:ACAD:23::/64, 2 successors, FD is 2681856
        via FE80::2 (2681856/2169856), Serial0/0/0
        via FE80::3 (2681856/2169856), Serial0/0/1
P 2001:DB8:ACAD:13::/64, 1 successors, FD is 2169856
        via Connected, Serial0/0/1
```

Compare the highlighted entries to the routing table. What can you conclude from the comparison?

____

____

____

Step 4: Verify the parameters and current state of the active IPv6 routing protocol processes.

Issue the **show ipv6 protocols** command to verify the configured parameter. From the output, EIGRP is the configured IPv6 routing protocol with 1.1.1.1 as the router ID for R1. This routing protocol is associated with autonomous system 1 with three active interfaces: G0/0, S0/0/0, and S0/0/1.

```
R1# show ipv6 protocols
IPv6 Routing Protocol is "connected"
IPv6 Routing Protocol is "ND"
IPv6 Routing Protocol is "eigrp 1"
EIGRP-IPv6 Protocol for AS(1)
  Metric weight K1=1, K2=0, K3=1, K4=0, K5=0
  NSF-aware route hold timer is 240
  Router-ID: 1.1.1.1
  Topology : 0 (base)
```

```
    Active Timer: 3 min

    Distance: internal 90 external 170

    Maximum path: 16

    Maximum hopcount 100

    Maximum metric variance 1


  Interfaces:
    GigabitEthernet0/0
    Serial0/0/0
    Serial0/0/1
  Redistribution:
    None
```

Part 4:   Configure and Verify Passive Interfaces

A passive interface does not allow outgoing and incoming routing updates over the configured interface. The **passive-interface** *interface* command causes the router to stop sending and receiving Hello packets over an interface.

Step 1:   Configure interface G0/0 as passive on R1 and R2.

```
R1(config)# ipv6 router eigrp 1
R1(config-rtr)# passive-interface g0/0


R2(config)# ipv6 router eigrp 1
R2(config-rtr)# passive-interface g0/0
```

Step 2:   Verify the passive interface configuration.

Issue the **show ipv6 protocols** command on R1 and verify that G0/0 has been configured as passive.

```
R1# show ipv6 protocols
IPv6 Routing Protocol is "connected"
IPv6 Routing Protocol is "ND"
IPv6 Routing Protocol is "eigrp 1"
EIGRP-IPv6 Protocol for AS(1)
  Metric weight K1=1, K2=0, K3=1, K4=0, K5=0
  NSF-aware route hold timer is 240
  Router-ID: 1.1.1.1
  Topology : 0 (base)
    Active Timer: 3 min
    Distance: internal 90 external 170
    Maximum path: 16
    Maximum hopcount 100
```

```
    Maximum metric variance 1


Interfaces:
  Serial0/0/0
  Serial0/0/1
  GigabitEthernet0/0 (passive)
Redistribution:
  None
```

Step 3:   Configure the G0/0 passive interface on R3.

If a few interfaces are configured as passive, use the **passive-interface default** command to configure all the interfaces on the router as passive. Use the **no passive-interface** *interface* command to allow EIGRP Hello messages in and out of the router interface.

a. Configure all interfaces as passive on R3.

```
R3(config)# ipv6 router eigrp 1

R3(config-rtr)# passive-interface default

R3(config-rtr)#

*Apr 13 00:07:03.267: %DUAL-5-NBRCHANGE: EIGRP-IPv6 1: Neighbor FE80::1 (Serial0/0/0)
is down: interface passive

*Apr 13 00:07:03.267: %DUAL-5-NBRCHANGE: EIGRP-IPv6 1: Neighbor FE80::2 (Serial0/0/1)
is down: interface passive
```

b. After you have issued the **passive-interface default** command, R3 no longer participates in the routing process. What command can you use to verify it?

____

c. What command can you use to display the passive interfaces on R3?

____

d. Configure the serial interfaces to participate in the routing process.

```
R3(config)# ipv6 router eigrp 1

R3(config-rtr)# no passive-interface s0/0/0

R3(config-rtr)# no passive-interface s0/0/1

R3(config-rtr)#

*Apr 13 00:21:23.807: %DUAL-5-NBRCHANGE: EIGRP-IPv6 1: Neighbor FE80::1 (Serial0/0/0)
is up: new adjacency

*Apr 13 00:21:25.567: %DUAL-5-NBRCHANGE: EIGRP-IPv6 1: Neighbor FE80::2 (Serial0/0/1)
is up: new adjacency
```

e. The neighbor relationships have been established again with R1 and R2. Verify that only G0/0 has been configured as passive. What command do you use to verify the passive interface?

____

Reflection

1. Where would you configure passive interfaces? Why?

2. What are some advantages with using EIGRP as the routing protocol in your network?

Router Interface Summary Table

Router Interface Summary				
Router Model	**Ethernet Interface #1**	**Ethernet Interface #2**	**Serial Interface #1**	**Serial Interface #2**
1800	Fast Ethernet 0/0 (F0/0)	Fast Ethernet 0/1 (F0/1)	Serial 0/0/0 (S0/0/0)	Serial 0/0/1 (S0/0/1)
1900	Gigabit Ethernet 0/0 (G0/0)	Gigabit Ethernet 0/1 (G0/1)	Serial 0/0/0 (S0/0/0)	Serial 0/0/1 (S0/0/1)
2801	Fast Ethernet 0/0 (F0/0)	Fast Ethernet 0/1 (F0/1)	Serial 0/1/0 (S0/1/0)	Serial 0/1/1 (S0/1/1)
2811	Fast Ethernet 0/0 (F0/0)	Fast Ethernet 0/1 (F0/1)	Serial 0/0/0 (S0/0/0)	Serial 0/0/1 (S0/0/1)
2900	Gigabit Ethernet 0/0 (G0/0)	Gigabit Ethernet 0/1 (G0/1)	Serial 0/0/0 (S0/0/0)	Serial 0/0/1 (S0/0/1)

Note: To find out how the router is configured, look at the interfaces to identify the type of router and how many interfaces the router has. There is no way to effectively list all the combinations of configurations for each router class. This table includes identifiers for the possible combinations of Ethernet and Serial interfaces in the device. The table does not include any other type of interface, even though a specific router may contain one. An example of this might be an ISDN BRI interface. The string in parenthesis is the legal abbreviation that can be used in Cisco IOS commands to represent the interface.

4.5.1.1 Class Activity – Portfolio RIP and EIGRP

Objectives

Configure EIGRP for IPv4 in a small routed network (review).

Scenario

You are preparing a portfolio file for comparison of RIP and EIGRP routing protocols.

Think of a network with three interconnected routers with each router providing a LAN for PCs, printers, and other end devices. The graphic on this page depicts one example of a topology like this.

In this modeling activity scenario, you will be creating, addressing and configuring a topology, using verification commands, and comparing/contrasting RIP and EIGRP routing protocol outputs.

Complete the PDF reflection questions. Save your work and be prepared to share your answers with the class. Also save a copy of this activity for later use within this course or for portfolio reference.

Resources

Packet Tracer and word processing software programs

Directions

Step 1: **WAN and LAN topology design.**

    a. Use Packet Tracer to design a network with three routers (1941 model, suggested). If necessary, add NIC cards to the routers to provide connectivity to the routers to provide for at least one LAN to each router. Add at least one PC to each LAN.

    b. Address the networks. You may use a flat addressing scheme or VLSM. Use only IPv4 networks for this entire activity.

Step 2: **Copy the topology.**

    a. Highlight the entire topology by using your cursor.

    b. Use Ctrl+C to make a copy of the highlighted topology.

    c. Use Ctrl+V to insert a full copy of the topology to the desktop of Packet Tracer. You will now have displayed two exact, IPv4-addressed topologies with which to work for routing protocols configurations.

    d. While highlighted, move the copied topology to a different location on the Packet Tracer desktop to create room between the two for configuration purposes.

Step 3: **Configure RIP and EIGRP on the separate topologies.**

    a. Configure the RIP routing protocol on the first topology and EIGRP on the second routing topology.

    b. Once you have successfully configured RIP on one topology and EIGRP on the other, check to make sure your PCs can ping each other.

    c. Save your work so no configuration information is lost.

Step 4:   Use verification commands to check output for the routing protocols.

a. To compare/contrast routing protocol information from the two topologies, issue the **show ip route** command on R1 for topology 1 and 2.

b. Copy the output into a table in your word processing program file. Label each column with RIP or EIGRP and place the output you received from the **show ip route** command.

c. Issue the **show ip protocols** command on R1 for topology table 1 and 2. Create another table in your word processing software file and place the output information below RIP or EIGRP.

d. Issue the **show cdp neighbors** command on R1s topology 1. Copy the output to a third table with RIP as the heading and issue the **show ip eigrp neighbors** R1s topology 2. Copy the output from this command in column 2 of table 3 under the heading EIGRP.

Reflection

1. Compare and contrast the output for the **show ip route** verification command.

---

2. Compare and contrast the output for the **show ip protocol** verification command.

---

3. Compare and contrast the **show cdp neighbors** command for the RIP topology and the **show ip eigrp neighbors** command for the EIGRP topology.

---

4. After comparing and contrasting the RIP and EIGRP output, which do you find most informative? Support your answer.

Chapter 5 — EIGRP Advanced Configurations and Troubleshooting

5.0.1.2 Class Activity EIGRP – Back to the Future

Objectives

Implement advanced EIGRP features to enhance operation in a small- to medium-sized business network.

Scenario

Many of these bulleted concepts were mentioned in the previous chapter's curriculum content and will be the focus of this chapter:

- Auto-summarization
- Load balancing
- Default routes
- Hold-down timers
- Authentication

With a partner, write 10 EIGRP review questions based on the previous chapter's curriculum content. Three of the questions must focus on the bulleted items above. Ideally, Multiple Choice, True/False, or Fill in the Blank question types will be designed. As you design your questions, make sure you record the curriculum section and page numbers of the supporting content in case you need to refer back for answer verification.

Save your work and then meet with another group, or the entire class, and quiz them using the questions you developed.

Resources

- Word processing software program
- Curriculum content from the previous chapter

5.1.5.5 Lab – Configuring Advanced EIGRP for IPv4 Features

Topology

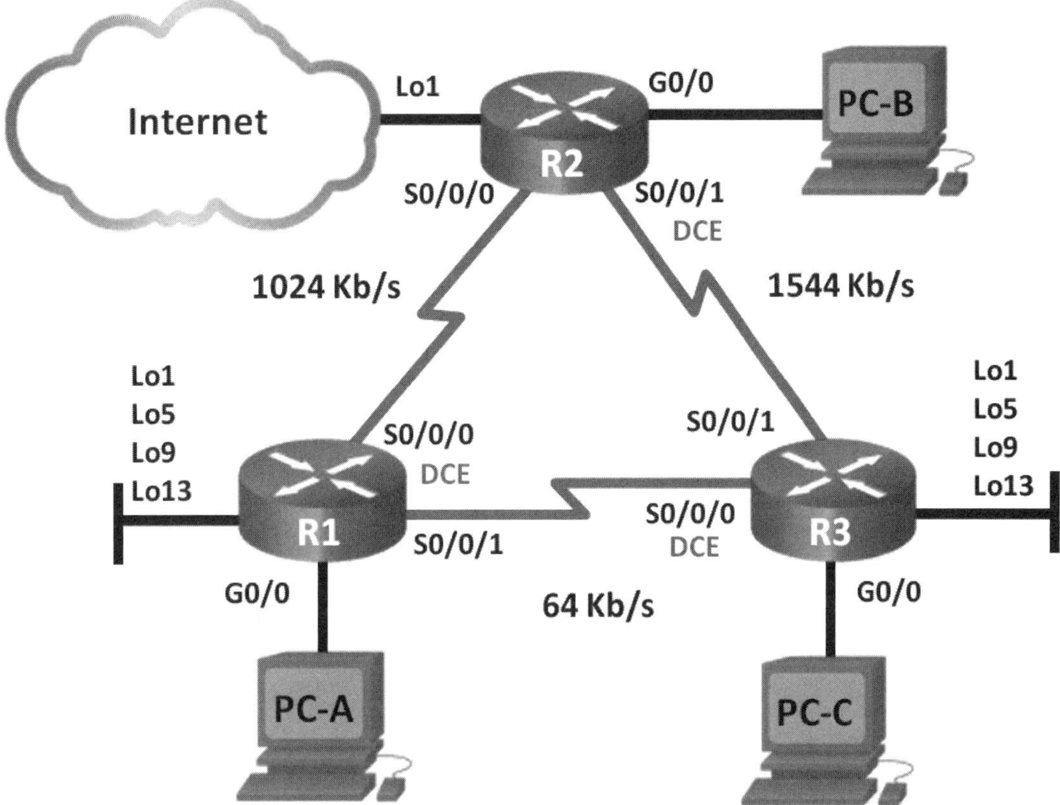

Addressing Table

Device	Interface	IP Address	Subnet Mask	Default Gateway
R1	G0/0	192.168.1.1	255.255.255.0	N/A
	S0/0/0 (DCE)	192.168.12.1	255.255.255.252	N/A
	S0/0/1	192.168.13.1	255.255.255.252	N/A
	Lo1	192.168.11.1	255.255.255.252	N/A
	Lo5	192.168.11.5	255.255.255.252	N/A
	Lo9	192.168.11.9	255.255.255.252	N/A
	Lo13	192.168.11.13	255.255.255.252	N/A
R2	G0/0	192.168.2.1	255.255.255.0	N/A
	S0/0/0	192.168.12.2	255.255.255.252	N/A
	S0/0/1 (DCE)	192.168.23.1	255.255.255.252	N/A
	Lo1	192.168.22.1	255.255.255.252	N/A
R3	G0/0	192.168.3.1	255.255.255.0	N/A
	S0/0/0 (DCE)	192.168.13.2	255.255.255.252	N/A
	S0/0/1	192.168.23.2	255.255.255.252	N/A
	Lo1	192.168.33.1	255.255.255.252	N/A
	Lo5	192.168.33.5	255.255.255.252	N/A
	Lo9	192.168.33.9	255.255.255.252	N/A
	Lo13	192.168.33.13	255.255.255.252	N/A
PC-A	NIC	192.168.1.3	255.255.255.0	192.168.1.1
PC-B	NIC	192.168.2.3	255.255.255.0	192.168.2.1
PC-C	NIC	192.168.3.3	255.255.255.0	192.168.3.1

Objectives

Part 1: Build the Network and Configure Basic Device Settings

Part 2: Configure EIGRP and Verify Connectivity

Part 3: Configure Summarization for EIGRP

- Configure EIGRP for automatic summarization.
- Configure manual summarization for EIGRP.

Part 4: Propagate a Default Route

Part 5: Fine-Tune EIGRP

- Configure bandwidth utilization for EIGRP.
- Configure Hello and Hold timers for EIGRP.

Part 6: Configure EIGRP Authentication

Background / Scenario

EIGRP has advanced features to allow changes related to summarization, default route propagation, bandwidth utilization, metrics, and security.

In this lab, you will configure automatic and manual summarization for EIGRP, configure EIGRP route propagation, fine-tune EIGRP metrics, and use MD5 authentication to secure EIGRP routing information.

Note: The routers used with CCNA hands-on labs are Cisco 1941 Integrated Services Routers (ISRs) with Cisco IOS Release 15.2(4)M3 (universalk9 image). Other routers and Cisco IOS versions can be used. Depending on the model and Cisco IOS version, the commands available and output produced might vary from what is shown in the labs. Refer to the Router Interface Summary Table at this end of the lab for the correct interface identifiers.

Note: Ensure that the routers have been erased and have no startup configurations. If you are unsure, contact your instructor.

Required Resources

- 3 Routers (Cisco 1941 with Cisco IOS Release 15.2(4)M3 universal image or comparable)
- 3 PCs (Windows 7, Vista, or XP with terminal emulation program, such as Tera Term)
- Console cables to configure the Cisco IOS devices via the console ports
- Ethernet and serial cables as shown in the topology

Part 1: Build the Network and Configure Basic Device Settings

In Part 1, you will set up the network topology and configure basic settings on the PC hosts and routers.

Step 1: Cable the network as shown in the topology.

Step 2: Configure PC hosts.

Step 3: Initialize and reload the routers as necessary.

Step 4: Configure basic settings for each router.

a. Disable DNS lookup.

b. Configure device name as shown in the topology.

c. Assign **cisco** as the console and vty passwords.

d. Assign **class** as the privileged EXEC password.

e. Configure **logging synchronous** to prevent console messages from interrupting command entry.

f. Configure the IP address listed in the Addressing Table for all interfaces.

Note: Do **NOT** configure the loopback interfaces at this time.

g. Copy the running configuration to the startup configuration.

Part 2: Configure EIGRP and Verify Connectivity

In Part 2, you will configure basic EIGRP for the topology and set bandwidths for the serial interfaces.

Note: This lab provides minimal assistance with the actual commands necessary to configure EIGRP. However, the required commands are provided in Appendix A. Test your knowledge by trying to configure the devices without referring to the appendix.

Step 1:   **Configure EIGRP.**

a.   On R1, configure EIGRP routing with an autonomous system (AS) ID of 1 for all directly connected networks. Write the commands used in the space below.

b.   For the LAN interface on R1, disable the transmission of EIGRP Hello packets. Write the command used in the space below.

c.   On R1, configure the bandwidth for S0/0/0 to 1024 Kb/s and the bandwidth for S0/0/1 to 64 Kb/s. Write the commands used in the space below. **Note**: The **bandwidth** command only affects the EIGRP metric calculation, not the actual bandwidth of the serial link.

d.   On R2, configure EIGRP routing with an AS ID of 1 for all networks, disable the transmission of EIGRP Hello packets for the LAN interface, and configure the bandwidth for S0/0/0 to 1024 Kb/s.

e.   On R3, configure EIGRP routing with an AS ID of 1 for all networks, disable the transmission of EIGRP Hello packets for the LAN interface, and configure the bandwidth for S0/0/0 to 64 Kb/s.

Step 2:   **Test connectivity.**

All PCs should be able to ping one another. Verify and troubleshoot if necessary.

Note: It may be necessary to disable the PC firewall to ping between PCs.

Part 3:   **Configure Summarization for EIGRP**

In Part 3, you will add loopback interfaces to R1, enable EIGRP automatic summarization on R1, and observe the effects on the routing table for R2. You will also add loopback interfaces on R3.

Step 1:   **Configure EIGRP for automatic summarization.**

a.   Issue the **show ip protocols** command on R1. What is the default status of automatic summarization in EIGRP?

b. Configure the loopback addresses on R1.

c. Add the appropriate network statements to the EIGRP process on R1. Record the commands used in the space below.

____

____

____

d. On R2, issue the **show ip route eigrp** command. How are the loopback networks represented in the output?

____

e. On R1, issue the **auto-summary** command inside the EIGRP process.

```
R1(config)# router eigrp 1
R1(config-router)# auto-summary
R1(config-router)#
*Apr 14 01:14:55.463: %DUAL-5-NBRCHANGE: EIGRP-IPv4 1: Neighbor 192.168.13.2
(Serial0/0/1) is resync: summary configured

*Apr 14 01:14:55.463: %DUAL-5-NBRCHANGE: EIGRP-IPv4 1: Neighbor 192.168.12.2
(Serial0/0/0) is resync: summary configured

*Apr 14 01:14:55.463: %DUAL-5-NBRCHANGE: EIGRP-IPv4 1: Neighbor 192.168.13.2
(Serial0/0/1) is resync: summary up, remove components

R1(config-router)#67: %DUAL-5-NBRCHANGE: EIGRP-IPv4 1: Neighbor 192.168.12.2
(Serial0/0/0) is resync: summary up, remove components

*Apr 14 01:14:55.467: %DUAL-5-NBRCHANGE: EIGRP-IPv4 1: Neighbor 192.168.12.2
(Serial0/0/0) is resync: summary up, remove components

*Apr 14 01:14:55.467: %DUAL-5-NBRCHANGE: EIGRP-IPv4 1: Neighbor 192.168.13.2
(Serial0/0/1) is resync: summary up, remove components
```

How does the routing table on R2 change?

____

____

Step 2: **Configure manual summarization for EIGRP.**

a. Configure the loopback addresses on R3.

b. Add the appropriate network statements to the EIGRP process on R3.

c. On R2, issue the **show ip route eigrp** command. How are the loopback networks from R3 represented in the output?

____

d. Determine the summary EIGRP route for the loopback addresses on R3. Write the summary route in the space below.

____

e. For the serial interfaces on R3, issue the **ip summary-address eigrp 1** *network address subnet mask* command to manually summarize the networks.

```
R3(config)# interface s0/0/0

R3(config-if)# ip summary-address eigrp 1 192.168.33.0 255.255.255.240

R3(config-if)# exit

R3(config)# interface s0/0/1

R3(config-if)# ip summary-address eigrp 1 192.168.33.0 255.255.255.240

*Apr 14 01:33:46.433: %DUAL-5-NBRCHANGE: EIGRP-IPv4 1: Neighbor 192.168.13.1 (Seri-
al0/0/0) is resync: summary configured

*Apr 14 01:33:46.433: %DUAL-5-NBRCHANGE: EIGRP-IPv4 1: Neighbor 192.168.23.1 (Seri-
al0/0/1) is resync: summary configured
```

How does the routing table on R2 change?

____

Part 4:   Configure and Propagate a Default Static Route

In Part 4, you will configure a default static route on R2 and propagate the route to all other routers.

a. Configure the loopback address on R2.

b. Configure a default static route with an exit interface of Lo1.

```
R2(config)# ip route 0.0.0.0 0.0.0.0 Lo1
```

c. Use the **redistribute static** command within the EIGRP process to propagate the default static route to other participating routers.

```
R2(config)# router eigrp 1

R2(config-router)# redistribute static
```

d. Use the **show ip protocols command** on R2 to verify the static route is being distributed.

```
R2# show ip protocols
*** IP Routing is NSF aware ***


Routing Protocol is "eigrp 1"
  Outgoing update filter list for all interfaces is not set
  Incoming update filter list for all interfaces is not set
  Default networks flagged in outgoing updates
  Default networks accepted from incoming updates
  Redistributing: static
  EIGRP-IPv4 Protocol for AS(1)
    Metric weight K1=1, K2=0, K3=1, K4=0, K5=0
    NSF-aware route hold timer is 240
    Router-ID: 192.168.23.1
    Topology : 0 (base)
      Active Timer: 3 min
      Distance: internal 90 external 170
      Maximum path: 4
      Maximum hopcount 100
      Maximum metric variance 1

  Automatic Summarization: disabled
  Maximum path: 4
  Routing for Networks:
    192.168.2.0
    192.168.12.0/30
    192.168.23.0/30
  Passive Interface(s):
    GigabitEthernet0/0
  Routing Information Sources:
    Gateway         Distance      Last Update
    192.168.12.1          90      00:13:20
    192.168.23.2          90      00:13:20
  Distance: internal 90 external 170
```

e. On R1, issue the **show ip route eigrp | include 0.0.0.0** command to view statements specific to the default route. How is the static default route represented in the output? What is the administrative distance (AD) for the propagated route?

____

____

Part 5:   **Fine-Tune EIGRP**

In Part 5, you will configure the percentage of bandwidth that can be used by an EIGRP interface and change the Hello and Hold timers for EIGRP interfaces.

Step 1:   **Configure bandwidth utilization for EIGRP.**

a.   Configure the serial link between R1 and R2 to allow only 75 percent of the link bandwidth for EIGRP traffic.

```
R1(config)# interface s0/0/0

R1(config-if)# ip bandwidth-percent eigrp 1 75

R2(config)# interface s0/0/0

R2(config-if)# ip bandwidth-percent eigrp 1 75
```

b.   Configure the serial link between R1 and R3 to allow 40 percent of the links bandwidth for EIGRP traffic.

Step 2:   **Configure Hello and Hold Timers for EIGRP.**

a.   On R2, use the **show ip eigrp interfaces detail** command to view the Hello and Hold timers for EIGRP.

```
R2# show ip eigrp interfaces detail
EIGRP-IPv4 Interfaces for AS(1)
                            Xmit Queue    PeerQ        Mean   Pacing Time   Multicast    Pending
Interface          Peers  Un/Reliable  Un/Reliable   SRTT   Un/Reliable   Flow Timer   Routes
Se0/0/0               1       0/0          0/0          1       0/15          50           0
  Hello-interval is 5, Hold-time is 15
  Split-horizon is enabled
  Next xmit serial <none>
  Packetized sent/expedited: 29/1
  Hello's sent/expedited: 390/2
  Un/reliable mcasts: 0/0  Un/reliable ucasts: 35/39
  Mcast exceptions: 0  CR packets: 0  ACKs suppressed: 0
  Retransmissions sent: 0  Out-of-sequence rcvd: 0
  Topology-ids on interface - 0
  Interface BW percentage is 75
  Authentication mode is not set
Se0/0/1               1       0/0          0/0          1       0/16          50           0
  Hello-interval is 5, Hold-time is 15
  Split-horizon is enabled
  Next xmit serial <none>
  Packetized sent/expedited: 34/5
  Hello's sent/expedited: 382/2
  Un/reliable mcasts: 0/0  Un/reliable ucasts: 31/42
  Mcast exceptions: 0  CR packets: 0  ACKs suppressed: 2
  Retransmissions sent: 0  Out-of-sequence rcvd: 0
  Topology-ids on interface - 0
  Authentication mode is not set
```

What is the default value for hello time? _______________________

What is the default value for hold time? ______________________

b. Configure S0/0/0 and S0/0/1 interfaces on R1 to use a Hello interval of 60 seconds and a Hold time of 180 seconds in that specific order.

```
R1(config)# interface s0/0/0
R1(config-if)# ip hello-interval eigrp 1 60
R1(config-if)# ip hold-time eigrp 1 180
R1(config)# interface s0/0/1
R1(config-if)# ip hello-interval eigrp 1 60
R1(config-if)# ip hold-time eigrp 1 180
```

c. Configure the serial interfaces on R2 and R3 to use a Hello interval of 60 seconds and a Hold time of 180 seconds.

d. Use the **show ip eigrp interfaces detail** command on R2 to verify configuration.

Part 6: Configure EIGRP Authentication

In Part 6, you will create an authentication key on all routers and configure router interfaces to use MD5 authentication for EIGRP message authentication.

Step 1: Configure authentication keys.

a. On R1, use the **key chain** *name* command in global configuration mode to create a key chain with the label EIGRP-KEYS.

```
R1(config)# key chain EIGRP-KEYS
R1(config-keychain)# key 1
R1(config-keychain-key)# key-string cisco
```

b. Complete the configuration on R2 and R3.

c. Issue the **show key chain** command. You should have the same output on every router.

Step 2: Configure EIGRP link authentication.

a. Apply the following commands to active EIGRP authentication on the serial interfaces on R1.

```
R1# conf t
R1(config)# interface s0/0/0
R1(config-if)# ip authentication key-chain eigrp 1 EIGRP-KEYS
R1(config-if)# ip authentication mode eigrp 1 md5
R1(config-if)# interface s0/0/1
R1(config-if)# ip authentication key-chain eigrp 1 EIGRP-KEYS
R1(config-if)# ip authentication mode eigrp 1 md5
```

b. Activate EIGRP authentication on the serial interfaces on R2 and R3.

c. On R2, use the **show ip eigrp interfaces detail** command to verify authentication.

```
R2# show ip eigrp interfaces detail
EIGRP-IPv4 Interfaces for AS(1)
                            Xmit Queue   PeerQ        Mean   Pacing Time   Multicast    Pending
Interface           Peers  Un/Reliable  Un/Reliable  SRTT   Un/Reliable   Flow Timer   Routes
Se0/0/0                 1      0/0          0/0          1      0/23          50           0
   Hello-interval is 60, Hold-time is 180
   Split-horizon is enabled
   Next xmit serial <none>
   Packetized sent/expedited: 30/5
   Hello's sent/expedited: 1163/5
   Un/reliable mcasts: 0/0  Un/reliable ucasts: 25/34
   Mcast exceptions: 0  CR packets: 0  ACKs suppressed: 0
   Retransmissions sent: 0  Out-of-sequence rcvd: 0
   Topology-ids on interface - 0
   Authentication mode is md5,  key-chain is "EIGRP-KEYS"
```

```
    Se0/0/1                      1         0/0       0/0          2       0/15        50            0
        Hello-interval is 60, Hold-time is 180
        Split-horizon is enabled
        Next xmit serial <none>
        Packetized sent/expedited: 31/1
        Hello's sent/expedited: 1354/3
        Un/reliable mcasts: 0/0  Un/reliable ucasts: 28/34
        Mcast exceptions: 0  CR packets: 0  ACKs suppressed: 4
        Retransmissions sent: 0  Out-of-sequence rcvd: 0
        Topology-ids on interface - 0
        Authentication mode is md5,  key-chain is "EIGRP-KEYS"
```

Reflection

1. What are the benefits of summarizing routes?

____

____

2. When setting EIGRP timers, why is it important to make the hold time value equal to or greater than the Hello interval?

____

____

3. Why is it important to configure authentication for EIGRP?

____

____

Router Interface Summary Table

Router Interface Summary				
Router Model	**Ethernet Interface #1**	**Ethernet Interface #2**	**Serial Interface #1**	**Serial Interface #2**
1800	Fast Ethernet 0/0 (F0/0)	Fast Ethernet 0/1 (F0/1)	Serial 0/0/0 (S0/0/0)	Serial 0/0/1 (S0/0/1)
1900	Gigabit Ethernet 0/0 (G0/0)	Gigabit Ethernet 0/1 (G0/1)	Serial 0/0/0 (S0/0/0)	Serial 0/0/1 (S0/0/1)
2801	Fast Ethernet 0/0 (F0/0)	Fast Ethernet 0/1 (F0/1)	Serial 0/1/0 (S0/1/0)	Serial 0/1/1 (S0/1/1)
2811	Fast Ethernet 0/0 (F0/0)	Fast Ethernet 0/1 (F0/1)	Serial 0/0/0 (S0/0/0)	Serial 0/0/1 (S0/0/1)
2900	Gigabit Ethernet 0/0 (G0/0)	Gigabit Ethernet 0/1 (G0/1)	Serial 0/0/0 (S0/0/0)	Serial 0/0/1 (S0/0/1)

Note: To find out how the router is configured, look at the interfaces to identify the type of router and how many interfaces the router has. There is no way to effectively list all the combinations of configurations for each router class. This table includes identifiers for the possible combinations of Ethernet and Serial interfaces in the device. The table does not include any other type of interface, even though a specific router may contain one. An example of this might be an ISDN BRI interface. The string in parenthesis is the legal abbreviation that can be used in Cisco IOS commands to represent the interface.

Appendix A: Configuration Commands

Router R1

```
R1(config)# router eigrp 1
R1(config-router)# network 192.168.1.0
R1(config-router)# network 192.168.12.0 0.0.0.3
R1(config-router)# network 192.168.13.0 0.0.0.3
R1(config-router)# network 192.168.11.0 0.0.0.3
R1(config-router)# network 192.168.11.4 0.0.0.3
R1(config-router)# network 192.168.11.8 0.0.0.3
R1(config-router)# network 192.168.11.12 0.0.0.3
R1(config-router)# passive-interface g0/0
R1(config)# int s0/0/0
R1(config-if)# bandwidth 1024
R1(config-if)# int s0/0/1
R1(config-if)# bandwidth 64
```

Router R2

```
R2(config)# router eigrp 1
R2(config-router)# network 192.168.2.0
R2(config-router)# network 192.168.12.0 0.0.0.3
R2(config-router)# network 192.168.23.0 0.0.0.3
R2(config-router)# passive-interface g0/0
R2(config)# int s0/0/0
R2(config-if)# bandwidth 1024
```

Router R3

```
R3(config)# router eigrp 1
R3(config-router)# network 192.168.3.0
R3(config-router)# network 192.168.13.0 0.0.0.3
R3(config-router)# network 192.168.23.0 0.0.0.3
R3(config-router)# network 192.168.33.0 0.0.0.3
R3(config-router)# network 192.168.33.4 0.0.0.3
R3(config-router)# network 192.168.33.8 0.0.0.3
R3(config-router)# network 192.168.33.12 0.0.0.3
R3(config-router)# passive-interface g0/0
R3(config)# int s0/0/0
R3(config-if)# bandwidth 64
```

5.2.3.6 Lab – Troubleshooting Basic EIGRP for IPv4 and IPv6

Topology

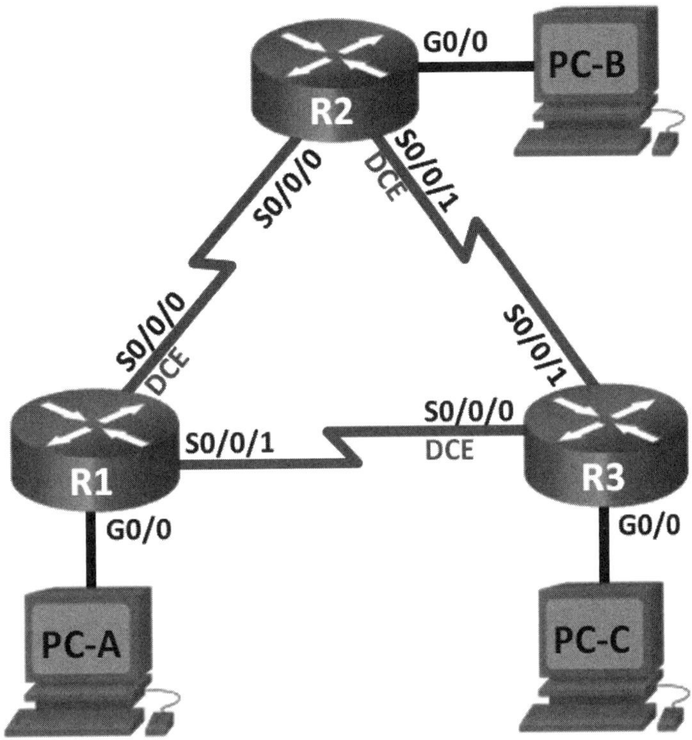

Addressing Table

Device	EIGRP Router ID	Interface	IP Address	Default Gateway
R1	1.1.1.1	G0/0	192.168.1.1/24 2001:DB8:ACAD:A::1/64 FE80::1 link-local	N/A
		S0/0/0 (DCE)	192.168.12.1/30 2001:DB8:ACAD:12::1/64 FE80::1 link-local	N/A
		S0/0/1	192.18.13.1/30 2001:DB8:ACAD:13::1/64 FE80::1 link-local	N/A
R2	2.2.2.2	G0/0	192.168.2.1/24 2001:DB8:ACAD:B::2/64 FE80::2 link-local	N/A
		S0/0/0	192.168.12.2/30 2001:DB8:ACAD:12::2/64 FE80::2 link-local	N/A
		S0/0/1 (DCE)	192.168.23.1/30 2001:DB8:ACAD:23::2/64 FE80::2 link-local	N/A
R3	3.3.3.3	G0/0	192.168.3.1/24 2001:DB8:ACAD:C::3/64 FE80::3 link-local	N/A
		S0/0/0 (DCE)	192.168.13.2/30 2001:DB8:ACAD:13::3/64 FE80::3 link-local	N/A
		S0/0/1	192.168.23.2/30 2001:DB8:ACAD:23::3/64 FE80::3 link-local	N/A
PC-A		NIC	192.168.1.3/24 2001:DB8:ACAD:A::A/64	192.168.1.1 FE80::1
PC-B		NIC	192.168.2.3/24 2001:DB8:ACAD:B::B/64	192.168.2.1 FE80::2
PC-C		NIC	192.168.3.3/24 2001:DB8:ACAD:C::C/64	192.168.3.1 FE80::3

Objectives

Part 1: Build the Network and Load Device Configurations

Part 2: Troubleshoot Layer 3 Connectivity

Part 3: Troubleshoot EIGRP for IPv4

Part 4: Troubleshoot EIGRP for IPv6

Background / Scenario

The Enhanced Interior Gateway Routing Protocol (EIGRP) is an advanced distance vector routing protocol developed by Cisco Systems. EIGRP routers discover neighbors and establish and maintain adjacencies with neighbor routers using Hello packets. An EIGRP router assumes that as long as it is receiving Hello packets from a neighboring router, that neighbor is up and its routes remain viable.

EIGRP for IPv4 runs over the IPv4 network layer, communicating with other EIGRP IPv4 peers, and advertising only IPv4 routes. EIGRP for IPv6 has the same functionality as EIGRP for IPv4 but uses IPv6 as the network layer protocol, communicating with EIGRP for IPv6 peers and advertising IPv6 routes.

In this lab, you will troubleshoot a network that runs EIGRP for IPv4 and EIGRP for IPv6 routing protocols. This network is experiencing problems and you are tasked with finding the problems and correcting them.

Note: The routers used with CCNA hands-on labs are Cisco 1941 Integrated Services Routers (ISRs) with Cisco IOS Release 15.2(4)M3 (universalk9 image). Other routers and Cisco IOS versions can be used. Depending on the model and Cisco IOS version, the commands available and output produced might vary from what is shown in the labs. Refer to the Router Interface Summary Table at the end of this lab for the correct interface identifiers.

Note: Make sure that the routers have been erased and have no startup configurations. If you are unsure, contact your instructor.

Required Resources

- 3 Router (Cisco 1941 with Cisco IOS Release 15.2(4)M3 universal image or comparable)
- 3 PCs (Windows 7, Vista, or XP with terminal emulation program, such as Tera Term)
- Console cables to configure the Cisco IOS devices via the console ports
- Ethernet and serial cables as shown in the topology

Part 1: Build the Network and Load Device Configurations

In Part 1, you will set up the network topology and configure basic settings on the PC hosts and routers.

Step 1: Cable the network as shown in the topology.

Step 2: Configure PC hosts.

Step 3: Load router configurations.

Load the following configurations into the appropriate router. All routers have the same passwords. The privileged EXEC password is **class**, and the console and vty password is **cisco**.

Router R1 Configuration:

```
conf t
service password-encryption
hostname R1
enable secret class
no ip domain lookup
```

```
ipv6 unicast-routing
interface GigabitEthernet0/0
 ip address 192.168.1.1 255.255.255.0
 duplex auto
 speed auto
 ipv6 address FE80::1 link-local
 ipv6 address 2001:DB8:ACAD:A::1/64
 ipv6 eigrp 1
 no shutdown
interface Serial0/0/0
 bandwidth 128
 ip address 192.168.21.1 255.255.255.252

 ipv6 address FE80::1 link-local
 ipv6 address 2001:DB8:ACAD:12::1/64
 ipv6 eigrp 1
 clock rate 128000
 no shutdown
interface Serial0/0/1

 ip address 192.168.13.1 255.255.255.252
 ipv6 address FE80::1 link-local
 ipv6 address 2001:DB8:ACAD:31::1/64

 ipv6 eigrp 1
 no shutdown
router eigrp 1
 network 192.168.1.0
 network 192.168.12.0 0.0.0.3
 network 192.168.13.0 0.0.0.3
 passive-interface GigabitEthernet0/0
 eigrp router-id 1.1.1.1
ipv6 router eigrp 1


 no shutdown
banner motd @
  Unauthorized Access is Prohibited! @
line con 0
```

```
 password cisco
 logging synchronous
line vty 0 4
 password cisco
login
 transport input all
end
```

Router R2 Configuration:

```
conf t
service password-encryption
hostname R2
enable secret class
no ip domain lookup
ipv6 unicast-routing
interface GigabitEthernet0/0
 ip address 192.168.2.1 255.255.255.0
 duplex auto
 speed auto
 ipv6 address FE80::2 link-local
 ipv6 address 2001:DB8:ACAD:B::2/64
 ipv6 eigrp 1


interface Serial0/0/0

 ip address 192.168.12.2 255.255.255.252
 ipv6 address FE80::2 link-local
 ipv6 address 2001:DB8:ACAD:12::2/64
 ipv6 eigrp 1
 no shutdown
interface Serial0/0/1
 bandwidth 128
 ip address 192.168.23.1 255.255.255.0

 ipv6 address FE80::2 link-local
 ipv6 address 2001:DB8:ACAD:23::2/64
 ipv6 eigrp 1
 clock rate 128000
 no shutdown
```

```
router eigrp 1

 network 192.168.12.0 0.0.0.3
 network 192.168.23.0 0.0.0.3
 passive-interface GigabitEthernet0/0
 eigrp router-id 2.2.2.2
ipv6 router eigrp 1

 no shutdown
 passive-interface GigabitEthernet0/0
banner motd @
  Unauthorized Access is Prohibited! @
line con 0
 password cisco
 login
 logging synchronous
line vty 0 4
 password cisco
 login
 transport input all
end
```

Router R3 Configuration:

```
conf t
service password-encryption
hostname R3
enable secret class
no ip domain lookup

interface GigabitEthernet0/0
 ip address 192.168.3.1 255.255.255.0
 duplex auto
 speed auto
 ipv6 address FE80::3 link-local
 ipv6 address 2001:DB8:ACAD:C::3/64
 ipv6 eigrp 1

interface Serial0/0/0
```

```
  ip address 192.168.13.2 255.255.255.252
  ipv6 address FE80::3 link-local
  ipv6 address 2001:DB8:ACAD:13::3/64
  ipv6 eigrp 1
  no shutdown

interface Serial0/0/1
 bandwidth 128
 ip address 192.168.23.2 255.255.255.252
 ipv6 address FE80::3 link-local
 ipv6 address 2001:DB8:ACAD:23::3/64
 ipv6 eigrp 1
 no shutdown
router eigrp 1
 network 192.168.3.0
 network 192.168.13.0 0.0.0.3

 passive-interface GigabitEthernet0/0
 eigrp router-id 3.3.3.3




banner motd @
  Unauthorized Access is Prohibited! @
line con 0
 password cisco
 login
 logging synchronous
line vty 0 4
 password cisco
 login
 transport input all
end
```

Step 4:   **Save the running configuration for all routers.**

Part 2:   Troubleshoot Layer 3 Connectivity

In Part 2, you will verify that Layer 3 connectivity is established on all interfaces. You will need to test both IPv4 and IPv6 connectivity for all device interfaces.

Note: All serial interfaces should be set with a bandwidth of 128 Kb/s. The clock rate on the DCE interface should be set to 128000.

Step 1:   Verify that the interfaces listed in the Addressing Table are active and configured with correct IP address information.

a.   Issue the **show ip interface brief** command on all routers to verify that the interfaces are in an up/up state. Record your findings.

b.   Issue the **show run interface** command to verify IP address assignments on all router interfaces. Compare the interface IP addresses against the Addressing Table and verify the subnet mask assignments. For IPv6, verify that the link-local address has been assigned. Record your findings.

c. Issue the **show interface** *interface-id* command to verify bandwidth setting on the serial interfaces. Record your findings.

d. Issue the **show controllers** *interface-id* command to verify that clock rates have been set to 128 Kb/s on all DCE serial interfaces. Issue the **show interface** *interface-id* command to verify bandwidth setting on the serial interfaces. Record your findings.

e. Resolve all problems found. Record the commands used to correct the issues.

Step 2: **Verify Layer 3 connectivity.**

Use the **ping** command and verify that each router has network connectivity with the serial interfaces on the neighbor routers. Verify that the PCs can ping their default gateways. If problems still exist, continue trouble-shooting Layer 3 issues.

Part 3: **Troubleshoot EIGRP for IPv4**

In Part 3, you will troubleshoot EIGRP for IPv4 problems and make the necessary changes needed to estab-lish EIGRP for IPv4 routes and end-to-end IPv4 connectivity.

Note: LAN (G0/0) interfaces should not advertise EIGRP routing information, but routes to these networks should be contained in the routing tables.

Step 1: **Test IPv4 end-to-end connectivity.**

From each PC host, ping the other PC hosts in the topology to verify end-to-end connectivity.

Note: It may be necessary to disable the PC firewall before testing, to ping between PCs.

a.   Ping from PC-A to PC-B. Were the pings successful? _______________

b.   Ping from PC-A to PC-C. Were the pings successful? _______________

c.   Ping from PC-B to PC-C. Were the pings successful? _______________

Step 2: **Verify that all interfaces are assigned to EIGRP for IPv4.**

a.   Issue the **show ip protocols** command to verify that EIGRP is running and that all networks are adver-tised. This command also allows you to verify that the router ID is set correctly, and that the LAN inter-faces are set as passive interfaces. Record your findings.

____

____

____

b. Make the necessary changes based on the output from the **show ip protocols** command. Record the
    commands that were used to correct the issues.

____

____

____

c. Re-issue the **show ip protocols** command to verify that your changes had the desired effect.

Step 3: Verify EIGRP neighbor information.

a. Issue the **show ip eigrp neighbor** command to verify that EIGRP adjacencies have been established
    between the neighboring routers.

b. Resolve any outstanding problems that were discovered.

Step 4: Verify EIGRP for IPv4 routing information.

a. Issue the **show ip route eigrp** command to verify that each router has EIGRP for IPv4 routes to all non-
    adjoining networks.

Are all EIGRP routes available? _________

If any EIGRP for IPv4 routes are missing, what is missing?

____

b.   If any routing information is missing, resolve these issues.

Step 5:   Verify IPv4 end-to-end connectivity.

From each PC, verify that IPv4 end-to-end connectivity exists. PCs should be able to ping the other PC hosts in the topology. If IPv4 end-to-end connectivity does not exist, then continue troubleshooting to resolve remaining issues.

Note: It may be necessary to disable the PCs firewall.

Part 4:   Troubleshoot EIGRP for IPv6

In Part 4, you will troubleshoot EIGRP for IPv6 problems and make the necessary changes needed to establish EIGRP for IPv6 routes and end-to-end IPv6 connectivity.

Note: LAN (G0/0) interfaces should not advertise EIGRP routing information, but routes to these networks should be contained in the routing tables.

Step 1:   Test IPv6 end-to-end connectivity.

From each PC host, ping the IPv6 addresses of the other PC hosts in the topology to verify end-to-end connectivity.

Step 2:   Verify that IPv6 unicast routing has been enabled on all routers.

a.   An easy way to verify that IPv6 routing has been enabled on a router is to use the **show run | section ipv6 unicast** command. By adding this pipe to the **show run** command, the **ipv6 unicast-routing** command is displayed if IPv6 routing has been enabled.

Note: The **show run** command can also be issued without any pipe, and then a manual search for the **ipv6 unicast-routing** command can be done.

Issue the command on each router. Record your findings.

____

____

____

c.   If IPv6 unicast routing is not enabled on one or more routers, enable it now. Record the commands that were used to correct the issues.

____

____

Step 3:   Verify that all interfaces are assigned to EIGRP for IPv6.

a.   Issue the **show ipv6 protocols** command and verify that the router ID is correct. This command also allows you to verify that the LAN interfaces are set as passive interfaces.

Note: If no output is generated from this command, then the EIGRP for IPv6 process has not been configured.

Record your findings.

____

____

____

b.   Make the necessary configuration changes. Record the commands used to correct the issues.

____

____

____

____

____

____

____

____

c.   Re-issue the **show ipv6 protocols** command to verify that your changes are correct.

Step 4:   Verify that all routers have correct neighbor adjacency information.

a.   Issue the **show ipv6 eigrp neighbor** command to verify that adjacencies have formed between neighboring routers.

b.   Resolve any EIGRP adjacency issues that still exist.

Step 5:   Verify EIGRP for IPv6 routing information.

a. Issue the **show ipv6 route eigrp** command, and verify that EIGRP for IPv6 routes exist to all non-adjoining networks.

Are all EIGRP routes available? _________

If any EIGRP for IPv6 routes are missing, what is missing?

____

b. Resolve any routing issues that still exist.

Step 6:   Test IPv6 end-to-end connectivity.

From each PC, verify that IPv6 end-to-end connectivity exists. PCs should be able to ping the other PC hosts in the topology. If IPv6 end-to-end connectivity does not exist, then continue troubleshooting to resolve remaining issues.

Note: It may be necessary to disable the PCs firewall.

Reflection

Why would you troubleshoot EIGRP for IPv4 and EIGRP for IPv6 separately?

____

Router Interface Summary Table

Router Interface Summary				
Router Model	**Ethernet Interface #1**	**Ethernet Interface #2**	**Serial Interface #1**	**Serial Interface #2**
1800	Fast Ethernet 0/0 (F0/0)	Fast Ethernet 0/1 (F0/1)	Serial 0/0/0 (S0/0/0)	Serial 0/0/1 (S0/0/1)
1900	Gigabit Ethernet 0/0 (G0/0)	Gigabit Ethernet 0/1 (G0/1)	Serial 0/0/0 (S0/0/0)	Serial 0/0/1 (S0/0/1)
2801	Fast Ethernet 0/0 (F0/0)	Fast Ethernet 0/1 (F0/1)	Serial 0/1/0 (S0/1/0)	Serial 0/1/1 (S0/1/1)
2811	Fast Ethernet 0/0 (F0/0)	Fast Ethernet 0/1 (F0/1)	Serial 0/0/0 (S0/0/0)	Serial 0/0/1 (S0/0/1)
2900	Gigabit Ethernet 0/0 (G0/0)	Gigabit Ethernet 0/1 (G0/1)	Serial 0/0/0 (S0/0/0)	Serial 0/0/1 (S0/0/1)

Note: To find out how the router is configured, look at the interfaces to identify the type of router and how many interfaces the router has. There is no way to effectively list all the combinations of configurations for each router class. This table includes identifiers for the possible combinations of Ethernet and Serial interfaces in the device. The table does not include any other type of interface, even though a specific router may contain one. An example of this might be an ISDN BRI interface. The string in parenthesis is the legal abbreviation that can be used in Cisco IOS commands to represent the interface.

5.2.3.7 Lab – Troubleshooting Advanced EIGRP

Topology

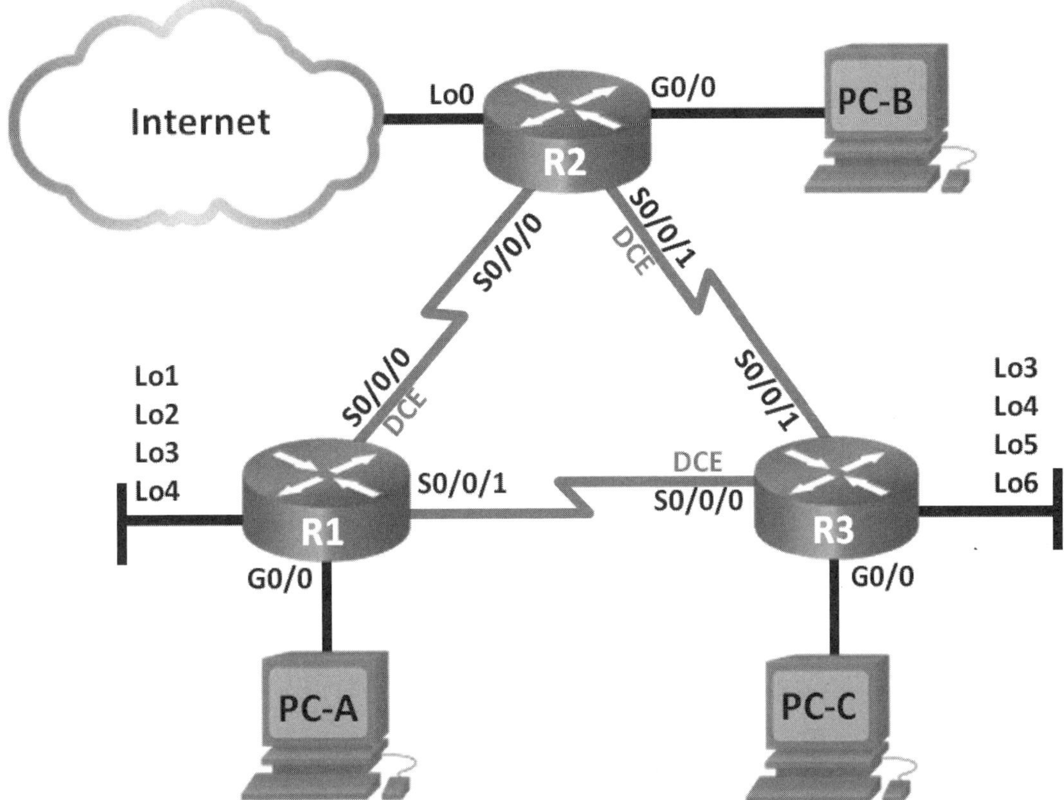

Addressing Table

Device	Interface	IP Address	Subnet Mask	Default Gateway
R1	G0/0	192.168.1.1	255.255.255.0	N/A
	Lo1	172.16.11.1	255.255.255.0	N/A
	Lo2	172.16.12.1	255.255.255.0	N/A
	Lo3	172.16.13.1	255.255.255.0	N/A
	Lo4	172.16.14.1	255.255.255.0	N/A
	S0/0/0 (DCE)	192.168.12.1	255.255.255.252	N/A
	S0/0/1	192.168.13.1	255.255.255.252	N/A
R2	G0/0	192.168.2.1	255.255.255.0	N/A
	Lo0	209.165.200.225	255.255.255.252	N/A
	S0/0/0	192.168.12.2	255.255.255.252	N/A
	S0/0/1 (DCE)	192.168.23.1	255.255.255.252	N/A
R3	G0/0	192.168.3.1	255.255.255.0	N/A
	Lo3	172.16.33.1	255.255.255.0	N/A
	Lo4	172.16.34.1	255.255.255.0	N/A
	Lo5	172.16.35.1	255.255.255.0	N/A
	Lo6	172.16.36.1	255.255.255.0	N/A
	S0/0/0 (DCE)	192.168.13.2	255.255.255.252	N/A
	S0/0/1	192.168.23.2	255.255.255.252	N/A
PC-A	NIC	192.168.1.3	255.255.255.0	192.168.1.1
PC-B	NIC	192.168.2.3	255.255.255.0	192.168.2.1
PC-C	NIC	192.168.3.3	255.255.255.0	192.168.3.1

Objectives

Part 1: Build the Network and Load Device Configurations

Part 2: Troubleshoot EIGRP

Background / Scenario

The Enhanced Interior Gateway Routing Protocol (EIGRP) has advanced features to allow changes related to summarization, default route propagation, bandwidth utilization, metrics, and security.

In this lab, you will troubleshoot a network that is running EIGRP. Advanced EIGRP features have been implemented, but the network is now experiencing problems. You are tasked with finding and correcting the network issues.

Note: The routers used with CCNA hands-on labs are Cisco 1941 Integrated Services Routers (ISRs) with Cisco IOS, Release 15.2(4)M3 (universalk9 image). Other routers and Cisco IOS versions can be used. Depending on the model and Cisco IOS version, the commands available and output produced might vary from what is shown in the labs. Refer to the Router Interface Summary Table at the end of this lab for the correct interface identifiers.

Note: Ensure that the routers have been erased and have no startup configurations. If you are unsure, contact your instructor.

Required Resources

- 3 Routers (Cisco 1941 with Cisco IOS Release 15.2(4)M3 universal image or comparable)
- 3 PCs (Windows 7, Vista, or XP with terminal emulation program, such as Tera Term)
- Console cables to configure the Cisco IOS devices via the console ports
- Ethernet cables as shown in the topology

Part 1: Build the Network and Load Device Configurations

Step 1: Cable the network as shown in the topology.

Step 2: Configure PC hosts.

Step 3: Load router configurations.

Load the following configurations into the appropriate router. All routers have the same passwords. The privileged EXEC password is **class**, and **cisco** is the console and vty password.

Router R1 Configuration:

```
conf t
hostname R1
enable secret class
no ip domain lookup
key chain EIGRP-KEYS
 key 1
  key-string cisco123

line con 0
 password cisco
 login
 logging synchronous
line vty 0 4
 password cisco
 login
banner motd @
  Unauthorized Access is Prohibited! @
interface lo1
 description Connection to Branch 11
 ip add 172.16.11.1 255.255.255.0
interface lo2
 description Connection to Branch 12
 ip add 172.16.12.1 255.255.255.0
```

```
interface lo3
 description Connection to Branch 13
 ip add 172.16.13.1 255.255.255.0
interface lo4
 description Connection to Branch 14
 ip add 172.16.14.1 255.255.255.0
interface g0/0
 description R1 LAN Connection
 ip add 192.168.1.1 255.255.255.0
 no shutdown
interface s0/0/0
 description Serial Link to R2
 clock rate 128000

 ip add 192.168.12.1 255.255.255.252
 ip authentication mode eigrp 1 md5
 ip authentication key-chain eigrp 1 EIGRP-KEYS
 ip hello-interval eigrp 1 30
 ip hold-time eigrp 1 90
 ip bandwidth-percent eigrp 1 40

 no shutdown
interface s0/0/1
 description Serial Link to R3
 bandwidth 128
 ip add 192.168.13.1 255.255.255.252
 ip authentication mode eigrp 1 md5
 ip authentication key-chain eigrp 1 EIGRP-KEYS
 ip bandwidth-percent eigrp 1 40



 no shutdown
router eigrp 1
 router-id 1.1.1.1
 network 192.168.1.0 0.0.0.255
 network 192.168.12.0 0.0.0.3
 network 192.168.13.0 0.0.0.3
 network 172.16.0.0 0.0.255.255
```

```
 passive-interface g0/0
 auto-summary

end
```

Router R2 Configuration:

```
conf t
hostname R2
enable secret class
no ip domain lookup
key chain EIGRP-KEYS
 key 1
  key-string Cisco123
line con 0
 password cisco
 login
 logging synchronous
line vty 0 4
 password cisco
 login
banner motd @
  Unauthorized Access is Prohibited! @
interface g0/0
 description R2 LAN Connection
 ip add 192.168.2.1 255.255.255.0
 no shutdown
interface s0/0/0
 description Serial Link to R1
 bandwidth 128
 ip add 192.168.12.2 255.255.255.252
 ip authentication mode eigrp 1 md5
 ip authentication key-chain eigrp 1 EIGRP-KEYS
 ip bandwidth-percent eigrp 1 40
 ip hello-interval eigrp 1 30
 ip hold-time eigrp 1 90
 no shutdown
interface s0/0/1
 description Serial Link to R3
 bandwidth 128
```

```
  ip add 192.168.23.1 255.255.255.252
  ip authentication mode eigrp 1 md5


  ip bandwidth-percent eigrp 1 40
  ip hello-interval eigrp 1 30
  ip hold-time eigrp 1 90
 no shutdown
interface lo0
  ip add 209.165.200.225 255.255.255.252
 description Connection to ISP
router eigrp 1
 router-id 2.2.2.2
 network 192.168.2.0 0.0.0.255
 network 192.168.12.0 0.0.0.3
 network 192.168.23.0 0.0.0.3
 passive-interface g0/0


ip route 0.0.0.0 0.0.0.0 lo0
end
```

Router R3 Configuration:

```
conf t
hostname R3
enable secret class
no ip domain lookup
key chain EIGRP-KEYS
 key 1
  key-string Cisco123
line con 0
 password cisco
 login
 logging synchronous
line vty 0 4
 password cisco
 login
banner motd @
  Unauthorized Access is Prohibited! @
interface lo3
 description Connection to Branch 33
```

```
 ip add 172.16.33.1 255.255.255.0
interface lo4
 description Connection to Branch 34
 ip add 172.16.34.1 255.255.255.0
interface lo5
 description Connection to Branch 35
 ip add 172.16.35.1 255.255.255.0
interface lo6
 description Connection to Branch 36
 ip add 172.16.36.1 255.255.255.0
interface g0/0
 description R3 LAN Connection
 ip add 192.168.3.1 255.255.255.0
 no shutdown
interface s0/0/0
 description Serial Link to R1
 ip add 192.168.13.2 255.255.255.252
 ip authentication mode eigrp 1 md5
 ip authentication key-chain eigrp 1 EIGRP-KEYS

 ip hello-interval eigrp 1 30
 ip hold-time eigrp 1 90

 clock rate 128000
 bandwidth 128
 no shutdown
interface s0/0/1
 description Serial Link to R2
 bandwidth 128
 ip add 192.168.23.2 255.255.255.252
 ip authentication mode eigrp 1 md5
 ip authentication key-chain eigrp 1 eigrp-keys

 ! ip bandwidth-percent eigrp 1 40
 ip hello-interval eigrp 1 30
 ip hold-time eigrp 1 90

 no shutdown
 router eigrp 1
```

```
router-id 3.3.3.3

network 192.168.3.0 0.0.0.255

network 192.168.13.0 0.0.0.3

network 192.168.23.0 0.0.0.3

network 172.16.0.0 0.0.255.255

passive-interface g0/0

auto-summary


end
```

Step 4:   **Verify end-to-end connectivity.**

Note: It may be necessary to disable the PC firewall to ping between PCs.

Step 5:   **Save the configuration on all routers.**

Part 2:   Troubleshoot EIGRP

In Part 2, verify that all routers have established neighbor adjacencies, and that all network routes are available.

Additional EIGRP Requirements:

- All serial interface clock rates should be set at 128 Kb/s and a matching bandwidth setting should be available to allow EIGRP cost metrics to be calculated correctly.

- Manual route summarization of the branch networks, simulated by using Loopback interfaces on R1 and R3, should be utilized. The automatic summarization feature of EIGRP should not be used.

- EIGRP should redistribute the static default route to the Internet. This is simulated by using Loopback interface 0 on R2.

- EIGRP should be configured to use no more than **40** percent of the available bandwidth on the serial interfaces.

- EIGRP Hello/Hold timer intervals should be set to **30/90** on all serial interfaces.

- All serial interfaces should be configured with MD5 authentication, using key chain **EIGRP-KEYS**, with a key-string of **Cisco123**.

List the commands used during your EIGRP troubleshooting process:

____

____

____

____

List the changes made to resolve the EIGRP issues. If no problems were found on the device, then respond with "no problems were found".

R1 Router:

R2 Router:

R3 Router:

Reflection

1. How can the **auto-summary** command create routing issues in EIGRP?

2. What advantages are provided by manually summarizing the branch routes (loopback interfaces on R1 and R3) in this network?

3.   Why would you want to change the EIGRP Hello and Hold time intervals on an interface?

____

____

Router Interface Summary Table

Router Interface Summary				
Router Model	**Ethernet Interface #1**	**Ethernet Interface #2**	**Serial Interface #1**	**Serial Interface #2**
1800	Fast Ethernet 0/0 (F0/0)	Fast Ethernet 0/1 (F0/1)	Serial 0/0/0 (S0/0/0)	Serial 0/0/1 (S0/0/1)
1900	Gigabit Ethernet 0/0 (G0/0)	Gigabit Ethernet 0/1 (G0/1)	Serial 0/0/0 (S0/0/0)	Serial 0/0/1 (S0/0/1)
2801	Fast Ethernet 0/0 (F0/0)	Fast Ethernet 0/1 (F0/1)	Serial 0/1/0 (S0/1/0)	Serial 0/1/1 (S0/1/1)
2811	Fast Ethernet 0/0 (F0/0)	Fast Ethernet 0/1 (F0/1)	Serial 0/0/0 (S0/0/0)	Serial 0/0/1 (S0/0/1)
2900	Gigabit Ethernet 0/0 (G0/0)	Gigabit Ethernet 0/1 (G0/1)	Serial 0/0/0 (S0/0/0)	Serial 0/0/1 (S0/0/1)

Note: To find out how the router is configured, look at the interfaces to identify the type of router and how many interfaces the router has. There is no way to effectively list all the combinations of configurations for each router class. This table includes identifiers for the possible combinations of Ethernet and Serial interfaces in the device. The table does not include any other type of interface, even though a specific router may contain one. An example of this might be an ISDN BRI interface. The string in parenthesis is the legal abbreviation that can be used in Cisco IOS commands to represent the interface.

5.3.1.1 Class Activity – Tweaking EIGRP

Objectives

Implement advanced EIGRP features to enhance operation in a small- to medium-sized business network.

Scenario

The purpose of this activity is to review EIGRP routing protocol fine-tuning concepts.

You will work with a partner to design one EIGRP topology. This topology will be the basis for two parts of the activity. The first will use default settings for all configurations and the second will incorporate, at least, three of the following fine-tuning EIGRP options:

- Manual summary route

- Default routes

- Default routes propagation

- Hello interval timer settings

    Refer to the labs, Packet Tracer activities, and interactive activities to help you as you progress through this modeling activity.

    Directions are listed on the PDF file for this activity. Share your completed work with another group. You may wish to save a copy of this activity to a portfolio.

Resources

- Packet Tracer software or real network lab equipment
- Word processing program

Directions

Step 1:   Design a WAN and LAN topology.

a. Use Packet Tracer to design a network with two routers (1941 model, suggested). If necessary, add NICs to the routers to provide connectivity to the routers to provide for, at least, two LANs for each router. Add, at least, one PC to each LAN.

b. Address the networks using either an IPv4 or IPv6 addressing scheme. VLSM may or may not be used per group discretion. If you use a full VLSM-addressed network, you will need to turn off auto-summarization from the beginning of your configuration design.

c. Configure the topology using basic EIGRP default settings.

d. Make sure all PCs can ping each other to prove connectivity. If not, work to make this so.

e. Save your work.

Step 2:   Copy the topology.

a. Using your cursor, highlight the entire EIGRP-configured topology.

b. Press **Ctrl+C** to copy the highlighted topology.

   c.   Use **Ctrl+V** to paste a full copy of the topology to the Packet Tracer desktop. You will now have displayed two exact EIGRP-configured topologies. You will use the topology copy to tweak the network.

   d.   While highlighted, move the copied topology to a different location on the Packet Tracer desktop to create room between the two for configuration purposes.

Step 3: Configure fine-tuning features on the copied topology.

   a.   Choose three of the bulleted items from the Scenario section of this activity. Configure your changes on the copied topology. **Note**: By changing the Hello interval times, network instability may occur. You should be able to configure it; however, notice adjacencies status changing if you do choose this configuration option.

   b.   Save your work to avoid losing your configuration.

Step 4: Use verification commands to compare and contrast your default and fine-tuned configurations.

   a.   Use, at least, three output commands to compare and contrast the two topologies, and copy them to a word processing software program. For example, some useful commands include:

- `show ip route`

- `show running-configuration`

- `show ip protocols, show ip eigrp neighbors`

   b.   Share your work with another group. Explain how you changed the second topology from the first configured example. Justify what happened when you configured the three EIGRP fine-tuning options.

Chapter 6 — Single-Area OSPF

6.2.4.5 Lab – Configuring Basic Single-Area OSPFv2

Topology

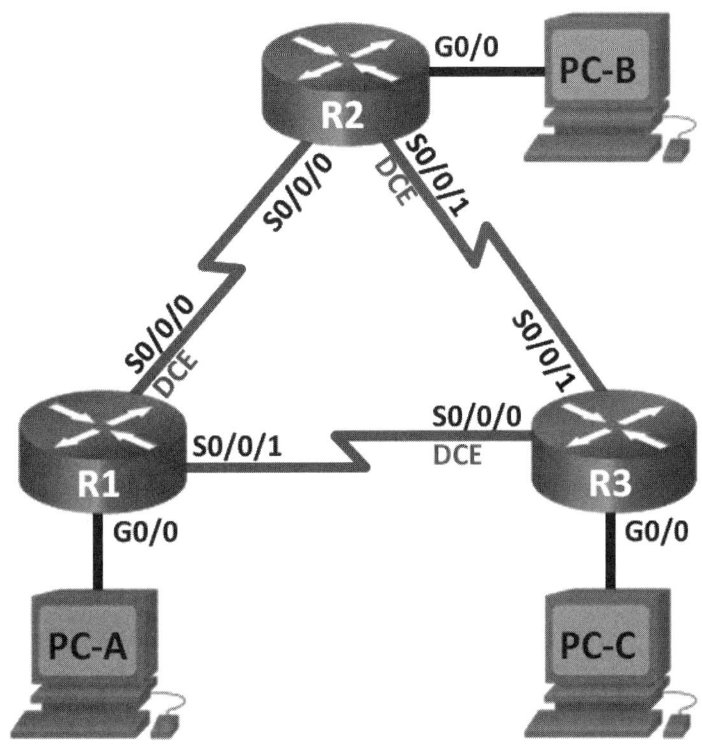

Addressing Table

Device	Interface	IP Address	Subnet Mask	Default Gateway
R1	G0/0	192.168.1.1	255.255.255.0	N/A
	S0/0/0 (DCE)	192.168.12.1	255.255.255.252	N/A
	S0/0/1	192.168.13.1	255.255.255.252	N/A
R2	G0/0	192.168.2.1	255.255.255.0	N/A
	S0/0/0	192.168.12.2	255.255.255.252	N/A
	S0/0/1 (DCE)	192.168.23.1	255.255.255.252	N/A
R3	G0/0	192.168.3.1	255.255.255.0	N/A
	S0/0/0 (DCE)	192.168.13.2	255.255.255.252	N/A
	S0/0/1	192.168.23.2	255.255.255.252	N/A
PC-A	NIC	192.168.1.3	255.255.255.0	192.168.1.1
PC-B	NIC	192.168.2.3	255.255.255.0	192.168.2.1
PC-C	NIC	192.168.3.3	255.255.255.0	192.168.3.1

Objectives

Part 1: Build the Network and Configure Basic Device Settings

Part 2: Configure and Verify OSPF Routing

Part 3: Change Router ID Assignments

Part 4: Configure OSPF Passive Interfaces

Part 5: Change OSPF Metrics

Background / Scenario

Open Shortest Path First (OSPF) is a link-state routing protocol for IP networks. OSPFv2 is defined for IPv4 networks, and OSPFv3 is defined for IPv6 networks. OSPF detects changes in the topology, such as link failures, and converges on a new loop-free routing structure very quickly. It computes each route using Dijkstra's algorithm, a shortest path first algorithm.

In this lab, you will configure the network topology with OSPFv2 routing, change the router ID assignments, configure passive interfaces, adjust OSPF metrics, and use a number of CLI commands to display and verify OSPF routing information.

Note: The routers used with CCNA hands-on labs are Cisco 1941 Integrated Services Routers (ISRs) with Cisco IOS Release 15.2(4)M3 (universalk9 image). Other routers and Cisco IOS versions can be used. Depending on the model and Cisco IOS version, the commands available and output produced might vary from what is shown in the labs. Refer to the Router Interface Summary Table at the end of this lab for the correct interface identifiers.

Note: Make sure that the routers have been erased and have no startup configurations. If you are unsure, contact your instructor.

Required Resources

- 3 Routers (Cisco 1941 with Cisco IOS Release 15.2(4)M3 universal image or comparable)
- 3 PCs (Windows 7, Vista, or XP with terminal emulation program, such as Tera Term)
- Console cables to configure the Cisco IOS devices via the console ports
- Ethernet and serial cables as shown in the topology

Part 1:   Build the Network and Configure Basic Device Settings

In Part 1, you set up the network topology and configure basic settings on the PC hosts and routers.

Step 1:   **Cable the network as shown in the topology.**

Step 2:   **Initialize and reload the routers as necessary.**

Step 3:   **Configure basic settings for each router.**

a.   Disable DNS lookup.

b.   Configure device name as shown in the topology.

c. Assign **class** as the privileged EXEC password.

d. Assign **cisco** as the console and vty passwords.

e. Configure a message of the day (MOTD) banner to warn users that unauthorized access is prohibited.

f. Configure **logging synchronous** for the console line.

g. Configure the IP address listed in the Addressing Table for all interfaces.

h. Set the clock rate for all DCE serial interfaces at **128000**.

i. Copy the running configuration to the startup configuration.

Step 4: **Configure PC hosts.**

Step 5: **Test connectivity.**

The routers should be able to ping one another, and each PC should be able to ping its default gateway. The PCs are unable to ping other PCs until OSPF routing is configured. Verify and troubleshoot if necessary.

Part 2: **Configure and Verify OSPF Routing**

In Part 2, you will configure OSPFv2 routing on all routers in the network and then verify that routing tables are updated correctly. After OSPF has been verified, you will configure OSPF authentication on the links for added security.

Step 1: **Configure OSPF on R1.**

a. Use the **router ospf** command in global configuration mode to enable OSPF on R1.

```
R1(config)# router ospf 1
```

Note: The OSPF process id is kept locally and has no meaning to other routers on the network.

b. Configure the **network** statements for the networks on R1. Use an area ID of 0.

```
R1(config-router)# network 192.168.1.0 0.0.0.255 area 0
R1(config-router)# network 192.168.12.0 0.0.0.3 area 0
R1(config-router)# network 192.168.13.0 0.0.0.3 area 0
```

Step 2: **Configure OSPF on R2 and R3.**

Use the **router ospf** command and add the **network** statements for the networks on R2 and R3. Neighbor adjacency messages display on R1 when OSPF routing is configured on R2 and R3.

```
R1#
00:22:29: %OSPF-5-ADJCHG: Process 1, Nbr 192.168.23.1 on Serial0/0/0 from LOADING to
FULL, Loading Done
R1#
00:23:14: %OSPF-5-ADJCHG: Process 1, Nbr 192.168.23.2 on Serial0/0/1 from LOADING to
FULL, Loading Done
R1#
```

Step 3:   Verify OSPF neighbors and routing information.

a. Issue the **show ip ospf neighbor** command to verify that each router lists the other routers in the network as neighbors.

```
R1# show ip ospf neighbor


Neighbor ID      Pri   State            Dead Time   Address        Interface
192.168.23.2      0    FULL/  -         00:00:33    192.168.13.2   Serial0/0/1
192.168.23.1      0    FULL/  -         00:00:30    192.168.12.2   Serial0/0/0
```

b. Issue the **show ip route** command to verify that all networks display in the routing table on all routers.

```
R1# show ip route
Codes: L - local, C - connected, S - static, R - RIP, M - mobile, B - BGP
       D - EIGRP, EX - EIGRP external, O - OSPF, IA - OSPF inter area
       N1 - OSPF NSSA external type 1, N2 - OSPF NSSA external type 2
       E1 - OSPF external type 1, E2 - OSPF external type 2, E - EGP
       i - IS-IS, L1 - IS-IS level-1, L2 - IS-IS level-2, ia - IS-IS inter area
       * - candidate default, U - per-user static route, o - ODR
       P - periodic downloaded static route


Gateway of last resort is not set


      192.168.1.0/24 is variably subnetted, 2 subnets, 2 masks
C        192.168.1.0/24 is directly connected, GigabitEthernet0/0
L        192.168.1.1/32 is directly connected, GigabitEthernet0/0
O     192.168.2.0/24 [110/65] via 192.168.12.2, 00:32:33, Serial0/0/0
O     192.168.3.0/24 [110/65] via 192.168.13.2, 00:31:48, Serial0/0/1
      192.168.12.0/24 is variably subnetted, 2 subnets, 2 masks
C        192.168.12.0/30 is directly connected, Serial0/0/0
L        192.168.12.1/32 is directly connected, Serial0/0/0
      192.168.13.0/24 is variably subnetted, 2 subnets, 2 masks
C        192.168.13.0/30 is directly connected, Serial0/0/1
L        192.168.13.1/32 is directly connected, Serial0/0/1
      192.168.23.0/30 is subnetted, 1 subnets
O        192.168.23.0/30 [110/128] via 192.168.12.2, 00:31:38, Serial0/0/0
                         [110/128] via 192.168.13.2, 00:31:38, Serial0/0/1
```

What command would you use to only see the OSPF routes in the routing table?

Step 4: **Verify OSPF protocol settings.**

The **show ip protocols** command is a quick way to verify vital OSPF configuration information. This information includes the OSPF process ID, the router ID, networks the router is advertising, the neighbors the router is receiving updates from, and the default administrative distance, which is 110 for OSPF.

```
R1# show ip protocols
*** IP Routing is NSF aware ***


Routing Protocol is "ospf 1"
  Outgoing update filter list for all interfaces is not set
  Incoming update filter list for all interfaces is not set
  Router ID 192.168.13.1
  Number of areas in this router is 1. 1 normal 0 stub 0 nssa
  Maximum path: 4
  Routing for Networks:
    192.168.1.0 0.0.0.255 area 0
    192.168.12.0 0.0.0.3 area 0
    192.168.13.0 0.0.0.3 area 0
  Routing Information Sources:
    Gateway         Distance      Last Update
    192.168.23.2         110      00:19:16
    192.168.23.1         110      00:20:03
  Distance: (default is 110)
```

Step 5: **Verify OSPF process information.**

Use the **show ip ospf command** to examine the OSPF process ID and router ID. This command displays the OSPF area information, as well as the last time the SPF algorithm was calculated.

```
R1# show ip ospf
 Routing Process "ospf 1" with ID 192.168.13.1
 Start time: 00:20:23.260, Time elapsed: 00:25:08.296
 Supports only single TOS(TOS0) routes
 Supports opaque LSA
 Supports Link-local Signaling (LLS)
 Supports area transit capability
 Supports NSSA (compatible with RFC 3101)
 Event-log enabled, Maximum number of events: 1000, Mode: cyclic
 Router is not originating router-LSAs with maximum metric
 Initial SPF schedule delay 5000 msecs
 Minimum hold time between two consecutive SPFs 10000 msecs
 Maximum wait time between two consecutive SPFs 10000 msecs
 Incremental-SPF disabled
 Minimum LSA interval 5 secs
```

```
    Minimum LSA arrival 1000 msecs
    LSA group pacing timer 240 secs
    Interface flood pacing timer 33 msecs
    Retransmission pacing timer 66 msecs
    Number of external LSA 0. Checksum Sum 0x000000
    Number of opaque AS LSA 0. Checksum Sum 0x000000
    Number of DCbitless external and opaque AS LSA 0
    Number of DoNotAge external and opaque AS LSA 0
    Number of areas in this router is 1. 1 normal 0 stub 0 nssa
    Number of areas transit capable is 0
    External flood list length 0
    IETF NSF helper support enabled
    Cisco NSF helper support enabled
    Reference bandwidth unit is 100 mbps
        Area BACKBONE(0)
            Number of interfaces in this area is 3
            Area has no authentication
            SPF algorithm last executed 00:22:53.756 ago
            SPF algorithm executed 7 times
            Area ranges are
            Number of LSA 3. Checksum Sum 0x019A61
            Number of opaque link LSA 0. Checksum Sum 0x000000
            Number of DCbitless LSA 0
            Number of indication LSA 0
            Number of DoNotAge LSA 0
            Flood list length 0
```

Step 6: Verify OSPF interface settings.

a. Issue the **show ip ospf interface brief** command to display a summary of OSPF-enabled interfaces.

```
R1# show ip ospf interface brief
Interface     PID    Area              IP Address/Mask      Cost   State  Nbrs F/C
Se0/0/1       1      0                 192.168.13.1/30      64     P2P    1/1
Se0/0/0       1      0                 192.168.12.1/30      64     P2P    1/1
Gi0/0         1      0                 192.168.1.1/24       1      DR     0/0
```

b. For a more detailed list of every OSPF-enabled interface, issue the **show ip ospf interface** command.

```
R1# show ip ospf interface
Serial0/0/1 is up, line protocol is up
  Internet Address 192.168.13.1/30, Area 0, Attached via Network Statement
  Process ID 1, Router ID 192.168.13.1, Network Type POINT_TO_POINT, Cost: 64
  Topology-MTID    Cost    Disabled    Shutdown    Topology Name
        0           64         no          no          Base
```

```
  Transmit Delay is 1 sec, State POINT_TO_POINT
  Timer intervals configured, Hello 10, Dead 40, Wait 40, Retransmit 5
    oob-resync timeout 40
    Hello due in 00:00:01
  Supports Link-local Signaling (LLS)
  Cisco NSF helper support enabled
  IETF NSF helper support enabled
  Index 3/3, flood queue length 0
  Next 0x0(0)/0x0(0)
  Last flood scan length is 1, maximum is 1
  Last flood scan time is 0 msec, maximum is 0 msec
  Neighbor Count is 1, Adjacent neighbor count is 1
    Adjacent with neighbor 192.168.23.2
  Suppress hello for 0 neighbor(s)
Serial0/0/0 is up, line protocol is up
  Internet Address 192.168.12.1/30, Area 0, Attached via Network Statement
  Process ID 1, Router ID 192.168.13.1, Network Type POINT_TO_POINT, Cost: 64
  Topology-MTID    Cost    Disabled    Shutdown      Topology Name
        0           64        no          no            Base
  Transmit Delay is 1 sec, State POINT_TO_POINT
  Timer intervals configured, Hello 10, Dead 40, Wait 40, Retransmit 5
    oob-resync timeout 40
    Hello due in 00:00:03
  Supports Link-local Signaling (LLS)
  Cisco NSF helper support enabled
  IETF NSF helper support enabled
  Index 2/2, flood queue length 0
  Next 0x0(0)/0x0(0)
  Last flood scan length is 1, maximum is 1
  Last flood scan time is 0 msec, maximum is 0 msec
  Neighbor Count is 1, Adjacent neighbor count is 1
    Adjacent with neighbor 192.168.23.1
  Suppress hello for 0 neighbor(s)
GigabitEthernet0/0 is up, line protocol is up
  Internet Address 192.168.1.1/24, Area 0, Attached via Network Statement
  Process ID 1, Router ID 192.168.13.1, Network Type BROADCAST, Cost: 1
  Topology-MTID    Cost    Disabled    Shutdown      Topology Name
        0            1        no          no            Base
  Transmit Delay is 1 sec, State DR, Priority 1
  Designated Router (ID) 192.168.13.1, Interface address 192.168.1.1
  No backup designated router on this network
```

```
    Timer intervals configured, Hello 10, Dead 40, Wait 40, Retransmit 5
      oob-resync timeout 40
      Hello due in 00:00:01
    Supports Link-local Signaling (LLS)
    Cisco NSF helper support enabled
    IETF NSF helper support enabled
    Index 1/1, flood queue length 0
    Next 0x0(0)/0x0(0)
    Last flood scan length is 0, maximum is 0
    Last flood scan time is 0 msec, maximum is 0 msec
    Neighbor Count is 0, Adjacent neighbor count is 0
    Suppress hello for 0 neighbor(s)
```

Step 7:   **Verify end-to-end connectivity.**

Each PC should be able to ping the other PCs in the topology. Verify and troubleshoot if necessary.

Note: It may be necessary to disable the PC firewall to ping between PCs.

Part 3:   **Change Router ID Assignments**

The OSPF router ID is used to uniquely identify the router in the OSPF routing domain. Cisco routers derive the router ID in one of three ways and with the following precedence:

1) IP address configured with the OSPF **router-id** command, if present

2) Highest IP address of any of the router's loopback addresses, if present

3) Highest active IP address on any of the router's physical interfaces

Because no router IDs or loopback interfaces have been configured on the three routers, the router ID for each router is determined by the highest IP address of any active interface.

In Part 3, you will change the OSPF router ID assignment using loopback addresses. You will also use the **router-id** command to change the router ID.

Step 1:   **Change router IDs using loopback addresses.**

a. Assign an IP address to loopback 0 on R1.

```
R1(config)# interface lo0
R1(config-if)# ip address 1.1.1.1 255.255.255.255
R1(config-if)# end
```

b. Assign IP addresses to Loopback 0 on R2 and R3. Use IP address 2.2.2.2/32 for R2 and 3.3.3.3/32 for R3.

c. Save the running configuration to the startup configuration on all three routers.

d. You must reload the routers in order to reset the router ID to the loopback address. Issue the **reload** command on all three routers. Press Enter to confirm the reload.

e. After the router completes the reload process, issue the **show ip protocols** command to view the new router ID.

```
R1# show ip protocols
*** IP Routing is NSF aware ***


Routing Protocol is "ospf 1"
  Outgoing update filter list for all interfaces is not set
  Incoming update filter list for all interfaces is not set
  Router ID 1.1.1.1
  Number of areas in this router is 1. 1 normal 0 stub 0 nssa
  Maximum path: 4
  Routing for Networks:
    192.168.1.0 0.0.0.255 area 0
    192.168.12.0 0.0.0.3 area 0
    192.168.13.0 0.0.0.3 area 0
  Routing Information Sources:
    Gateway         Distance      Last Update
    3.3.3.3              110      00:01:00
    2.2.2.2              110      00:01:14
  Distance: (default is 110)
```

f. Issue the **show ip ospf neighbor** command to display the router ID changes for the neighboring routers.

```
R1# show ip ospf neighbor


Neighbor ID     Pri   State          Dead Time   Address         Interface
3.3.3.3          0    FULL/  -       00:00:35    192.168.13.2    Serial0/0/1
2.2.2.2          0    FULL/  -       00:00:32    192.168.12.2    Serial0/0/0
R1#
```

Step 2: Change the router ID on R1 using the router-id command.

The preferred method for setting the router ID is with the **router-id** command.

a. Issue the **router-id 11.11.11.11** command on R1 to reassign the router ID. Notice the informational message that appears when issuing the **router-id** command.

```
R1(config)# router ospf 1
R1(config-router)# router-id 11.11.11.11
Reload or use "clear ip ospf process" command, for this to take effect
R1(config)# end
```

b. You will receive an informational message telling you that you must either reload the router or use the **clear ip ospf process** command for the change to take effect. Issue the **clear ip ospf process** command on all three routers. Type **yes** to reply to the reset verification message, and press ENTER.

c. Set the router ID for R2 to **22.22.22.22** and the router ID for R3 to **33.33.33.33**. Then use **clear ip ospf process** command to reset ospf routing process.

d. Issue the **show ip protocols** command to verify that the router ID changed on R1.

```
R1# show ip protocols
*** IP Routing is NSF aware ***


Routing Protocol is "ospf 1"
  Outgoing update filter list for all interfaces is not set
  Incoming update filter list for all interfaces is not set
  Router ID 11.11.11.11
  Number of areas in this router is 1. 1 normal 0 stub 0 nssa
  Maximum path: 4
  Routing for Networks:
     192.168.1.0 0.0.0.255 area 0
     192.168.12.0 0.0.0.3 area 0
     192.168.13.0 0.0.0.3 area 0
  Passive Interface(s):
     GigabitEthernet0/1
  Routing Information Sources:
     Gateway         Distance      Last Update
     33.33.33.33          110      00:00:19
     22.22.22.22          110      00:00:31
     3.3.3.3              110      00:00:41
     2.2.2.2              110      00:00:41
  Distance: (default is 110)
```

e. Issue the **show ip ospf neighbor** command on R1 to verify that new router ID for R2 and R3 is listed.

```
R1# show ip ospf neighbor

Neighbor ID     Pri   State         Dead Time   Address        Interface
33.33.33.33      0    FULL/  -      00:00:36    192.168.13.2   Serial0/0/1
22.22.22.22      0    FULL/  -      00:00:32    192.168.12.2   Serial0/0/0
```

Part 4: Configure OSPF Passive Interfaces

The **passive-interface** command prevents routing updates from being sent through the specified router interface. This is commonly done to reduce traffic on the LANs as they do not need to receive dynamic routing protocol communication. In Part 4, you will use the **passive-interface** command to configure a single interface as passive. You will also configure OSPF so that all interfaces on the router are passive by default, and then enable OSPF routing advertisements on selected interfaces.

Step 1: Configure a passive interface.

a. Issue the **show ip ospf interface g0/0** command on R1. Notice the timer indicating when the next Hello packet is expected. Hello packets are sent every 10 seconds and are used between OSPF routers to verify that their neighbors are up.

```
R1# show ip ospf interface g0/0
GigabitEthernet0/0 is up, line protocol is up
  Internet Address 192.168.1.1/24, Area 0, Attached via Network Statement
  Process ID 1, Router ID 11.11.11.11, Network Type BROADCAST, Cost: 1
  Topology-MTID    Cost    Disabled    Shutdown      Topology Name
       0            1         no          no            Base
  Transmit Delay is 1 sec, State DR, Priority 1
  Designated Router (ID) 11.11.11.11, Interface address 192.168.1.1
  No backup designated router on this network
  Timer intervals configured, Hello 10, Dead 40, Wait 40, Retransmit 5
    oob-resync timeout 40
    Hello due in 00:00:02
  Supports Link-local Signaling (LLS)
  Cisco NSF helper support enabled
  IETF NSF helper support enabled
  Index 1/1, flood queue length 0
  Next 0x0(0)/0x0(0)
  Last flood scan length is 0, maximum is 0
  Last flood scan time is 0 msec, maximum is 0 msec
  Neighbor Count is 0, Adjacent neighbor count is 0
  Suppress hello for 0 neighbor(s)
```

b. Issue the **passive-interface** command to change the G0/0 interface on R1 to passive.

```
R1(config)# router ospf 1
R1(config-router)# passive-interface g0/0
```

c. Re-issue the **show ip ospf interface g0/0** command to verify that G0/0 is now passive.

```
R1# show ip ospf interface g0/0
GigabitEthernet0/0 is up, line protocol is up
  Internet Address 192.168.1.1/24, Area 0, Attached via Network Statement
  Process ID 1, Router ID 11.11.11.11, Network Type BROADCAST, Cost: 1
  Topology-MTID    Cost    Disabled    Shutdown      Topology Name
       0            1         no          no            Base
  Transmit Delay is 1 sec, State DR, Priority 1
  Designated Router (ID) 11.11.11.11, Interface address 192.168.1.1
  No backup designated router on this network
  Timer intervals configured, Hello 10, Dead 40, Wait 40, Retransmit 5
    oob-resync timeout 40
    No Hellos (Passive interface)
  Supports Link-local Signaling (LLS)
  Cisco NSF helper support enabled
  IETF NSF helper support enabled
```

```
Index 1/1, flood queue length 0

Next 0x0(0)/0x0(0)

Last flood scan length is 0, maximum is 0

Last flood scan time is 0 msec, maximum is 0 msec

Neighbor Count is 0, Adjacent neighbor count is 0

Suppress hello for 0 neighbor(s)
```

d. Issue the **show ip route** command on R2 and R3 to verify that a route to the 192.168.1.0/24 network is still available.

```
R2# show ip route
Codes: L - local, C - connected, S - static, R - RIP, M - mobile, B - BGP
       D - EIGRP, EX - EIGRP external, O - OSPF, IA - OSPF inter area
       N1 - OSPF NSSA external type 1, N2 - OSPF NSSA external type 2
       E1 - OSPF external type 1, E2 - OSPF external type 2
       i - IS-IS, su - IS-IS summary, L1 - IS-IS level-1, L2 - IS-IS level-2
       ia - IS-IS inter area, * - candidate default, U - per-user static route
       o - ODR, P - periodic downloaded static route, H - NHRP, l - LISP
       + - replicated route, % - next hop override


Gateway of last resort is not set


      2.0.0.0/32 is subnetted, 1 subnets
C        2.2.2.2 is directly connected, Loopback0
O     192.168.1.0/24 [110/65] via 192.168.12.1, 00:58:32, Serial0/0/0
      192.168.2.0/24 is variably subnetted, 2 subnets, 2 masks
C        192.168.2.0/24 is directly connected, GigabitEthernet0/0
L        192.168.2.1/32 is directly connected, GigabitEthernet0/0
O     192.168.3.0/24 [110/65] via 192.168.23.2, 00:58:19, Serial0/0/1
      192.168.12.0/24 is variably subnetted, 2 subnets, 2 masks
C        192.168.12.0/30 is directly connected, Serial0/0/0
L        192.168.12.2/32 is directly connected, Serial0/0/0
      192.168.13.0/30 is subnetted, 1 subnets
O        192.168.13.0 [110/128] via 192.168.23.2, 00:58:19, Serial0/0/1
                      [110/128] via 192.168.12.1, 00:58:32, Serial0/0/0
      192.168.23.0/24 is variably subnetted, 2 subnets, 2 masks
C        192.168.23.0/30 is directly connected, Serial0/0/1
L        192.168.23.1/32 is directly connected, Serial0/0/1
```

Step 2:   Set passive interface as the default on a router.

a. Issue the **show ip ospf neighbor** command on R1 to verify that R2 is listed as an OSPF neighbor.

```
R1# show ip ospf neighbor
```

```
Neighbor ID      Pri   State          Dead Time    Address          Interface
33.33.33.33       0   FULL/  -        00:00:31     192.168.13.2     Serial0/0/1
22.22.22.22       0   FULL/  -        00:00:32     192.168.12.2     Serial0/0/0
```

b. Issue the **passive-interface default** command on R2 to set the default for all OSPF interfaces as passive.

```
R2(config)# router ospf 1
R2(config-router)# passive-interface default
R2(config-router)#
*Apr  3 00:03:00.979: %OSPF-5-ADJCHG: Process 1, Nbr 11.11.11.11 on Serial0/0/0 from
FULL to DOWN, Neighbor Down: Interface down or detached
*Apr  3 00:03:00.979: %OSPF-5-ADJCHG: Process 1, Nbr 33.33.33.33 on Serial0/0/1 from
FULL to DOWN, Neighbor Down: Interface down or detached
```

c. Re-issue the **show ip ospf neighbor** command on R1. After the dead timer expires, R2 will no longer be listed as an OSPF neighbor.

```
R1# show ip ospf neighbor

Neighbor ID      Pri   State          Dead Time    Address          Interface
33.33.33.33       0   FULL/  -        00:00:34     192.168.13.2     Serial0/0/1
```

d. Issue the **show ip ospf interface S0/0/0** command on R2 to view the OSPF status of interface S0/0/0.

```
R2# show ip ospf interface s0/0/0
Serial0/0/0 is up, line protocol is up
  Internet Address 192.168.12.2/30, Area 0, Attached via Network Statement
  Process ID 1, Router ID 22.22.22.22, Network Type POINT_TO_POINT, Cost: 64
  Topology-MTID    Cost    Disabled    Shutdown      Topology Name
        0           64        no          no            Base
  Transmit Delay is 1 sec, State POINT_TO_POINT
  Timer intervals configured, Hello 10, Dead 40, Wait 40, Retransmit 5
    oob-resync timeout 40
    No Hellos (Passive interface)
  Supports Link-local Signaling (LLS)
  Cisco NSF helper support enabled
  IETF NSF helper support enabled
  Index 2/2, flood queue length 0
  Next 0x0(0)/0x0(0)
  Last flood scan length is 0, maximum is 0
  Last flood scan time is 0 msec, maximum is 0 msec
  Neighbor Count is 0, Adjacent neighbor count is 0
  Suppress hello for 0 neighbor(s)
```

e. If all interfaces on R2 are passive, then no routing information is being advertised. In this case, R1 and R3 should no longer have a route to the 192.168.2.0/24 network. You can verify this by using the **show ip route** command.

f. On R2, issue the **no passive-interface** command so the router will send and receive OSPF routing up-
    dates. After entering this command, you will see an informational message that a neighbor adjacency has
    been established with R1.

```
R2(config)# router ospf 1

R2(config-router)# no passive-interface s0/0/0

R2(config-router)#

*Apr  3 00:18:03.463: %OSPF-5-ADJCHG: Process 1, Nbr 11.11.11.11 on Serial0/0/0 from
LOADING to FULL, Loading Done
```

g. Re-issue the **show ip route** and **show ipv6 ospf neighbor** commands on R1 and R3, and look for a
    route to the 192.168.2.0/24 network.

What interface is R3 using to route to the 192.168.2.0/24 network? ______________

What is the accumulated cost metric for the 192.168.2.0/24 network on R3? __________

Does R2 show up as an OSPF neighbor on R1? __________

Does R2 show up as an OSPF neighbor on R3? __________

What does this information tell you?

____

____

____

____

h. Change interface S0/0/1 on R2 to allow it to advertise OSPF routes. Record the commands used below.

____

____

i. Re-issue the **show ip route** command on R3.

What interface is R3 using to route to the 192.168.2.0/24 network? ______________

What is the accumulated cost metric for the 192.168.2.0/24 network on R3 now and how is this calculated?

____

Is R2 listed as an OSPF neighbor to R3? __________

Part 5:   Change OSPF Metrics

In Part 5, you will change OSPF metrics using the **auto-cost reference-bandwidth** command, the **band-width** command, and the **ip ospf cost** command.

Note: All DCE interfaces should have been configured with a clocking rate of 128000 in Part 1.

Step 1:   Change the reference bandwidth on the routers.

The default reference-bandwidth for OSPF is 100Mb/s (Fast Ethernet speed). However, most modern infrastructure devices have links that are faster than 100Mb/s. Because the OSPF cost metric must be an integer, all links with transmission speeds of 100Mb/s or higher have a cost of 1. This results in Fast Ethernet, Gigabit Ethernet and 10G Ethernet interfaces all having the same cost. Therefore, the reference-bandwidth must be changed to a higher value to accommodate networks with links faster that 100Mb/s.

a.   Issue the **show interface** command on R1 to view the default bandwidth setting for the G0/0 interface.

```
R1# show interface g0/0
GigabitEthernet0/0 is up, line protocol is up
  Hardware is CN Gigabit Ethernet, address is c471.fe45.7520 (bia c471.fe45.7520)
  MTU 1500 bytes, BW 1000000 Kbit/sec, DLY 100 usec,
     reliability 255/255, txload 1/255, rxload 1/255
  Encapsulation ARPA, loopback not set
  Keepalive set (10 sec)
  Full Duplex, 100Mbps, media type is RJ45
  output flow-control is unsupported, input flow-control is unsupported
  ARP type: ARPA, ARP Timeout 04:00:00
  Last input never, output 00:17:31, output hang never
  Last clearing of "show interface" counters never
  Input queue: 0/75/0/0 (size/max/drops/flushes); Total output drops: 0
  Queueing strategy: fifo
  Output queue: 0/40 (size/max)
  5 minute input rate 0 bits/sec, 0 packets/sec
  5 minute output rate 0 bits/sec, 0 packets/sec
     0 packets input, 0 bytes, 0 no buffer
     Received 0 broadcasts (0 IP multicasts)
     0 runts, 0 giants, 0 throttles
     0 input errors, 0 CRC, 0 frame, 0 overrun, 0 ignored
     0 watchdog, 0 multicast, 0 pause input
     279 packets output, 89865 bytes, 0 underruns
     0 output errors, 0 collisions, 1 interface resets
     0 unknown protocol drops
     0 babbles, 0 late collision, 0 deferred
     1 lost carrier, 0 no carrier, 0 pause output
     0 output buffer failures, 0 output buffers swapped out
```

Note: The bandwidth setting on G0/0 may differ from what is shown above if the PC host interface can only support Fast Ethernet speed. If the PC host interface is not capable of supporting gigabit speed, then the bandwidth will most likely be displayed as 100000 Kbit/sec.

b. Issue the **show ip route ospf** command on R1 to determine the route to the 192.168.3.0/24 network.

```
R1# show ip route ospf
Codes: L - local, C - connected, S - static, R - RIP, M - mobile, B - BGP
       D - EIGRP, EX - EIGRP external, O - OSPF, IA - OSPF inter area
       N1 - OSPF NSSA external type 1, N2 - OSPF NSSA external type 2
       E1 - OSPF external type 1, E2 - OSPF external type 2
       i - IS-IS, su - IS-IS summary, L1 - IS-IS level-1, L2 - IS-IS level-2
       ia - IS-IS inter area, * - candidate default, U - per-user static route
       o - ODR, P - periodic downloaded static route, H - NHRP, l - LISP
       + - replicated route, % - next hop override


Gateway of last resort is not set


O       192.168.3.0/24 [110/65] via 192.168.13.2, 00:00:57, Serial0/0/1
        192.168.23.0/30 is subnetted, 1 subnets
O          192.168.23.0 [110/128] via 192.168.13.2, 00:00:57, Serial0/0/1
                        [110/128] via 192.168.12.2, 00:01:08, Serial0/0/0
```

Note: The accumulated cost to the 192.168.3.0/24 network from R1 is 65.

c. Issue the **show ip ospf interface** command on R3 to determine the routing cost for G0/0.

```
R3# show ip ospf interface g0/0
GigabitEthernet0/0 is up, line protocol is up
  Internet Address 192.168.3.1/24, Area 0, Attached via Network Statement
  Process ID 1, Router ID 3.3.3.3, Network Type BROADCAST, Cost: 1
  Topology-MTID    Cost    Disabled    Shutdown      Topology Name
        0            1        no          no             Base
  Transmit Delay is 1 sec, State DR, Priority 1
  Designated Router (ID) 192.168.23.2, Interface address 192.168.3.1
  No backup designated router on this network
  Timer intervals configured, Hello 10, Dead 40, Wait 40, Retransmit 5
    oob-resync timeout 40
    Hello due in 00:00:05
  Supports Link-local Signaling (LLS)
  Cisco NSF helper support enabled
  IETF NSF helper support enabled
  Index 1/1, flood queue length 0
  Next 0x0(0)/0x0(0)
  Last flood scan length is 0, maximum is 0
  Last flood scan time is 0 msec, maximum is 0 msec
```

```
    Neighbor Count is 0, Adjacent neighbor count is 0
    Suppress hello for 0 neighbor(s)
```

d. Issue the **show ip ospf interface s0/0/1** command on R1 to view the routing cost for S0/0/1.

```
R1# show ip ospf interface s0/0/1
Serial0/0/1 is up, line protocol is up
  Internet Address 192.168.13.1/30, Area 0, Attached via Network Statement
  Process ID 1, Router ID 1.1.1.1, Network Type POINT_TO_POINT, Cost: 64
  Topology-MTID    Cost    Disabled    Shutdown      Topology Name
        0           64        no          no             Base
  Transmit Delay is 1 sec, State POINT_TO_POINT
  Timer intervals configured, Hello 10, Dead 40, Wait 40, Retransmit 5
    oob-resync timeout 40
    Hello due in 00:00:04
  Supports Link-local Signaling (LLS)
  Cisco NSF helper support enabled
  IETF NSF helper support enabled
  Index 3/3, flood queue length 0
  Next 0x0(0)/0x0(0)
  Last flood scan length is 1, maximum is 1
  Last flood scan time is 0 msec, maximum is 0 msec
  Neighbor Count is 1, Adjacent neighbor count is 1
    Adjacent with neighbor 192.168.23.2
  Suppress hello for 0 neighbor(s)
```

The sum of the costs of these two interfaces is the accumulated cost for the route to the 192.168.3.0/24 network on R3 (1 + 64 = 65), as can be seen in the output from the **show ip route** command.

e. Issue the **auto-cost reference-bandwidth 10000** command on R1 to change the default reference bandwidth setting. With this setting, 10Gb/s interfaces will have a cost of 1, 1 Gb/s interfaces will have a cost of 10, and 100Mb/s interfaces will have a cost of 100.

```
R1(config)# router ospf 1
R1(config-router)# auto-cost reference-bandwidth 10000
% OSPF: Reference bandwidth is changed.
        Please ensure reference bandwidth is consistent across all routers.
```

f. Issue the **auto-cost reference-bandwidth 10000** command on routers R2 and R3.

g. Re-issue the **show ip ospf interface** command to view the new cost of G0/0 on R3, and S0/0/1 on R1.

```
R3# show ip ospf interface g0/0
GigabitEthernet0/0 is up, line protocol is up
  Internet Address 192.168.3.1/24, Area 0, Attached via Network Statement
  Process ID 1, Router ID 3.3.3.3, Network Type BROADCAST, Cost: 10
  Topology-MTID    Cost    Disabled    Shutdown      Topology Name
        0           10        no          no             Base
```

```
    Transmit Delay is 1 sec, State DR, Priority 1

    Designated Router (ID) 192.168.23.2, Interface address 192.168.3.1

    No backup designated router on this network

    Timer intervals configured, Hello 10, Dead 40, Wait 40, Retransmit 5

      oob-resync timeout 40

      Hello due in 00:00:02

    Supports Link-local Signaling (LLS)

    Cisco NSF helper support enabled

    IETF NSF helper support enabled

    Index 1/1, flood queue length 0

    Next 0x0(0)/0x0(0)

    Last flood scan length is 0, maximum is 0

    Last flood scan time is 0 msec, maximum is 0 msec

    Neighbor Count is 0, Adjacent neighbor count is 0

    Suppress hello for 0 neighbor(s)
```

Note: If the device connected to the G0/0 interface does not support Gigabit Ethernet speed, the cost will be different than the output display. For example, the cost will be 100 for Fast Ethernet speed (100Mb/s).

```
R1# show ip ospf interface s0/0/1

Serial0/0/1 is up, line protocol is up

    Internet Address 192.168.13.1/30, Area 0, Attached via Network Statement

    Process ID 1, Router ID 1.1.1.1, Network Type POINT_TO_POINT, Cost: 6476

    Topology-MTID    Cost    Disabled    Shutdown      Topology Name
         0            6476      no          no            Base

    Transmit Delay is 1 sec, State POINT_TO_POINT

    Timer intervals configured, Hello 10, Dead 40, Wait 40, Retransmit 5

      oob-resync timeout 40

      Hello due in 00:00:05

    Supports Link-local Signaling (LLS)

    Cisco NSF helper support enabled

    IETF NSF helper support enabled

    Index 3/3, flood queue length 0

    Next 0x0(0)/0x0(0)

    Last flood scan length is 1, maximum is 1

    Last flood scan time is 0 msec, maximum is 0 msec

    Neighbor Count is 1, Adjacent neighbor count is 1

      Adjacent with neighbor 192.168.23.2

    Suppress hello for 0 neighbor(s)
```

h. Re-issue the **show ip route ospf** command to view the new accumulated cost for the 192.168.3.0/24 route (10 + 6476 = 6486).

Note: If the device connected to the G0/0 interface does not support Gigabit Ethernet speed, the total cost will be different than the output display. For example, the accumulated cost will be 6576 if G0/0 is operating at Fast Ethernet speed (100Mb/s).

```
R1# show ip route ospf
Codes: L - local, C - connected, S - static, R - RIP, M - mobile, B - BGP
       D - EIGRP, EX - EIGRP external, O - OSPF, IA - OSPF inter area
       N1 - OSPF NSSA external type 1, N2 - OSPF NSSA external type 2
       E1 - OSPF external type 1, E2 - OSPF external type 2
       i - IS-IS, su - IS-IS summary, L1 - IS-IS level-1, L2 - IS-IS level-2
       ia - IS-IS inter area, * - candidate default, U - per-user static route
       o - ODR, P - periodic downloaded static route, H - NHRP, l - LISP
       + - replicated route, % - next hop override


Gateway of last resort is not set


O       192.168.2.0/24 [110/6486] via 192.168.12.2, 00:05:40, Serial0/0/0
O       192.168.3.0/24 [110/6486] via 192.168.13.2, 00:01:08, Serial0/0/1
        192.168.23.0/30 is subnetted, 1 subnets
O          192.168.23.0 [110/12952] via 192.168.13.2, 00:05:17, Serial0/0/1
                        [110/12952] via 192.168.12.2, 00:05:17, Serial0/0/
```

Note: Changing the default reference-bandwidth on the routers from 100 to 10,000 in effect changed the accumulated costs of all routes by a factor of 100, but the cost of each interface link and route is now more accurately reflected.

i.   To reset the reference-bandwidth back to its default value, issue the **auto-cost reference-bandwidth 100** command on all three routers.

```
R1(config)# router ospf 1
R1(config-router)# auto-cost reference-bandwidth 100
% OSPF: Reference bandwidth is changed.
        Please ensure reference bandwidth is consistent across all routers.
```

Why would you want to change the OSPF default reference-bandwidth?

____

____

Step 2:   **Change the bandwidth for an interface.**

On most serial links, the bandwidth metric will default to 1544 Kbits (that of a T1). If this is not the actual speed of the serial link, the bandwidth setting will need to be changed to match the actual speed to allow the route cost to be calculated correctly in OSPF. Use the **bandwidth** command to adjust the bandwidth setting on an interface.

Note: A common misconception is to assume that the **bandwidth** command will change the physical bandwidth, or speed, of the link. The command modifies the bandwidth metric used by OSPF to calculate routing costs, and does not modify the actual bandwidth (speed) of the link.

a. Issue the **show interface s0/0/0** command on R1 to view the current bandwidth setting on S0/0/0. Even though the clock rate, link speed on this interface was set to 128Kb/s, the bandwidth is still showing 1544Kb/s.

```
R1# show interface s0/0/0
Serial0/0/0 is up, line protocol is up
  Hardware is WIC MBRD Serial
  Internet address is 192.168.12.1/30
  MTU 1500 bytes, BW 1544 Kbit/sec, DLY 20000 usec,
     reliability 255/255, txload 1/255, rxload 1/255
  Encapsulation HDLC, loopback not set
  Keepalive set (10 sec)
<Output omitted>
```

b. Issue the **show ip route ospf** command on R1 to view the accumulated cost for the route to network 192.168.23.0/24 using S0/0/0. Note that there are two equal-cost (128) routes to the 192.168.23.0/24 network, one via S0/0/0 and one via S0/0/1.

```
R1# show ip route ospf
Codes: L - local, C - connected, S - static, R - RIP, M - mobile, B - BGP
       D - EIGRP, EX - EIGRP external, O - OSPF, IA - OSPF inter area
       N1 - OSPF NSSA external type 1, N2 - OSPF NSSA external type 2
       E1 - OSPF external type 1, E2 - OSPF external type 2
       i - IS-IS, su - IS-IS summary, L1 - IS-IS level-1, L2 - IS-IS level-2
       ia - IS-IS inter area, * - candidate default, U - per-user static route
       o - ODR, P - periodic downloaded static route, H - NHRP, l - LISP
       + - replicated route, % - next hop override


Gateway of last resort is not set


O       192.168.3.0/24 [110/65] via 192.168.13.2, 00:00:26, Serial0/0/1
        192.168.23.0/30 is subnetted, 1 subnets
O          192.168.23.0 [110/128] via 192.168.13.2, 00:00:26, Serial0/0/1
                        [110/128] via 192.168.12.2, 00:00:42, Serial0/0/0
```

c. Issue the **bandwidth 128** command to set the bandwidth on S0/0/0 to 128Kb/s.

```
R1(config)# interface s0/0/0
R1(config-if)# bandwidth 128
```

d. Re-issue the **show ip route ospf** command. The routing table no longer displays the route to the 192.168.23.0/24 network over the S0/0/0 interface. This is because the best route, the one with the lowest cost, is now via S0/0/1.

```
R1# show ip route ospf
Codes: L - local, C - connected, S - static, R - RIP, M - mobile, B - BGP
       D - EIGRP, EX - EIGRP external, O - OSPF, IA - OSPF inter area
       N1 - OSPF NSSA external type 1, N2 - OSPF NSSA external type 2
```

```
        E1 - OSPF external type 1, E2 - OSPF external type 2

        i - IS-IS, su - IS-IS summary, L1 - IS-IS level-1, L2 - IS-IS level-2

        ia - IS-IS inter area, * - candidate default, U - per-user static route

        o - ODR, P - periodic downloaded static route, H - NHRP, l - LISP

        + - replicated route, % - next hop override


Gateway of last resort is not set


O       192.168.3.0/24 [110/65] via 192.168.13.2, 00:04:51, Serial0/0/1

        192.168.23.0/30 is subnetted, 1 subnets

O          192.168.23.0 [110/128] via 192.168.13.2, 00:04:51, Serial0/0/1
```

e. Issue the **show ip ospf interface brief** command. The cost for S0/0/0 has changed from 64 to 781 which is an accurate cost representation of the link speed.

```
R1# show ip ospf interface brief
Interface     PID    Area          IP Address/Mask     Cost   State  Nbrs F/C
Se0/0/1       1      0             192.168.13.1/30     64     P2P    1/1
Se0/0/0       1      0             192.168.12.1/30     781    P2P    1/1
Gi0/0         1      0             192.168.1.1/24      1      DR     0/0
```

f. Change the bandwidth for interface S0/0/1 to the same setting as S0/0/0 on R1.

g. Re-issue the **show ip route ospf** command to view the accumulated cost of both routes to the 192.168.23.0/24 network. Note that there are again two equal-cost (845) routes to the 192.168.23.0/24 network, one via S0/0/0 and one via S0/0/1.

```
R1# show ip route ospf
Codes: L - local, C - connected, S - static, R - RIP, M - mobile, B - BGP
       D - EIGRP, EX - EIGRP external, O - OSPF, IA - OSPF inter area
       N1 - OSPF NSSA external type 1, N2 - OSPF NSSA external type 2
       E1 - OSPF external type 1, E2 - OSPF external type 2
       i - IS-IS, su - IS-IS summary, L1 - IS-IS level-1, L2 - IS-IS level-2
       ia - IS-IS inter area, * - candidate default, U - per-user static route
       o - ODR, P - periodic downloaded static route, H - NHRP, l - LISP
       + - replicated route, % - next hop override


Gateway of last resort is not set


O       192.168.3.0/24 [110/782] via 192.168.13.2, 00:00:09, Serial0/0/1

        192.168.23.0/30 is subnetted, 1 subnets

O          192.168.23.0 [110/845] via 192.168.13.2, 00:00:09, Serial0/0/1
                         [110/845] via 192.168.12.2, 00:00:09, Serial0/0/0
```

Explain how the costs to the 192.168.3.0/24 and 192.168.23.0/30 networks from R1 were calculated.

____

____

____

h.   Issue the **show ip route ospf** command on R3. The accumulated cost of the 192.168.1.0/24 is still show-ing as 65. Unlike the **clock rate** command, the **bandwidth** command needs to be applied on each side of a serial link.

```
R3# show ip route ospf
Codes: L - local, C - connected, S - static, R - RIP, M - mobile, B - BGP
       D - EIGRP, EX - EIGRP external, O - OSPF, IA - OSPF inter area
       N1 - OSPF NSSA external type 1, N2 - OSPF NSSA external type 2
       E1 - OSPF external type 1, E2 - OSPF external type 2
       i - IS-IS, su - IS-IS summary, L1 - IS-IS level-1, L2 - IS-IS level-2
       ia - IS-IS inter area, * - candidate default, U - per-user static route
       o - ODR, P - periodic downloaded static route, H - NHRP, l - LISP
       + - replicated route, % - next hop override


Gateway of last resort is not set


O    192.168.1.0/24 [110/65] via 192.168.13.1, 00:30:58, Serial0/0/0
     192.168.12.0/30 is subnetted, 1 subnets
O       192.168.12.0 [110/128] via 192.168.23.1, 00:30:58, Serial0/0/1
                     [110/128] via 192.168.13.1, 00:30:58, Serial0/0/0
```

i.   Issue the **bandwidth 128** command on all remaining serial interfaces in the topology.

What is the new accumulated cost to the 192.168.23.0/24 network on R1? Why?

____

____

Step 3:   Change the route cost.

OSPF uses the bandwidth setting to calculate the cost for a link by default. However, you can override this calculation by manually setting the cost of a link using the **ip ospf cost** command. Like the **bandwidth** com-mand, **the ip ospf cost** command only affects the side of the link where it was applied.

a.   Issue the **show ip route ospf** on R1.

```
R1# show ip route ospf
Codes: L - local, C - connected, S - static, R - RIP, M - mobile, B - BGP
```

```
              D - EIGRP, EX - EIGRP external, O - OSPF, IA - OSPF inter area
              N1 - OSPF NSSA external type 1, N2 - OSPF NSSA external type 2
              E1 - OSPF external type 1, E2 - OSPF external type 2
              i - IS-IS, su - IS-IS summary, L1 - IS-IS level-1, L2 - IS-IS level-2
              ia - IS-IS inter area, * - candidate default, U - per-user static route
              o - ODR, P - periodic downloaded static route, H - NHRP, l - LISP
              + - replicated route, % - next hop override


Gateway of last resort is not set


O        192.168.2.0/24 [110/782] via 192.168.12.2, 00:00:26, Serial0/0/0
O        192.168.3.0/24 [110/782] via 192.168.13.2, 00:02:50, Serial0/0/1
         192.168.23.0/30 is subnetted, 1 subnets
O           192.168.23.0 [110/1562] via 192.168.13.2, 00:02:40, Serial0/0/1
                         [110/1562] via 192.168.12.2, 00:02:40, Serial0/0/0
```

b. Apply the **ip ospf cost 1565** command to the S0/0/1 interface on R1. A cost of 1565 is higher than the accumulated cost of the route through R2 which is 1562.

```
R1(config)# int s0/0/1
R1(config-if)# ip ospf cost 1565
```

c. Re-issue the **show ip route ospf** command on R1 to display the effect this change has made on the routing table. All OSPF routes for R1 are now being routed through R2.

```
R1# show ip route ospf
Codes: L - local, C - connected, S - static, R - RIP, M - mobile, B - BGP
       D - EIGRP, EX - EIGRP external, O - OSPF, IA - OSPF inter area
       N1 - OSPF NSSA external type 1, N2 - OSPF NSSA external type 2
       E1 - OSPF external type 1, E2 - OSPF external type 2
       i - IS-IS, su - IS-IS summary, L1 - IS-IS level-1, L2 - IS-IS level-2
       ia - IS-IS inter area, * - candidate default, U - per-user static route
       o - ODR, P - periodic downloaded static route, H - NHRP, l - LISP
       + - replicated route, % - next hop override


Gateway of last resort is not set


O        192.168.2.0/24 [110/782] via 192.168.12.2, 00:02:06, Serial0/0/0
O        192.168.3.0/24 [110/1563] via 192.168.12.2, 00:05:31, Serial0/0/0
         192.168.23.0/30 is subnetted, 1 subnets
O           192.168.23.0 [110/1562] via 192.168.12.2, 01:14:02, Serial0/0/0
```

Note: Manipulating link costs using the **ip ospf cost** command is the easiest and preferred method for changing OSPF route costs. In addition to changing the cost based on bandwidth, a network administrator may have other reasons for changing the cost of a route, such as preference for a particular service provider or the actual monetary cost of a link or route.

Explain why the route to the 192.168.3.0/24 network on R1 is now going through R2?

____

____

____

Reflection

1. Why is it important to control the router ID assignment when using the OSPF protocol?

____

____

____

____

2. Why is the DR/BDR election process not a concern in this lab?

____

____

____

3. Why would you want to set an OSPF interface to passive?

____

____

____

Router Interface Summary Table

Router Interface Summary				
Router Model	**Ethernet Interface #1**	**Ethernet Interface #2**	**Serial Interface #1**	**Serial Interface #2**
1800	Fast Ethernet 0/0 (F0/0)	Fast Ethernet 0/1 (F0/1)	Serial 0/0/0 (S0/0/0)	Serial 0/0/1 (S0/0/1)
1900	Gigabit Ethernet 0/0 (G0/0)	Gigabit Ethernet 0/1 (G0/1)	Serial 0/0/0 (S0/0/0)	Serial 0/0/1 (S0/0/1)
2801	Fast Ethernet 0/0 (F0/0)	Fast Ethernet 0/1 (F0/1)	Serial 0/1/0 (S0/1/0)	Serial 0/1/1 (S0/1/1)
2811	Fast Ethernet 0/0 (F0/0)	Fast Ethernet 0/1 (F0/1)	Serial 0/0/0 (S0/0/0)	Serial 0/0/1 (S0/0/1)
2900	Gigabit Ethernet 0/0 (G0/0)	Gigabit Ethernet 0/1 (G0/1)	Serial 0/0/0 (S0/0/0)	Serial 0/0/1 (S0/0/1)

Note: To find out how the router is configured, look at the interfaces to identify the type of router and how many interfaces the router has. There is no way to effectively list all the combinations of configurations for each router class. This table includes identifiers for the possible combinations of Ethernet and Serial interfaces in the device. The table does not include any other type of interface, even though a specific router may contain one. An example of this might be an ISDN BRI interface. The string in parenthesis is the legal abbreviation that can be used in Cisco IOS commands to represent the interface.

6.3.3.6 Lab – Configuring Basic Single-Area OSPFv3

Topology

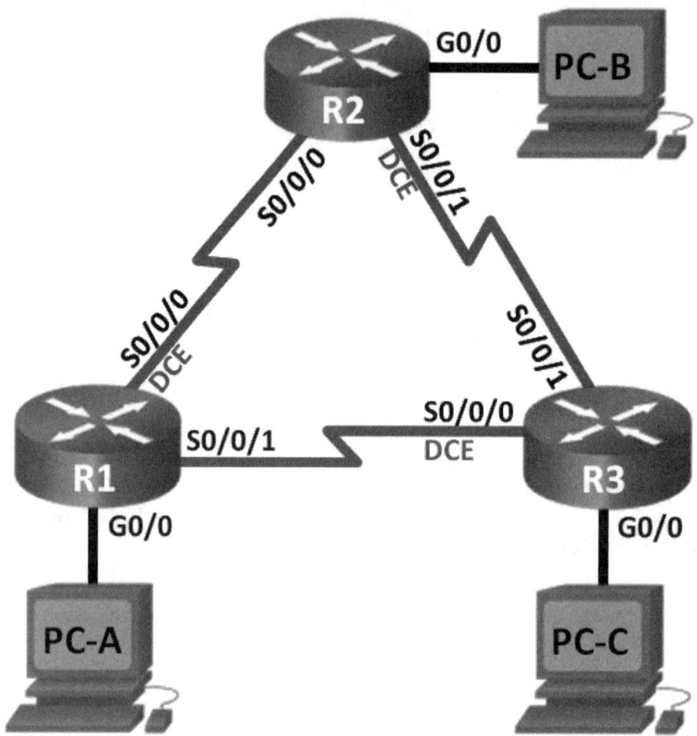

Addressing Table

Device	Interface	IPv6 Address	Default Gateway
R1	G0/0	2001:DB8:ACAD:A::1/64 FE80::1 link-local	N/A
	S0/0/0 (DCE)	2001:DB8:ACAD:12::1/64 FE80::1 link-local	N/A
	S0/0/1	2001:DB8:ACAD:13::1/64 FE80::1 link-local	N/A
R2	G0/0	2001:DB8:ACAD:B::2/64 FE80::2 link-local	N/A
	S0/0/0	2001:DB8:ACAD:12::2/64 FE80::2 link-local	N/A
	S0/0/1 (DCE)	2001:DB8:ACAD:23::2/64 FE80::2 link-local	N/A
R3	G0/0	2001:DB8:ACAD:C::3/64 FE80::3 link-local	N/A
	S0/0/0 (DCE)	2001:DB8:ACAD:13::3/64 FE80::3 link-local	N/A
	S0/0/1	2001:DB8:ACAD:23::3/64 FE80::3 link-local	N/A
PC-A	NIC	2001:DB8:ACAD:A::A/64	FE80::1
PC-B	NIC	2001:DB8:ACAD:B::B/64	FE80::2
PC-C	NIC	2001:DB8:ACAD:C::C/64	FE80::3

Objectives

Part 1: Build the Network and Configure Basic Device Settings

Part 2: Configure and Verify OSPFv3 Routing

Part 3: Configure OSPFv3 Passive Interfaces

Background / Scenario

Open Shortest Path First (OSPF) is a link-state routing protocol for IP networks. OSPFv2 is defined for IPv4 networks, and OSPFv3 is defined for IPv6 networks.

In this lab, you will configure the network topology with OSPFv3 routing, assign router IDs, configure passive interfaces, and use a number of CLI commands to display and verify OSPFv3 routing information.

Note: The routers used with CCNA hands-on labs are Cisco 1941 Integrated Services Routers (ISRs) with Cisco IOS Release 15.2(4)M3 (universalk9 image). Other routers and Cisco IOS versions can be used. Depending on the model and Cisco IOS version, the commands available and output produced might vary from what is shown in the labs. Refer to the Router Interface Summary Table at the end of this lab for the correct interface identifiers.

Note: Make sure that the routers have been erased and have no startup configurations. If you are unsure, contact your instructor.

Required Resources

- 3 Routers (Cisco 1941 with Cisco IOS Release 15.2(4)M3 universal image or comparable)
- 3 PCs (Windows 7, Vista, or XP with terminal emulation program, such as Tera Term)
- Console cables to configure the Cisco IOS devices via the console ports
- Ethernet and serial cables as shown in the topology

Part 1: Build the Network and Configure Basic Device Settings

In Part 1, you will set up the network topology and configure basic settings on the PC hosts and routers.

Step 1: Cable the network as shown in the topology.

Step 2: Initialize and reload the routers as necessary.

Step 3: Configure basic settings for each router.

a.   Disable DNS lookup.

b.   Configure device name as shown in the topology.

c.   Assign **class** as the privileged EXEC password.

d.   Assign **cisco** as the vty password.

e.   Configure a MOTD banner to warn users that unauthorized access is prohibited.

f.   Configure **logging synchronous** for the console line.

g.   Encrypt plain text passwords.

h.   Configure the IPv6 unicast and link-local addresses listed in the Addressing Table for all interfaces.

i.   Enable IPv6 unicast routing on each router.

j.   Copy the running configuration to the startup configuration.

Step 4: Configure PC hosts.

Step 5: Test connectivity.

The routers should be able to ping one another, and each PC should be able to ping its default gateway. The PCs are unable to ping other PCs until OSPFv3 routing is configured. Verify and troubleshoot if necessary.

Part 2: Configure OSPFv3 Routing

In Part 2, you will configure OSPFv3 routing on all routers in the network and then verify that routing tables are updated correctly.

Step 1:   **Assign router IDs.**

OSPFv3 continues to use a 32 bit address for the router ID. Because there are no IPv4 addresses configured on the routers, you will manually assign the router ID using the **router-id** command.

a.   Issue the **ipv6 router ospf** command to start an OSPFv3 process to the router.

```
R1(config)# ipv6 router ospf 1
```

Note: The OSPF process ID is kept locally and has no meaning to other routers on the network.

b.   Assign the OSPFv3 router ID **1.1.1.1** to the R1.

```
R1(config-rtr)# router-id 1.1.1.1
```

c.   Start the OSPFv3 routing process and assign a router ID of **2.2.2.2** to R2 and a router ID of **3.3.3.3** to R3.

d.   Issue the **show ipv6 ospf** command to verify the router IDs on all routers.

```
R2# show ipv6 ospf
 Routing Process "ospfv3 1" with ID 2.2.2.2
 Event-log enabled, Maximum number of events: 1000, Mode: cyclic
 Router is not originating router-LSAs with maximum metric
 <output omitted>
```

Step 2:   **Configure OSPFv6 on R1.**

With IPv6, it is common to have multiple IPv6 addresses configured on an interface. The network statement has been eliminated in OSPFv3. OSPFv3 routing is enabled at the interface level instead.

a.   Issue the **ipv6 ospf 1 area 0** command for each interface on R1 that is to participate in OSPFv3 routing.

```
R1(config)# interface g0/0
R1(config-if)# ipv6 ospf 1 area 0
R1(config-if)# interface s0/0/0
R1(config-if)# ipv6 ospf 1 area 0
R1(config-if)# interface s0/0/1
R1(config-if)# ipv6 ospf 1 area 0
```

Note: The process ID must match the process ID you used in Step1a.

b.   Assign the interfaces on R2 and R3 to OSPFv3 area 0. You should see neighbor adjacency messages display when adding the interfaces to area 0.

```
R1#
*Mar 19 22:14:43.251: %OSPFv3-5-ADJCHG: Process 1, Nbr 2.2.2.2 on Serial0/0/0 from
LOADING to FULL, Loading Done

R1#
*Mar 19 22:14:46.763: %OSPFv3-5-ADJCHG: Process 1, Nbr 3.3.3.3 on Serial0/0/1 from
LOADING to FULL, Loading Done
```

Step 3:   Verify OSPFv3 neighbors.

Issue the **show ipv6 ospf neighbor** command to verify that the router has formed an adjacency with its neighboring routers. If the router ID of the neighboring router is not displayed, or if its state does not show as FULL, the two routers have not formed an OSPF adjacency.

```
R1# show ipv6 ospf neighbor


             OSPFv3 Router with ID (1.1.1.1) (Process ID 1)


Neighbor ID     Pri   State          Dead Time   Interface ID   Interface
3.3.3.3           0   FULL/  -       00:00:39    6              Serial0/0/1
2.2.2.2           0   FULL/  -       00:00:36    6              Serial0/0/0
```

Step 4:   Verify OSPFv3 protocol settings.

The **show ipv6 protocols** command is a quick way to verify vital OSPFv3 configuration information, including the OSPF process ID, the router ID, and the interfaces enabled for OSPFv3.

```
R1# show ipv6 protocols
IPv6 Routing Protocol is "connected"
IPv6 Routing Protocol is "ND"
IPv6 Routing Protocol is "ospf 1"
  Router ID 1.1.1.1
  Number of areas: 1 normal, 0 stub, 0 nssa
  Interfaces (Area 0):
    Serial0/0/1
    Serial0/0/0
    GigabitEthernet0/0
  Redistribution:
    None
```

Step 5:   Verify OSPFv3 interfaces.

a.   Issue the **show ipv6 ospf interface** command to display a detailed list for every OSPF-enabled interface.

```
R1# show ipv6 ospf interface
Serial0/0/1 is up, line protocol is up
  Link Local Address FE80::1, Interface ID 7
  Area 0, Process ID 1, Instance ID 0, Router ID 1.1.1.1
  Network Type POINT_TO_POINT, Cost: 64
  Transmit Delay is 1 sec, State POINT_TO_POINT
  Timer intervals configured, Hello 10, Dead 40, Wait 40, Retransmit 5
     Hello due in 00:00:05
  Graceful restart helper support enabled
  Index 1/3/3, flood queue length 0
  Next 0x0(0)/0x0(0)/0x0(0)
  Last flood scan length is 1, maximum is 1
```

```
    Last flood scan time is 0 msec, maximum is 0 msec
   Neighbor Count is 1, Adjacent neighbor count is 1
     Adjacent with neighbor 3.3.3.3
   Suppress hello for 0 neighbor(s)
 Serial0/0/0 is up, line protocol is up
   Link Local Address FE80::1, Interface ID 6
   Area 0, Process ID 1, Instance ID 0, Router ID 1.1.1.1
   Network Type POINT_TO_POINT, Cost: 64
   Transmit Delay is 1 sec, State POINT_TO_POINT
   Timer intervals configured, Hello 10, Dead 40, Wait 40, Retransmit 5
     Hello due in 00:00:00
   Graceful restart helper support enabled
   Index 1/2/2, flood queue length 0
   Next 0x0(0)/0x0(0)/0x0(0)
   Last flood scan length is 1, maximum is 2
   Last flood scan time is 0 msec, maximum is 0 msec
   Neighbor Count is 1, Adjacent neighbor count is 1
     Adjacent with neighbor 2.2.2.2
   Suppress hello for 0 neighbor(s)
 GigabitEthernet0/0 is up, line protocol is up
   Link Local Address FE80::1, Interface ID 3
   Area 0, Process ID 1, Instance ID 0, Router ID 1.1.1.1
   Network Type BROADCAST, Cost: 1
   Transmit Delay is 1 sec, State DR, Priority 1
   Designated Router (ID) 1.1.1.1, local address FE80::1
   No backup designated router on this network
   Timer intervals configured, Hello 10, Dead 40, Wait 40, Retransmit 5
     Hello due in 00:00:03
   Graceful restart helper support enabled
   Index 1/1/1, flood queue length 0
   Next 0x0(0)/0x0(0)/0x0(0)
   Last flood scan length is 0, maximum is 0
   Last flood scan time is 0 msec, maximum is 0 msec
   Neighbor Count is 0, Adjacent neighbor count is 0
   Suppress hello for 0 neighbor(s)
```

b. To display a summary of OSPFv3-enabled interfaces, issue the **show ipv6 ospf interface brief** command.

```
R1# show ipv6 ospf interface brief
Interface    PID    Area          Intf ID    Cost   State Nbrs F/C
Se0/0/1      1      0             7          64     P2P   1/1
Se0/0/0      1      0             6          64     P2P   1/1
Gi0/0        1      0             3          1      DR    0/0
```

Step 6:   Verify the IPv6 routing table.

Issue the **show ipv6 route** command to verify that all networks are appearing in the routing table.

```
R2# show ipv6 route
IPv6 Routing Table - default - 10 entries
Codes: C - Connected, L - Local, S - Static, U - Per-user Static route
       B - BGP, R - RIP, I1 - ISIS L1, I2 - ISIS L2
       IA - ISIS interarea, IS - ISIS summary, D - EIGRP, EX - EIGRP external
       ND - ND Default, NDp - ND Prefix, DCE - Destination, NDr - Redirect
       O - OSPF Intra, OI - OSPF Inter, OE1 - OSPF ext 1, OE2 - OSPF ext 2
       ON1 - OSPF NSSA ext 1, ON2 - OSPF NSSA ext 2
O   2001:DB8:ACAD:A::/64 [110/65]
       via FE80::1, Serial0/0/0
C   2001:DB8:ACAD:B::/64 [0/0]
       via GigabitEthernet0/0, directly connected
L   2001:DB8:ACAD:B::2/128 [0/0]
       via GigabitEthernet0/0, receive
O   2001:DB8:ACAD:C::/64 [110/65]
       via FE80::3, Serial0/0/1
C   2001:DB8:ACAD:12::/64 [0/0]
       via Serial0/0/0, directly connected
L   2001:DB8:ACAD:12::2/128 [0/0]
       via Serial0/0/0, receive
O   2001:DB8:ACAD:13::/64 [110/128]
       via FE80::3, Serial0/0/1
       via FE80::1, Serial0/0/0
C   2001:DB8:ACAD:23::/64 [0/0]
       via Serial0/0/1, directly connected
L   2001:DB8:ACAD:23::2/128 [0/0]
       via Serial0/0/1, receive
L   FF00::/8 [0/0]
       via Null0, receive
```

What command would you use to only see the OSPF routes in the routing table?

____

Step 7:   Verify end-to-end connectivity.

Each PC should be able to ping the other PCs in the topology. Verify and troubleshoot if necessary.

Note: It may be necessary to disable the PC firewall to ping between PCs.

Part 3:   Configure OSPFv3 Passive Interfaces

The **passive-interface** command prevents routing updates from being sent through the specified router interface. This is commonly done to reduce traffic on the LANs as they do not need to receive dynamic routing protocol communication. In Part 3, you will use the **passive-interface** command to configure a single interface as passive. You will also configure OSPFv3 so that all interfaces on the router are passive by default, and then enable OSPF routing advertisements on selected interfaces.

Step 1:   Configure a passive interface.

a.   Issue the **show ipv6 ospf interface g0/0** command on R1. Notice the timer indicating when the next Hello packet is expected. Hello packets are sent every 10 seconds and are used between OSPF routers to verify that their neighbors are up.

```
R1# show ipv6 ospf interface g0/0
GigabitEthernet0/0 is up, line protocol is up
  Link Local Address FE80::1, Interface ID 3
  Area 0, Process ID 1, Instance ID 0, Router ID 1.1.1.1
  Network Type BROADCAST, Cost: 1
  Transmit Delay is 1 sec, State DR, Priority 1
  Designated Router (ID) 1.1.1.1, local address FE80::1
  No backup designated router on this network
  Timer intervals configured, Hello 10, Dead 40, Wait 40, Retransmit 5
    Hello due in 00:00:05
  Graceful restart helper support enabled
  Index 1/1/1, flood queue length 0
  Next 0x0(0)/0x0(0)/0x0(0)
  Last flood scan length is 0, maximum is 0
  Last flood scan time is 0 msec, maximum is 0 msec
  Neighbor Count is 0, Adjacent neighbor count is 0
  Suppress hello for 0 neighbor(s)
```

b.   Issue the **passive-interface** command to change the G0/0 interface on R1 to passive.

```
R1(config)# ipv6 router ospf 1
R1(config-rtr)# passive-interface g0/0
```

c.   Re-issue the **show ipv6 ospf interface g0/0** command to verify that G0/0 is now passive.

```
R1# show ipv6 ospf interface g0/0
GigabitEthernet0/0 is up, line protocol is up
  Link Local Address FE80::1, Interface ID 3
  Area 0, Process ID 1, Instance ID 0, Router ID 1.1.1.1
  Network Type BROADCAST, Cost: 1
  Transmit Delay is 1 sec, State WAITING, Priority 1
  No designated router on this network
  No backup designated router on this network
  Timer intervals configured, Hello 10, Dead 40, Wait 40, Retransmit 5
```

```
No Hellos (Passive interface)
  Wait time before Designated router selection 00:00:34
Graceful restart helper support enabled
Index 1/1/1, flood queue length 0
Next 0x0(0)/0x0(0)/0x0(0)
Last flood scan length is 0, maximum is 0
Last flood scan time is 0 msec, maximum is 0 msec
Neighbor Count is 0, Adjacent neighbor count is 0
Suppress hello for 0 neighbor(s)
```

d. Issue the **show ipv6 route ospf** command on R2 and R3 to verify that a route to the 2001:DB8:ACAD:A::/64 network is still available.

```
R2# show ipv6 route ospf
IPv6 Routing Table - default - 10 entries
Codes: C - Connected, L - Local, S - Static, U - Per-user Static route
       B - BGP, R - RIP, I1 - ISIS L1, I2 - ISIS L2
       IA - ISIS interarea, IS - ISIS summary, D - EIGRP, EX - EIGRP external
       ND - ND Default, NDp - ND Prefix, DCE - Destination, NDr - Redirect
       O - OSPF Intra, OI - OSPF Inter, OE1 - OSPF ext 1, OE2 - OSPF ext 2
       ON1 - OSPF NSSA ext 1, ON2 - OSPF NSSA ext 2
O    2001:DB8:ACAD:A::/64 [110/65]
     via FE80::1, Serial0/0/0
O    2001:DB8:ACAD:C::/64 [110/65]
     via FE80::3, Serial0/0/1
O    2001:DB8:ACAD:13::/64 [110/128]
     via FE80::3, Serial0/0/1
     via FE80::1, Serial0/0/0
```

Step 2:   Set passive interface as the default on the router.

a. Issue the **passive-interface default** command on R2 to set the default for all OSPFv3 interfaces as passive.

```
R2(config)# ipv6 router ospf 1
R2(config-rtr)# passive-interface default
```

b. Issue the **show ipv6 ospf neighbor** command on R1. After the dead timer expires, R2 is no longer listed as an OSPF neighbor.

```
R1# show ipv6 ospf neighbor


            OSPFv3 Router with ID (1.1.1.1) (Process ID 1)


Neighbor ID     Pri   State           Dead Time    Interface ID     Interface
3.3.3.3           0   FULL/  -        00:00:37     6                Serial0/0/1
```

c. On R2, issue the **show ipv6 ospf interface s0/0/0** command to view the OSPF status of interface S0/0/0.

```
R2# show ipv6 ospf interface s0/0/0
Serial0/0/0 is up, line protocol is up
  Link Local Address FE80::2, Interface ID 6
  Area 0, Process ID 1, Instance ID 0, Router ID 2.2.2.2
  Network Type POINT_TO_POINT, Cost: 64
  Transmit Delay is 1 sec, State POINT_TO_POINT
  Timer intervals configured, Hello 10, Dead 40, Wait 40, Retransmit 5
    No Hellos (Passive interface)
  Graceful restart helper support enabled
  Index 1/2/2, flood queue length 0
  Next 0x0(0)/0x0(0)/0x0(0)
  Last flood scan length is 2, maximum is 3
  Last flood scan time is 0 msec, maximum is 0 msec
  Neighbor Count is 0, Adjacent neighbor count is 0
  Suppress hello for 0 neighbor(s)
```

d. If all OSPFv3 interfaces on R2 are passive, then no routing information is being advertised. If this is the case, then R1 and R3 should no longer have a route to the 2001:DB8:ACAD:B::/64 network. You can verify this by using the **show ipv6 route** command.

e. Change S0/0/1 on R2 by issuing the **no passive-interface** command, so that it sends and receives OSPFv3 routing updates. After entering this command, an informational message displays stating that a neighbor adjacency has been established with R3.

```
R2(config)# ipv6 router ospf 1
R2(config-rtr)# no passive-interface s0/0/1
*Apr  8 19:21:57.939: %OSPFv3-5-ADJCHG: Process 1, Nbr 3.3.3.3 on Serial0/0/1
from LOADING to FULL, Loading Done
```

f. Re-issue the **show ipv6 route** and **show ipv6 ospf neighbor** commands on R1 and R3, and look for a route to the 2001:DB8:ACAD:B::/64 network.

What interface is R1 using to route to the 2001:DB8:ACAD:B::/64 network? __________

What is the accumulated cost metric for the 2001:DB8:ACAD:B::/64 network on R1? ________

Does R2 show up as an OSPFv3 neighbor on R1? __________

Does R2 show up as an OSPFv3 neighbor on R3? __________

What does this information tell you?

____

____

____

____

g. On R2, issue the **no passive-interface S0/0/0** command to allow OSPFv3 routing updates to be advertised on that interface.

h. Verify that R1 and R2 are now OSPFv3 neighbors.

Reflection

1. If the OSPFv6 configuration for R1 had a process ID of 1, and the OSPFv3 configuration for R2 had a process ID of 2, can routing information be exchanged between the two routers? Why?

____

____

2. What may have been the reasoning for removing the **network** command in OSPFv3?

____

____

____

____

Router Interface Summary Table

Router Interface Summary				
Router Model	**Ethernet Interface #1**	**Ethernet Interface #2**	**Serial Interface #1**	**Serial Interface #2**
1800	Fast Ethernet 0/0 (F0/0)	Fast Ethernet 0/1 (F0/1)	Serial 0/0/0 (S0/0/0)	Serial 0/0/1 (S0/0/1)
1900	Gigabit Ethernet 0/0 (G0/0)	Gigabit Ethernet 0/1 (G0/1)	Serial 0/0/0 (S0/0/0)	Serial 0/0/1 (S0/0/1)
2801	Fast Ethernet 0/0 (F0/0)	Fast Ethernet 0/1 (F0/1)	Serial 0/1/0 (S0/1/0)	Serial 0/1/1 (S0/1/1)
2811	Fast Ethernet 0/0 (F0/0)	Fast Ethernet 0/1 (F0/1)	Serial 0/0/0 (S0/0/0)	Serial 0/0/1 (S0/0/1)
2900	Gigabit Ethernet 0/0 (G0/0)	Gigabit Ethernet 0/1 (G0/1)	Serial 0/0/0 (S0/0/0)	Serial 0/0/1 (S0/0/1)
Note: To find out how the router is configured, look at the interfaces to identify the type of router and how many interfaces the router has. There is no way to effectively list all the combinations of configurations for each router class. This table includes identifiers for the possible combinations of Ethernet and Serial interfaces in the device. The table does not include any other type of interface, even though a specific router may contain one. An example of this might be an ISDN BRI interface. The string in parenthesis is the legal abbreviation that can be used in Cisco IOS commands to represent the interface.				

6.4.1.1 Class Activity – Stepping Through OSPFv3

Objectives

Explain the process by which link-state routers learn about other networks.

Scenario

This class activity is designed for groups of three students. The objective is to review the Shortest Path First (SPF) routing process.

You will design and address a network, communicate the network address scheme and operation of network links to your group members, and compute the SPF.

Complete the steps as shown on the PDF for this class activity. If you have time, share your network design and Open Shortest Path First (OSPF) process with another group.

Resources

In preparation of this activity, you will need two different IPv6 network and cost numbers. The IPv6 network numbers must be chosen with the following format: 2002:DB8:AAAA:?::0/64, where**?** is a student-selected network number. You have two choices for *cost* – 10 (Fast Ethernet network), or 1 (Gigabit Ethernet network).

Bring your two IPv6 network and cost numbers to the group setting. One student in your group will act as the recorder, will draw three circles, and connect them on paper. Each circle will represent a student's router and the connecting lines will represent the networks and links to be agreed upon.

Each group member should follow Steps 1 to 4 (below) in the order listed. As the group progresses through the activity, you should keep personal notes about your own router, including information about neighbor adjacency, link-state advertisements, topology table entries, and the SPF algorithm.

Directions

Step 1:

a. Speak to the classmate to your left. Compare network and cost numbers brought to the group. Agree upon an IPv6 network, links, and cost numbers you would like to use between your two routers. Remember, you may only use 1 (Gigabit Ethernet) or 10 (Fast Ethernet) for cost. When you have agreed upon your network, link numbers, and determined the cost of the route, record the information on the paper graphic created by the recorder.

b. Complete the same process with the classmate to your right.

c. After speaking with both of your direct neighbors, you have agreed upon two networks with link addresses and the cost of the route. Record the information you agreed upon on the paper graphic.

Step 2:

a. Each student will speak only to their direct neighbors. They will share all of their IPv6 network and link numbers and the cost of the networks to which they are connected. Almost immediately, everyone in the group will know about all networks, their links, and the cost of the individual networks between neighbors.

b. Check with the group members to ascertain all group members have the same information with which to work for Step 3.

Step 3:

    a.   On your own paper, create a table listing possible paths to all other networks. Use the formula supplied with this chapter $n(n-1)/2$. You will have a total of four possible routes to list on your table.

    b.   On the table created in the Step 3 a., add a column with the headings, IPv6 Network Number and Cost.

    c.   Fill in the table with information you know about the networks on your group's topology.

Step 4:

    a.   Go back to the table created in Step 3.

    b.   Place a star by the lowest-cost routes to all other routers.

When these four steps are complete, you have established neighbor adjacencies, exchanged link-state advertisements, built a topology table, and created a routing table with the best cost to all other networks within your group or area.

If you have the time, refer to your topology table and build the network on real equipment or Packet Tracer. Use some or all of the commands listed below to prove OSPF's operation:

```
R1# show ipv6 interface brief
R1# show ipv6 protocols
R1# show ip protocols
R1# show ipv6 route
```

Reflection

1.   Which OSPFv3 processing step is reviewed in Step 1 of this activity?

2.   Which OSPFv3 processing step is reviewed in Step 2 of this activity?

3.   Which process for OSPFv3 is reviewed in Step 3 of this activity?

4.   Which process step for OSPFv3 is reviewed in Step 4 of this activity?

Chapter 7 — Adjust and Troubleshoot Single-Area OSPF

7.0.1.2 Class Activity – DR and BDR Elections

Objectives

Modify the OSPF interface priority to influence the Designated Router (DR) and Backup Designated Router (BDR) election.

Scenario

You are trying to decide how to influence the selection of the designated router and backup designated router for your OSPF network. This activity simulates that process.

Three separate designated-router election scenarios will be presented. The focus is on electing a DR and BDR for your group. Refer to the PDF for this activity for the remaining instructions.

If additional time is available, two groups can be combined to simulate DR and BDR elections.

Required Resources

- Router priorities paper sign example (student developed)
- Router ID paper sign example (student developed)

Directions

This is a group activity with four classmates comprising each group. Before reporting to the group, each student will prepare router priority and router ID signs to bring to the group.

Step 1:   Decide the router priority.

a.   Prior to joining your group, use a clean sheet of paper. On one side of the paper, write DEFAULT ROUTER PRIORITY = 1.

b.   On the other side of the same sheet of paper, write ROUTER PRIORITY = (choose a number between 0 and 255).

Step 2:   Decide the router ID.

a.   On a second clean sheet of paper, on one side, write ROUTER ID = (any IPv4 number).

b.   On the other side, write ROUTER ID = Loopback (any IPv4) number.

Step 3:   Begin DR and BDR elections.

a.   Start the first election process.

1)   Students within the group will show each other the router priority numbers they selected for Step 1b.

2)   After comparing their priority numbers, the student with the highest priority number is elected the DR and the student with the second-highest priority number is elected the BDR. Any student, who wrote 0 as their priority number, cannot participate in the election.

3) The elected DR student will announce the elections by saying "I am the DR for all of you in this group. Please send me any changes to your networks or interfaces to IP address 224.0.0.6. I will then forward those changes to all of you at IP address 224.0.0.5. Stay tuned for future updates."

4) The BDR's elected student will say, "I am your BDR. Please send all changes to your router interfaces or networks to the DR. If the DR does not announce your changes, I will step in and do that from that point onward."

b. Start the second election process.

1) Students will hold up their DEFAULT ROUTER PRIORITY = 1 sign first. When it is agreed that all of the students have the same router priority, they will put that paper down.

2) Next, students will display their ROUTER ID = Loopback (IPv4) address signs.

3) The student with the highest loopback IPv4 address wins the election and repeats "I am the DR for all of you in this group. Our priorities are the same, but I have the highest loopback address on my router as compared to all of you; therefore, you have elected me as your DR. Please send all changes to your network addresses or interfaces to 224.0.0.6. I will then report any changes to all of you via 224.0.0.5."

4) The BDR will repeat his/her respective phrase from Step 4a.

c. Start the third election process, but this time, all students can choose which sides of their papers to display. The DR/BDR election process uses the highest router priority first, highest loopback router ID second, and highest IPv4 router ID third, and elects a DR and BDR.

1) Elect a DR and BDR.

2) Justify your elections.

3) If you have time, get together with another group and go through the scenario processes again to solidify DR and BDR elections.

7.1.1.13 Lab – Configuring OSPFv2 on a Multiaccess Network

Topology

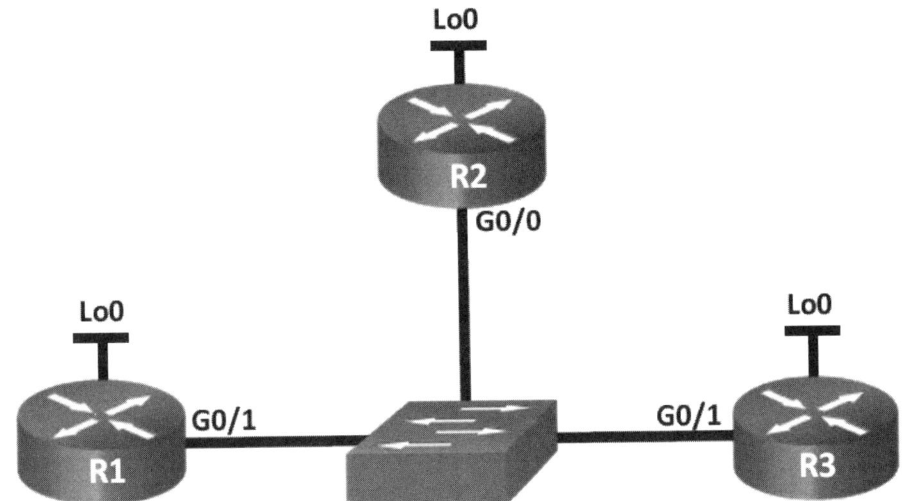

Addressing Table

Device	Interface	IP Address	Subnet Mask
R1	G0/1	192.168.1.1	255.255.255.0
	Lo0	192.168.31.11	255.255.255.255
R2	G0/0	192.168.1.2	255.255.255.0
	Lo0	192.168.31.22	255.255.255.255
R3	G0/1	192.168.1.3	255.255.255.0
	Lo0	192.168.31.33	255.255.255.255

Objectives

Part 1: Build the Network and Configure Basic Device Settings

Part 2: Configure and Verify OSPFv2 on the DR, BDR, and DROther

Part 3: Configure OSPFv2 Interface Priority to Determine the DR and BDR

Background / Scenario

A multiaccess network is a network with more than two devices on the same shared media. Examples include Ethernet and Frame Relay. On multiaccess networks, OSPFv2 elects a Designated Router (DR) to be the collection and distribution point for link-state advertisements (LSAs) that are sent and received. A Backup Designated Router (BDR) is also elected in case the DR fails. All other routers become DROthers as this indicates a router that is neither the DR nor the BDR.

Because the DR acts as a focal point for OSPF routing protocol communication, the router chosen should be capable of supporting a heavier traffic load than other routers in the network. A router with a powerful CPU and adequate DRAM is typically the best choice for the DR.

In this lab, you will configure OSPFv2 on the DR, BDR and DROther. You will then modify the priority of routers to control the outcome of the DR/BDR election process and ensure that the desired router becomes the DR.

Note: The routers used with CCNA hands-on labs are Cisco 1941 Integrated Services Routers (ISRs) with Cisco IOS Release 15.2(4)M3 (universalk9 image). The switches used are Cisco Catalyst 2960s with Cisco IOS Release 15.0(2) (lanbasek9 image). Other routers, switches, and Cisco IOS versions can be used. Depending on the model and Cisco IOS version, the commands available and output produced might vary from what is shown in the labs. Refer to the Router Interface Summary Table at the end of this lab for the correct interface identifiers.

Note: Make sure that the routers and switches have been erased and have no startup configurations. If you are unsure, contact your instructor.

Required Resources

- 3 Routers (Cisco 1941 with Cisco IOS Release 15.2(4)M3 universal image or comparable)
- 1 Switch (Cisco 2960 with Cisco IOS Release 15.0(2) lanbasek9 image or comparable)
- Console cables to configure the Cisco IOS devices via the console ports
- Ethernet cables as shown in the topology

Part 1:   Build the Network and Configure Basic Device Settings

In Part 1, you will set up the network topology and configure basic settings on the routers.

Step 1:   Cable the network as shown in the topology.

Attach the devices shown in the topology diagram, and cable as necessary.

Step 2:   Initialize and reload the routers.

Step 3:   Configure basic settings for each router.

a.   Disable DNS lookup.

b.   Configure device names as shown in the topology.

c.   Assign **class** as the privileged EXEC password.

d.   Assign **cisco** as the console and vty passwords.

e.   Encrypt the plain text passwords.

f.   Configure a MOTD banner to warn users that unauthorized access is prohibited.

g.   Configure **logging synchronous** for the console line.

h.   Configure the IP addresses listed in the Addressing Table for all interfaces.

i.   Use the **show ip interface brief** command to verify that the IP addressing is correct and that the interfaces are active.

j.   Copy the running configuration to the startup configuration.

Part 2:   Configure and Verify OSPFv2 on the DR, BDR and DROther

In Part 2, you will configure OSPFv2 on the DR, BDR, and DROther. The DR and BDR election process takes place as soon as the first router has its interface enabled on the multiaccess network. This can happen as the routers are powered-on or when the OSPF **network** command for that interface is configured. If a new router enters the network after the DR and BDR have already been elected, it does not become the DR or BDR, even if it has a higher OSPF interface priority or router ID than the current DR or BDR. Configure the OSPF process on the router with the highest router ID first to ensure that this router becomes the DR.

Step 1:   Configure OSPF on R3.

Configure the OSPF process on R3 (the router with the highest router ID) to ensure that this router becomes the DR.

a. Assign 1 as the process ID for the OSPF process. Configure the router to advertise the 192.168.1.0/24 network. Use an area ID of 0 for the OSPF *area-id* parameter in the **network** statement.

What factor determined that R3 has the highest router ID?

____

b. Verify that OSPF has been configured and R3 is the DR.

What command would you use to verify that OSPF has been configured correctly and R3 is the DR?

____

Step 2:   Configure OSPF on R2.

Configure the OSPF process on R2 (the router with the second highest router ID) to ensure that this router becomes the BDR.

a. Assign 1 as the process ID for the OSPF process. Configure the router to advertise the 192.168.1.0/24 network. Use an area ID of 0 for the OSPF *area-id* parameter in the **network** statement.

b. Verify that the OSPF has been configured and that R2 is the BDR. Record the command used for verification.

____

c. Issue the **show ip ospf neighbor** command to view information about the other routers in the OSPF area.

```
R2# show ip ospf neighbor

Neighbor ID      Pri   State          Dead Time   Address        Interface
192.168.31.33     1    FULL/DR        00:00:33    192.168.1.3    GigabitEthernet0/0
```

Notice that R3 is the DR.

Step 3: Configure OSPF on R1.

Configure the OSPF process on R1 (the router with the lowest router ID). This router will be designated as DROther instead of DR or BDR.

a. Assign 1 as the process ID for the OSPF process. Configure the router to advertise the 192.168.1.0/24 network. Use an area ID of 0 for the OSPF *area-id* parameter in the **network** statement.

b. Issue **show ip ospf interface brief** command to verify that OSPF has been configured and R1 is the DROther.

```
R1# show ip ospf interface brief

Interface    PID    Area          IP Address/Mask     Cost   State Nbrs F/C
Gi0/1         1      0            192.168.1.1/24       1     DROTH 2/2
```

c. Issue the **show ip ospf neighbor** command to view information about the other routers in the OSPF area.

```
R1# show ip ospf neighbor

Neighbor ID      Pri   State          Dead Time   Address        Interface
192.168.31.22     1    FULL/BDR       00:00:35    192.168.1.2    GigabitEthernet0/1
192.168.31.33     1    FULL/DR        00:00:30    192.168.1.3    GigabitEthernet0/1
```

What priority are both the DR and BDR routers? __________

Part 3: Configure OSPFv2 Interface Priority to Determine the DR and BDR

In Part 3, you will configure router interface priority to determine the DR/BDR election, reset the OSPFv2 process, and then verify that the DR and BDR routers have changed. OSPF interface priority overrides all other settings in determining which routers become the DR and BDR.

Step 1: Configure R1 G0/1 with OSPF priority 255.

A value of 255 is the highest possible interface priority.

```
R1(config)# interface g0/1
R1(config-if)# ip ospf priority 255
R1(config-if)# end
```

Step 2: Configure R3 G0/1 with OSPF priority 100.

```
R3(config)# interface g0/1
R3(config-if)# ip ospf priority 100
R3(config-if)# end
```

Step 3:   **Configure R2 G0/0 with OSPF priority 0.**

A priority of 0 causes the router to be ineligible to participate in an OSPF election and does not become a DR or BDR.

```
R2(config)# interface g0/0
R2(config-if)# ip ospf priority 0
R2(config-if)# end
```

Step 4:   **Reset the OSPF process.**

a. Issue the **show ip ospf neighbor** command to determine the DR and BDR.

b. Has the DR designation changed? ______________   Which router is the DR? ______________

Has the BDR designation changed? ______________   Which router is the BDR? ______________

What is the role of R2 now? ______________

Explain the immediate effects caused by the **ip ospf priority** command.

____

____

____

Note: If the DR and BDR designations did not change, issue the **clear ip ospf 1 process** command on all of the routers to reset the OSPF processes and force a new election.

If the **clear ip ospf process** command does not reset the DR and BDR, issue the **reload** command on all routers after saving the running configuration to the startup configuration.

c. Issue the **show ip ospf interface** command on R1 and R3 to confirm the priority settings and DR/BDR status on the routers.

```
R1# show ip ospf interface
GigabitEthernet0/1 is up, line protocol is up
  Internet Address 192.168.1.1/24, Area 0
  Process ID 1, Router ID 192.168.31.11, Network Type BROADCAST, Cost: 1
  Transmit Delay is 1 sec, State DR, Priority 255
  Designated Router (ID) 192.168.31.11, Interface address 192.168.1.1
  Backup Designated router (ID) 192.168.31.33, Interface address 192.168.1.3
  Timer intervals configured, Hello 10, Dead 40, Wait 40, Retransmit 5
    oob-resync timeout 40
    Hello due in 00:00:00
  Supports Link-local Signaling (LLS)
  Index 1/1, flood queue length 0
  Next 0x0(0)/0x0(0)
  Last flood scan length is 1, maximum is 2
```

```
      Last flood scan time is 0 msec, maximum is 0 msec
      Neighbor Count is 2, Adjacent neighbor count is 2
        Adjacent with neighbor 192.168.31.22
        Adjacent with neighbor 192.168.31.33   (Backup Designated Router)
      Suppress hello for 0 neighbor(s)


   R3# show ip ospf interface
   GigabitEthernet0/1 is up, line protocol is up
      Internet Address 192.168.1.3/24, Area 0
      Process ID 1, Router ID 192.168.31.33, Network Type BROADCAST, Cost: 1
      Transmit Delay is 1 sec, State BDR, Priority 100
      Designated Router (ID) 192.168.31.11, Interface address 192.168.1.1
      Backup Designated router (ID) 192.168.31.33, Interface address 192.168.1.3
      Timer intervals configured, Hello 10, Dead 40, Wait 40, Retransmit 5
        oob-resync timeout 40
        Hello due in 00:00:00
      Supports Link-local Signaling (LLS)
      Index 1/1, flood queue length 0
      Next 0x0(0)/0x0(0)
      Last flood scan length is 0, maximum is 2
      Last flood scan time is 0 msec, maximum is 0 msec
      Neighbor Count is 2, Adjacent neighbor count is 2
        Adjacent with neighbor 192.168.31.22
        Adjacent with neighbor 192.168.31.11   (Designated Router)
      Suppress hello for 0 neighbor(s)
```

Which router is now the DR? _____________

Which router is now the BDR? ___________

Did the interface priority override the router ID in determining the DR/BDR? ___________

Reflection

1. List the criteria used from highest to lowest for determining the DR on an OSPF network.

    ____

    ____

    ____

2. What is the significance of a 255 interface priority?

    ____

Router Interface Summary Table

Router Interface Summary				
Router Model	**Ethernet Interface #1**	**Ethernet Interface #2**	**Serial Interface #1**	**Serial Interface #2**
1800	Fast Ethernet 0/0 (F0/0)	Fast Ethernet 0/1 (F0/1)	Serial 0/0/0 (S0/0/0)	Serial 0/0/1 (S0/0/1)
1900	Gigabit Ethernet 0/0 (G0/0)	Gigabit Ethernet 0/1 (G0/1)	Serial 0/0/0 (S0/0/0)	Serial 0/0/1 (S0/0/1)
2801	Fast Ethernet 0/0 (F0/0)	Fast Ethernet 0/1 (F0/1)	Serial 0/1/0 (S0/1/0)	Serial 0/1/1 (S0/1/1)
2811	Fast Ethernet 0/0 (F0/0)	Fast Ethernet 0/1 (F0/1)	Serial 0/0/0 (S0/0/0)	Serial 0/0/1 (S0/0/1)
2900	Gigabit Ethernet 0/0 (G0/0)	Gigabit Ethernet 0/1 (G0/1)	Serial 0/0/0 (S0/0/0)	Serial 0/0/1 (S0/0/1)

Note: To find out how the router is configured, look at the interfaces to identify the type of router and how many interfaces the router has. There is no way to effectively list all the combinations of configurations for each router class. This table includes identifiers for the possible combinations of Ethernet and Serial interfaces in the device. The table does not include any other type of interface, even though a specific router may contain one. An example of this might be an ISDN BRI interface. The string in parenthesis is the legal abbreviation that can be used in Cisco IOS commands to represent the interface.

7.1.4.8 Lab – Configuring OSFPv2 Advanced Features

Topology

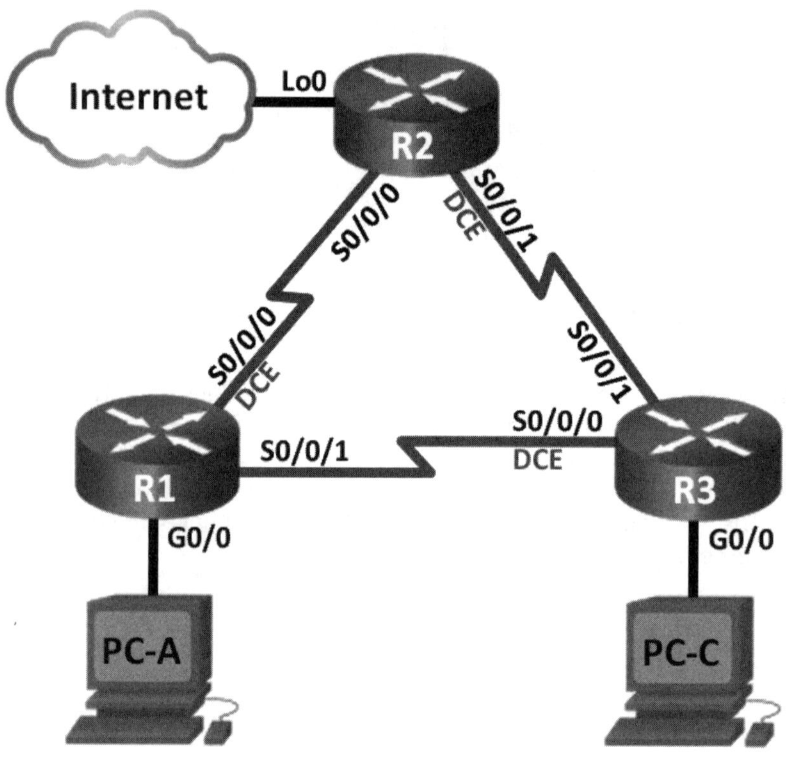

Addressing Table

Device	Interface	IP Address	Subnet Mask	Default Gateway
R1	G0/0	192.168.1.1	255.255.255.0	N/A
	S0/0/0 (DCE)	192.168.12.1	255.255.255.252	N/A
	S0/0/1	192.168.13.1	255.255.255.252	N/A
R2	Lo0	209.165.200.225	255.255.255.252	N/A
	S0/0/0	192.168.12.2	255.255.255.252	N/A
	S0/0/1 (DCE)	192.168.23.1	255.255.255.252	N/A
R3	G0/0	192.168.3.1	255.255.255.0	N/A
	S0/0/0 (DCE)	192.168.13.2	255.255.255.252	N/A
	S0/0/1	192.168.23.2	255.255.255.252	N/A
PC-A	NIC	192.168.1.3	255.255.255.0	192.168.1.1
PC-C	NIC	192.168.3.3	255.255.255.0	192.168.3.1

Objectives

Part 1: Build the Network and Configure Basic Device Settings

Part 2: Configure and Verify OSPF Routing

Part 3: Change OSPF Metrics

Part 4: Configure and Propagate a Static Default Route

Part 5: Configure OSPF Authentication

Background / Scenario

Open Shortest Path First (OSPF) has advanced features to allow changes to be made to control metrics, default route propagation, and security.

In this lab, you will adjust OSPF metrics on the router interfaces, configure OSPF route propagation, and use Message Digest 5 (MD5) authentication to secure OSPF routing information.

Note: The routers used with CCNA hands-on labs are Cisco 1941 Integrated Services Routers (ISRs) with Cisco IOS Release 15.2(4)M3 (universalk9 image). Other routers and Cisco IOS versions can be used. Depending on the model and Cisco IOS version, the commands available and output produced might vary from what is shown in the labs. Refer to the Router Interface Summary Table at the end of this lab for the correct interface identifiers.

Note: Make sure that the routers have been erased and have no startup configurations. If you are unsure, contact your instructor.

Required Resources

- 3 Routers (Cisco 1941 with Cisco IOS Release 15.2(4)M3 universal image or comparable)
- 2 PCs (Windows 7, Vista, or XP with terminal emulation program, such as Tera Term)
- Console cables to configure the Cisco IOS devices via the console ports
- Ethernet and serial cables as shown in the topology

Part 1:   Build the Network and Configure Basic Device Settings

In Part 1, you will set up the network topology and configure basic settings on the PC hosts and routers.

Step 1:   Cable the network as shown in the topology.

Step 2:   Initialize and reload the routers as necessary.

Step 3:   Configure basic settings for each router.

a.   Disable DNS lookup.

b.   Configure device name as shown in the topology.

c.   Assign **class** as the privileged EXEC password.

d.   Assign **cisco** as the console and vty passwords.

e.   Encrypt the clear text passwords.

f.   Configure a MOTD banner to warn users that unauthorized access is prohibited.

g.   Configure **logging synchronous** for the console line.

h.   Configure the IP addresses listed in the Addressing Table for all interfaces.

i.   Set the clock rate for all DCE serial interfaces at 128000.

j.   Copy the running configuration to the startup configuration.

Step 4:   **Configure PC hosts.**

Refer to the Addressing Table for PC host address information.

Step 5:   **Test connectivity.**

At this point, the PCs are unable to ping each other. However, the routers should be able to ping the directly connected neighbor interfaces, and the PCs should be able to ping their default gateway. Verify and troubleshoot if necessary.

Part 2:   **Configure and Verify OSPF Routing**

In Part 2, you will configure OSPFv2 routing on all routers in the network and then verify that routing tables are updated correctly.

Step 1:   **Configure the router ID on all routers.**

Assign 1 as the process ID for this OSPF process. Each router should be given the following router ID assignments:

- R1 Router ID: **1.1.1.1**
- R2 Router ID: **2.2.2.2**
- R3 Router ID: **3.3.3.3**

Step 2:   **Configure OSPF network information on the routers.**

Step 3:   **Verify OSPF routing.**

a.   Issue the **show ip ospf neighbor** command to verify that each router is listing the other routers in the network.

b.   Issue the **show ip route ospf** command to verify that all OSPF networks are present in the routing table on all routers.

Step 4:   **Test end-to-end connectivity.**

Ping PC-C from PC-A to verify end-to-end connectivity. The pings should be successful. If they are not, troubleshoot as necessary.

Note: It may be necessary to disable the PC firewall for the pings to be successful.

Part 3:   **Change OSPF Metrics**

In Part 3, you will change OSPF metrics using the **bandwidth** command, the **auto-cost reference-bandwidth** command, and the **ip ospf cost** command. Making these changes will provide more accurate metrics to OSPF.

Note: All DCE interfaces should have been configured with a clocking rate of 128000 in Part 1.

Step 1:   Change the bandwidth on all serial interfaces to 128Kb/s.

a.   Issue the **show ip ospf interface brief** command to view the default cost settings on the router interfaces.

```
R1# show ip ospf interface brief
Interface    PID   Area             IP Address/Mask     Cost   State Nbrs F/C
Se0/0/1      1     0                192.168.13.1/30     64     P2P    1/1
Se0/0/0      1     0                192.168.12.1/30     64     P2P    1/1
Gi0/0        1     0                192.168.1.1/24      1      DR     0/0
```

b.   Use the **bandwidth 128** interface command on all serial interfaces.

c.   Issue the **show ip ospf interface brief** command to view the new cost settings.

```
R1# show ip ospf interface brief
Interface    PID   Area             IP Address/Mask     Cost   State Nbrs F/C
Se0/0/1      1     0                192.168.13.1/30     781    P2P    1/1
Se0/0/0      1     0                192.168.12.1/30     781    P2P    1/1
Gi0/0        1     0                192.168.1.1/24      1      DR     0/0
```

Step 2:   Change the reference bandwidth on the routers.

a.   Issue the **auto-cost reference-bandwidth 1000** command on the routers to change the default reference bandwidth setting to account for Gigabit Ethernet Interfaces.

b.   Re-issue the **show ip ospf interface brief** command to view how this command has changed cost values.

```
R1# show ip ospf interface brief
Interface    PID   Area             IP Address/Mask     Cost   State Nbrs F/C
Se0/0/1      1     0                192.168.13.1/30     7812   P2P    0/0
Se0/0/0      1     0                192.168.12.1/30     7812   P2P    0/0
Gi0/0        1     0                192.168.1.1/24      1      DR     0/0
```

Note: If the router had Fast Ethernet interfaces instead of Gigabit Ethernet interfaces, then the cost would now be 10 on those interfaces.

Step 3:   Change the route cost.

a.   Issue the **show ip route ospf** command to display the current OSPF routes on R1. Notice that there are currently two routes in the table that use the S0/0/1 interface.

```
R1# show ip route ospf
Codes: L - local, C - connected, S - static, R - RIP, M - mobile, B - BGP
       D - EIGRP, EX - EIGRP external, O - OSPF, IA - OSPF inter area
       N1 - OSPF NSSA external type 1, N2 - OSPF NSSA external type 2
       E1 - OSPF external type 1, E2 - OSPF external type 2
       i - IS-IS, su - IS-IS summary, L1 - IS-IS level-1, L2 - IS-IS level-2
       ia - IS-IS inter area, * - candidate default, U - per-user static route
       o - ODR, P - periodic downloaded static route, H - NHRP, l - LISP
```

```
        + - replicated route, % - next hop override


Gateway of last resort is not set


O       192.168.3.0/24 [110/7822] via 192.168.13.2, 00:00:12, Serial0/0/1
        192.168.23.0/30 is subnetted, 1 subnets
O          192.168.23.0 [110/15624] via 192.168.13.2, 00:00:12, Serial0/0/1
                        [110/15624] via 192.168.12.2, 00:20:03, Serial0/0/0
```

b. Apply the **ip ospf cost 16000** command to the S0/0/1 interface on R1. A cost of 16,000 is higher than the accumulated cost of the route through R2 which is 15,624.

c. Issue the **show ip ospf interface brief** command on R1 to view the cost change to S0/0/1.

```
R1# show ip ospf interface brief
Interface      PID    Area            IP Address/Mask      Cost   State Nbrs F/C
Se0/0/1        1      0               192.168.13.1/30      16000  P2P    1/1
Se0/0/0        1      0               192.168.12.1/30      7812   P2P    1/1
Gi0/0          1      0               192.168.1.1/24       1      DR     0/0
```

d. Re-issue the **show ip route ospf** command on R1 to display the effect this change has made on the routing table. All OSPF routes for R1 are now being routed through R2.

```
R1# show ip route ospf
Codes: L - local, C - connected, S - static, R - RIP, M - mobile, B - BGP
       D - EIGRP, EX - EIGRP external, O - OSPF, IA - OSPF inter area
       N1 - OSPF NSSA external type 1, N2 - OSPF NSSA external type 2
       E1 - OSPF external type 1, E2 - OSPF external type 2
       i - IS-IS, su - IS-IS summary, L1 - IS-IS level-1, L2 - IS-IS level-2
       ia - IS-IS inter area, * - candidate default, U - per-user static route
       o - ODR, P - periodic downloaded static route, H - NHRP, l - LISP
       + - replicated route, % - next hop override


Gateway of last resort is not set


O       192.168.3.0/24 [110/15625] via 192.168.12.2, 00:05:31, Serial0/0/0
        192.168.23.0/30 is subnetted, 1 subnets
O          192.168.23.0 [110/15624] via 192.168.12.2, 01:14:02, Serial0/0/0
```

Explain why the route to the 192.168.3.0/24 network on R1 is now going through R2?

____

____

____

Part 4:   Configure and Propagate a Static Default Route

In Part 4, you will use a loopback interface on R2 to simulate an ISP connection to the Internet. You will create a static default route on R2, and then OSPF will propagate that route to the other two routers on the network.

Step 1:   Configure a static default route on R2 to loopback 0.

Configure a default route using the loopback interface configured in Part 1, to simulate a connection to an ISP.

Step 2:   Have OSPF propagate the default static route.

Issue the **default-information originate** command to include the static default route in the OSPF updates that are sent from R2.

```
R2(config)# router ospf 1
R2(config-router)# default-information originate
```

Step 3:   Verify OSPF static route propagation.

a. Issue the **show ip route static** command on R2.

```
R2# show ip route static
Codes: L - local, C - connected, S - static, R - RIP, M - mobile, B - BGP
       D - EIGRP, EX - EIGRP external, O - OSPF, IA - OSPF inter area
       N1 - OSPF NSSA external type 1, N2 - OSPF NSSA external type 2
       E1 - OSPF external type 1, E2 - OSPF external type 2
       i - IS-IS, su - IS-IS summary, L1 - IS-IS level-1, L2 - IS-IS level-2
       ia - IS-IS inter area, * - candidate default, U - per-user static route
       o - ODR, P - periodic downloaded static route, H - NHRP, l - LISP
       + - replicated route, % - next hop override


Gateway of last resort is 0.0.0.0 to network 0.0.0.0


S*      0.0.0.0/0 is directly connected, Loopback0
```

b. Issue the **show ip route** command on R1 to verify the propagation of the static route from R2.

```
R1# show ip route
Codes: L - local, C - connected, S - static, R - RIP, M - mobile, B - BGP
       D - EIGRP, EX - EIGRP external, O - OSPF, IA - OSPF inter area
       N1 - OSPF NSSA external type 1, N2 - OSPF NSSA external type 2
       E1 - OSPF external type 1, E2 - OSPF external type 2
       i - IS-IS, su - IS-IS summary, L1 - IS-IS level-1, L2 - IS-IS level-2
       ia - IS-IS inter area, * - candidate default, U - per-user static route
       o - ODR, P - periodic downloaded static route, H - NHRP, l - LISP
       + - replicated route, % - next hop override
```

```
Gateway of last resort is 192.168.12.2 to network 0.0.0.0


O*E2  0.0.0.0/0 [110/1] via 192.168.12.2, 00:02:57, Serial0/0/0
         192.168.1.0/24 is variably subnetted, 2 subnets, 2 masks
C           192.168.1.0/24 is directly connected, GigabitEthernet0/0
L           192.168.1.1/32 is directly connected, GigabitEthernet0/0
O          192.168.3.0/24 [110/15634] via 192.168.12.2, 00:03:35, Serial0/0/0
         192.168.12.0/24 is variably subnetted, 2 subnets, 2 masks
C           192.168.12.0/30 is directly connected, Serial0/0/0
L           192.168.12.1/32 is directly connected, Serial0/0/0
         192.168.13.0/24 is variably subnetted, 2 subnets, 2 masks
C           192.168.13.0/30 is directly connected, Serial0/0/1
L           192.168.13.1/32 is directly connected, Serial0/0/1
         192.168.23.0/30 is subnetted, 1 subnets
O           192.168.23.0 [110/15624] via 192.168.12.2, 00:05:18, Serial0/0/0
```

    c.   Verify end-to-end connectivity by issuing a ping from PC-A to the ISP interface address 209.165.200.225.

       Were the pings successful? ___________________

Part 5: Configure OSPF Authentication

OSPF authentication can be set up at the link level or the area level. There are three authentication types available for OSPF authentication: Null, plain text, or MD5. In Part 5, you will set up OSPF MD5 authentication, which is the strongest available.

Step 1: Set up MD5 OSPF authentication on a single link.

    a.   Issue the **debug ip ospf adj** command on R2 to view OSPF adjacency messages.

```
R2# debug ip ospf adj
OSPF adjacency debugging is on
```

    b.   Assign an MD5 key for OSPF Authentication on R1, interface S0/0/0.

```
R1(config)# interface s0/0/0
R1(config-if)# ip ospf message-digest-key 1 md5 MD5KEY
```

    c.   Activate MD5 authentication on R1, interface S0/0/0.

```
R1(config-if)# ip ospf authentication message-digest
```

       OSPF debug messages informing you of a Mismatched Authentication type displays on R2.

```
*Mar 19 00:03:18.187: OSPF-1 ADJ   Se0/0/0: Rcv pkt from 192.168.12.1 : Mismatched Au-
thentication type. Input packet specified type 2, we use type 0
```

    d.   Issue the **u all** command, which is the shortest version of the **undebug all** command on R2 to disable debugging.

    e.   Configure OSPF authentication on R2, interface S0/0/0. Use the same MD5 password you entered for R1.

f. Issue a **show ip ospf interface s0/0/0** command on R2. This command displays the type of authentication at the bottom of the output.

```
R2# show ip ospf interface s0/0/0
Serial0/0/0 is up, line protocol is up
  Internet Address 192.168.12.2/30, Area 0, Attached via Network Statement
  Process ID 1, Router ID 2.2.2.2, Network Type POINT_TO_POINT, Cost: 7812
  Topology-MTID    Cost    Disabled    Shutdown       Topology Name
        0           7812      no          no               Base
  Transmit Delay is 1 sec, State POINT_TO_POINT
  Timer intervals configured, Hello 10, Dead 40, Wait 40, Retransmit 5
    oob-resync timeout 40
    Hello due in 00:00:03
  Supports Link-local Signaling (LLS)
  Cisco NSF helper support enabled
  IETF NSF helper support enabled
  Index 1/1, flood queue length 0
  Next 0x0(0)/0x0(0)
  Last flood scan length is 1, maximum is 1
  Last flood scan time is 0 msec, maximum is 0 msec
  Neighbor Count is 1, Adjacent neighbor count is 1
    Adjacent with neighbor 1.1.1.1
  Suppress hello for 0 neighbor(s)
  Message digest authentication enabled
    Youngest key id is 1
```

Step 2: **Set up OSPF Authentication at the area level.**

a. Issue the **area 0 authentication** command to set MD5 authentication for OSPF Area 0 on R1.

```
R1(config)# router ospf 1
R1(config-router)# area 0 authentication message-digest
```

b. This option still requires that you assign the MD5 password at the interface level.

```
R1(config)# interface s0/0/1
R1(config-if)# ip ospf message-digest-key 1 md5 MD5KEY
```

c. Issue the **show ip ospf neighbor** command on R3. R1 no longer has an adjacency with R3.

```
R3# show ip ospf neighbor


Neighbor ID     Pri   State           Dead Time   Address         Interface
2.2.2.2          0    FULL/  -        00:00:31    192.168.23.1    Serial0/0/1
```

d. Set up area authentication on R3 and assign the same MD5 password to interface S0/0/0.

```
R3(config)# router ospf 1
```

```
R3(config-router)# area 0 authentication message-digest
R3(config-router)# interface s0/0/0
R3(config-if)# ip ospf message-digest-key 1 md5 MD5KEY
```

e. Issue the **show ip ospf neighbor** command on R3. Notice that R1 is now showing as a neighbor, but R2 is missing.

```
R3# show ip ospf neighbor


Neighbor ID     Pri   State         Dead Time   Address        Interface
1.1.1.1      0   FULL/  -       00:00:38    192.168.13.1   Serial0/0/0
```

Why is R2 no longer showing as an OSPF neighbor?

____

____

f. Configure R2 to perform area-level MD5 authentication.

```
R2(config)# router ospf 1
R2(config-router)# area 0 authentication message-digest
```

g. Assign **MD5KEY** as the MD5 password for the link between R2 and R3.

h. Issue the **show ip ospf neighbor** command on all routers to verify that all adjacencies have been re-established.

```
R1# show ip ospf neighbor


Neighbor ID     Pri   State         Dead Time   Address        Interface
3.3.3.3         0   FULL/  -       00:00:39    192.168.13.2   Serial0/0/1
2.2.2.2         0   FULL/  -       00:00:35    192.168.12.2   Serial0/0/0


R2# show ip ospf neighbor


Neighbor ID     Pri   State         Dead Time   Address        Interface
3.3.3.3         0   FULL/  -       00:00:36    192.168.23.2   Serial0/0/1
1.1.1.1         0   FULL/  -       00:00:32    192.168.12.1   Serial0/0/0


R3# show ip ospf neighbor


Neighbor ID     Pri   State         Dead Time   Address        Interface
2.2.2.2         0   FULL/  -       00:00:33    192.168.23.1   Serial0/0/1
1.1.1.1         0   FULL/  -       00:00:39    192.168.13.1   Serial0/0/0
```

Reflection

1. What is the easiest and preferred method of manipulating OSPF route costs?

____

____

2. What does the **default-information originate** command do for a network using the OSPF routing protocol?

____

3. Why is it a good idea to use OSPF authentication?

____

____

____

Router Interface Summary Table

Router Interface Summary				
Router Model	**Ethernet Interface #1**	**Ethernet Interface #2**	**Serial Interface #1**	**Serial Interface #2**
1800	Fast Ethernet 0/0 (F0/0)	Fast Ethernet 0/1 (F0/1)	Serial 0/0/0 (S0/0/0)	Serial 0/0/1 (S0/0/1)
1900	Gigabit Ethernet 0/0 (G0/0)	Gigabit Ethernet 0/1 (G0/1)	Serial 0/0/0 (S0/0/0)	Serial 0/0/1 (S0/0/1)
2801	Fast Ethernet 0/0 (F0/0)	Fast Ethernet 0/1 (F0/1)	Serial 0/1/0 (S0/1/0)	Serial 0/1/1 (S0/1/1)
2811	Fast Ethernet 0/0 (F0/0)	Fast Ethernet 0/1 (F0/1)	Serial 0/0/0 (S0/0/0)	Serial 0/0/1 (S0/0/1)
2900	Gigabit Ethernet 0/0 (G0/0)	Gigabit Ethernet 0/1 (G0/1)	Serial 0/0/0 (S0/0/0)	Serial 0/0/1 (S0/0/1)

Note: To find out how the router is configured, look at the interfaces to identify the type of router and how many interfaces the router has. There is no way to effectively list all the combinations of configurations for each router class. This table includes identifiers for the possible combinations of Ethernet and Serial interfaces in the device. The table does not include any other type of interface, even though a specific router may contain one. An example of this might be an ISDN BRI interface. The string in parenthesis is the legal abbreviation that can be used in Cisco IOS commands to represent the interface.

7.2.3.3 Lab – Troubleshooting Basic Single-Area OSPFv2 and OSPFv3

Topology

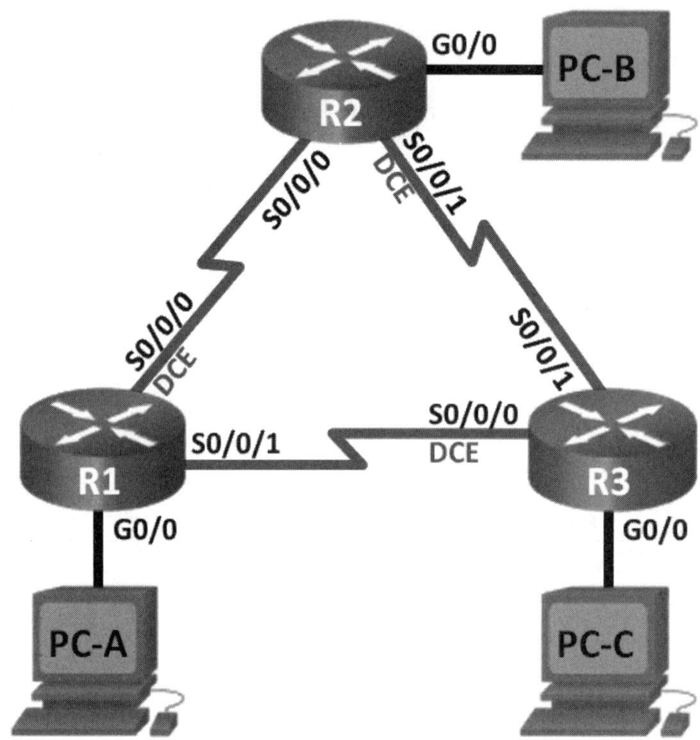

Addressing Table

Device	OSPF Router ID	Interface	Address	Default Gateway
R1	1.1.1.1	G0/0	192.168.1.1/24 2001:DB8:ACAD:A::1/64 FE80::1 link-local	N/A
		S0/0/0	192.168.12.1/30 2001:DB8:ACAD:12::1/64 FE80::1 link-local	N/A
		S0/0/1	192.18.13.1/30 2001:DB8:ACAD:13::1/64 FE80::1 link-local	N/A
R2	2.2.2.2	G0/0	192.168.2.1/24 2001:DB8:ACAD:B::2/64 FE80::2 link-local	N/A
		S0/0/0	192.168.12.2/30 2001:DB8:ACAD:12::2/64 FE80::2 link-local	N/A
		S0/0/1	192.168.23.1/30 2001:DB8:ACAD:23::2/64 FE80::2 link-local	N/A
R3	3.3.3.3	G0/0	192.168.3.1/24 2001:DB8:ACAD:C::3/64 FE80::3 link-local	N/A
		S0/0/0	192.168.13.2/30 2001:DB8:ACAD:13::3/64 FE80::3 link-local	N/A
		S0/0/1	192.168.23.2/30 2001:DB8:ACAD:23::3/64 FE80::3 link-local	N/A
PC-A		NIC	192.168.1.3/24 2001:DB8:ACAD:A::A/64	192.168.1.1 FE80::1
PC-B		NIC	192.168.2.3/24 2001:DB8:ACAD:B::B/64	192.168.2.1 FE80::2
PC-C		NIC	192.168.3.3/24 2001:DB8:ACAD:C::C/64	192.168.3.1 FE80::3

Objectives

Part 1: Build the Network and Load Device Configurations

Part 2: Troubleshoot Layer 3 Connectivity

Part 3: Troubleshoot OSPFv2

Part 4: Troubleshoot OSPFv3

Background / Scenario

Open Shortest Path First (OSPF) is a link-state routin... ...etworks. OSPFv2 is defined for IPv4 networks, and OSPFv3 is defined for IPv6 networks. OSP... ...SPFv3 are completely isolated routing protocols, changes in OSPFv2 do not affect OSPFv3 routin... ...d vice versa.

In this lab, a single-area OSPF network running OSPFv2 and OSPFv3 is experiencing problems. You have been assigned to find the problems with the network and correct them.

Note: The routers used with CCNA hands-on labs are Cisco 1941 Integrated Services Routers (ISRs) with Cisco IOS Release 15.2(4)M3 (universalk9 image). Other routers and Cisco IOS versions can be used. Depending on the model and Cisco IOS version, the commands available and output produced might vary from what is shown in the labs. Refer to the Router Interface Summary Table at the end of this lab for the correct interface identifiers.

Note: Make sure that the routers have been erased and have no startup configurations. If you are unsure, contact your instructor.

Required Resources

- 3 Routers (Cisco 1941 with Cisco IOS Release 15.2(4)M3 universal image or comparable)
- 3 PCs (Windows 7, Vista, or XP with terminal emulation program, such as Tera Term)
- Console cables to configure the Cisco IOS devices via the console ports
- Ethernet and serial cables as shown in the topology

Part 1: Build the Network and Load Device Configurations

In Part 1, you will set up the network topology and configure basic settings on the PC hosts and routers.

Step 1: **Cable the network as shown in the topology.**

Step 2: **Configure PC hosts.**

Step 3: **Load router configurations.**

Load the following configurations into the appropriate router. All routers have the same passwords. The privileged EXEC password is **cisco**. The password for console and vty access is **class**.

Router R1 Configuration:

```
conf t
service password-encryption
no ip domain lookup
hostname R1
enable secret class
line con 0
 logging synchronous
 password cisco
 login
line vty 0
```

```
 password cisco
 login
banner motd @Unauthorized Access is Prohibited!@
ipv6 unicast-routing
ipv6 router ospf 1
 router-id 1.1.1.1
 passive-interface g0/0
interface g0/0
 ip address 192.168.1.1 255.255.255.0
 ipv6 address 2001:db8:acad:a::1/64
 ipv6 address fe80::1 link-local


interface s0/0/0
 clock rate 128000
 ip address 192.168.12.1 255.255.255.0

 ipv6 address 2001:db8:acad:12::1/64
 ipv6 address fe80::1 link-local
 ipv6 ospf 1 area 0
 no shutdown
interface s0/0/1
 ip address 192.168.13.1 255.255.255.0

 ipv6 address 2001:db8:acad:13::1/64
 ipv6 address fe80::1 link-local
 ipv6 ospf 1 area 0
 no shutdown
router ospf 1
 network 192.168.1.0 0.0.0.255 area 0
 network 129.168.12.0 0.0.0.3 area 0

 network 192.168.13.0 0.0.0.3 area 0
 passive-interface g0/0


end
```

Router R2 Configuration:

```
 conf t
```

```
service password-encryption
no ip domain lookup
hostname R2
enable secret class
line con 0
 logging synchronous
 password cisco
 login
line vty 0
 password cisco
 login
banner motd @Unauthorized Access is Prohibited!@
ipv6 unicast-routing
ipv6 router ospf 1
 router-id 2.2.2.2

interface g0/0
ip address 192.168.2.1 255.255.255.0
 ipv6 address 2001:db8:acad:B::2/64
 ipv6 address fe80::1 link-local



 no shutdown
interface s0/0/0
 ip address 192.168.12.2 255.255.255.252
 ipv6 address 2001:db8:acad:12::2/64
 ipv6 address fe80::2 link-local
 ipv6 ospf 1 area 0
 no shutdown
interface s0/0/1
 clock rate 128000

 ipv6 address 2001:db8:acad:23::2/64
 ipv6 address fe80::2 link-local

 no shutdown
router ospf 1
 network 192.168.2.0 0.0.0.255 area 0
```

```
network 192.168.12.0 0.0.0.3 area 0
network 192.168.23.0 0.0.0.3 area 0


end
```

Router R3 Configuration:

```
conf t
service password-encryption
no ip domain lookup
enable secret class
hostname R3
line con 0
 logging synchronous
 password cisco
 login
line vty 0
 password cisco
 login
banner motd @Unauthorized Access is Prohibited!@
interface g0/0


 ipv6 address 2001:db8:acad:c::3/64
 ipv6 address fe80::3 link-local



interface s0/0/0
 clock rate 128000
 ip address 192.168.13.1 255.255.255.252


 ipv6 address 2001:db8:acad:13::3/64
 ipv6 address fe80::3 link-local


 no shutdown
interface s0/0/1
 ip address 192.168.23.2 255.255.255.252
 ipv6 address 2001:db8:acad:23::3/64
 ipv6 address fe80::3 link-local
```

```
router ospf 1
 network 192.168.3.0 0.0.0.255 area 0



 passive-interface g0/0
end
```

Part 2:   Troubleshoot Layer 3 Connectivity

In Part 2, you will verify that Layer 3 connectivity is established on all interfaces. You will need to test both IPv4 and IPv6 connectivity for all device interfaces.

Step 1:   Verify that the interfaces listed in the Addressing Table are active and configured with the correct IP address information.

a.   Issue the **show ip interface brief** command on all routers to verify that the interfaces are in an up/up state. Record your findings.

____

____

____

____

b.   Issue the **show run interface** command to verify IP address assignments on all router interfaces. Compare the interface IP addresses against the Addressing Table and verify the subnet mask assignments. For IPv6, verify that the link-local address has been assigned. Record your findings.

____

____

____

____

c. Resolve all problems that are found. Record the commands used to correct the issues.

____

____

____

____

____

____

____

____

d. Using the **ping** command, verify that each router has network connectivity with the serial interfaces on the neighbor routers. Verify that the PCs can ping their default gateways. If problems still exist, continue troubleshooting Layer 3 issues.

Part 3: Troubleshoot OSPFv2

In Part 3, you will troubleshoot OSPFv2 problems and make the necessary changes needed to establish OS-PFv2 routes and end-to-end IPv4 connectivity.

Note: LAN (G0/0) interfaces should not advertise OSPF routing information, but routes to these networks should be in the routing tables.

Step 1: Test IPv4 end-to-end connectivity.

From each PC host, ping the other PC hosts in the topology to verify end-to-end connectivity.

Note: It may be necessary to disable the PC firewall before testing, to ping between PCs.

a. Ping from PC-A to PC-B. Were the pings successful? ________________

b. Ping from PC-A to PC-C. Were the pings successful? ________________

c. Ping from PC-B to PC-C. Were the pings successful? ________________

Step 2: Verify that all interfaces are assigned to OSPFv2 area 0 on R1.

a. Issue the **show ip protocols** command to verify that OSPF is running and that all networks are advertised in area 0. Verify that the router ID is set correctly. Record your findings.

____

____

____

b. Make the necessary changes to the configuration on R1 based on the output from the **show ip protocols** command. Record the commands used to correct the issues.

____

____

____

c. Issue the **clear ip ospf process** command if necessary.

d. Re-issue the **show ip protocols** command to verify that your changes had the desired effect.

e. Issue the **show ip ospf interface brief** command to verify that all interfaces are listed as OSPF networks assigned to area 0.

f. Issue the **show ip ospf interface g0/0** command to verify that G0/0 is a passive interface.

Note: This information is also in the **show ip protocols** command.

g. Resolve any problems discovered on R1. List any additional changes made to R1. If no problems were found on the device, then respond with "no problems were found".

____

Step 3:   Verify that all interfaces are assigned to OSPFv2 area 0 on R2.

a. Issue the **show ip protocols** command to verify that OSPF is running and that all networks are being advertised in area 0. Verify that the router ID is set correctly. Record your findings.

____

____

____

b. Make the necessary changes to the configuration on R2 based on the output from the **show ip protocols** command. Record the commands used to correct the issues.

____

____

____

c. Issue the **clear ip ospf process** command if necessary.

d. Re-issue the **show ip protocols** command to verify that your changes had the desired effect.

e. Issue the **show ip ospf interface brief** command to verify that all interfaces are listed as OSPF networks assigned to area 0.

f. Issue the **show ip ospf interface g0/0** command to verify that G0/0 is a passive interface.

   Note: This information is also available from the **show ip protocols** command.

g. Resolve any problems discovered on R2. List any additional changes made to R2. If no problems were found on the device, then respond with "no problems were found".

____

____

Step 4:   Verify that all interfaces are assigned to OSPFv2 area 0 on R3.

a. Issue the **show ip protocols** command to verify that OSPF is running and that all networks are being advertised in area 0. Verify that the router ID is set correctly as well. Record your findings.

____

____

____

b. Make the necessary changes to the configuration on R3 based on the output from the **show ip protocols** command. Record the commands used to correct the issues.

____

____

____

c. Issue the **clear ip ospf process** command if necessary.

d. Re-issue the **show ip protocols** command to verify that your changes had the desired effect.

e. Issue the **show ip ospf interface brief** command to verify that all interfaces are listed as OSPF networks assigned to area 0.

f. Issue the **show ip ospf interface g0/0** command to verify that G0/0 is a passive interface.

    Note: This information is also in the **show ip protocols** command.

g. Resolve any problems discovered on R3. List any additional changes made to R3. If no problems were found on the device, then respond with "no problems were found".

____

Step 5:   Verify OSPF neighbor information.

a. Issue the **show ip ospf neighbor** command on all routers to view the OSPF neighbor information.

Step 6: Verify OSPFv2 Routing Information.

a.   Issue the **show ip route ospf** command to verify that each router has OSPFv2 routes to all non-adjoining networks.

Are all OSPFv2 routes available? _________

If any OSPFv2 routes are missing, what is missing?

____

b.   If any routing information is missing, resolve these issues.

Step 7: Verify IPv4 end-to-end connectivity.

From each PC, verify that IPv4 end-to-end connectivity exists. PCs should be able to ping the other PC hosts in the topology. If IPv4 end-to-end connectivity does not exist, then continue troubleshooting to resolve any remaining issues.

Note: It may be necessary to disable the PC firewall to ping between PCs.

Part 4: Troubleshoot OSPFv3

In Part 4, you will troubleshoot OSPFv3 problems and make the necessary changes needed to establish OS-PFv3 routes and end-to-end IPv6 connectivity.

Note: LAN (G0/0) interfaces should not advertise OSPFv3 routing information, but routes to these networks should be contained in the routing tables.

Step 1: Test IPv6 end-to-end connectivity.

From each PC host, ping the IPv6 addresses of the other PC hosts in the topology to verify IPv6 end-to-end connectivity.

Note: It may be necessary to disable the PC firewall to ping between PCs.

Step 2: Verify that IPv6 unicast routing has been enabled on all routers.

a.   An easy way to verify that IPv6 routing has been enabled on a router is to use the **show run | section ipv6 unicast** command. By adding this pipe (|) section to the **show run** command, the **ipv6 unicast-routing** command displays if IPv6 routing has been enabled.

Note: The **show run** command can also be issued without any pipe, and then a manual search for the **ipv6 unicast-routing** command can be done.

Issue the command on each router. Record your findings.

____

____

____

b. If IPv6 unicast routing is not enabled on one or more routers, enable it now. Record the commands used to correct the issues.

____

____

Step 3:   Verify that all interfaces are assigned to OSPFv3 area 0 on R1.

a. Issue the **show ipv6 protocols** command and verify that the router ID is correct. Also verify that the expected interfacesdisplay under area 0.

Note: If no output is generated from this command, then the OSPFv3 process has not been configured.

Record your findings.

____

____

____

b. Make the necessary configuration changes to R1. Record the commands used to correct the issues.

____

____

____

c. Issue the **clear ipv6 ospf process** command if necessary.

d. Re-issue the **show ipv6 protocols** command to verify that your changes had the desired effect.

e. Issue the show ipv6 ospf interface brief command to verify that all interfaces are listed as OSPF networks assigned to area 0.

f. Issue the **show ipv6 ospf interface g0/0** command to verify that this interface is set not to advertise OSPFv3 routes.

g. Resolve any problems discovered on R1. List any additional changes made to R1. If no problems were found on the device, then respond with "no problems were found".

____

Step 4:   Verify that all interfaces are assigned to OSPFv3 area 0 on R2.

a. Issue the **show ipv6 protocols** command and verify the router ID is correct. Also verify that the expected interfaces display under area 0.

   Note: If no output is generated from this command, then the OSPFv3 process has not been configured.

   Record your findings.

   ____

   ____

   ____

b. Make the necessary configuration changes to R2. Record the commands used to correct the issues.

   ____

   ____

   ____

c. Issue the **clear ipv6 ospf process** command if necessary.

d. Re-issue the **show ipv6 protocols** command to verify that your changes had the desired effect.

e. Issue the **show ipv6 ospf interface brief** command to verify that all interfaces are listed as OSPF networks assigned to area 0.

f. Issue the **show ipv6 ospf interface g0/0** command to verify that this interface is not set to advertise OSPFv3 routes.

g. List any additional changes made to R2. If no problems were found on the device, then respond with "no problems were found".

Step 5:   Verify that all interfaces are assigned to OSPFv3 area 0 on R3.

a. Issue the **show ipv6 protocols** command and verify that the router ID is correct. Also verify that the expected interfaces display under area 0.

Note: If no output is generated from this command, then the OSPFv3 process has not been configured.

Record your findings.

OSPFv3 has not been configured on this router.

b. Make the necessary configuration changes to R3. Record the commands used to correct the issues.

c. Issue the **clear ipv6 ospf process** command if necessary.

d. Re-issue the **show ipv6 protocols** command to verify that your changes had the desired effect.

e. Issue the show ipv6 ospf interface brief command to verify that all interfaces are listed as OSPF networks assigned to area 0.

f. Issue the **show ipv6 ospf interface g0/0** command to verify that this interface is set not to advertise OSPFv3 routes.

g. Resolve any problems discovered on R3. List any additional changes made to R3. If no problems were found on the device, then respond with "no problems were found".

No problems were found as long as G0/0 was configured as a passive OSPFv3 interface in Step 5b.

Step 6:   **Verify that all routers have correct neighbor adjacency information.**

a. Issue the **show ipv6 ospf neighbor** command to verify that adjacencies have formed between neighboring routers.

b. Resolve any OSPFv3 adjacency issues that still exist.

Step 7:   **Verify OSPFv3 routing information.**

a. Issue the **show ipv6 route ospf** command, and verify that OSPFv3 routes exist to all non-adjoining networks.

Are all OSPFv3 routes available? _________

If any OSPFv3 routes are missing, what is missing?

____

b.   Resolve any routing issues that still exist.

Step 8:   **Verify IPv6 end-to-end connectivity.**

From each PC, verify that IPv6 end-to-end connectivity exists. PCs should be able to ping each interface on the network. If IPv6 end-to-end connectivity does not exist, then continue troubleshooting to resolve remaining issues.

Note: It may be necessary to disable the PC firewall to ping between PCs.

Reflection

Why would you troubleshoot OSPFv2 and OSPFv3 separately?

____

____

Router Interface Summary Table

Router Interface Summary				
Router Model	**Ethernet Interface #1**	**Ethernet Interface #2**	**Serial Interface #1**	**Serial Interface #2**
1800	Fast Ethernet 0/0 (F0/0)	Fast Ethernet 0/1 (F0/1)	Serial 0/0/0 (S0/0/0)	Serial 0/0/1 (S0/0/1)
1900	Gigabit Ethernet 0/0 (G0/0)	Gigabit Ethernet 0/1 (G0/1)	Serial 0/0/0 (S0/0/0)	Serial 0/0/1 (S0/0/1)
2801	Fast Ethernet 0/0 (F0/0)	Fast Ethernet 0/1 (F0/1)	Serial 0/1/0 (S0/1/0)	Serial 0/1/1 (S0/1/1)
2811	Fast Ethernet 0/0 (F0/0)	Fast Ethernet 0/1 (F0/1)	Serial 0/0/0 (S0/0/0)	Serial 0/0/1 (S0/0/1)
2900	Gigabit Ethernet 0/0 (G0/0)	Gigabit Ethernet 0/1 (G0/1)	Serial 0/0/0 (S0/0/0)	Serial 0/0/1 (S0/0/1)
Note: To find out how the router is configured, look at the interfaces to identify the type of router and how many interfaces the router has. There is no way to effectively list all the combinations of configurations for each router class. This table includes identifiers for the possible combinations of Ethernet and Serial interfaces in the device. The table does not include any other type of interface, even though a specific router may contain one. An example of this might be an ISDN BRI interface. The string in parenthesis is the legal abbreviation that can be used in Cisco IOS commands to represent the interface.				

7.2.3.4 Lab – Troubleshooting Advanced Single-Area OSPFv2

Topology

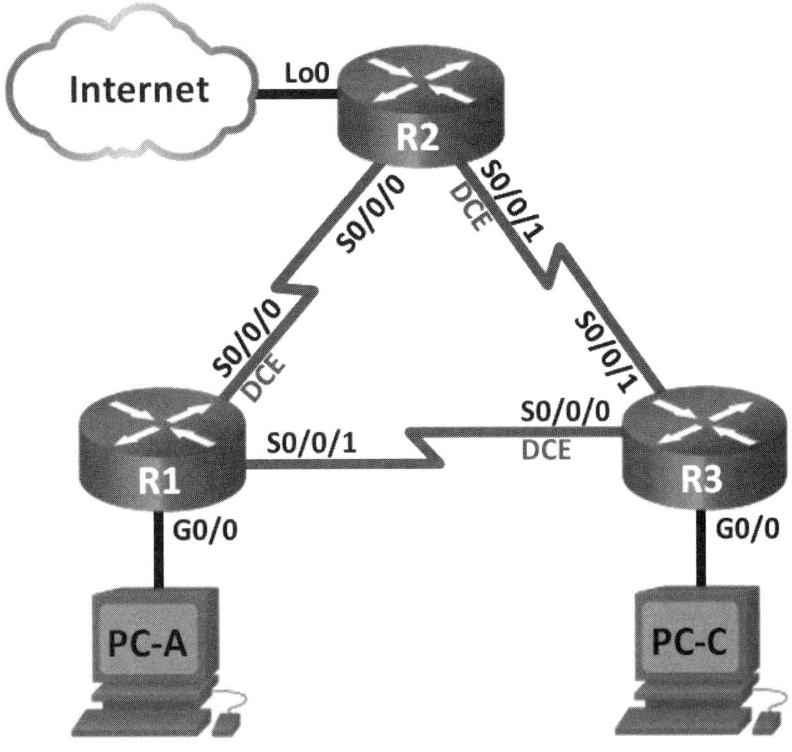

Addressing Table

Device	Interface	IP Address	Subnet Mask	Default Gateway
R1	G0/0	192.168.1.1	255.255.255.0	N/A
	S0/0/0 (DCE)	192.168.12.1	255.255.255.252	N/A
	S0/0/1	192.168.13.1	255.255.255.252	N/A
R2	Lo0	209.165.200.225	255.255.255.252	N/A
	S0/0/0	192.168.12.2	255.255.255.252	N/A
	S0/0/1 (DCE)	192.168.23.1	255.255.255.252	N/A
R3	G0/0	192.168.3.1	255.255.255.0	N/A
	S0/0/0 (DCE)	192.168.13.2	255.255.255.252	N/A
	S0/0/1	192.168.23.2	255.255.255.252	N/A
PC-A	NIC	192.168.1.3	255.255.255.0	192.168.1.1
PC-C	NIC	192.168.3.3	255.255.255.0	192.168.3.1

Objectives

Part 1: Build the Network and Load Device Configurations

Part 2: Troubleshoot OSPF

Background / Scenario

OSPF is a popular routing protocol used by businesses worldwide. A Network Administrator should be able to isolate OSPF issues and resolve those issues in a timely manner.

In this lab, you will troubleshoot a single-area OSPFv2 network and resolve all issues that exist.

Note: The routers used with CCNA hands-on labs are Cisco 1941 Integrated Services Routers (ISRs) with Cisco IOS Release 15.2(4)M3 (universalk9 image). Other routers and Cisco IOS versions can be used. Depending on the model and Cisco IOS version, the commands available and output produced might vary from what is shown in the labs. Refer to the Router Interface Summary Table at the end of this lab for the correct interface identifiers.

Note: Make sure that the routers have been erased and have no startup configurations. If you are unsure, contact your instructor.

Required Resources

- 3 Routers (Cisco 1941 with Cisco IOS Release 15.2(4)M3 universal image or comparable)
- 3 PCs (Windows 7, Vista, or XP with terminal emulation program, such as Tera Term)
- Console cables to configure the Cisco IOS devices via the console ports
- Ethernet and serial cables, as shown in the topology

Part 1:   Build the Network and Load Device Configurations

In Part 1, you will set up the network topology and configure basic settings on the PC hosts and routers.

Step 1:   Cable the network as shown in the topology.

Step 2:   Configure PC hosts.

Step 3:   Load router configurations.

Load the following configurations into the appropriate router. All routers have the same passwords. The privileged EXEC password is **class**. The password for console and vty lines is **cisco**.

Router R1 Configuration:

```
conf t
hostname R1
enable secret class
no ip domain lookup
interface GigabitEthernet0/0
 ip address 192.168.1.1 255.255.255.0
 duplex auto
 speed auto
 no shut
interface Serial0/0/0
 bandwidth 128
```

```
 ip address 192.168.12.1 255.255.255.252
 ip ospf message-digest-key 1 md5 MD5LINKS
 clock rate 128000
 no shut
interface Serial0/0/1
 bandwidth 64

 ip ospf message-digest-key 1 md5 MD5LINKS
 ip address 192.168.13.1 255.255.255.252
 no shut
router ospf 1
 auto-cost reference-bandwidth 1000

 area 0 authentication message-digest
 passive-interface g0/0
 network 192.168.1.0 0.0.0.255 area 0
 network 192.168.12.0 0.0.0.3 area 0
 network 192.168.13.0 0.0.0.3 area 0
banner motd ^
  Unauthorized Access is Prohibited!
^
line con 0
 password cisco
 logging synchronous
 login
line vty 0 4
 password cisco
 login
 transport input all
 end
```

Router R2 Configuration:

```
conf t
hostname R2
enable secret class
no ip domain lookup
interface Loopback0
  ip address 209.165.200.225 255.255.255.252
interface Serial0/0/0
```

```
  bandwidth 182

  ip ospf message-digest-key 1 md5 MD5LINKS
  ip address 192.168.12.2 255.255.255.252
  no shut
interface Serial0/0/1
 bandwidth 128
 ip ospf message-digest-key 1 md5 MD5LINKS
 ip address 192.168.23.1 255.255.255.252
 clock rate 128000
 no shut
router ospf 1
 router-id 2.2.2.2
 auto-cost reference-bandwidth 1000
 area 0 authentication message-digest
 passive-interface g0/0
 network 192.168.12.0 0.0.0.3 area 0
 network 192.168.23.0 0.0.0.3 area 0

ip route 0.0.0.0 0.0.0.0 Loopback0
banner motd ^
  Unauthorized Access is Prohibited!
^
line con 0
 password cisco
 logging synchronous
 login
line vty 0 4
 password cisco
 login
 transport input all
end
```

Router R3 Configuration:

```
conf t
hostname R3
enable secret class
no ip domain lookup
interface GigabitEthernet0/0
 ip address 192.168.3.1 255.255.255.0
```

```
 duplex auto
 speed auto
 no shut
interface Serial0/0/0
 bandwidth 128
 ip ospf message-digest-key 1 md5 MD5LINKS
 ip address 192.168.13.2 255.255.255.252
 clock rate 128000
 no shut
interface Serial0/0/1
 bandwidth 128
 ip address 192.168.23.2 255.255.255.252

 no shut
router ospf 1
 router-id 3.3.3.3

 area 0 authentication message-digest
 passive-interface g0/0
 network 192.168.3.0 0.0.0.255 area 0
 network 192.168.13.0 0.0.0.3 area 0
 network 192.168.23.0 0.0.0.3 area 0
banner motd ^
  Unauthorized Access is Prohibited!
^
line con 0
 password cisco
 logging synchronous
 login
line vty 0 4
 password cisco
 login
 transport input all
end
```

Step 4:   **Test end-to-end connectivity.**

All interfaces should be up and the PCs should be able to ping the default gateway.

Part 2:   **Troubleshoot OSPF**

In Part 2, verify that all routers have established neighbor adjacencies, and that all network routes are available.

Additional OSPF Requirements:

- Each router should have the following router ID assignments:
    - R1 Router ID: **1.1.1.1**
    - R2 Router ID: **2.2.2.2**
    - R3 Router ID: **3.3.3.3**
- All serial interface clocking rates should be set at 128 Kb/s and a matching bandwidth setting should be available to allow OSPF cost metrics to be calculated correctly.
- The 1941 routers have Gigabit interfaces, so the default OSPF reference bandwidth should be adjusted to allow cost metrics to reflect appropriate costs for all interfaces.
- OSPF should propagate a default route to the Internet. This is simulated by using Loopback interface 0 on R2.
- All interfaces advertising OSPF routing information should be configured with MD5 authentication, using **MD5LINKS** as the key.

List the commands used during your OSPF troubleshooting process:

____

____

____

____

List the changes made to resolve the OSPF issues. If no problems were found on the device, then respond with "no problems were found".

R1 Router:

____

____

____

____

R2 Router:

____

____

____

____

R3 Router:

____

____

____

Reflection

How would you change the network in this lab so all LAN traffic was routed through R2?

____

____

____

____

Router Interface Summary Table

Router Interface Summary				
Router Model	**Ethernet Interface #1**	**Ethernet Interface #2**	**Serial Interface #1**	**Serial Interface #2**
1800	Fast Ethernet 0/0 (F0/0)	Fast Ethernet 0/1 (F0/1)	Serial 0/0/0 (S0/0/0)	Serial 0/0/1 (S0/0/1)
1900	Gigabit Ethernet 0/0 (G0/0)	Gigabit Ethernet 0/1 (G0/1)	Serial 0/0/0 (S0/0/0)	Serial 0/0/1 (S0/0/1)
2801	Fast Ethernet 0/0 (F0/0)	Fast Ethernet 0/1 (F0/1)	Serial 0/1/0 (S0/1/0)	Serial 0/1/1 (S0/1/1)
2811	Fast Ethernet 0/0 (F0/0)	Fast Ethernet 0/1 (F0/1)	Serial 0/0/0 (S0/0/0)	Serial 0/0/1 (S0/0/1)
2900	Gigabit Ethernet 0/0 (G0/0)	Gigabit Ethernet 0/1 (G0/1)	Serial 0/0/0 (S0/0/0)	Serial 0/0/1 (S0/0/1)

Note: To find out how the router is configured, look at the interfaces to identify the type of router and how many interfaces the router has. There is no way to effectively list all the combinations of configurations for each router class. This table includes identifiers for the possible combinations of Ethernet and Serial interfaces in the device. The table does not include any other type of interface, even though a specific router may contain one. An example of this might be an ISDN BRI interface. The string in parenthesis is the legal abbreviation that can be used in Cisco IOS commands to represent the interface.

7.3.1.1 Class Activity – OSPF Troubleshooting Mastery

Objective

Explain the process and tools used to troubleshoot a single-area OSPF network.

Scenario

You have decided to change your routing protocol from RIPv2 to OSPFv2. Your small- to medium-sized business network topology will not change from its original physical settings. Use the diagram on the PDF for this activity as your company's small- to medium- business network design.

Your addressing design is complete and you then configure your routers with IPv4 and VLSM. OSPF has been applied as the routing protocol. However, some routers are sharing routing information with each other and some are not.

Open the PDF file that accompanies this modeling activity and follow the directions to complete the activity.

When the steps in the directions are complete, regroup as a class and compare recorded activity correction times. The group taking the shortest time to find and fix the configuration error will be declared the winner only after successfully explaining how they found the error, fixed it, and proved that the topology is now working.

Required Resources

- Topology diagram
- Packet Tracer software
- Timer

Topology Diagram

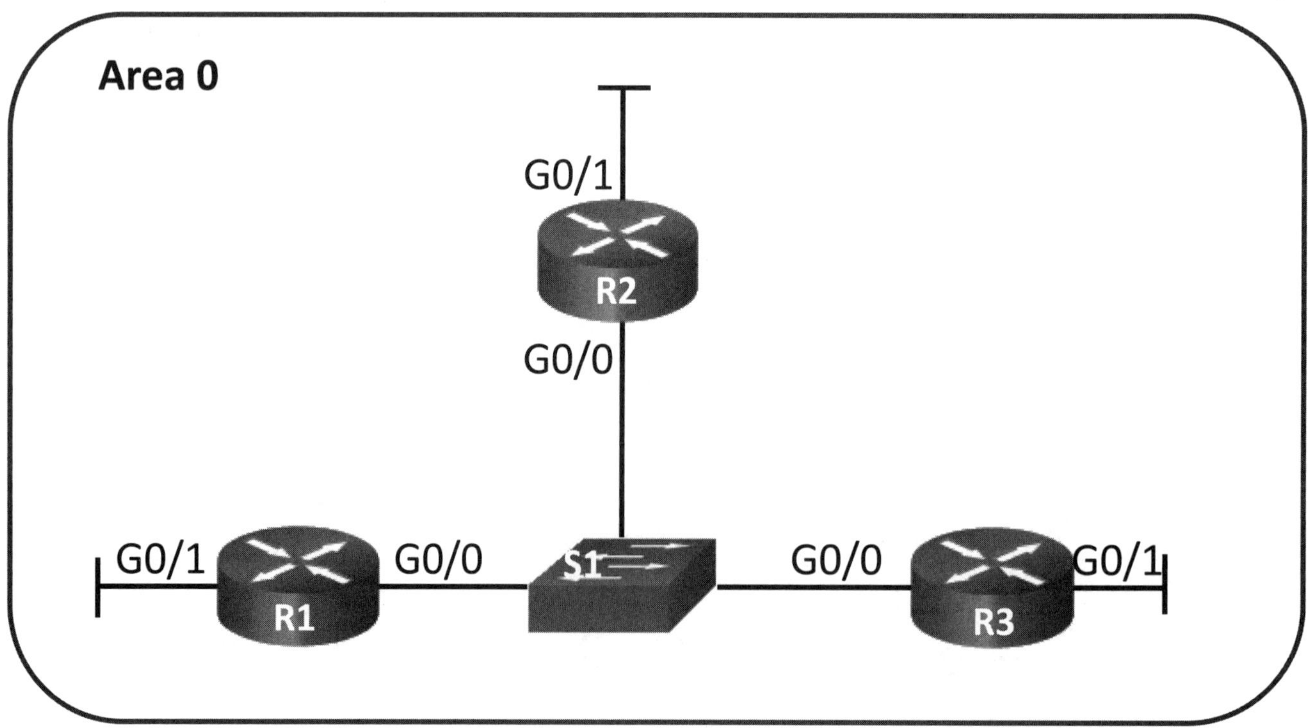

Directions

Choose a partner from the class with whom to work on this activity. Use Packet Tracer to create the topology diagram shown for this activity.

Step 1:   Build the topology based on the modeling activity page for this scenario.

Step 2:   Configure the routers.

    a.   Use IPv4 for all interfaces.

    b.   Incorporate VLSM into the addressing scheme.

    c.   Make one intentional configuration error.

    d.   Verify that the network does not work based upon the intentional error.

    e.   Save your file to be used with Step 3.

Step 3:   Exchange your Packet Tracer file with another group.

    a.   Find the configuration error on the Packet Tracer network file you received from another group.

    b.   Fix the OSPF configuration error so that the network operates fully.

    c.   Record the time it took to find and fix the OSPF network error.

    d.   When complete, meet with your class to determine the Master Troubleshooter for the day.

Chapter 8 — Multi-Area OSPF

8.0.1.2 Class Activity – Leaving on a Jet Plane

Objective

Explain the operation of multiarea OSPF to enable internetworking in a small- to medium-sized business network.

Scenario

You and a classmate are starting a new airline to serve your continent. In addition to your core area or headquarters airport, you will locate and map four intra-continental airport service areas and one trans-continental airport service area that can be used for additional source and destination travel.

Use the blank world map provided to design your airport locations. Additional instructions for completing this activity can be found in the accompanying PDF.

Required Resources

- Blank world map diagram
- Word processing software or alternative graphics software for marking airport locations and their connections

Blank World Map Diagram

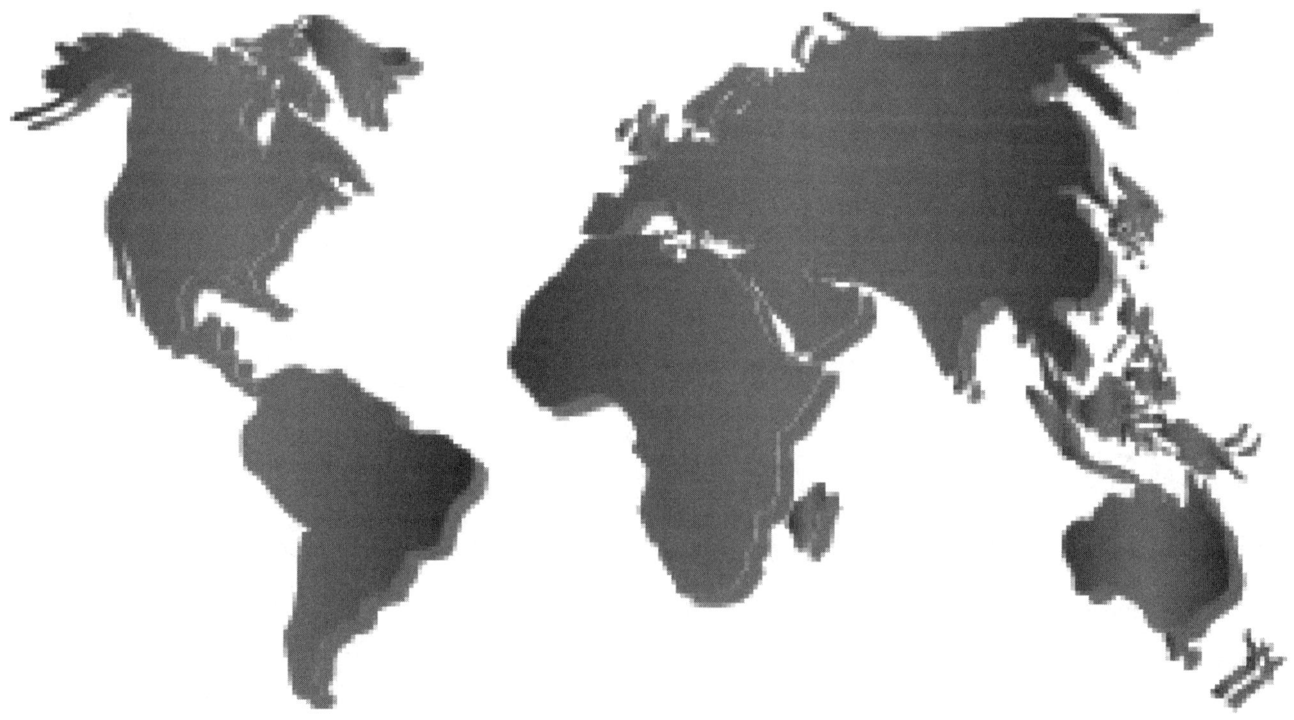

Directions

Step 1:   Design the airport locations.

a.   Use the blank world map diagram provided.

b.   On your map, place a star in the center of the continent in which you live. This is now the Airport Core Site and will serve as your core transit location. Label it as Airport Core Site. This is your first area of intra-continental service and all airports will be connected to the Airport Core Site.

Step 2:   Map airports within your continent to serve your passengers.

a.   Map four airport locations within your continent to connect to the Airport Core Site. Call them North, South, East, and West Airport Sites.

b.   Place four circles on your continent's map to represent the North, South, East, and West Airport Sites. Some circles may overlap due to the size of the continent and the sites placement on the map.

c.   Draw a straight line from each of these airports to the Airport Core Site. These intra-continent locations are your first level of service for your airlines. They are also known as area border airport sites.

Step 3:   Identify another continent your airline will serve.

a.   On the world map, locate another continent you would like to provide service to and from the Airlines Core Site.

b.   Place a circle in the center of the continent you chose for second-level service. This airport will be called Transcontinental Airport Site.

c.   Draw a line from your Airlines Core Site to the Transcontinental Airport Site. This airport will be known as an autonomous system border router (ASBR) airport site.

Summary

After completing Step 3, you should be able to see that the airport connections resemble a network topology. Complete the reflection questions, save your work, and be prepared to share your answers with the class.

Reflection

1.   While designing your airline travel routes, did you pay close attention to the headquarters location? Why would it be important to have a core site for airline travel?

2.   Would networks incorporate core, border, and ASBRs into area sites? Justify your answer.

3. What is the significance of mapping transcontinental areas?

4. What is the significance of mapping internal airline destination routes? Compare this to a routing topology.

5. Is it possible that the Airlines Core Site could serve several functions for your airlines (network)? Explain your answer.

8.2.3.8 Lab – Configuring Multiarea OSPFv2

Topology

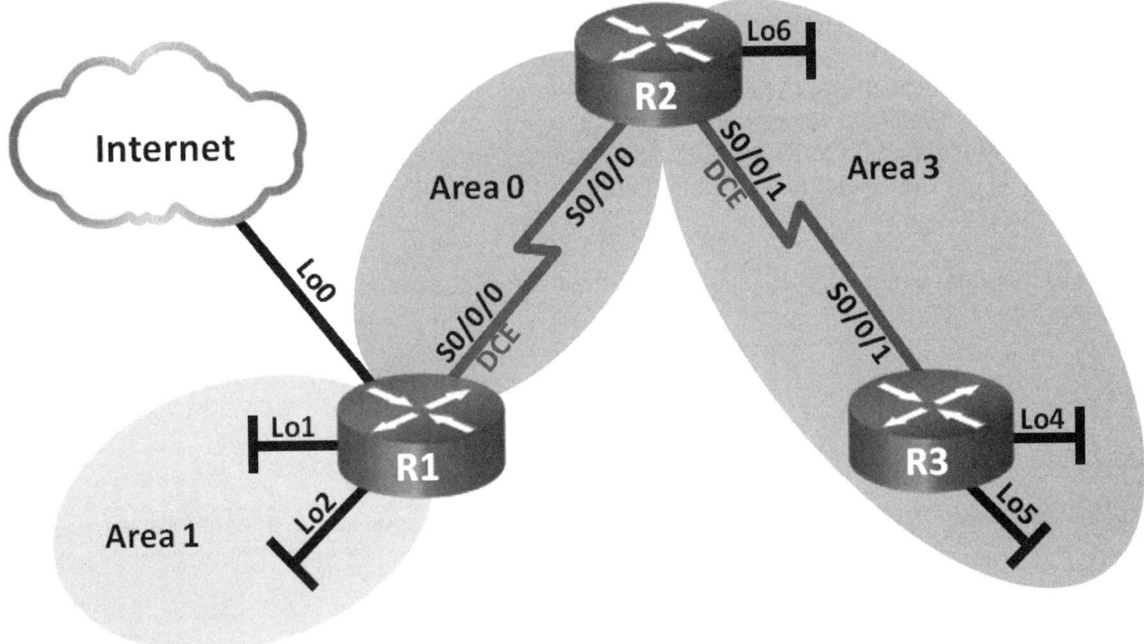

Addressing Table

Device	Interface	IP Address	Subnet Mask
R1	Lo0	209.165.200.225	255.255.255.252
	Lo1	192.168.1.1	255.255.255.0
	Lo2	192.168.2.1	255.255.255.0
	S0/0/0 (DCE)	192.168.12.1	255.255.255.252
R2	Lo6	192.168.6.1	255.255.255.0
	S0/0/0	192.168.12.2	255.255.255.252
	S0/0/1 (DCE)	192.168.23.1	255.255.255.252
R3	Lo4	192.168.4.1	255.255.255.0
	Lo5	192.168.5.1	255.255.255.0
	S0/0/1	192.168.23.2	255.255.255.252

Objectives

Part 1: Build the Network and Configure Basic Device Settings

Part 2: Configure a Multiarea OSPFv2 Network

Part 3: Configure Interarea Summary Routes

Background / Scenario

To make OSPF more efficient and scalable, OSPF supports hierarchical routing using the concept of areas. An OSPF area is a group of routers that share the same link-state information in their link-state databases (LSDBs). When a large OSPF area is divided into smaller areas, it is called multiarea OSPF. Multiarea OSPF is useful in larger network deployments to reduce processing and memory overhead.

In the lab, you will configure a multiarea OSPFv2 network with interarea summary routes.

Note: The routers used with CCNA hands-on labs are Cisco 1941 Integrated Services Routers (ISRs) with Cisco IOS Release 15.2(4)M3 (universalk9 image). Other routers and Cisco IOS versions can be used. Depending on the model and Cisco IOS version, the commands available and output produced might vary from what is shown in the labs. Refer to the Router Interface Summary Table at the end of this lab for the correct interface identifiers.

Note: Make sure that the routers have been erased and have no startup configurations. If you are unsure, contact your instructor.

Required Resources

- 3 Routers (Cisco 1941 with Cisco IOS Release 15.2(4)M3 universal image or comparable)
- Console cables to configure the Cisco IOS devices via the console ports
- Serial cables as shown in the topology

Part 1:   Build the Network and Configure Basic Device Settings

In Part 1, you will set up the network topology and configure basic settings on the routers.

Step 1:   Cable the network as shown in the topology.

Step 2:   Initialize and reload the routers as necessary.

Step 3:   Configure basic settings for each router.

a.   Disable DNS lookup.

b.   Configure device name, as shown in the topology.

c.   Assign **class** as the privileged EXEC password.

d.   Assign **cisco** as the console and vty passwords.

e.   Configure **logging synchronous** for the console line.

f.   Configure an MOTD banner to warn users that unauthorized access is prohibited.

g.   Configure the IP addresses listed in the Addressing Table for all interfaces. DCE interfaces should be configured with a clock rate of 128000. Bandwidth should be set to 128 Kb/s on all serial interfaces.

h.   Copy the running configuration to the startup configuration.

Step 4: **Verify Layer 3 connectivity.**

Use the **show ip interface brief** command to verify that the IP addressing is correct and that the interfaces are active. Verify that each router can ping their neighbor's serial interface.

Part 2: **Configure a Multiarea OSPFv2 Network**

In Part 2, you will configure a multiarea OSPFv2 network with process ID of 1. All LAN loopback interfaces should be passive, and all serial interfaces should be configured with MD5 authentication using **Cisco123** as the key.

Step 1: **Identify the OSPF router types in the topology.**

Identify the Backbone router(s): ______________________________

Identify the Autonomous System Boundary Router(s) (ASBR): __________________

Identify the Area Border Router(s) (ABR): ____________________

Identify the Internal router(s): ___________________________

Step 2: **Configure OSPF on R1.**

a. Configure a router ID of 1.1.1.1 with OSPF process ID of 1.

b. Add the networks for R1 to OSPF.

```
R1(config-router)# network 192.168.1.0 0.0.0.255 area 1
R1(config-router)# network 192.168.2.0 0.0.0.255 area 1
R1(config-router)# network 192.168.12.0 0.0.0.3 area 0
```

c. Set all LAN loopback interfaces, Lo1 and Lo2, as passive.

d. Create a default route to the Internet using exit interface Lo0.

Note: You may see the "%Default route without gateway, if not a point-to-point interface, may impact performance" message. This is normal behavior if using a Loopback interface to simulate a default route.

e. Configure OSPF to propagate the routes throughout the OSPF areas.

Step 3: **Configure OSPF on R2.**

a. Configure a router ID of 2.2.2.2 with OSPF process ID of 1.

b.   Add the networks for R2 to OSPF. Add the networks to the correct area. Write the commands used in the space below.

____

____

____

c.   Set all LAN loopback interfaces as passive.

Step 4:   Configure OSPF on R3.

a.   Configure a router ID of 3.3.3.3 with OSPF process ID of 1.

b.   Add the networks for R3 to OSPF. Write the commands used in the space below.

____

____

____

c.   Set all LAN loopback interfaces as passive.

Step 5:   Verify that OSPF settings are correct and adjacencies have been established between routers.

a.   Issue the `show ip protocols` command to verify OSPF settings on each router. Use this command to identify the OSPF router types and to determine the networks assigned to each area.

```
R1# show ip protocols

*** IP Routing is NSF aware ***

Routing Protocol is "ospf 1"
  Outgoing update filter list for all interfaces is not set
  Incoming update filter list for all interfaces is not set
  Router ID 1.1.1.1
```

```
     It is an area border and autonomous system boundary router
Redistributing External Routes from,
    Number of areas in this router is 2. 2 normal 0 stub 0 nssa
    Maximum path: 4
    Routing for Networks:
        192.168.1.0 0.0.0.255 area 1
        192.168.2.0 0.0.0.255 area 1
        192.168.12.0 0.0.0.3 area 0
    Passive Interface(s):
      Loopback1
      Loopback2
    Routing Information Sources:
      Gateway           Distance       Last Update
      2.2.2.2               110        00:01:45
    Distance: (default is 110)
```

R2# **show ip protocols**

```
*** IP Routing is NSF aware ***


Routing Protocol is "ospf 1"
    Outgoing update filter list for all interfaces is not set
    Incoming update filter list for all interfaces is not set
    Router ID 2.2.2.2
    It is an area border router
    Number of areas in this router is 2. 2 normal 0 stub 0 nssa
    Maximum path: 4
    Routing for Networks:
        192.168.6.0 0.0.0.255 area 3
        192.168.12.0 0.0.0.3 area 0
        192.168.23.0 0.0.0.3 area 3
    Passive Interface(s):
      Loopback6
    Routing Information Sources:
      Gateway           Distance       Last Update
      3.3.3.3               110        00:01:20
      1.1.1.1               110        00:10:12
    Distance: (default is 110)
```

R3# **show ip protocols**

```
*** IP Routing is NSF aware ***


Routing Protocol is "ospf 1"
    Outgoing update filter list for all interfaces is not set
    Incoming update filter list for all interfaces is not set
```

```
    Router ID 3.3.3.3
    Number of areas in this router is 1. 1 normal 0 stub 0 nssa
    Maximum path: 4
    Routing for Networks:
        192.168.4.0 0.0.0.255 area 3
        192.168.5.0 0.0.0.255 area 3
        192.168.23.0 0.0.0.3 area 3
    Passive Interface(s):
        Loopback4
        Loopback5
    Routing Information Sources:
        Gateway          Distance        Last Update
        1.1.1.1               110        00:07:46
        2.2.2.2               110        00:07:46
    Distance: (default is 110)
```

What is the OSPF router type for each router?

R1: ____

R2: ____

R3: ____

b.   Issue the **show ip ospf neighbor** command to verify that OSPF adjacencies have been established between routers.

```
R1# show ip ospf neighbor


Neighbor ID      Pri    State          Dead Time    Address          Interface
2.2.2.2            0    FULL/  -       00:00:34     192.168.12.2     Serial0/0/0


R2# show ip ospf neighbor


Neighbor ID      Pri    State          Dead Time    Address          Interface
1.1.1.1            0    FULL/  -       00:00:36     192.168.12.1     Serial0/0/0
3.3.3.3            0    FULL/  -       00:00:36     192.168.23.2     Serial0/0/1


R3# show ip ospf neighbor


Neighbor ID      Pri    State          Dead Time    Address          Interface
2.2.2.2            0    FULL/  -       00:00:38     192.168.23.1     Serial0/0/1
```

c.   Issue the **show ip ospf interface brief** command to display a summary of interface route costs.

```
R1# show ip ospf interface brief
Interface    PID    Area        IP Address/Mask     Cost   State Nbrs F/C
Se0/0/0      1      0           192.168.12.1/30     781    P2P    1/1
Lo1          1      1           192.168.1.1/24      1      LOOP   0/0
Lo2          1      1           192.168.2.1/24      1      LOOP   0/0


R2# show ip ospf interface brief
Interface    PID    Area        IP Address/Mask     Cost   State Nbrs F/C
Se0/0/0      1      0           192.168.12.2/30     781    P2P    1/1
Lo6          1      3           192.168.6.1/24      1      LOOP   0/0
Se0/0/1      1      3           192.168.23.1/30     781    P2P    1/1


R3# show ip ospf interface brief
Interface    PID    Area        IP Address/Mask     Cost   State Nbrs F/C
Lo4          1      3           192.168.4.1/24      1      LOOP   0/0
Lo5          1      3           192.168.5.1/24      1      LOOP   0/0
Se0/0/1      1      3           192.168.23.2/30     781    P2P    1/1
```

Step 6:   **Configure MD5 authentication on all serial interfaces.**

Configure OSPF MD5 authentication at the interface level with an authentication key of **Cisco123**.

Why is it a good idea to verify that OSPF is functioning correctly before configuring OSPF authentication?

____

____

Step 7:   Verify OSPF adjacencies have been re-established.

Issue the **show ip ospf neighbor** command again to verify that adjacencies have been re-established after MD5 authentication was implemented. Troubleshoot any issues found before moving on to Part 3.

Part 3:   Configure Interarea Summary Routes

OSPF does not perform automatic summarization. Interarea summarization must be manually configured on ABRs. In Part 3, you will apply interarea summary routes on the ABRs. Using **show** commands, you will be able to observe how summarization affects the routing table and LSDBs.

Step 1:   Display the OSPF routing tables on all routers.

a.   Issue the **show ip route ospf** command on R1. OSPF routes that originate from a different area have a descriptor (O IA) indicating that these are interarea routes.

```
R1# show ip route ospf

Codes: L - local, C - connected, S - static, R - RIP, M - mobile, B - BGP
       D - EIGRP, EX - EIGRP external, O - OSPF, IA - OSPF inter area
       N1 - OSPF NSSA external type 1, N2 - OSPF NSSA external type 2
       E1 - OSPF external type 1, E2 - OSPF external type 2
       i - IS-IS, su - IS-IS summary, L1 - IS-IS level-1, L2 - IS-IS level-2
       ia - IS-IS inter area, * - candidate default, U - per-user static route
       o - ODR, P - periodic downloaded static route, H - NHRP, l - LISP
       + - replicated route, % - next hop override


Gateway of last resort is 0.0.0.0 to network 0.0.0.0


      192.168.4.0/32 is subnetted, 1 subnets
O IA     192.168.4.1 [110/1563] via 192.168.12.2, 00:23:49, Serial0/0/0
      192.168.5.0/32 is subnetted, 1 subnets
O IA     192.168.5.1 [110/1563] via 192.168.12.2, 00:23:49, Serial0/0/0
      192.168.23.0/30 is subnetted, 1 subnets
O IA     192.168.6.1 [110/782] via 192.168.12.2, 00:02:01, Serial0/0/0
      192.168.23.0/30 is subnetted, 1 subnets
O IA     192.168.23.0 [110/1562] via 192.168.12.2, 00:23:49, Serial0/0/0
```

b.   Repeat the **show ip route ospf** command for R2 and R3. Record the OSPF interarea routes for each router.

R2:

____

____

____

R3:

____

____

____

Step 2:   Display the LSDB on all routers.

a. Issue the **show ip ospf database** command on R1. A router maintains a separate LSDB for every area that it is a member.

```
R1# show ip ospf database


            OSPF Router with ID (1.1.1.1) (Process ID 1)


                Router Link States (Area 0)


Link ID          ADV Router      Age          Seq#          Checksum Link count
1.1.1.1          1.1.1.1         1295         0x80000003 0x0039CD 2
2.2.2.2          2.2.2.2         1282         0x80000002 0x00D430 2


                Summary Net Link States (Area 0)


Link ID          ADV Router      Age          Seq#          Checksum
192.168.1.1      1.1.1.1         1387         0x80000002 0x00AC1F
192.168.2.1      1.1.1.1         1387         0x80000002 0x00A129
192.168.4.1      2.2.2.2         761          0x80000001 0x000DA8
192.168.5.1      2.2.2.2         751          0x80000001 0x0002B2
192.168.6.1      2.2.2.2         1263         0x80000001 0x00596A
192.168.23.0     2.2.2.2         1273         0x80000001 0x00297E


                Router Link States (Area 1)


Link ID          ADV Router      Age          Seq#          Checksum Link count
1.1.1.1          1.1.1.1         1342         0x80000006 0x0094A4 2


                Summary Net Link States (Area 1)


Link ID          ADV Router      Age          Seq#          Checksum
192.168.4.1      1.1.1.1         760          0x80000001 0x00C8E0
192.168.5.1      1.1.1.1         750          0x80000001 0x00BDEA
192.168.6.1      1.1.1.1         1262         0x80000001 0x0015A2
```

```
192.168.12.0    1.1.1.1         1387        0x80000001 0x00C0F5
192.168.23.0    1.1.1.1         1272        0x80000001 0x00E4B6


                Type-5 AS External Link States


Link ID         ADV Router      Age         Seq#        Checksum Tag
0.0.0.0           1.1.1.1       1343        0x80000001 0x001D91 1
```

b. Repeat the **show ip ospf database** command for R2 and R3. Record the Link IDs for the Summary Net Link States for each area.

    R2:

____

____

    R3:

____

____

Step 3:   Configure the interarea summary routes.

a. Calculate the summary route for the networks in area 1.

b. Configure the summary route for area 1 on R1.

```
R1(config)# router ospf 1
R1(config-router)# area 1 range 192.168.0.0 255.255.252.0
```

c. Calculate the summary route for the networks in area 3. Record your results.

____

d. Configure the summary route for area 3 on R2. Write the commands you used in the space below.

____

____

Step 4:   Re-display the OSPF routing tables on all routers.

Issue the **show ip route ospf** command on each router. Record the results for the summary and interarea routes.

R1:

R2:

R3:

Step 5:   Display the LSDB on all routers.

Issue the **show ip ospf database** command again on each router. Record the Link IDs for the Summary Net Link States for each area.

R1:

R2:

R3:

What type of LSA is injected into the backbone by the ABR when interarea summarization is enabled?

Step 6:   **Verify end-to-end connectivity.**

Verify that all networks can be reached from each router. If any issues exist, troubleshoot until they have been resolved.

Reflection

What are three advantages for designing a network with multiarea OSPF?

____

____

____

Router Interface Summary Table

Router Interface Summary				
Router Model	**Ethernet Interface #1**	**Ethernet Interface #2**	**Serial Interface #1**	**Serial Interface #2**
1800	Fast Ethernet 0/0 (F0/0)	Fast Ethernet 0/1 (F0/1)	Serial 0/0/0 (S0/0/0)	Serial 0/0/1 (S0/0/1)
1900	Gigabit Ethernet 0/0 (G0/0)	Gigabit Ethernet 0/1 (G0/1)	Serial 0/0/0 (S0/0/0)	Serial 0/0/1 (S0/0/1)
2801	Fast Ethernet 0/0 (F0/0)	Fast Ethernet 0/1 (F0/1)	Serial 0/1/0 (S0/1/0)	Serial 0/1/1 (S0/1/1)
2811	Fast Ethernet 0/0 (F0/0)	Fast Ethernet 0/1 (F0/1)	Serial 0/0/0 (S0/0/0)	Serial 0/0/1 (S0/0/1)
2900	Gigabit Ethernet 0/0 (G0/0)	Gigabit Ethernet 0/1 (G0/1)	Serial 0/0/0 (S0/0/0)	Serial 0/0/1 (S0/0/1)

Note: To find out how the router is configured, look at the interfaces to identify the type of router and how many interfaces the router has. There is no way to effectively list all the combinations of configurations for each router class. This table includes identifiers for the possible combinations of Ethernet and Serial interfaces in the device. The table does not include any other type of interface, even though a specific router may contain one. An example of this might be an ISDN BRI interface. The string in parenthesis is the legal abbreviation that can be used in Cisco IOS commands to represent the interface.

8.2.3.9 Lab – Configuring Multiarea OSPFv3

Topology

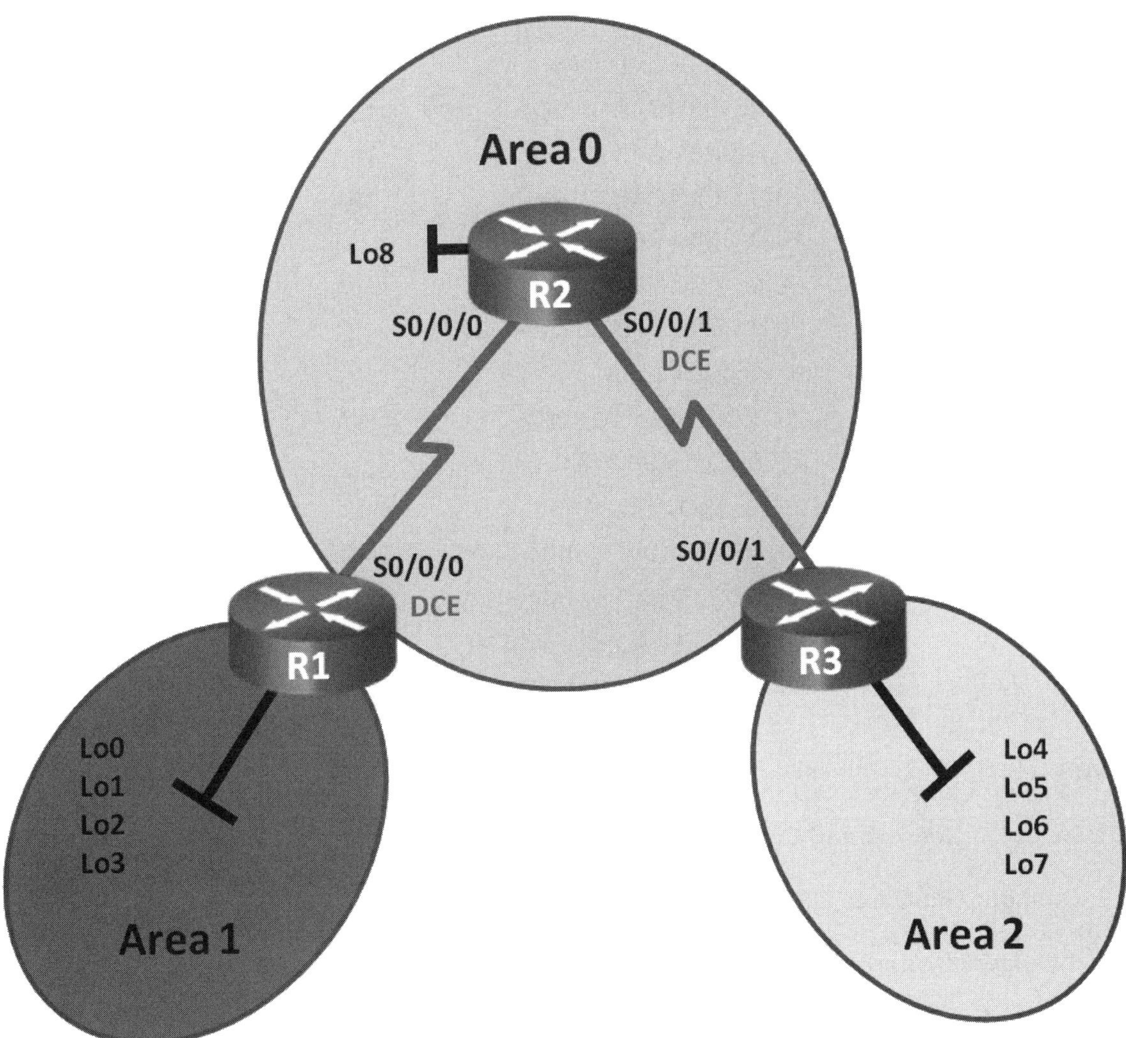

Addressing Table

Device	Interface	IPv6 Address	Default Gateway
R1	S0/0/0 (DCE)	2001:DB8:ACAD:12::1/64	
		FE80::1 link-local	N/A
	Lo0	2001:DB8:ACAD::1/64	N/A
	Lo1	2001:DB8:ACAD:1::1/64	N/A
	Lo2	2001:DB8:ACAD:2::1/64	N/A
	Lo3	2001:DB8:ACAD:3::1/64	N/A
R2	S0/0/0	2001:DB8:ACAD:12::2/64	
		FE80::2 link-local	N/A
	S0/0/1 (DCE)	2001:DB8:ACAD:23::2/64	
		FE80::2 link-local	N/A
	Lo8	2001:DB8:ACAD:8::1/64	N/A
R3	S0/0/1	2001:DB8:ACAD:23::3/64	
		FE80::3 link-local	N/A
	Lo4	2001:DB8:ACAD:4::1/64	N/A
	Lo5	2001:DB8:ACAD:5::1/64	N/A
	Lo6	2001:DB8:ACAD:6::1/64	N/A
	Lo7	2001:DB8:ACAD:7::1/64	N/A

Objectives

Part 1: Build the Network and Configure Basic Device Settings

Part 2: Configure Multiarea OSPFv3 Routing

Part 3: Configure Interarea Route Summarization

Background / Scenario

Using multiarea OSPFv3 in large IPv6 network deployments can reduce router processing by creating smaller routing tables and requiring less memory overhead. In multiarea OSPFv3, all areas are connected to the backbone area (area 0) through area border routers (ABRs).

In this lab, you will implement OSPFv3 routing for multiple areas and configure interarea route summarizations on the Area Border Routers (ABRs). You will also use a number of **show** commands to display and verify OSPFv3 routing information. This lab uses loopback addresses to simulate networks in multiple OSPFv3 areas.

Note: The routers used with CCNA hands-on labs are Cisco 1941 Integrated Services Routers (ISRs) with Cisco IOS Release 15.2(4)M3 (universalk9 image). Other routers and Cisco IOS versions can be used. Depending on the model and Cisco IOS version, the commands available and output produced might vary from what is shown in the labs. Refer to the Router Interface Summary Table at this end of this lab for the correct interface identifiers.

Note: Make sure that the routers have been erased and have no startup configurations. If you are unsure, contact your instructor.

Required Resources

- 3 Routers (Cisco 1941 with Cisco IOS Release 15.2(4)M3 universal image or comparable)
- 3 PCs (Windows 7, Vista, or XP with terminal emulation program, such as Tera Term)
- Console cables to configure the Cisco IOS devices via the console ports
- Serial cables as shown in the topology

Part 1: Build the Network and Configure Basic Device Settings

In Part 1, you will set up the network topology and configure basic settings on the routers.

Step 1: Cable the network as shown in the topology.

Step 2: Initialize and reload the routers as necessary.

Step 3: Configure basic settings for each router.

a. Disable DNS lookup.

b. Configure device name as shown in the topology.

c. Assign **class** as the privileged EXEC password.

d. Assign **cisco** as the vty password.

e. Configure a MOTD banner to warn users that unauthorized access is prohibited.

f. Configure **logging synchronous** for the console line.

g. Encrypt plain text passwords.

h. Configure the IPv6 unicast and link-local addresses listed in the Addressing Table for all interfaces.

i. Enable IPv6 unicast routing on each router.

j. Copy the running configuration to the startup configuration.

Step 4: Test connectivity.

The routers should be able to ping one another. The routers are unable to ping distant loopbacks until OS-PFv3 routing is configured. Verify and troubleshoot if necessary.

Part 2: Configure Multiarea OSPFv3 Routing

In Part 2, you will configure OSPFv3 routing on all routers to separate the network domain into three distinct areas, and then verify that routing tables are updated correctly.

Step 1: Assign router IDs.

a. On R1, issue the **ipv6 router ospf** command to start an OSPFv3 process on the router.

```
R1(config)# ipv6 router ospf 1
```

Note: The OSPF process ID is kept locally and has no meaning to other routers on the network.

b. Assign the OSPFv3 router ID **1.1.1.1** to R1.

```
R1(config-rtr)# router-id 1.1.1.1
```

c. Assign a router ID of **2.2.2.2** to R2 and a router ID of **3.3.3.3** to R3.

d. Issue the **show ipv6 ospf** command to verify the router IDs on all routers.

```
R2# show ipv6 ospf
Routing Process "ospfv3 1" with ID 2.2.2.2
Event-log enabled, Maximum number of events: 1000, Mode: cyclic
Router is not originating router-LSAs with maximum metric
<output omitted>
```

Step 2:   Configure multiarea OSPFv3.

a. Issue the **ipv6 ospf 1 area** *area-id* command for each interface on R1 that is to participate in OSPFv3 routing. The loopback interfaces are assigned to area 1 and the serial interface is assigned to area 0. You will change the network type on the loopback interfaces to ensure that the correct subnet is advertised.

```
R1(config)# interface lo0
R1(config-if)# ipv6 ospf 1 area 1
R1(config-if)# ipv6 ospf network point-to-point
R1(config-if)# interface lo1
R1(config-if)# ipv6 ospf 1 area 1
R1(config-if)# ipv6 ospf network point-to-point
R1(config-if)# interface lo2
R1(config-if)# ipv6 ospf 1 area 1
R1(config-if)# ipv6 ospf network point-to-point
R1(config-if)# interface lo3
R1(config-if)# ipv6 ospf 1 area 1
R1(config-if)# ipv6 ospf network point-to-point
R1(config-if)# interface s0/0/0
R1(config-if)# ipv6 ospf 1 area 0
```

b. Use the **show ipv6 protocols** command to verify multiarea OSPFv3 status.

```
R1# show ipv6 protocols
IPv6 Routing Protocol is "connected"
IPv6 Routing Protocol is "ND"
IPv6 Routing Protocol is "ospf 1"
  Router ID 1.1.1.1
  Area border router
  Number of areas: 2 normal, 0 stub, 0 nssa
  Interfaces (Area 0):
    Serial0/0/0
  Interfaces (Area 1):
    Loopback0
    Loopback1
    Loopback2
```

```
    Loopback3

  Redistribution:

    None
```

c. Assign all interfaces on R2 to participate in OSPFv3 area 0. For the loopback interface, change the network type to point-to point. Write the commands used in the space below.

____

____

____

____

____

____

d. Use the **show ipv6 ospf interface brief** command to view OSPFv3 enabled interfaces.

```
R2# show ipv6 ospf interface brief
Interface    PID   Area              Intf ID    Cost   State Nbrs F/C
Lo8          1     0                 13         1      P2P   0/0
Se0/0/1      1     0                 7          64     P2P   1/1
Se0/0/0      1     0                 6          64     P2P   1/1
```

e. Assign the loopback interfaces on R3 to participate in OSPFv3 area 2 and change the network type to point-to-point. Assign the serial interface to participate in OSPFv3 area 0. Write the commands used in the space below.

____

____

____

____

____

____

____

____

f.   Use the **show ipv6 ospf** command to verify configurations.

```
R3# show ipv6 ospf
Routing Process "ospfv3 1" with ID 3.3.3.3
Event-log enabled, Maximum number of events: 1000, Mode: cyclic
It is an area border router
Router is not originating router-LSAs with maximum metric
Initial SPF schedule delay 5000 msecs
Minimum hold time between two consecutive SPFs 10000 msecs
Maximum wait time between two consecutive SPFs 10000 msecs
Minimum LSA interval 5 secs
Minimum LSA arrival 1000 msecs
LSA group pacing timer 240 secs
Interface flood pacing timer 33 msecs
Retransmission pacing timer 66 msecs
Number of external LSA 0. Checksum Sum 0x000000
Number of areas in this router is 2. 2 normal 0 stub 0 nssa
Graceful restart helper support enabled
Reference bandwidth unit is 100 mbps
RFC1583 compatibility enabled
    Area BACKBONE(0)
        Number of interfaces in this area is 1
        SPF algorithm executed 2 times
        Number of LSA 16. Checksum Sum 0x0929F8
        Number of DCbitless LSA 0
        Number of indication LSA 0
        Number of DoNotAge LSA 0
        Flood list length 0
    Area 2
        Number of interfaces in this area is 4
        SPF algorithm executed 2 times
        Number of LSA 13. Checksum Sum 0x048E3C
        Number of DCbitless LSA 0
        Number of indication LSA 0
        Number of DoNotAge LSA 0
        Flood list length 0
```

Step 3:   Verify OSPFv3 neighbors and routing information.

a.   Issue the **show ipv6 ospf neighbor** command on all routers to verify that each router is listing the correct routers as neighbors.

```
R1# show ipv6 ospf neighbor
```

```
        OSPFv3 Router with ID (1.1.1.1) (Process ID 1)


  Neighbor ID     Pri   State            Dead Time   Interface ID   Interface
  2.2.2.2          0    FULL/  -         00:00:39    6              Serial0/0/0
```

b. Issue the **show ipv6 route ospf** command on all routers to verify that each router has learned routes to all networks in the Addressing Table.

```
R1# show ipv6 route ospf

IPv6 Routing Table - default - 16 entries

Codes: C - Connected, L - Local, S - Static, U - Per-user Static route
       B - BGP, R - RIP, H - NHRP, I1 - ISIS L1
       I2 - ISIS L2, IA - ISIS interarea, IS - ISIS summary, D - EIGRP
       EX - EIGRP external, ND - ND Default, NDp - ND Prefix, DCE - Destination
       NDr - Redirect, O - OSPF Intra, OI - OSPF Inter, OE1 - OSPF ext 1
       OE2 - OSPF ext 2, ON1 - OSPF NSSA ext 1, ON2 - OSPF NSSA ext 2
OI   2001:DB8:ACAD:4::/64 [110/129]
        via FE80::2, Serial0/0/0
OI   2001:DB8:ACAD:5::/64 [110/129]
        via FE80::2, Serial0/0/0
OI   2001:DB8:ACAD:6::/64 [110/129]
        via FE80::2, Serial0/0/0
OI   2001:DB8:ACAD:7::/64 [110/129]
        via FE80::2, Serial0/0/0
O    2001:DB8:ACAD:8::/64 [110/65]
        via FE80::2, Serial0/0/0
O    2001:DB8:ACAD:23::/64 [110/128]
        via FE80::2, Serial0/0/0
```

What is the significance of an OI route?

____

c. Issue the **show ipv6 ospf database** command on all routers.

```
R1# show ipv6 ospf database


        OSPFv3 Router with ID (1.1.1.1) (Process ID 1)


            Router Link States (Area 0)


  ADV Router      Age       Seq#          Fragment ID  Link count  Bits
  1.1.1.1         908       0x80000001    0            1           B
  2.2.2.2         898       0x80000003    0            2           None
  3.3.3.3         899       0x80000001    0            1           B
```

Inter Area Prefix Link States (Area 0)

ADV Router	Age	Seq#	Prefix
1.1.1.1	907	0x80000001	2001:DB8:ACAD::/62
3.3.3.3	898	0x80000001	2001:DB8:ACAD:4::/62

Link (Type-8) Link States (Area 0)

ADV Router	Age	Seq#	Link ID	Interface
1.1.1.1	908	0x80000001	6	Se0/0/0
2.2.2.2	909	0x80000002	6	Se0/0/0

Intra Area Prefix Link States (Area 0)

ADV Router	Age	Seq#	Link ID	Ref-lstype	Ref-LSID
1.1.1.1	908	0x80000001	0	0x2001	0
2.2.2.2	898	0x80000003	0	0x2001	0
3.3.3.3	899	0x80000001	0	0x2001	0

Router Link States (Area 1)

ADV Router	Age	Seq#	Fragment ID	Link count	Bits
1.1.1.1	908	0x80000001	0	0	B

Inter Area Prefix Link States (Area 1)

ADV Router	Age	Seq#	Prefix
1.1.1.1	907	0x80000001	2001:DB8:ACAD:12::/64
1.1.1.1	907	0x80000001	2001:DB8:ACAD:8::/64
1.1.1.1	888	0x80000001	2001:DB8:ACAD:23::/64
1.1.1.1	888	0x80000001	2001:DB8:ACAD:4::/62

Link (Type-8) Link States (Area 1)

ADV Router	Age	Seq#	Link ID	Interface
1.1.1.1	908	0x80000001	13	Lo0
1.1.1.1	908	0x80000001	14	Lo1
1.1.1.1	908	0x80000001	15	Lo2
1.1.1.1	908	0x80000001	16	Lo3

Intra Area Prefix Link States (Area 1)

```
ADV Router        Age         Seq#         Link ID     Ref-lstype   Ref-LSID
  1.1.1.1         908         0x80000001   0           0x2001       0
```

How many link state databases are found on R1? ______

How many link state databases are found on R2? ______

How many link state databases are found on R3? ______

Part 3:   **Configure Interarea Route Summarization**

In Part 3, you will manually configure interarea route summarization on the ABRs.

Step 1:   **Summarize networks on R1.**

    a.   List the network addresses for the loopback interfaces and identify the hextet section where the addresses differ.

        2001:DB8:ACAD:0000::1/64

        2001:DB8:ACAD:0001::1/64

        2001:DB8:ACAD:0002::1/64

        2001:DB8:ACAD:0003::1/64

    b.   Convert the differing section from hex to binary.

        2001:DB8:ACAD: 0000 0000 0000 0000::1/64

        2001:DB8:ACAD: 0000 0000 0000 0001::1/64

        2001:DB8:ACAD: 0000 0000 0000 0010::1/64

        2001:DB8:ACAD: 0000 0000 0000 0011::1/64

    c.   Count the number of leftmost matching bits to determine the prefix for the summary route.

        2001:DB8:ACAD: 0000 0000 0000 0000::1/64

        2001:DB8:ACAD: 0000 0000 0000 0001::1/64

        2001:DB8:ACAD: 0000 0000 0000 0010::1/64

        2001:DB8:ACAD: 0000 0000 0000 0011::1/64

        How many bits match? ______

    d.   Copy the matching bits and then add zero bits to determine the summarized network address.

        2001:DB8:ACAD: 0000 0000 0000 0000::0

    e.   Convert the binary section back to hex.

        2001:DB8:ACAD::

    f.   Append the prefix of the summary route (result of Step 1c).

        2001:DB8:ACAD::/62

Step 2:   Configure interarea route summarization on R1.

a. To manually configure interarea route summarization on R1, use the **area** *area-id* **range** *address mask* command.

```
R1(config)# ipv6 router ospf 1
R1(config-rtr)# area 1 range 2001:DB8:ACAD::/62
```

b. View the OSPFv3 routes on R3.

```
R3# show ipv6 route ospf
IPv6 Routing Table - default - 14 entries
Codes: C - Connected, L - Local, S - Static, U - Per-user Static route
       B - BGP, R - RIP, H - NHRP, I1 - ISIS L1
       I2 - ISIS L2, IA - ISIS interarea, IS - ISIS summary, D - EIGRP
       EX - EIGRP external, ND - ND Default, NDp - ND Prefix, DCE - Destination
       NDr - Redirect, O - OSPF Intra, OI - OSPF Inter, OE1 - OSPF ext 1
       OE2 - OSPF ext 2, ON1 - OSPF NSSA ext 1, ON2 - OSPF NSSA ext 2
OI  2001:DB8:ACAD::/62 [110/129]
      via FE80::2, Serial0/0/1
O   2001:DB8:ACAD:8::/64 [110/65]
      via FE80::2, Serial0/0/1
O   2001:DB8:ACAD:12::/64 [110/128]
      via FE80::2, Serial0/0/1
```

Compare this output to the output from Part 2, Step 3b. How are the networks in area 1 now expressed in the routing table on R3?

____

c. View the OSPFv3 routes on R1.

```
R1# show ipv6 route ospf
IPv6 Routing Table - default - 18 entries
Codes: C - Connected, L - Local, S - Static, U - Per-user Static route
       B - BGP, R - RIP, H - NHRP, I1 - ISIS L1
       I2 - ISIS L2, IA - ISIS interarea, IS - ISIS summary, D - EIGRP
       EX - EIGRP external, ND - ND Default, NDp - ND Prefix, DCE - Destination
       NDr - Redirect, O - OSPF Intra, OI - OSPF Inter, OE1 - OSPF ext 1
       OE2 - OSPF ext 2, ON1 - OSPF NSSA ext 1, ON2 - OSPF NSSA ext 2
O   2001:DB8:ACAD::/62 [110/1]
      via Null0, directly connected
OI  2001:DB8:ACAD:4::/64 [110/129]
      via FE80::2, Serial0/0/0
OI  2001:DB8:ACAD:5::/64 [110/129]
      via FE80::2, Serial0/0/0
OI  2001:DB8:ACAD:6::/64 [110/129]
```

```
          via FE80::2, Serial0/0/0
OI   2001:DB8:ACAD:7::/64 [110/129]
          via FE80::2, Serial0/0/0
O    2001:DB8:ACAD:8::/64 [110/65]
          via FE80::2, Serial0/0/0
O    2001:DB8:ACAD:23::/64 [110/128]
          via FE80::2, Serial0/0/0
```

Compare this output to the output from Part 2, Step 3b. How are the summarized networks expressed in the routing table on R1?

____

Step 3:   **Summarize networks and configure interarea route summarization on R3.**

  a.   Summarize the loopback interfaces on R3.

    1)   List the network addresses and identify the hextet section where the addresses differ.

    2)   Convert the differing section from hex to binary.

    3)   Count the number of left-most matching bits to determine the prefix for the summary route.

    4)   Copy the matching bits and then add zero bits to determine the summarized network address.

    5)   Convert the binary section back to hex.

    6)   Append the prefix of the summary route.

    7)   Write the summary address in the space provided.

____

  b.   Manually configure interarea route summarization on R3. Write the commands in the space provided.

____

  c.   Verify that area 2 routes are summarized on R1. What command was used?

____

  d.   Record the routing table entry on R1 for the summarized route advertised from R3.

____

Reflection

1. Why would multiarea OSPFv3 be used?

    ____

    ____

2. What is the benefit of configuring interarea route summarization?

    ____

    ____

Router Interface Summary Table

Router Interface Summary				
Router Model	**Ethernet Interface #1**	**Ethernet Interface #2**	**Serial Interface #1**	**Serial Interface #2**
1800	Fast Ethernet 0/0 (F0/0)	Fast Ethernet 0/1 (F0/1)	Serial 0/0/0 (S0/0/0)	Serial 0/0/1 (S0/0/1)
1900	Gigabit Ethernet 0/0 (G0/0)	Gigabit Ethernet 0/1 (G0/1)	Serial 0/0/0 (S0/0/0)	Serial 0/0/1 (S0/0/1)
2801	Fast Ethernet 0/0 (F0/0)	Fast Ethernet 0/1 (F0/1)	Serial 0/1/0 (S0/1/0)	Serial 0/1/1 (S0/1/1)
2811	Fast Ethernet 0/0 (F0/0)	Fast Ethernet 0/1 (F0/1)	Serial 0/0/0 (S0/0/0)	Serial 0/0/1 (S0/0/1)
2900	Gigabit Ethernet 0/0 (G0/0)	Gigabit Ethernet 0/1 (G0/1)	Serial 0/0/0 (S0/0/0)	Serial 0/0/1 (S0/0/1)

Note: To find out how the router is configured, look at the interfaces to identify the type of router and how many interfaces the router has. There is no way to effectively list all the combinations of configurations for each router class. This table includes identifiers for the possible combinations of Ethernet and Serial interfaces in the device. The table does not include any other type of interface, even though a specific router may contain one. An example of this might be an ISDN BRI interface. The string in parenthesis is the legal abbreviation that can be used in Cisco IOS commands to represent the interface.

8.2.3.10 Lab – Troubleshooting Multiarea OSPFv2 and OSPFv3

Topology

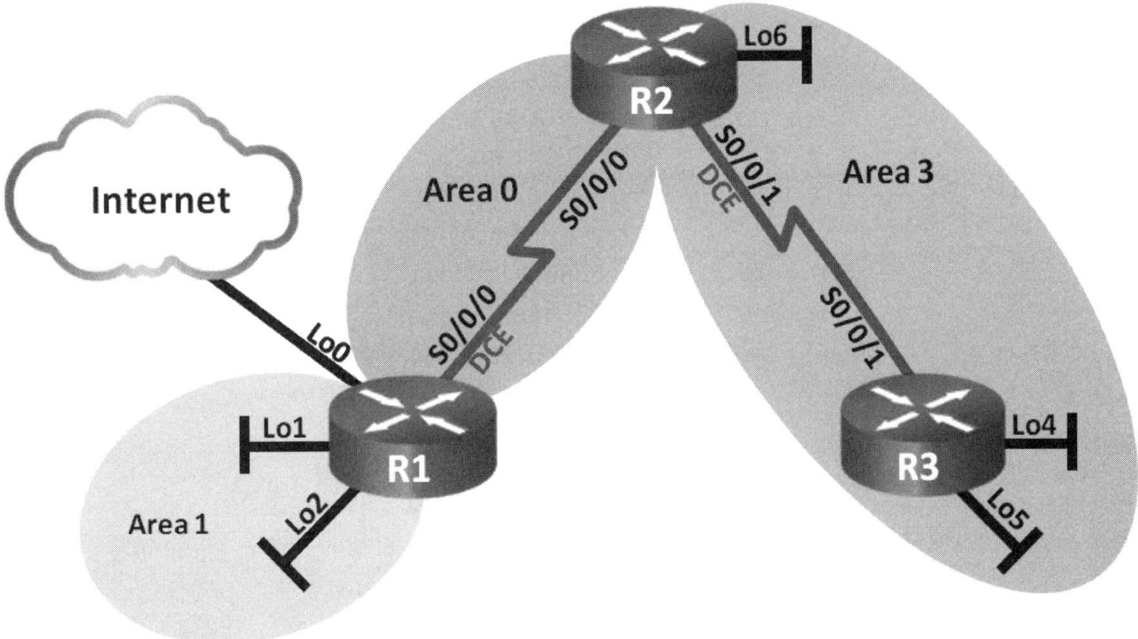

Addressing Table

Device	Interface	IP Address
R1	Lo0	209.165.200.225/30
	Lo1	192.168.1.1/24 2001:DB8:ACAD:1::1/64 FE80::1 link-local
	Lo2	192.168.2.1/24 2001:DB8:ACAD:2::1/64 FE80::1 link-local
	S0/0/0 (DCE)	192.168.12.1/30 2001:DB8:ACAD:12::1/64 FE80::1 link-local
R2	S0/0/0	192.168.12.2/30 2001:DB8:ACAD:12::2/64 FE80::2 link-local
	S0/0/1 (DCE)	192.168.23.2/30 2001:DB8:ACAD:23::2/64 FE80::2 link-local
	Lo6	192.168.6.1/24 2001:DB8:ACAD:6::1/64 FE80::2 link-local
R3	Lo4	192.168.4.1/24 2001:DB8:ACAD:4::1/64 FE80::3 link-local
	Lo5	192.168.5.1/24 2001:DB8:ACAD:5::1/64 FE80::3 link-local
	S0/0/1	192.168.23.1/30 2001:DB8:ACAD:23::1/64 FE80::3 link-local

Objectives

Part 1: Build the Network and Load Device Configurations

Part 2: Troubleshoot Layer 3 Connectivity

Part 3: Troubleshoot OSPFv2

Part 4: Troubleshoot OSPFv3

Background / Scenario

Open Shortest Path First (OSPF) is an open-standard link-state routing protocol for IP networks. OSPFv2 is defined for IPv4 networks, while OSPFv3 is defined for IPv6 networks. OSPFv2 and OSPFv3 are completely isolated routing protocols, meaning changes in OSPFv2 do not affect OSPFv3 routing, and vice versa.

In this lab, a multiarea OSPF network running OSPFv2 and OSPFv3 is experiencing problems. You have been assigned to find the problems with the network and correct them.

Note: The routers used with CCNA hands-on labs are Cisco 1941 Integrated Services Routers (ISRs) with Cisco IOS Release 15.2(4)M3 (universalk9 image). Other routers and Cisco IOS versions can be used. Depending on the model and Cisco IOS version, the commands available and output produced might vary from what is shown in the labs. Refer to the Router Interface Summary Table at the end of this lab for the correct interface identifiers.

Note: Make sure that the routers have been erased and have no startup configurations. If you are unsure, contact your instructor.

Required Resources

- 3 Routers (Cisco 1941 with Cisco IOS Release 15.2(4)M3 universal image or comparable)
- Console cables to configure the Cisco IOS devices via the console ports
- Serial cables as shown in the topology

Part 1: Build the Network and Load Device Configurations

Step 1: Cable the network as shown in the topology.

Step 2: Load router configuration files.

Load the following configurations into the appropriate router. All routers have the same passwords. The enable password is **class**, and the line password is **cisco**.

Router R1 Configuration:

```
enable
conf t
hostname R1
enable secret class
ipv6 unicast-routing
no ip domain lookup
interface Loopback0
 ip address 209.165.200.225 255.255.255.252
interface Loopback1
 ip address 192.168.1.1 255.255.255.0
 ipv6 address 2001:DB80:ACAD:1::1/64



 ipv6 ospf network point-to-point
interface Loopback2
 ip address 192.168.2.1 255.255.255.0
 ipv6 address 2001:DB8:ACAD:2::1/64
 ipv6 ospf 1 area 1
 ipv6 ospf network point-to-point
```

```
interface Serial0/0/0
  ip address 192.168.21.1 255.255.255.252

  ipv6 address FE80::1 link-local
  ipv6 address 2001:DB8:ACAD:12::1/64
  ipv6 ospf 1 area 0
  clock rate 128000
  shutdown

router ospf 1
  router-id 1.1.1.1
  passive-interface Loopback1
  passive-interface Loopback2

  network 192.168.2.0 0.0.0.255 area 1
  network 192.168.12.0 0.0.0.3 area 0
  default-information originate
ipv6 router ospf 1

  area 1 range 2001:DB8:ACAD::/61

ip route 0.0.0.0 0.0.0.0 Loopback0
banner motd @
  Unauthorized Access is Prohibited! @
line con 0
 password cisco
 logging synchronous
 login
line vty 0 4
 password cisco
 logging synchronous
 login
 transport input all
end
```

Router R2 Configuration:

```
enable
conf t
hostname R2
ipv6 unicast-routing
no ip domain lookup
```

```
enable secret class
interface Loopback6
 ip address 192.168.6.1 255.255.255.0
 ipv6 address 2001:DB8:CAD:6::1/64


interface Serial0/0/0
 ip address 192.168.12.2 255.255.255.252
 ipv6 address FE80::2 link-local
 ipv6 address 2001:DB8:ACAD:12::2/64
 ipv6 ospf 1 area 0
 no shutdown
interface Serial0/0/1
 ip address 192.168.23.2 255.255.255.252
 ipv6 address FE80::2 link-local
 ipv6 address 2001:DB8:ACAD:23::2/64
 ipv6 ospf 1 area 3
 clock rate 128000
 no shutdown
router ospf 1
 router-id 2.2.2.2
 passive-interface Loopback6
 network 192.168.6.0 0.0.0.255 area 3
 network 192.168.12.0 0.0.0.3 area 0
 network 192.168.23.0 0.0.0.3 area 3
ipv6 router ospf 1
 router-id 2.2.2.2
banner motd @
  Unauthorized Access is Prohibited! @
line con 0
 password cisco
 logging synchronous
 login
line vty 0 4
 password cisco
 logging synchronous
 login
 transport input all
end
```

Router R3 Configuration:

```
enable
conf t
hostname R3
no ip domain lookup
ipv6 unicast-routing
enable secret class
interface Loopback4
 ip address 192.168.4.1 255.255.255.0
 ipv6 address 2001:DB8:ACAD:4::1/64
 ipv6 ospf 1 area 3
interface Loopback5
 ip address 192.168.5.1 255.255.255.0
 ipv6 address 2001:DB8:ACAD:5::1/64
 ipv6 ospf 1 area 3
interface Serial0/0/1
 ip address 192.168.23.1 255.255.255.252
 ipv6 address FE80::3 link-local
 ipv6 address 2001:DB8:ACAD:23::1/64
 ipv6 ospf 1 area 3
 no shutdown
router ospf 1
 router-id 3.3.3.3
 passive-interface Loopback4
 passive-interface Loopback5
 network 192.168.4.0 0.0.0.255 area 3
 network 192.168.5.0 0.0.0.255 area 3

ipv6 router ospf 1
 router-id 3.3.3.3
banner motd @
  Unauthorized Access is Prohibited! @
line con 0
 password cisco
 logging synchronous
 login
line vty 0 4
 password cisco
 logging synchronous
 login
 transport input all
end
```

Step 3:   **Save your configuration.**

Part 2:   **Troubleshoot Layer 3 Connectivity**

In Part 2, you will verify that Layer 3 connectivity is established on all interfaces. You will need to test both IPv4 and IPv6 connectivity for all device interfaces.

Step 1:   **Verify the interfaces listed in the Addressing Table are active and configured with correct IP address information.**

    a.   Issue the **show ip interface brief** command on all three routers to verify that the interfaces are in an up/up state.

    b.   Issue the **show run | section interface** command to view all the commands related to interfaces.

c.   Resolve all problems found. Record the commands used to correct the configuration.

____

____

____

____

____

____

____

d.   Using the **ping** command, verify that IPv4 and IPv6 connectivity has been established on all directly connected router interfaces. If problems still exist, continue troubleshooting Layer 3 issues.

Part 3:   Troubleshoot OSPFv2

Note: LAN (loopback) interfaces should not advertise OSPF routing information, but routes to these networks
should be contained in the routing tables.

Step 1:   Test IPv4 end-to-end connectivity.

From each router, ping all interfaces on the other routers. Record your results below as IPv4 OSPFv2 connectivity problems do exist.

____

____

____

____

Step 2:   Verify that all interfaces are assigned to the proper OSPFv2 areas on R1.

a.   Issue the **show ip protocols** command to verify that OSPF is running and that all networks are being
advertised in the correct areas. Verify that the router ID is set correctly, as well for OSPF.

b.   If required, make the necessary changes needed to the configuration on R1 based on the output from the **show ip protocols** command. Record the commands used to correct the configuration.

____

____

____

c.   If required, re-issue the **show ip protocols** command to verify that your changes had the desired effect.

d.   Issue the **show ip ospf interface brief** command to verify that the serial interface and loopback interfaces 1 and 2 are listed as OSPF networks assigned to their respective areas.

e.   Resolve any problems discovered on R1 for OSPFv2.

Step 3:   **Verify that all interfaces are assigned to the proper OSPFv2 areas on R2.**

a.   Issue the **show ip protocols** command to verify that OSPF is running and that all networks are being advertised in their proper respective areas. Verify that the router ID is also set correctly.

b. If required, make any necessary changes to the configuration on R2 based on the output from the **show ip protocols** command. Record the commands used to correct the configuration.

____

____

____

c. If required, re-issue the **show ip protocols** command to verify that your changes had the desired effect.

d. Issue the **show ip ospf interface brief** command to verify that all interfaces are listed as OSPF networks assigned to their proper respective areas.

e. Resolve any problems discovered on R2 for OSPFv2.

Step 4:   Verify that all interfaces are assigned to the proper OSPFv2 areas on R3.

a. Issue the **show ip protocols** command to verify that OSPF is running and that all networks are being advertised in their respective areas. Verify that the router ID is also set correctly.

b. If required, make the necessary changes to the configuration on R3 based on the output from the **show ip protocols** command. Record the commands used to correct the configuration.

____

____

____

c. If required, re-issue the **show ip protocols** command to verify that your changes had the desired effect.

d. Issue the **show ip ospf interface brief** command to verify that all interfaces are listed as OSPF networks assigned to their proper areas.

e. Resolve any problems discovered on R3 for OSPFv2.

Step 5:   Verify OSPFv2 neighbor information.

Issue the **show ip ospf neighbor** command to verify that each router has all OSPFv2 neighbors listed.

Step 6:   Verify OSPFv2 routing information.

a. Issue the **show ip route ospf** command to verify that each router has all OSPFv2 routes in their respective routing tables.

b.   If any OSPFv2 routes are missing, troubleshoot and resolve the problems.

Step 7:   Verify IPv4 end-to-end connectivity.

From each router, ping all interfaces on other routers. If IPv4 end-to-end connectivity does not exist, then continue troubleshooting to resolve any remaining issues.

Part 4:   Troubleshoot OSPFv3

Note: LAN (loopback) interfaces should not advertise OSPFv3 routing information, but routes to these networks should be contained in the routing tables.

Step 1:   Test IPv6 end-to-end connectivity.

From each router, ping all interfaces on the other routers. Record your results as IPv6 connectivity problems do exist.

____

____

____

____

Step 2:   Verify that IPv6 unicast routing has been enabled on all routers.

a.   An easy way to verify that IPv6 routing has been enabled on a router is to use the **show run | section ipv6 unicast** command. By adding the pipe section to the **show run** command, the **ipv6 unicast-routing** command is displayed if IPv6 routing has been enabled.

b. If IPv6 unicast routing is not enabled on one or more routers, enable it now. If required, record the commands used to correct the configuration.

____

____

Step 3: Verify that all interfaces are assigned to the proper OSPFv3 areas on R1.

a. Issue the **show ipv6 protocols** command to verify that the router ID is correct and the expected interfaces display in their proper areas.

b. If required, make any necessary changes to the configuration on R1 based on the output from the **show ipv6 protocols** command. Record the commands used to correct the configuration. It may be necessary to reset OSPF process by issuing the **clear ipv6 ospf process** command.

____

____

____

c. Re-issue the **show ipv6 protocols** command on R1 to make sure changes took effect.

d. Enter the **show ipv6 route ospf** command on R1 to verify that the interarea route summarization is configured correctly.

```
R1# show ipv6 route ospf

IPv6 Routing Table - default - 12 entries

Codes: C - Connected, L - Local, S - Static, U - Per-user Static route

       B - BGP, R - RIP, I1 - ISIS L1, I2 - ISIS L2

       IA - ISIS interarea, IS - ISIS summary, D - EIGRP, EX - EIGRP external

       ND - ND Default, NDp - ND Prefix, DCE - Destination, NDr - Redirect

       O - OSPF Intra, OI - OSPF Inter, OE1 - OSPF ext 1, OE2 - OSPF ext 2

       ON1 - OSPF NSSA ext 1, ON2 - OSPF NSSA ext 2

O   2001:DB8:ACAD::/61 [110/1]

       via Null0, directly connected

OI  2001:DB8:ACAD:4::/64 [110/129]

       via FE80::2, Serial0/0/0

OI  2001:DB8:ACAD:5::/64 [110/129]

       via FE80::2, Serial0/0/0

OI  2001:DB8:ACAD:23::/64 [110/128]

       via FE80::2, Serial0/0/0
```

e. Which IPv6 networks are included in the interarea route summarization shown in the routing table?

____

____

f. If required, make the necessary configuration changes on R1. Record the commands used to correct the configuration.

____

____

g. If required, re-issue the **show ipv6 route ospf** command on R1 to verify the changes.

```
R1# show ipv6 route ospf

IPv6 Routing Table - default - 11 entries

Codes: C - Connected, L - Local, S - Static, U - Per-user Static route

       B - BGP, R - RIP, I1 - ISIS L1, I2 - ISIS L2

       IA - ISIS interarea, IS - ISIS summary, D - EIGRP, EX - EIGRP external

       ND - ND Default, NDp - ND Prefix, DCE - Destination, NDr - Redirect

       O - OSPF Intra, OI - OSPF Inter, OE1 - OSPF ext 1, OE2 - OSPF ext 2

       ON1 - OSPF NSSA ext 1, ON2 - OSPF NSSA ext 2

O   2001:DB8:ACAD::/62 [110/1]

       via Null0, directly connected

OI  2001:DB8:ACAD:4::1/128 [110/128]

       via FE80::2, Serial0/0/0

OI  2001:DB8:ACAD:5::1/128 [110/128]
```

```
    via FE80::2, Serial0/0/0
OI  2001:DB8:ACAD:23::/64 [110/128]
    via FE80::2, Serial0/0/0
```

Step 4: Verify that all interfaces are assigned to the proper OSPFv3 areas on R2.

a. Issue the **show ipv6 protocols** command and verify that the router ID is correct and that the expected interfaces are showing up under their proper areas.

b. If required, make any necessary changes to the configuration on R2 based on the output from the **show ipv6 protocols** command. Record the commands used to correct the configuration. It may be necessary to reset OSPF process by issuing the **clear ipv6 ospf process** command.

____

____

____

c. Verify that the configuration change has the desired effect.

Step 5: Verify that all interfaces are assigned to the proper OSPFv3 areas on R3.

a. Issue the **show ipv6 protocols** command to verify that the router ID is correct and the expected interfaces display under their respective areas.

b. If required, make any necessary changes to the configuration on R3 based on the output from the **show ipv6 protocols** command. Record the commands used to correct the configuration. It may be necessary to reset OSPF process by issuing the **clear ipv6 ospf process** command.

____

____

____

c. Verify that the configuration changes have the desired effect.

Step 6: Verify that all routers have correct neighbor adjacency information.

a. Issue the **show ipv6 ospf neighbor** command to verify that adjacencies have formed between neighboring routers.

Step 7: Verify OSPFv3 routing information.

a. Issue the **show ipv6 route ospf** command, and verify that OSPFv3 routes exist to all networks.

b. Resolve any routing issues that still exist.

Step 8: Verify IPv6 end-to-end connectivity.

From each router, ping all of the IPv6 interfaces on the other routers. If IPv6 end-to-end issues still exist, continue troubleshooting to resolve any remaining issues.

Reflection

Why not just use the **show running-config** command to resolve all issues?

____

Router Interface Summary Table

Router Interface Summary				
Router Model	**Ethernet Interface #1**	**Ethernet Interface #2**	**Serial Interface #1**	**Serial Interface #2**
1800	Fast Ethernet 0/0 (F0/0)	Fast Ethernet 0/1 (F0/1)	Serial 0/0/0 (S0/0/0)	Serial 0/0/1 (S0/0/1)
1900	Gigabit Ethernet 0/0 (G0/0)	Gigabit Ethernet 0/1 (G0/1)	Serial 0/0/0 (S0/0/0)	Serial 0/0/1 (S0/0/1)
2801	Fast Ethernet 0/0 (F0/0)	Fast Ethernet 0/1 (F0/1)	Serial 0/1/0 (S0/1/0)	Serial 0/1/1 (S0/1/1)
2811	Fast Ethernet 0/0 (F0/0)	Fast Ethernet 0/1 (F0/1)	Serial 0/0/0 (S0/0/0)	Serial 0/0/1 (S0/0/1)
2900	Gigabit Ethernet 0/0 (G0/0)	Gigabit Ethernet 0/1 (G0/1)	Serial 0/0/0 (S0/0/0)	Serial 0/0/1 (S0/0/1)
Note: To find out how the router is configured, look at the interfaces to identify the type of router and how many interfaces the router has. There is no way to effectively list all the combinations of configurations for each router class. This table includes identifiers for the possible combinations of Ethernet and Serial interfaces in the device. The table does not include any other type of interface, even though a specific router may contain one. An example of this might be an ISDN BRI interface. The string in parenthesis is the legal abbreviation that can be used in Cisco IOS commands to represent the interface.				

8.3.1.1 Class Activity – Digital Trolleys

Objective

Use CLI commands to verify operational status of a multiarea OSPF network.

Scenario

Your city has an aging digital trolley system based on a one-area design. All communications within this one area are taking longer to process as trolleys are being added to routes serving the population of your growing city. Trolley departures and arrivals are also taking a little longer, because each trolley must check large routing tables to determine where to pick up and deliver residents from their source and destination streets.

A concerned citizen has come up with the idea of dividing the city into different areas for a more efficient way to determine trolley routing information. It is thought that if the trolley maps are smaller, the system might be improved because of faster and smaller updates to the routing tables.

Your city board approves and implements the new area-based, digital trolley system. But to ensure the new area routes are more efficient, the city board needs data to show the results at the next open board meeting.

Complete the activity directions as stated below.

Save your work and explain the differences between the old, single area and new, multiarea system to another group or the entire class.

Required Resources

- Packet Tracer software
- Word processing software

Directions

Step 1:   **Map the single-area city trolley routing topology.**

    a.   Use Packet Tracer to map the old routing topology for the city. Cisco 1941 Integrated Services Routers (ISRs) are preferred.

    b.   Create a core area and place one of the routers in the core area.

    c.   Connect at least two routers to the core area router.

    d.   Choose to connect two more routers to the routers from Step 1c or create loopback addresses for the LAN interfaces on the routers from Step 1c.

    e.   Address the connected links or interfaces using IPv4 and VLSM.

    f.   Configure OSPF on each router for area 0 only.

    g.   Ping all routers to ensure full connectivity within the entire area.

Step 2:   **Map the multiarea city trolley routing topology.**

    a.   Use your cursor to highlight all devices from Step 1, and copy and paste them to another area of the Packet Tracer desktop.

    b.   Assign at least three areas to your topology. One must be the backbone (or core area) and the other two areas will be joined to the backbone area using current routers, which will now become area border routers.

c.   Configure the appropriate routers to their new area assignments. Remove old area configuration commands and assign new area commands to the appropriate interfaces.

d.   Save each router's changes as you make changes.

e.   When complete, you should have three areas represented on the topology and all routers should be able to ping each other throughout the network.

f.   Use the drawing tool and identify your areas by drawing circles or rectangles around the three areas.

g.   Save your work.

Step 3:   **Verify the network for city council members.**

a.   Use at least three commands learned (or used in this chapter) to help the city council prove that the new area, digital trolley routing topology works.

b.   Save a copy of topology graphics and verification commands comparisons in table format to a word processing file.

c.   Share your work with another group or the class. You may also want to add this activity and its files to a portfolio for this course.

Chapter 9 — Access Control Lists

9.0.1.2 Class Activity – Permit Me to Assist You

Objective

Explain the purpose and operation of ACLs.

Scenario

- Each individual in the class will record five questions they would ask a candidate who is applying for a security clearance for a network assistant position within a small- to medium-sized business. The list of questions should be listed in order of importance to selecting a good candidate for the job. The preferred answers will also be recorded.

- After three minutes of brainstorming the list of questions, the instructor will ask two students to serve as interviewers. These two students will use only their list of questions and answers for the next part of this activity. The instructor will explain to only the two interviewers that they have the discretion, at any time, to stop the process and state "you are all permitted to the next level of interviews" or "I am sorry, but you do not have the qualifications to continue to the next level of interviews." The interviewer does not need to complete all of the questions on the list.

- The rest of the class will be split in half and assigned to one of the interviewers.

- Once everyone is settled into their group with an interviewer, the group application interviews will begin.

- The two selected interviewers will ask the first question on the list that they created; an example would be "are you over the age of 18?" If the applicant does not meet the age requirement, as specified by the interviewer's original questions and answers, the applicant will be eliminated from the pool of applicants and must move to another area within the room where they will observe the rest of the application process.

The next question will then be asked by the interviewer. If applicants answer correctly, they may stay with the applicant group. The entire class will then get together and discuss their observations regarding the process to permit or deny them the opportunity to continue on to the next level of interviews.

Reflection

1. What factors did you consider when devising your list of criteria for network assistant security clearance?

2. How difficult was it to devise five security questions to deliver during the interviews? Why were you asked to list your questions in order of importance to selecting a good candidate?

3. Why would the process of elimination be stopped, even if there were still a few applicants available?

4. How could this scenario and the results be applied to network traffic?

9.2.2.7 Lab – Configuring and Verifying Standard ACLs

Topology

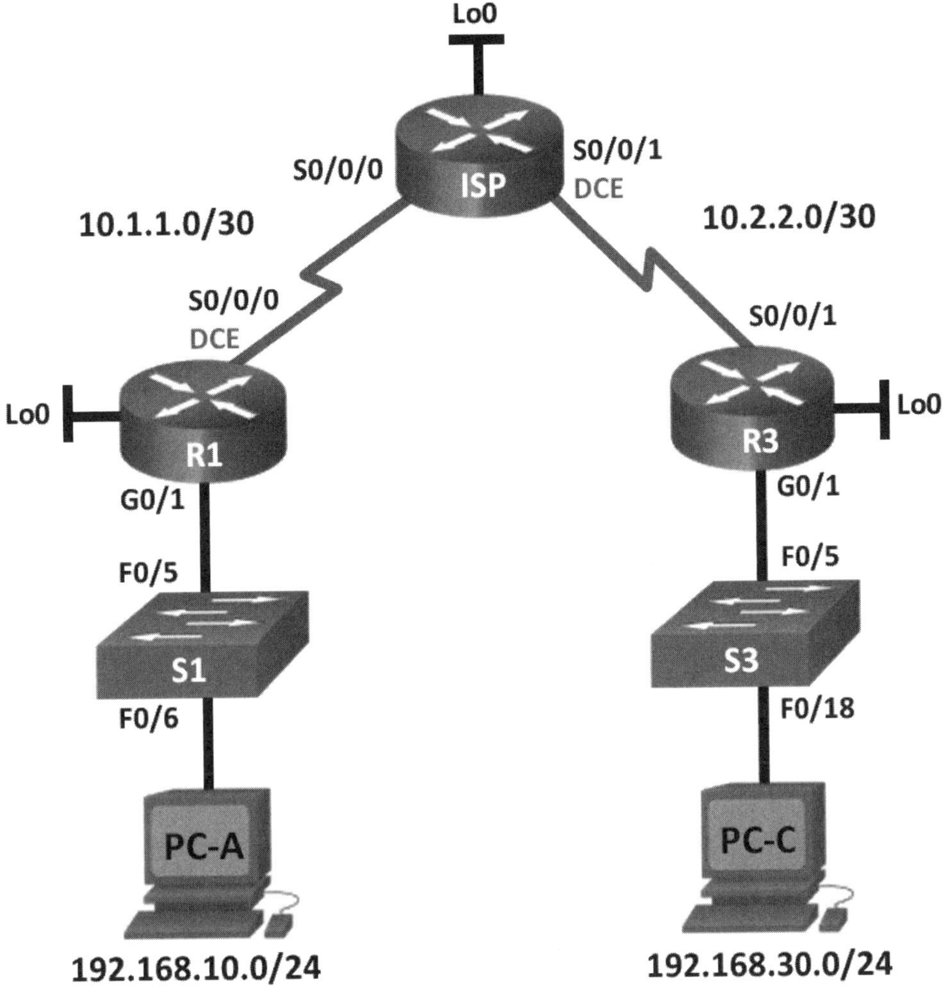

Addressing Table

Device	Interface	IP Address	Subnet Mask	Default Gateway
R1	G0/1	192.168.10.1	255.255.255.0	N/A
	Lo0	192.168.20.1	255.255.255.0	N/A
	S0/0/0 (DCE)	10.1.1.1	255.255.255.252	N/A
ISP	S0/0/0	10.1.1.2	255.255.255.252	N/A
	S0/0/1 (DCE)	10.2.2.2	255.255.255.252	N/A
	Lo0	209.165.200.225	255.255.255.224	N/A
R3	G0/1	192.168.30.1	255.255.255.0	N/A
	Lo0	192.168.40.1	255.255.255.0	N/A
	S0/0/1	10.2.2.1	255.255.255.252	N/A
S1	VLAN 1	192.168.10.11	255.255.255.0	192.168.10.1
S3	VLAN 1	192.168.30.11	255.255.255.0	192.168.30.1
PC-A	NIC	192.168.10.3	255.255.255.0	192.168.10.1
PC-C	NIC	192.168.30.3	255.255.255.0	192.168.30.1

Objectives

Part 1: Set Up the Topology and Initialize Devices

- Set up equipment to match the network topology.
- Initialize and reload the routers and switches.

Part 2: Configure Devices and Verify Connectivity

- Assign a static IP address to PCs.
- Configure basic settings on routers.
- Configure basic settings on switches.
- Configure EIGRP routing on R1, ISP, and R3.
- Verify connectivity between devices.

Part 3: Configure and Verify Standard Numbered and Named ACLs

- Configure, apply, and verify a numbered standard ACL.
- Configure, apply, and verify a named ACL.

Part 4: Modify a Standard ACL

- Modify and verify a named standard ACL.
- Test the ACL.

Background / Scenario

Network security is an important issue when designing and managing IP networks. The ability to configure proper rules to filter packets, based on established security policies, is a valuable skill.

In this lab, you will set up filtering rules for two offices represented by R1 and R3. Management has established some access policies between the LANs located at R1 and R3, which you must implement. The ISP router sitting between R1 and R3 will not have any ACLs placed on it. You would not be allowed any administrative access to an ISP router because you can only control and manage your own equipment.

Note: The routers used with CCNA hands-on labs are Cisco 1941 Integrated Services Routers (ISRs) with Cisco IOS Release 15.2(4)M3 (universalk9 image). The switches used are Cisco Catalyst 2960s with Cisco IOS Release 15.0(2) (lanbasek9 image). Other routers, switches, and Cisco IOS versions can be used. Depending on the model and Cisco IOS version, the commands available and output produced might vary from what is shown in the labs. Refer to the Router Interface Summary Table at the end of the lab for the correct interface identifiers.

Note: Make sure that the routers and switches have been erased and have no startup configurations. If you are unsure, contact your instructor.

Required Resources

- 3 Routers (Cisco 1941 with Cisco IOS Release 15.2(4)M3 universal image or comparable)
- 2 Switches (Cisco 2960 with Cisco IOS Release 15.0(2) lanbasek9 image or comparable)
- 2 PCs (Windows 7, Vista, or XP with terminal emulation program, such as Tera Term)
- Console cables to configure the Cisco IOS devices via the console ports
- Ethernet and serial cables as shown in the topology

Part 1: Set Up the Topology and Initialize Devices

In Part 1, you set up the network topology and clear any configurations, if necessary.

Step 1: Cable the network as shown in the topology.

Step 2: Initialize and reload the routers and switches.

Part 2: Configure Devices and Verify Connectivity

In Part 2, you configure basic settings on the routers, switches, and PCs. Refer to the Topology and Addressing Table for device names and address information.

Step 1: Configure IP addresses on PC-A and PC-C.

Step 2: Configure basic settings for the routers.

a. Disable DNS lookup.

b. Configure the device names as shown in the topology.

c. Create loopback interfaces on each router as shown in the Addressing Table.

d. Configure interface IP addresses as shown in the Topology and Addressing Table.

e. Configure a privileged EXEC mode password of **class**.

f. Assign a clock rate of **128000** to the DCE serial interfaces.

g. Assign **cisco** as the console password.

h. Assign **cisco** as the vty password and enable Telnet access.

Step 3:   (Optional) Configure basic settings on the switches.

a.   Disable DNS lookup.

b.   Configure the device names as shown in the topology.

c.   Configure the management interface IP address as shown in the Topology and Addressing Table.

d.   Configure a privileged EXEC mode password of **class**.

e.   Configure a default gateway.

f.   Assign **cisco** as the console password.

g.   Assign **cisco** as the vty password and enable Telnet access.

Step 4:   Configure EIGRP routing on R1, ISP, and R3.

a.   Configure autonomous system (AS) number 10 and advertise all networks on R1, ISP, and R3. Disable automatic summarization.

b.   After configuring EIGRP on R1, ISP, and R3, verify that all routers have complete routing tables listing all networks. Troubleshoot if this is not the case.

Step 5:   Verify connectivity between devices.

Note: It is very important to test whether connectivity is working **before** you configure and apply access lists! You want to ensure that your network is properly functioning before you start to filter traffic.

a.   From PC-A, ping PC-C and the loopback interface on R3. Were your pings successful? _________

b.   From R1, ping PC-C and the loopback interface on R3. Were your pings successful? _________

c.   From PC-C, ping PC-A and the loopback interface on R1. Were your pings successful? _________

d.   From R3, ping PC-A and the loopback interface on R1. Were your pings successful? _________

Part 3:   Configure and Verify Standard Numbered and Named ACLs

Step 1:   Configure a numbered standard ACL.

Standard ACLs filter traffic based on the source IP address only. A typical best practice for standard ACLs is to configure and apply it as close to the destination as possible. For the first access list, create a standard numbered ACL that allows traffic from all hosts on the 192.168.10.0/24 network and all hosts on the 192.168.20.0/24 network to access all hosts on the 192.168.30.0/24 network. The security policy also states that a **deny any** access control entry (ACE), also referred to as an ACL statement, should be present at the end of all ACLs.

What wildcard mask would you use to allow all hosts on the 192.168.10.0/24 network to access the 192.168.30.0/24 network?

____

Following Cisco's recommended best practices, on which router would you place this ACL? ____________

On which interface would you place this ACL? In what direction would you apply it?

---

a. Configure the ACL on R3. Use 1 for the access list number.

```
R3(config)# access-list 1 remark Allow R1 LANs Access
R3(config)# access-list 1 permit 192.168.10.0 0.0.0.255
R3(config)# access-list 1 permit 192.168.20.0 0.0.0.255
R3(config)# access-list 1 deny any
```

b. Apply the ACL to the appropriate interface in the proper direction.

```
R3(config)# interface g0/1
R3(config-if)# ip access-group 1 out
```

c. Verify a numbered ACL.

The use of various **show** commands can aid you in verifying both the syntax and placement of your ACLs in your router.

To see access list 1 in its entirety with all ACEs, which command would you use?

What command would you use to see where the access list was applied and in what direction?

---

1) On R3, issue the **show access-lists 1** command.

```
R3# show access-list 1
Standard IP access list 1
    10 permit 192.168.10.0, wildcard bits 0.0.0.255
    20 permit 192.168.20.0, wildcard bits 0.0.0.255
    30 deny    any
```

2) On R3, issue the **show ip interface g0/1** command.

```
R3# show ip interface g0/1
GigabitEthernet0/1 is up, line protocol is up
  Internet address is 192.168.30.1/24
  Broadcast address is 255.255.255.255
  Address determined by non-volatile memory
  MTU is 1500 bytes
  Helper address is not set
  Directed broadcast forwarding is disabled
  Multicast reserved groups joined: 224.0.0.10
  Outgoing access list is 1
  Inbound access list is not set
  Output omitted
```

3) Test the ACL to see if it allows traffic from the 192.168.10.0/24 network access to the 192.168.30.0/24 network. From the PC-A command prompt, ping the PC-C IP address. Were the pings successful? ________

4) Test the ACL to see if it allows traffic from the 192.168.20.0/24 network access to the 192.168.30.0/24 network. You must do an extended ping and use the loopback 0 address on R1 as your source. Ping PC-C's IP address. Were the pings successful? ________

```
R1# ping

Protocol [ip]:

Target IP address: 192.168.30.3

Repeat count [5]:

Datagram size [100]:

Timeout in seconds [2]:

Extended commands [n]: y

Source address or interface: 192.168.20.1

Type of service [0]:

Set DF bit in IP header? [no]:

Validate reply data? [no]:

Data pattern [0xABCD]:

Loose, Strict, Record, Timestamp, Verbose[none]:

Sweep range of sizes [n]:

Type escape sequence to abort.

Sending 5, 100-byte ICMP Echos to 192.168.30.3, timeout is 2 seconds:

Packet sent with a source address of 192.168.20.1

!!!!!

Success rate is 100 percent (5/5), round-trip min/avg/max = 28/29/32 ms
```

d. From the R1 prompt, ping PC-C's IP address again.

```
R1# ping 192.168.3.3
```

Was the ping successful? Why or why not?

____

____

____

Step 2: Configure a named standard ACL.

Create a named standard ACL that conforms to the following policy: allow traffic from all hosts on the 192.168.40.0/24 network access to all hosts on the 192.168.10.0/24 network. Also, only allow host PC-C access to the 192.168.10.0/24 network. The name of this access list should be called BRANCH-OFFICE-POLICY.

Following Cisco's recommended best practices, on which router would you place this ACL? ____________

On which interface would you place this ACL? In what direction would you apply it?

a. Create the standard named ACL BRANCH-OFFICE-POLICY on R1.

```
R1(config)# ip access-list standard BRANCH-OFFICE-POLICY
R1(config-std-nacl)# permit host 192.168.30.3
R1(config-std-nacl)# permit 192.168.40.0 0.0.0.255
R1(config-std-nacl)# end
R1#
*Feb 15 15:56:55.707: %SYS-5-CONFIG_I: Configured from console by console
```

Looking at the first permit ACE in the access list, what is another way to write this?

b. Apply the ACL to the appropriate interface in the proper direction.

```
R1# config t
R1(config)# interface g0/1
R1(config-if)# ip access-group BRANCH-OFFICE-POLICY out
```

c. Verify a named ACL.

1) On R1, issue the **show access-lists** command.

```
R1# show access-lists
Standard IP access list BRANCH-OFFICE-POLICY
    10 permit 192.168.30.3
    20 permit 192.168.40.0, wildcard bits 0.0.0.255
```

Is there any difference between this ACL on R1 with the ACL on R3? If so, what is it?

2) On R1, issue the **show ip interface g0/1** command.

```
R1# show ip interface g0/1
GigabitEthernet0/1 is up, line protocol is up
   Internet address is 192.168.10.1/24
   Broadcast address is 255.255.255.255
   Address determined by non-volatile memory
   MTU is 1500 bytes
   Helper address is not set
   Directed broadcast forwarding is disabled
   Multicast reserved groups joined: 224.0.0.10
   Outgoing access list is BRANCH-OFFICE-POLICY
   Inbound access list is not set
<Output omitted>
```

3) Test the ACL. From the command prompt on PC-C, ping PC-A's IP address. Were the pings success-
    ful? _______

4) Test the ACL to ensure that only the PC-C host is allowed access to the 192.168.10.0/24 network.
    You must do an extended ping and use the G0/1 address on R3 as your source. Ping PC-A's IP ad-
    dress. Were the pings successful? _______

5) Test the ACL to see if it allows traffic from the 192.168.40.0/24 network access to the 192.168.10.0/24 network. You must perform an extended ping and use the loopback 0 address on R3 as your source. Ping PC-A's IP address. Were the pings successful? ________

Part 4: **Modify a Standard ACL**

It is common in business for security policies to change. For this reason, ACLs may need to be modified. In Part 4, you will change one of the previous ACLs you configured, to match a new management policy being put in place.

Management has decided that users from the 209.165.200.224/27 network should be allowed full access to the 192.168.10.0/24 network. Management also wants ACLs on all of their routers to follow consistent rules. A **deny any** ACE should be placed at the end of all ACLs. You must modify the BRANCH-OFFICE-POLICY ACL.

You will add two additional lines to this ACL. There are two ways you could do this:

OPTION 1: Issue a **no ip access-list standard BRANCH-OFFICE-POLICY** command in global configuration mode. This would effectively take the whole ACL out of the router. Depending upon the router IOS, one of the following scenarios would occur: all filtering of packets would be cancelled and all packets would be allowed through the router; or, because you did not take off the **ip access-group** command on the G0/1 interface, filtering is still in place. Regardless, when the ACL is gone, you could retype the whole ACL, or cut and paste it in from a text editor.

OPTION 2: You can modify ACLs in place by adding or deleting specific lines within the ACL itself. This can come in handy, especially with ACLs that have many lines of code. The retyping of the whole ACL or cutting and pasting can easily lead to errors. Modifying specific lines within the ACL is easily accomplished.

Note: For this lab, use Option 2.

Step 1:   Modify a named standard ACL.

a. From R1 privilege EXEC mode, issue a **show access-lists** command.

```
R1# show access-lists
Standard IP access list BRANCH-OFFICE-POLICY
    10 permit 192.168.30.3 (8 matches)
    20 permit 192.168.40.0, wildcard bits 0.0.0.255 (5 matches)
```

b. Add two additional lines at the end of the ACL. From global config mode, modify the ACL, BRANCH-OF-FICE-POLICY.

```
R1#(config)# ip access-list standard BRANCH-OFFICE-POLICY
R1(config-std-nacl)# 30 permit 209.165.200.224 0.0.0.31
R1(config-std-nacl)# 40 deny any
R1(config-std-nacl)# end
```

c. Verify the ACL.

1) On R1, issue the **show access-lists** command.

```
R1# show access-lists
Standard IP access list BRANCH-OFFICE-POLICY
    10 permit 192.168.30.3 (8 matches)
    20 permit 192.168.40.0, wildcard bits 0.0.0.255 (5 matches)
    30 permit 209.165.200.224, wildcard bits 0.0.0.31
    40 deny    any
```

Do you have to apply the BRANCH-OFFICE-POLICY to the G0/1 interface on R1?

____

____

2) From the ISP command prompt, issue an extended ping. Test the ACL to see if it allows traffic from the 209.165.200.224/27 network access to the 192.168.10.0/24 network. You must do an extended ping and use the loopback 0 address on ISP as your source. Ping PC-A's IP address. Were the pings successful? ________

Reflection

1. As you can see, standard ACLs are very powerful and work quite well. Why would you ever have the need for using extended ACLs?

2. Typically, more typing is required when using a named ACL as opposed to a numbered ACL. Why would you choose named ACLs over numbered?

Router Interface Summary Table

Router Interface Summary				
Router Model	**Ethernet Interface #1**	**Ethernet Interface #2**	**Serial Interface #1**	**Serial Interface #2**
1800	Fast Ethernet 0/0 (F0/0)	Fast Ethernet 0/1 (F0/1)	Serial 0/0/0 (S0/0/0)	Serial 0/0/1 (S0/0/1)
1900	Gigabit Ethernet 0/0 (G0/0)	Gigabit Ethernet 0/1 (G0/1)	Serial 0/0/0 (S0/0/0)	Serial 0/0/1 (S0/0/1)
2801	Fast Ethernet 0/0 (F0/0)	Fast Ethernet 0/1 (F0/1)	Serial 0/1/0 (S0/1/0)	Serial 0/1/1 (S0/1/1)
2811	Fast Ethernet 0/0 (F0/0)	Fast Ethernet 0/1 (F0/1)	Serial 0/0/0 (S0/0/0)	Serial 0/0/1 (S0/0/1)
2900	Gigabit Ethernet 0/0 (G0/0)	Gigabit Ethernet 0/1 (G0/1)	Serial 0/0/0 (S0/0/0)	Serial 0/0/1 (S0/0/1)

Note: To find out how the router is configured, look at the interfaces to identify the type of router and how many interfaces the router has. There is no way to effectively list all the combinations of configurations for each router class. This table includes identifiers for the possible combinations of Ethernet and Serial interfaces in the device. The table does not include any other type of interface, even though a specific router may contain one. An example of this might be an ISDN BRI interface. The string in parenthesis is the legal abbreviation that can be used in Cisco IOS commands to represent the interface.

9.2.3.4 Lab – Configuring and Verifying VTY Restrictions

Topology

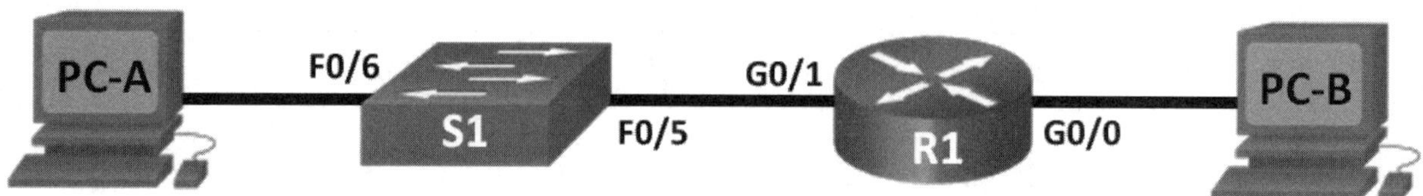

Addressing Table

Device	Interface	IP Address	Subnet Mask	Default Gateway
R1	G0/0	192.168.0.1	255.255.255.0	N/A
	G0/1	192.168.1.1	255.255.255.0	N/A
S1	VLAN 1	192.168.1.2	255.255.255.0	192.168.1.1
PC-A	NIC	192.168.1.3	255.255.255.0	192.168.1.1
PC-B	NIC	192.168.0.3	255.255.255.0	192.168.0.1

Objectives

Part 1: Configure Basic Device Settings

Part 2: Configure and Apply the Access Control List on R1

Part 3: Verify the Access Control List Using Telnet

Part 4: Challenge - Configure and Apply the Access Control List on S1

Background / Scenario

It is a good practice to restrict access to the router management interfaces, such as the console and vty lines. An access control list (ACL) can be used to allow access for specific IP addresses, ensuring that only the administrator PCs have permission to telnet or SSH into the router.

Note: In the Cisco device outputs, ACL are abbreviated as access-list.

In this lab, you will create and apply a named standard ACL to restrict remote access to the router vty lines.

After the ACL has been created and applied, you will test and verify the ACL by accessing the router from different IP addresses using Telnet.

This lab will provide the commands necessary for creating and applying the ACL.

Note: The routers used with CCNA hands-on labs are Cisco 1941 Integrated Services Routers (ISRs) with Cisco IOS Release 15.2(4)M3 (universalk9 image). The switches used are Cisco Catalyst 2960s with Cisco IOS Release 15.0(2) (lanbasek9 image). Other routers, switches, and Cisco IOS versions can be used. Depending on the model and Cisco IOS version, the commands available and output produced might vary from what is shown in the labs. Refer to the Router Interface Summary Table at the end of the lab for the correct interface identifiers.

Note: Make sure that the routers and switches have been erased and have no startup configurations. If you are unsure, contact your instructor.

Required Resources

- 1 Router (Cisco 1941 with Cisco IOS Release 15.2(4)M3 universal image or comparable)
- 1 Switch (Cisco 2960 with Cisco IOS Release 15.0(2) lanbasek9 image or comparable)
- 2 PCs (Windows 7, Vista, or XP with terminal emulation program, such as Tera Term)
- Console cables to configure the Cisco IOS devices via the console ports
- Ethernet cables as shown in the topology

Note: The Gigabit Ethernet interfaces on Cisco 1941 routers are autosensing and an Ethernet straight-through cable may be used between the router and PC-B. If using another model Cisco router, it may be necessary to use an Ethernet crossover cable.

Part 1: Configure Basic Device Settings

In Part 1, you will set up the network topology and configure the interface IP addresses, device access, and passwords on the router.

Step 1: Cable the network as shown in the topology diagram.

Step 2: Configure the PC-A and PC-B network settings according to the Addressing Table.

Step 3: Initialize and reload the router and switch.

a. Disable DNS lookup.

b. Configure device names according to the Topology diagram.

c. Assign **class** as the privileged EXEC encrypted password.

d. Assign **cisco** as the console password, activate logging synchronous, and enable login.

e. Assign **cisco** as the vty password, activate logging synchronous, and enable login.

f. Encrypt the plain text passwords.

g. Create a banner that warns anyone accessing the device that unauthorized access is prohibited.

h. Configure IP addresses on the interfaces listed in the Addressing Table.

i. Configure the default gateway for the switch.

j. Save the running configuration to the startup configuration file.

Part 2: Configure and Apply the Access Control List on R1

In Part 2, you will configure a named standard ACL and apply it to the router virtual terminal lines to restrict remote access to the router.

Step 1:   **Configure and apply a standard named ACL.**

a.   Console into the router R1 and enable privileged EXEC mode.

b.   From global configuration mode, view the command options under **ip access-list** by using a space and a question mark.

```
R1(config)# ip access-list ?
  extended     Extended Access List
  helper       Access List acts on helper-address
  log-update   Control access list log updates
  logging      Control access list logging
  resequence   Resequence Access List
  standard     Standard Access List
```

c.   View the command options under **ip access-list standard** by using a space and a question mark.

```
R1(config)# ip access-list standard ?
  <1-99>       Standard IP access-list number
  <1300-1999>  Standard IP access-list number (expanded range)
  WORD         Access-list name
```

d.   Add **ADMIN-MGT** to the end of the **ip access-list standard** command and press Enter. You are now in the standard named access-list configuration mode (config-std-nacl).

```
R1(config)# ip access-list standard ADMIN-MGT
R1(config-std-nacl)#
```

e.   Enter your ACL permit or deny access control entry (ACE), also known as an ACL statement, one line at a time. Remember that there is an implicit **deny any** at the end of the ACL, which effectively denies all traffic. Enter a question mark to view your command options.

```
R1(config-std-nacl)# ?
Standard Access List configuration commands:
  <1-2147483647>  Sequence Number
  default         Set a command to its defaults
  deny            Specify packets to reject
  exit            Exit from access-list configuration mode
  no              Negate a command or set its defaults
  permit          Specify packets to forward
  remark          Access list entry comment
```

f.   Create a permit ACE for Administrator PC-A at 192.168.1.3, and an additional permit ACE to allow other reserved administrative IP addresses from 192.168.1.4 to 192.168.1.7. Notice how the first permit ACE signifies a single host, by using the **host** keyword, the ACE **permit 192.168.1.3 0.0.0.0** could have been used instead. The second permit ACE allows hosts 192.168.1.4 through 192.168.1.7, by using the 0.0.0.3 wildcard, which is the inverse of a 255.255.255.252 subnet mask.

```
R1(config-std-nacl)# permit host 192.168.1.3
R1(config-std-nacl)# permit 192.168.1.4 0.0.0.3
R1(config-std-nacl)# exit
```

You do not need to enter a deny ACE because there is an implicit **deny any** ACE at the end of the ACL.

g.   Now that the named ACL is created, apply it to the vty lines.

```
R1(config)# line vty 0 4
R1(config-line)# access-class ADMIN-MGT in
R1(config-line)# exit
```

Part 3:   Verify the Access Control List Using Telnet

In Part 3, you will use Telnet to access the router, verifying that the named ACL is functioning correctly.

Note: SSH is more secure than Telnet; however, SSH requires that the network device be configured to accept SSH connections. Telnet is used with this lab for convenience.

a.   Open a command prompt on PC-A and verify that you can communicate with the router by issuing a **ping** command.

```
C:\Users\user1> ping 192.168.1.1

Pinging 192.168.1.1 with 32 bytes of data:
Reply from 192.168.1.1: bytes=32 time=5ms TTL=64
Reply from 192.168.1.1: bytes=32 time=1ms TTL=64
Reply from 192.168.1.1: bytes=32 time=1ms TTL=64
Reply from 192.168.1.1: bytes=32 time=1ms TTL=64

Ping statistics for 192.168.1.1:
    Packets: Sent = 4, Received = 4, Lost = 0 (0% loss),
Approximate round trip times in milli-seconds:
    Minimum = 1ms, Maximum = 5ms, Average = 2ms
C:\Users\user1>
```

b.   Using the command prompt on PC-A, launch the Telnet client program to telnet into the router. Enter the login and then the enable passwords. You should be successfully logged in, see the banner message, and receive an R1 router command prompt.

```
C:\Users\user1> telnet 192.168.1.1

Unauthorized access is prohibited!

User Access Verification

Password:
R1>enable
Password:
R1#
```

Was the Telnet connection successful? ____

c.   Type **exit** at the command prompt and press Enter to exit the Telnet session.

d.   Change your IP address to test if the named ACL blocks non-permitted IP addresses. Change the IPv4 address to 192.168.1.100 on PC-A.

e.   Attempt to telnet into R1 at 192.168.1.1 again. Was the Telnet session successful?

What message was received? ____

f.   Change the IP address on PC-A to test if the named ACL permits a host with an IP address from the 192.168.1.4 to 192.168.1.7 range to telnet into the router. After changing the IP address on PC-A, open a Windows command prompt and attempt to telnet into router R1.

Was the Telnet session successful?

g.   From privileged EXEC mode on R1, type the **show ip access-lists** command and press Enter. From the command output, notice how the Cisco IOS automatically assigns line numbers to the ACL ACEs in increments of 10 and shows the number of times each permit ACE has been successfully matched (in parenthesis).

```
R1# show ip access-lists
Standard IP access list ADMIN-MGT
    10 permit 192.168.1.3 (2 matches)
    20 permit 192.168.1.4, wildcard bits 0.0.0.3 (2 matches)
```

Because two successful Telnet connections to the router were established, and each Telnet session was initiated from an IP address that matches one of the permit ACEs, there are matches for each permit ACE.

Why do you think that there are two matches for each permit ACE when only one connection from each IP address was initiated?

How would you determine at what point the Telnet protocol causes the two matches during the Telnet connection?

h. On R1, enter into global configuration mode.

i. Enter into access-list configuration mode for the ADMIN-MGT named access list and add a **deny any** ACE to the end of the access list.

```
R1(config)# ip access-list standard ADMIN-MGT

R1(config-std-nacl)# deny any

R1(config-std-nacl)# exit
```

Note: Because there is an implicit **deny any** ACE at the end of all ACLs, adding an explicit **deny any** ACE is unnecessary, yet can still be useful to the network administrator to log or simply know how many times the **deny any** access-list ACE was matched.

j. Try to telnet from PC-B to R1. This creates a match to the **deny any** ACE in the ADMIN-MGT named access list.

k. From privileged EXEC mode, type **show ip access-lists** command and press Enter. You should now see multiple matches to the **deny any** ACE.

```
R1# show ip access-lists

Standard IP access list ADMIN-MGT

     10 permit 192.168.1.3 (2 matches)

     20 permit 192.168.1.4, wildcard bits 0.0.0.3 (2 matches)

     30 deny any (3 matches)
```

The failed Telnet connection produces more matches to the explicit deny ACE than a successful one. Why do you think this happens?

____

____

Part 4:   Challenge - Configure and Apply the Access Control List on S1

Step 1:   Configure and apply a standard named ACL for the vty lines on S1.

a. Without referring back to the R1 configuration commands, try to configure the ACL on S1, allowing only the PC-A IP address.

b. Apply the ACL to the S1 vty lines. Remember that there are more vty lines on a switch than a router.

Step 2:   Test the vty ACL on S1.

Telnet from each of the PCs to verify that the vty ACL is working properly. You should be able to telnet to S1 from PC-A, but not from PC-B.

Reflection

1. As evidenced by the remote vty access, ACLs are powerful content filters that can be applied to more than just inbound and outbound network interfaces. It what other ways might ACLs be applied?

2. Does an ACL applied to a vty remote management interface improve the security of Telnet connection? Does this make Telnet a more viable remote access management tool?

3. Why does it make sense to apply an ACL to vty lines instead of specific interfaces?

Router Interface Summary Table

Router Interface Summary				
Router Model	Ethernet Interface #1	Ethernet Interface #2	Serial Interface #1	Serial Interface #2
1800	Fast Ethernet 0/0 (F0/0)	Fast Ethernet 0/1 (F0/1)	Serial 0/0/0 (S0/0/0)	Serial 0/0/1 (S0/0/1)
1900	Gigabit Ethernet 0/0 (G0/0)	Gigabit Ethernet 0/1 (G0/1)	Serial 0/0/0 (S0/0/0)	Serial 0/0/1 (S0/0/1)
2801	Fast Ethernet 0/0 (F0/0)	Fast Ethernet 0/1 (F0/1)	Serial 0/1/0 (S0/1/0)	Serial 0/1/1 (S0/1/1)
2811	Fast Ethernet 0/0 (F0/0)	Fast Ethernet 0/1 (F0/1)	Serial 0/0/0 (S0/0/0)	Serial 0/0/1 (S0/0/1)
2900	Gigabit Ethernet 0/0 (G0/0)	Gigabit Ethernet 0/1 (G0/1)	Serial 0/0/0 (S0/0/0)	Serial 0/0/1 (S0/0/1)

Note: To find out how the router is configured, look at the interfaces to identify the type of router and how many interfaces the router has. There is no way to effectively list all the combinations of configurations for each router class. This table includes identifiers for the possible combinations of Ethernet and Serial interfaces in the device. The table does not include any other type of interface, even though a specific router may contain one. An example of this might be an ISDN BRI interface. The string in parenthesis is the legal abbreviation that can be used in Cisco IOS commands to represent the interface.

9.3.2.13 Lab – Configuring and Verifying Extended ACLs

Topology

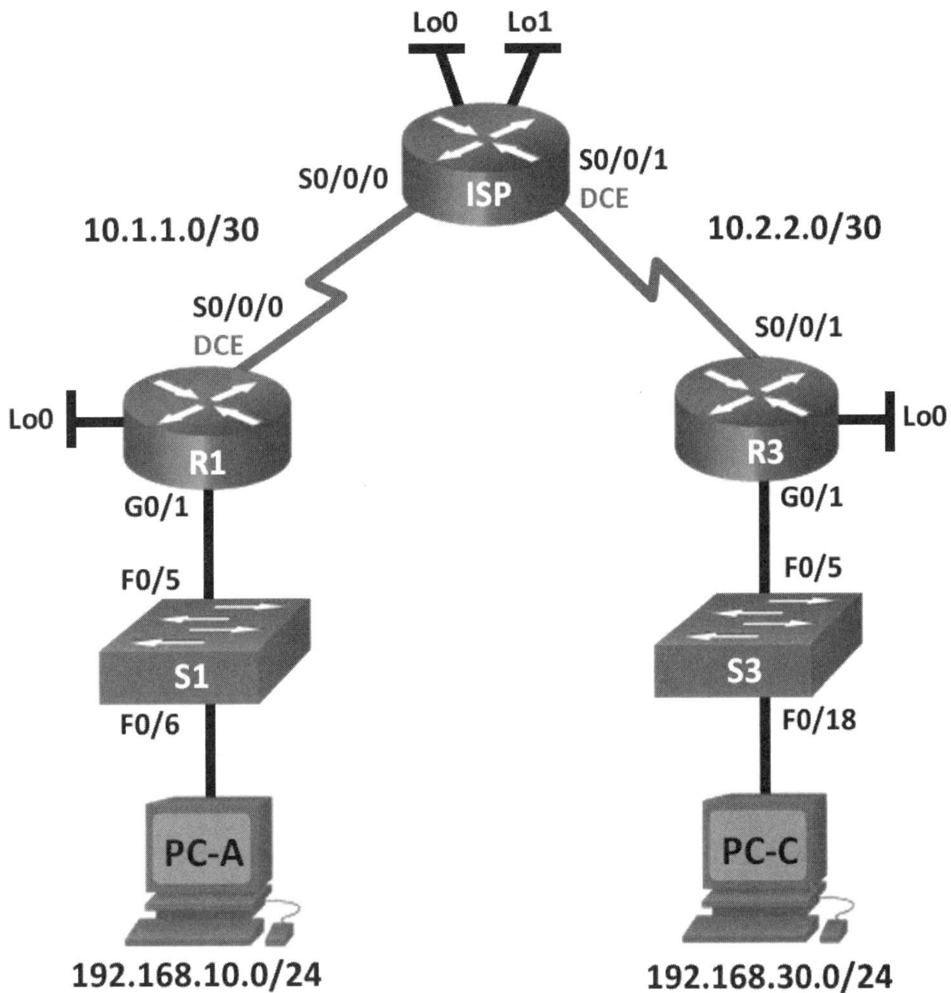

Addressing Table

Device	Interface	IP Address	Subnet Mask	Default Gateway
R1	G0/1	192.168.10.1	255.255.255.0	N/A
	Lo0	192.168.20.1	255.255.255.0	N/A
	S0/0/0 (DCE)	10.1.1.1	255.255.255.252	N/A
ISP	S0/0/0	10.1.1.2	255.255.255.252	N/A
	S0/0/1 (DCE)	10.2.2.2	255.255.255.252	N/A
	Lo0	209.165.200.225	255.255.255.224	N/A
	Lo1	209.165.201.1	255.255.255.224	N/A
R3	G0/1	192.168.30.1	255.255.255.0	N/A

	Lo0	192.168.40.1	255.255.255.0	N/A
	S0/0/1	10.2.2.1	255.255.255.252	N/A
S1	VLAN 1	192.168.10.11	255.255.255.0	192.168.10.1
S3	VLAN 1	192.168.30.11	255.255.255.0	192.168.30.1
PC-A	NIC	192.168.10.3	255.255.255.0	192.168.10.1
PC-C	NIC	192.168.30.3	255.255.255.0	192.168.30.1

Objectives

Part 1: Set Up the Topology and Initialize Devices

Part 2: Configure Devices and Verify Connectivity

- Configure basic settings on PCs, routers, and switches.

- Configure EIGRP routing on R1, ISP, and R3.

Part 3: Configure and Verify Extended Numbered and Named ACLs

- Configure, apply, and verify a numbered extended ACL.

- Configure, apply, and verify a named extended ACL.

Part 4: Modify and Verify Extended ACLs

Background / Scenario

Extended access control lists (ACLs) are extremely powerful. They offer a much greater degree of control than standard ACLs as to the types of traffic that can be filtered, as well as where the traffic originated and where it is going.

In this lab, you will set up filtering rules for two offices represented by R1 and R3. Management has established some access policies between the LANs located at R1 and R3, which you must implement. The ISP router between R1 and R3 does not have any ACLs placed on it. You would not be allowed any administrative access to an ISP router as you can only control and manage your own equipment.

Note: The routers used with CCNA hands-on labs are Cisco 1941 Integrated Services Routers (ISRs) with Cisco IOS Release 15.2(4)M3 (universalk9 image). The switches used are Cisco Catalyst 2960s with Cisco IOS Release 15.0(2) (lanbasek9 image). Other routers, switches, and Cisco IOS versions can be used. Depending on the model and Cisco IOS version, the commands available and output produced might vary from what is shown in the labs. Refer to the Router Interface Summary Table at the end of the lab for the correct interface identifiers.

Note: Make sure that the routers and switches have been erased and have no startup configurations. If you are unsure, contact your instructor.

Required Resources

- 3 Routers (Cisco 1941 with Cisco IOS Release 15.2(4)M3 universal image or comparable)

- 2 Switches (Cisco 2960 with Cisco IOS Release 15.0(2) lanbasek9 image or comparable)

- 2 PCs (Windows 7, Vista, or XP with terminal emulation program, such as Tera Term)

- Console cables to configure the Cisco IOS devices via the console ports

- Ethernet and serial cables as shown in the topology

Part 1:   Set Up the Topology and Initialize Devices

In Part 1, you will set up the network topology and clear any configurations if necessary.

Step 1:   Cable the network as shown in the topology.

Step 2:   Initialize and reload the routers and switches.

Part 2:   Configure Devices and Verify Connectivity

In Part 2, you will configure basic settings on the routers, switches, and PCs. Refer to the Topology and Addressing Table for device names and address information.

Step 1:   Configure IP addresses on PC-A and PC-C.

Step 2:   Configure basic settings on R1.

a.   Disable DNS lookup.

b.   Configure the device name as shown in the topology.

c.   Create a loopback interface on R1.

d.   Configure interface IP addresses as shown in the Topology and Addressing Table.

e.   Configure a privileged EXEC mode password of **class**.

f.   Assign a clock rate of **128000** to the S0/0/0 interface.

g.   Assign **cisco** as the console and vty password and enable Telnet access. Configure **logging synchronous** for both the console and vty lines.

h.   Enable web access on R1 to simulate a web server with local authentication for user **admin**.

```
R1(config)# ip http server
R1(config)# ip http authentication local
R1(config)# username admin privilege 15 secret class
```

Step 3:   Configure basic settings on ISP.

a.   Configure the device name as shown in the topology.

b.   Create the loopback interfaces on ISP.

c.   Configure interface IP addresses as shown in the Topology and Addressing Table.

d.   Disable DNS lookup.

e.   Assign **class** as the privileged EXEC mode password.

f.   Assign a clock rate of **128000** to the S0/0/1 interface.

g.   Assign **cisco** as the console and vty password and enable Telnet access. Configure **logging synchronous** for both console and vty lines.

h.   Enable web access on the ISP. Use the same parameters as in Step 2h.

Step 4:   Configure basic settings on R3.

a.   Configure the device name as shown in the topology.

b.   Create a loopback interface on R3.

c.   Configure interface IP addresses as shown in the Topology and Addressing Table.

d.   Disable DNS lookup.

e.   Assign **class** as the privileged EXEC mode password.

f.   Assign **cisco** as the console password and configure **logging synchronous** on the console line.

g.   Enable SSH on R3.

```
R3(config)# ip domain-name cisco.com
R3(config)# crypto key generate rsa modulus 1024
R3(config)# line vty 0 4
R3(config-line)# login local
R3(config-line)# transport input ssh
```

h.   Enable web access on R3. Use the same parameters as in Step 2h.

Step 5:   (Optional) Configure basic settings on S1 and S3.

a.   Configure the hostnames as shown in the topology.

b.   Configure the management interface IP addresses as shown in the Topology and Addressing Table.

c.   Disable DNS lookup.

d.   Configure a privileged EXEC mode password of **class**.

e.   Configure a default gateway address.

Step 6:   Configure EIGRP routing on R1, ISP, and R3.

a.   Configure autonomous system (AS) number 10 and advertise all networks on R1, ISP, and R3. Disable automatic summarization.

b.   After configuring EIGRP on R1, ISP, and R3, verify that all routers have complete routing tables listing all networks. Troubleshoot if this is not the case.

Step 7:   Verify connectivity between devices.

Note: It is very important to verify connectivity **before** you configure and apply ACLs! Ensure that your network is properly functioning before you start to filter out traffic.

a.   From PC-A, ping PC-C and the loopback and serial interfaces on R3.

Were your pings successful? _________

b. From R1, ping PC-C and the loopback and serial interface on R3.

   Were your pings successful? _________

c. From PC-C, ping PC-A and the loopback and serial interface on R1.

   Were your pings successful? _________

d. From R3, ping PC-A and the loopback and serial interface on R1.

   Were your pings successful? _________

e. From PC-A, ping the loopback interfaces on the ISP router.

   Were your pings successful? _________

f. From PC-C, ping the loopback interfaces on the ISP router.

   Were your pings successful? _________

g. Open a web browser on PC-A and go to http://209.165.200.225 on ISP. You will be prompted for a user-name and password. Use **admin** for the username and **class** for the password. If you are prompted to accept a signature, accept it. The router will load the Cisco Configuration Professional (CCP) Express in a separate window. You may be prompted for a username and password. Use **admin** for the username and **class** for the password.

h. Open a web browser on PC-C and go to http://10.1.1.1 on R1. You will be prompted for a username and password. Use **admin** for username and **class** for the password. If you are prompted to accept a sig-nature, accept it. The router will load CCP Express in a separate window. You may be prompted for a username and password. Use **admin** for the username and **class** for the password.

Part 3:   Configure and Verify Extended Numbered and Named ACLs

Extended ACLs can filter traffic in many different ways. Extended ACLs can filter on source IP addresses, source ports, destination IP addresses, destination ports, as well as various protocols and services.

Security policies are as follows:

1. Allow web traffic originating from the 192.168.10.0/24 network to go to any network.

2. Allow an SSH connection to the R3 serial interface from PC-A.

3. Allow users on 192.168.10.0.24 network access to 192.168.20.0/24 network.

4. Allow web traffic originating from the 192.168.30.0/24 network to access R1 via the web interface and the 209.165.200.224/27 network on ISP. The 192.168.30.0/24 network should NOT be allowed to access any other network via the web.

In looking at the security policies listed above, you will need at least two ACLs to fulfill the security policies. A best practice is to place extended ACLs as close to the source as possible. We will follow this practice for these policies.

Step 1:   Configure a numbered extended ACL on R1 for security policy numbers 1 and 2.

You will use a numbered extended ACL on R1. What are the ranges for extended ACLs?

____

a. Configure the ACL on R1. Use 100 for the ACL number.

```
R1(config)# access-list 100 remark Allow Web & SSH Access
R1(config)# access-list 100 permit tcp host 192.168.10.3 host 10.2.2.1 eq 22
R1(config)# access-list 100 permit tcp any any eq 80
```

What does the 80 signify in the command output listed above?

To what interface should ACL 100 be applied?

In what direction should ACL 100 be applied?

b. Apply ACL 100 to the S0/0/0 interface.

```
R1(config)# int s0/0/0
R1(config-if)# ip access-group 100 out
```

c. Verify ACL 100.

1) Open up a web browser on PC-A, and access http://209.165.200.225 (the ISP router). It should be successful; troubleshoot, if not.

2) Establish an SSH connection from PC-A to R3 using 10.2.2.1 for the IP address. Log in with **admin** and **class** for your credentials. It should be successful; troubleshoot, if not.

3) From privileged EXEC mode prompt on R1, issue the **show access-lists** command.

```
R1# show access-lists
Extended IP access list 100
    10 permit tcp host 192.168.10.3 host 10.2.2.1 eq 22 (22 matches)
    20 permit tcp any any eq www (111 matches)
```

4) From the PC-A command prompt, issue a ping to 10.2.2.1. Explain your results?

Step 2:   Configure a named extended ACL on R3 for security policy number 3.

a.   Configure the policy on R3. Name the ACL WEB-POLICY.

```
R3(config)# ip access-list extended WEB-POLICY
R3(config-ext-nacl)# permit tcp 192.168.30.0 0.0.0.255 host 10.1.1.1 eq 80
R3(config-ext-nacl)# permit tcp 192.168.30.0 0.0.0.255 209.165.200.224 0.0.0.31
eq 80
```

b.   Apply ACL WEB-POLICY to the S0/0/1 interface.

```
R3(config-ext-nacl)# int S0/0/1
R3(config-if)# ip access-group WEB-POLICY out
```

c.   Verify the ACL WEB-POLICY.

1)   From R3 privileged EXEC mode command prompt, issue the **show ip interface s0/0/1** command.

What, if any, is the name of the ACL? _______________________________________

In what direction is the ACL applied? _______________________________________

2)   Open up a web browser on PC-C and access http://209.165.200.225 (the ISP router). It should be successful; troubleshoot, if not.

3)   From PC-C, open a web session to http://10.1.1.1 (R1). It should be successful; troubleshoot, if not.

4)   From PC-C, open a web session to http://209.165.201.1 (ISP router). It should fail; troubleshoot, if not.

5)   From a PC-C command prompt, ping PC-A. What was your result and why?

Part 4:   Modify and Verify Extended ACLs

Because of the ACLs applied on R1 and R3, no pings or any other kind of traffic is allowed between the LAN networks on R1 and R3. Management has decided that all traffic between the 192.168.10.0/24 and 192.168.30.0/24 networks should be allowed. You must modify both ACLs on R1 and R3.

Step 1:   Modify ACL 100 on R1.

a.   From R1 privileged EXEC mode, issue the **show access-lists** command.

How many lines are there in this access list? ___________________

b.   Enter global configuration mode and modify the ACL on R1.

```
R1(config)# ip access-list extended 100
R1(config-ext-nacl)# 30 permit ip 192.168.10.0 0.0.0.255 192.168.30.0 0.0.0.255
R1(config-ext-nacl)# end
```

   c.   Issue the **show access-lists** command.

      Where did the new line that you just added appear in ACL 100?

Step 2: Modify ACL WEB-POLICY on R3.

   a.   From R3 privileged EXEC mode, issue the **show access-lists** command.

      How many lines are there in this access list? ___________________________

   b.   Enter global configuration mode and modify the ACL on R3.

```
R3(config)# ip access-list extended WEB-POLICY
R3(config-ext-nacl)# 30 permit ip 192.168.30.0 0.0.0.255 192.168.10.0 0.0.0.255
R3(config-ext-nacl)# end
```

   c.   Issue the **show access-lists** command to verify that the new line was added at the end of the ACL.

Step 3: Verify modified ACLs.

   a.   From PC-A, ping the IP address of PC-C. Were the pings successful? _______________

   b.   From PC-C, ping the IP address of PC-A. Were the pings successful? _______________

      Why did the ACLs work immediately for the pings after you changed them?

Reflection

1.   Why is careful planning and testing of ACLs required?

2.   Which type of ACL is better: standard or extended?

3.   Why are EIGRP hello packets and routing updates not blocked by the implicit **deny any** access control entry (ACE) or ACL statement of the ACLs applied to R1 and R3?

Router Interface Summary Table

Router Interface Summary				
Router Model	**Ethernet Interface #1**	**Ethernet Interface #2**	**Serial Interface #1**	**Serial Interface #2**
1800	Fast Ethernet 0/0 (F0/0)	Fast Ethernet 0/1 (F0/1)	Serial 0/0/0 (S0/0/0)	Serial 0/0/1 (S0/0/1)
1900	Gigabit Ethernet 0/0 (G0/0)	Gigabit Ethernet 0/1 (G0/1)	Serial 0/0/0 (S0/0/0)	Serial 0/0/1 (S0/0/1)
2801	Fast Ethernet 0/0 (F0/0)	Fast Ethernet 0/1 (F0/1)	Serial 0/1/0 (S0/1/0)	Serial 0/1/1 (S0/1/1)
2811	Fast Ethernet 0/0 (F0/0)	Fast Ethernet 0/1 (F0/1)	Serial 0/0/0 (S0/0/0)	Serial 0/0/1 (S0/0/1)
2900	Gigabit Ethernet 0/0 (G0/0)	Gigabit Ethernet 0/1 (G0/1)	Serial 0/0/0 (S0/0/0)	Serial 0/0/1 (S0/0/1)

Note: To find out how the router is configured, look at the interfaces to identify the type of router and how many interfaces the router has. There is no way to effectively list all the combinations of configurations for each router class. This table includes identifiers for the possible combinations of Ethernet and Serial interfaces in the device. The table does not include any other type of interface, even though a specific router may contain one. An example of this might be an ISDN BRI interface. The string in parenthesis is the legal abbreviation that can be used in Cisco IOS commands to represent the interface.

9.4.2.7 Lab – Troubleshooting ACL Configuration and Placement

Topology

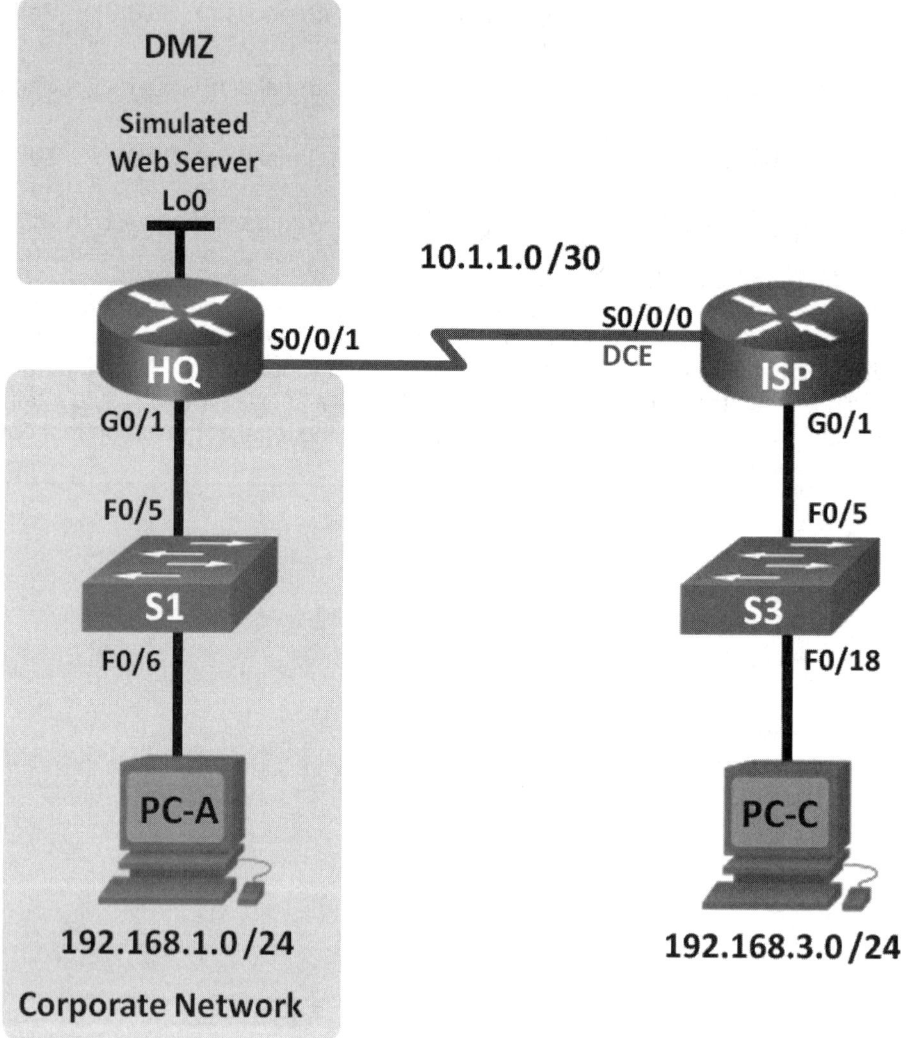

Addressing Table

Device	Interface	IP Address	Subnet Mask	Default Gateway
HQ	G0/1	192.168.1.1	255.255.255.0	N/A
	S0/0/1	10.1.1.2	255.255.255.252	N/A
	Lo0	192.168.4.1	255.255.255.0	N/A
ISP	G0/1	192.168.3.1	255.255.255.0	N/A
	S0/0/0 (DCE)	10.1.1.1	255.255.255.252	N/A
S1	VLAN 1	192.168.1.11	255.255.255.0	192.168.1.1
S3	VLAN 1	192.168.3.11	255.255.255.0	192.168.3.1
PC-A	NIC	192.168.1.3	255.255.255.0	192.168.1.1
PC-C	NIC	192.168.3.3	255.255.255.0	192.168.3.1

Objectives

Part 1: Build the Network and Configure Basic Device Settings

Part 2: Troubleshoot Internal Access

Part 3: Troubleshoot Remote Access

Background / Scenario

An access control list (ACL) is a series of IOS commands that can provide basic traffic filtering on a Cisco router. ACLs are used to select the types of traffic to be processed. A single ACL statement is called and access control entry (ACE). The ACEs in the ACL are evaluated from top to bottom with an implicit deny all ACE at the end of the list. ACLs can also control the types of traffic into or out of a network by the source and destination hosts or network. To process the desired traffic correctly, the placement of the ACLs is critical.

In this lab, a small company has just added a web server to the network to allow customers to access confidential information. The company network is divided into two zones: Corporate network zone and Demilitarized Zone (DMZ). The corporate network zone houses private servers and internal clients. The DMZ houses the externally accessible web server (simulated by Lo0 on HQ). Because the company can only administer its own HQ router, all ACLs must be applied to the HQ router.

- ACL 101 is implemented to limit the traffic out of the corporate network zone. This zone houses the private servers and internal clients (192.168.1.0/24). No other network should be able to access it.

- ACL 102 is used to limit the traffic into the corporate network. Only responses to requests that originated from within the corporate network are allowed back into that network. This includes TCP-based requests from internal hosts such as Web and FTP. ICMP is allowed into the network for troubleshooting purposes so that incoming ICMP messages generated in response to pings can be received by internal hosts.

- ACL 121 controls outside traffic to the DMZ and corporate network. Only HTTP traffic is allowed to the DMZ web server (simulated by Lo0 on R1). Other network related traffic, such as EIGRP, is allowed from outside networks. Furthermore, valid internal private addresses, such as 192.168.1.0, loopback address such as 127.0.0.0 and multicast addresses are denied entrance to the corporate network to prevent malicious network attacks from outside users.

Note: The routers used with CCNA hands-on labs are Cisco 1941 Integrated Services Routers (ISRs) with Cisco IOS Release 15.2(4)M3 (universalk9 image). The switches used are Cisco Catalyst 2960s with Cisco IOS Release 15.0(2) (lanbasek9 image). Other routers, switches and Cisco IOS versions can be used. Depending on the model and Cisco IOS version, the commands available and output produced might vary from what is shown in the labs. Refer to the Router Interface Summary Table at the end of the lab for the correct interface identifiers.

Note: Make sure that the routers and switches have been erased and have no startup configurations. If you are unsure, contact your instructor.

Required Resources

- 2 Routers (Cisco 1941 with Cisco IOS Release 15.2(4)M3 universal image or comparable)
- 2 Switches (Cisco 2960 with Cisco IOS Release 15.0(2) lanbasek9 image or comparable)
- 2 PCs (Windows 7, Vista, or XP with terminal emulation program, such as Tera Term)
- Console cables to configure the Cisco IOS devices via the console ports
- Ethernet and serial cables as shown in the topology

Part 1:   Build the Network and Configure Basic Device Settings

In Part 1, you set up the network topology and configure the routers and switches with some basic settings, such as passwords and IP addresses. Preset configurations are also provided for you for the initial router configurations. You will also configure the IP settings for the PCs in the topology.

Step 1:   Cable the network as shown in the topology.

Step 2:   Configure PC hosts.

Step 3:   Initialize and reload the routers and switches as necessary.

Step 4:   (Optional) Configure basic settings for each switch.

   a.   Disable DNS lookup.

   b.   Configure host names as shown in the Topology.

   c.   Configure IP address and default gateway in Addressing Table.

   d.   Assign **cisco** as the console and vty passwords.

   e.   Assign **class** as the privileged EXEC password.

   f.   Configure **logging synchronous** to prevent console messages from interrupting command entry.

Step 5:   Configure basic settings for each router.

   a.   Disable DNS lookup.

   b.   Configure host names as shown in the topology.

   c.   Assign **cisco** as the console and vty passwords.

   d.   Assign **class** as the privileged EXEC password.

   e.   Configure **logging synchronous** to prevent console messages from interrupting command entry.

Step 6:   Configure HTTP access and user credentials on HQ router.

Local user credentials are configured to access the simulated web server (192.168.4.1).

```
HQ(config)# ip http server
HQ(config)# username admin privilege 15 secret adminpass
HQ(config)# ip http authentication local
```

Step 7:   Load router configurations.

The configurations for the routers ISP and HQ are provided for you. There are errors within these configurations, and it is your job to determine the incorrect configurations and correct them.

Router ISP

```
hostname ISP
interface GigabitEthernet0/1
 ip address 192.168.3.1 255.255.255.0
 no shutdown
interface Serial0/0/0
 ip address 10.1.1.1 255.255.255.252
 clock rate 128000
 no shutdown
router eigrp 1
 network 10.1.1.0 0.0.0.3
 network 192.168.3.0
 no auto-summary
end
```

Router HQ

```
hostname HQ
interface Loopback0
 ip address 192.168.4.1 255.255.255.0
interface GigabitEthernet0/1
 ip address 192.168.1.1 255.255.255.0
 ip access-group 101 out

 ip access-group 102 in

 no shutdown
interface Serial0/0/1
 ip address 10.1.1.2 255.255.255.252
 ip access-group 121 in
 no shutdown
router eigrp 1
 network 10.1.1.0 0.0.0.3
 network 192.168.1.0
 network 192.168.4.0
 no auto-summary
access-list 101 permit ip 192.168.11.0 0.0.0.255 any

access-list 101 deny ip any any
access-list 102 permit tcp any any established
access-list 102 permit icmp any any echo-reply
```

```
access-list 102 permit icmp any any unreachable
access-list 102 deny ip any any
access-list 121 permit tcp any host 192.168.4.1 eq 89

access-list 121 deny icmp any host 192.168.4.11

access-list 121 deny ip 192.168.1.0 0.0.0.255 any
access-list 121 deny ip 127.0.0.0 0.255.255.255 any
access-list 121 deny ip 224.0.0.0 31.255.255.255 any
access-list 121 permit ip any any
access-list 121 deny ip any any
end
```

Part 2:   Troubleshoot Internal Access

In Part 2, the ACLs on router HQ are examined to determine if they are configured correctly.

Step 1:   Troubleshoot ACL 101

ACL 101 is implemented to limit the traffic out of the corporate network zone. This zone houses only internal clients and private servers. Only 192.168.1.0/24 network can exit this corporate network zone.

a.   Can PC-A ping its default gateway? _______________

b.   After verifying that the PC-A was configured correctly, examine the HQ router to find possible configuration errors by viewing the summary of ACL 101. Enter the command **show access-lists 101**.

```
HQ# show access-lists 101
Extended IP access list 101
    10 permit ip 192.168.11.0 0.0.0.255 any
    20 deny ip any any
```

c.   Are there any problems with ACL 101?

____

d.   Examine the default gateway interface for the 192.168.1.0 /24 network. Verify that the ACL 101 is applied in the correct direction on the G0/1 interface. Enter the **show ip interface g0/1** command.

```
HQ# show ip interface g0/1
GigabitEthernet0/1 is up, line protocol is up
  Internet address is 192.168.1.1/24
  Broadcast address is 255.255.255.255
  Address determined by setup command
  MTU is 1500 bytes
  Helper address is not set
  Directed broadcast forwarding is disabled
  Multicast reserved groups joined: 224.0.0.10
```

```
Outgoing access list is 101
Inbound  access list is 102
```

Is the direction for interface G0/1 configured correctly for ACL 101?

____

e. Correct the errors found regarding ACL 101 and verify the traffic from network 192.168.1.0 /24 can exit the corporate network. Record the commands used to correct the errors.

____

____

____

____

f. Verify PC-A can ping its default gateway interface.

Step 2:   Troubleshoot ACL 102

ACL 102 is implemented to limit traffic into the corporate network. Traffic originating from the outside network is not allowed onto the corporate network. Remote traffic is allowed into the corporate network if the established traffic originated from the internal network. ICMP reply messages are allowed for troubleshooting purposes.

a. Can PC-A ping PC-C? ________________

b. Examine the HQ router to find possible configuration errors by viewing the summary of ACL 102. Enter the command **show access-lists 102**.

```
HQ# show access-lists 102
Extended IP access list 102
    10 permit tcp any any established
    20 permit icmp any any echo-reply
    30 permit icmp any any unreachable
    40 deny ip any any (57 matches)
```

c. Are there any problems with ACL 102?

____

d. Verify that the ACL 102 is applied in the correct direction on G0/1 interface. Enter the **show ip interface g0/1** command.

```
HQ# show ip interface g0/1
GigabitEthernet0/1 is up, line protocol is up
  Internet address is 192.168.1.1/24
  Broadcast address is 255.255.255.255
  Address determined by setup command
  MTU is 1500 bytes
```

```
Helper address is not set
Directed broadcast forwarding is disabled
Multicast reserved groups joined: 224.0.0.10
Outgoing access list is 101
Inbound  access list is 101
```

e. Are there any problems with the application of ACL 102 to interface G0/1?

____

f. Correct any errors found regarding ACL 102. Record the commands used to correct the errors.

g. Can PC-A ping PC-C now? ____________

Part 3:   Troubleshoot Remote Access

In Part 3, ACL 121 is configured to prevent spoofing attacks from the outside networks and allow only remote HTTP access to the web server (192.168.4.1) in DMZ.

a. Verify ACL 121 has been configured correctly. Enter the **show ip access-list 121** command.

```
HQ# show ip access-lists 121
Extended IP access list 121
    10 permit tcp any host 192.168.4.1 eq 89
    20 deny icmp any host 192.168.4.11
    30 deny ip 192.168.1.0 0.0.0.255 any
    40 deny ip 127.0.0.0 0.255.255.255 any
    50 deny ip 224.0.0.0 31.255.255.255 any
    60 permit ip any any (354 matches)
    70 deny ip any any
```

Are there any problems with this ACL?

____

____

b. Verify that the ACL 121 is applied in the correct direction on the R1 S0/0/1 interface. Enter the **show ip interface s0/0/1** command.

```
HQ# show ip interface s0/0/1
Serial0/0/1 is up, line protocol is up
  Internet address is 10.1.1.2/30
  Broadcast address is 255.255.255.255
<output omitted>
  Multicast reserved groups joined: 224.0.0.10
  Outgoing access list is not set
  Inbound  access list is 121
```

Are there any problems with the application of this ACL?

c.   If any errors were found, make and record the necessary configuration changes to ACL 121.

d.   Verify that PC-C can only access the simulated web server on HQ by using the web browser. Provide the username **admin** and password **adminpass** to access the web server (192.168.4.1).

Reflection

1.   How should the ACL statement be ordered? From general to specific or vice versa?

2.   If you delete an ACL by using the **no access-list** command and the ACL is still applied to the interface, what happens?

Router Interface Summary Table

Router Interface Summary				
Router Model	**Ethernet Interface #1**	**Ethernet Interface #2**	**Serial Interface #1**	**Serial Interface #2**
1800	Fast Ethernet 0/0 (F0/0)	Fast Ethernet 0/1 (F0/1)	Serial 0/0/0 (S0/0/0)	Serial 0/0/1 (S0/0/1)
1900	Gigabit Ethernet 0/0 (G0/0)	Gigabit Ethernet 0/1 (G0/1)	Serial 0/0/0 (S0/0/0)	Serial 0/0/1 (S0/0/1)
2801	Fast Ethernet 0/0 (F0/0)	Fast Ethernet 0/1 (F0/1)	Serial 0/1/0 (S0/1/0)	Serial 0/1/1 (S0/1/1)
2811	Fast Ethernet 0/0 (F0/0)	Fast Ethernet 0/1 (F0/1)	Serial 0/0/0 (S0/0/0)	Serial 0/0/1 (S0/0/1)
2900	Gigabit Ethernet 0/0 (G0/0)	Gigabit Ethernet 0/1 (G0/1)	Serial 0/0/0 (S0/0/0)	Serial 0/0/1 (S0/0/1)

Note: To find out how the router is configured, look at the interfaces to identify the type of router and how many interfaces the router has. There is no way to effectively list all the combinations of configurations for each router class. This table includes identifiers for the possible combinations of Ethernet and Serial interfaces in the device. The table does not include any other type of interface, even though a specific router may contain one. An example of this might be an ISDN BRI interface. The string in parenthesis is the legal abbreviation that can be used in Cisco IOS commands to represent the interface.

9.5.2.7 Lab – Configuring and Verifying IPv6 ACLs

Topology

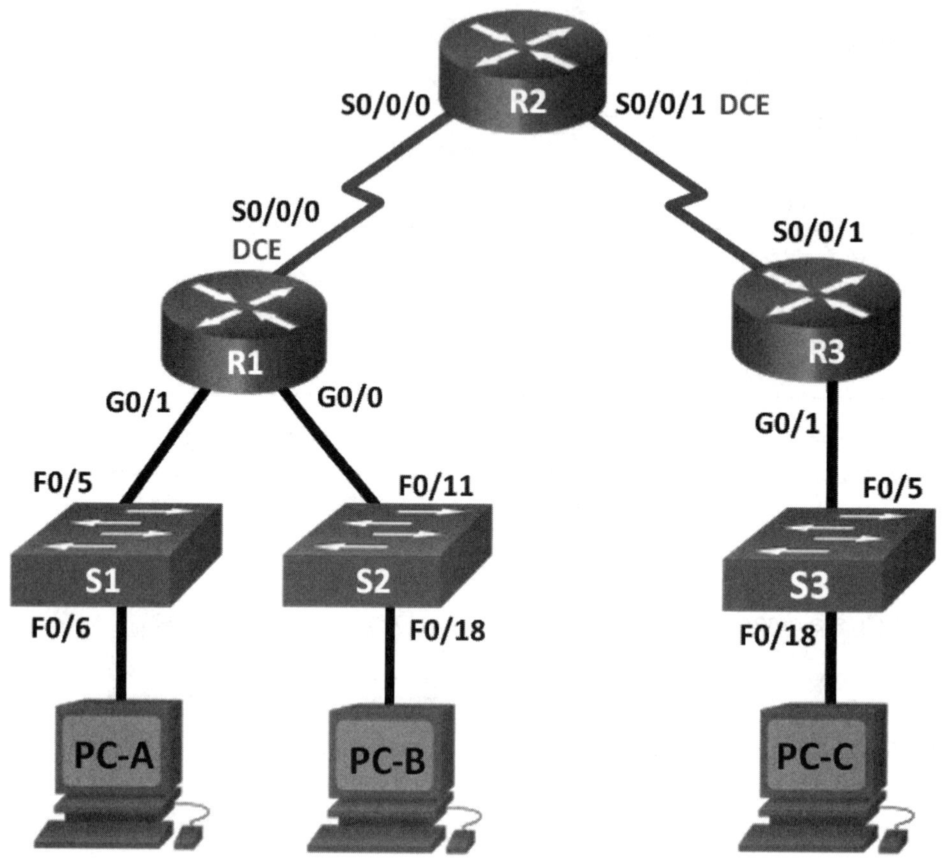

Addressing Table

Device	Interface	IP Address	Default Gateway
R1	G0/0	2001:DB8:ACAD:B::1/64	N/A
	G0/1	2001:DB8:ACAD:A::1/64	N/A
	S0/0/0 (DCE)	2001:DB8:AAAA:1::1/64	N/A
R2	S0/0/0	2001:DB8:AAAA:1::2/64	N/A
	S0/0/1 (DCE)	2001:DB8:AAAA:2::2/64	N/A
R3	G0/1	2001:DB8:CAFE:C::1/64	N/A
	S0/0/1	2001:DB8:AAAA:2::1/64	N/A
S1	VLAN1	2001:DB8:ACAD:A::A/64	N/A
S2	VLAN1	2001:DB8:ACAD:B::A/64	N/A
S3	VLAN1	2001:DB8:CAFE:C::A/64	N/A
PC-A	NIC	2001:DB8:ACAD:A::3/64	FE80::1
PC-B	NIC	2001:DB8:ACAD:B::3/64	FE80::1
PC-C	NIC	2001:DB8:CAFE:C::3/64	FE80::1

Objectives

Part 1: Set Up the Topology and Initialize Devices

Part 2: Configure Devices and Verify Connectivity

Part 3: Configure and Verify IPv6 ACLs

Part 4: Edit IPv6 ACLs

Background / Scenario

You can filter IPv6 traffic by creating IPv6 access control lists (ACLs) and applying them to interfaces similarly to the way that you create IPv4 named ACLs. IPv6 ACL types are extended and named. Standard and numbered ACLs are no longer used with IPv6. To apply an IPv6 ACL to a vty interface, you use the new **ipv6 traffic-filter** command. The **ipv6 access-class** command is still used to apply an IPv6 ACL to interfaces.

In this lab, you will apply IPv6 filtering rules and then verify that they are restricting access as expected. You will also edit an IPv6 ACL and clear the match counters.

Note: The routers used with CCNA hands-on labs are Cisco 1941 Integrated Services Routers (ISRs) with Cisco IOS Release 15.2(4)M3 (universalk9 image). The switches used are Cisco Catalyst 2960s with Cisco IOS Release 15.0(2) (lanbasek9 image). Other routers, switches and Cisco IOS versions can be used. Depending on the model and Cisco IOS version, the commands available and output produced might vary from what is shown in the labs. Refer to the Router Interface Summary Table at the end of the lab for the correct interface identifiers.

Note: Make sure that the routers and switches have been erased and have no startup configurations. If you are unsure, contact your instructor.

Required Resources

- 3 Routers (Cisco 1941 with Cisco IOS Release 15.2(4)M3 universal image or comparable)
- 3 Switches (Cisco 2960 with Cisco IOS Release 15.0(2) lanbasek9 image or comparable)
- 3 PCs (Windows 7, Vista, or XP with terminal emulation program, such as Tera Term)
- Console cables to configure the Cisco IOS devices via the console ports
- Ethernet and serial cables as shown in the topology

Part 1: Set Up the Topology and Initialize Devices

In Part 1, you set up the network topology and clear any configurations if necessary.

Step 1: Cable the network as shown in the topology.

Step 2: Initialize and reload the routers and switches.

Part 2: Configure Devices and Verify Connectivity

In Part 2, you configure basic settings on the routers, switches and PCs. Refer to the Topology and Addressing Table at the beginning of this lab for device names and address information.

Step 1:   **Configure IPv6 addresses on all PCs.**

Configure IPv6 global unicast addresses according to the Addressing Table. Use the link-local address of **FE80::1** for the default-gateway on all PCs.

Step 2:   **Configure the switches.**

a.   Disable DNS lookup.

b.   Assign the hostname.

c.   Assign a domain-name of **ccna-lab.com**.

d.   Encrypt plain text passwords.

e.   Create a MOTD banner warning users that unauthorized access is prohibited.

f.   Create a local user database with a username of **admin** and password as **classadm**.

g.   Assign **class** as the privileged EXEC encrypted password.

h.   Assign **cisco** as the console password and enable login.

i.   Enable login on the VTY lines using the local database.

j.   Generate a crypto rsa key for ssh using a modulus size of 1024 bits.

k.   Change the transport input VTY lines to all for SSH and Telnet only.

l.   Assign an IPv6 address to VLAN 1 according to the Addressing Table.

m.   Administratively disable all inactive interfaces.

Step 3:   **Configure basic settings on all routers.**

a.   Disable DNS lookup.

b.   Assign the hostname.

c.   Assign a domain-name of **ccna-lab.com**.

d.   Encrypt plain text passwords.

e.   Create a MOTD banner warning users that unauthorized access is prohibited.

f.   Create a local user database with a username of **admin** and password as **classadm**.

g.   Assign **class** as the privileged EXEC encrypted password.

h.   Assign **cisco** as the console password and enable login.

i.   Enable login on the VTY lines using the local database.

j.   Generate a crypto rsa key for ssh using a modulus size of 1024 bits.

k.   Change the transport input VTY lines to all for SSH and Telnet only.

Step 4:   **Configure IPv6 settings on R1.**

a.   Configure the IPv6 unicast address on interface G0/0, G0/1, and S0/0/0.

b.   Configure the IPv6 link-local address on interface G0/0, G0/1, and S0/0/0. Use **FE80::1** for the link-local address on all three interfaces.

c.   Set the clock rate on S0/0/0 to 128000.

d.   Enable the interfaces.

e.   Enable IPv6 unicast routing.

f.   Configure an IPv6 default route to use interface S0/0/0.

```
R1(config)# ipv6 route ::/0 s0/0/0
```

Step 5:   **Configure IPv6 settings on R2.**

a.   Configure the IPv6 unicast address on interface S0/0/0 and S0/0/1.

b.   Configure the IPv6 link-local address on interface S0/0/0 and S0/0/1. Use **FE80::2** for the link-local address on both interfaces.

c.   Set the clock rate on S0/0/1 to 128000.

d.   Enable the interfaces.

e.   Enable IPv6 unicast routing.

f.   Configure static IPv6 routes for traffic handling of R1 and R3 LAN subnets. ·

```
R2(config)# ipv6 route 2001:db8:acad::/48 s0/0/0
R2(config)# ipv6 route 2001:db8:cafe:c::/64 s0/0/1
```

Step 6:   **Configure IPv6 settings on R3.**

a.   Configure the IPv6 unicast address on interface G0/1 and S0/0/1.

b.   Configure the IPv6 link-local address on interface G0/1 and S0/0/1. Use **FE80::1** for the link-local address on both interfaces.

c.   Enable the interfaces.

d.   Enable IPv6 unicast routing.

e.   Configure an IPv6 default route to use interface S0/0/1.

```
R3(config)# ipv6 route ::/0 s0/0/1
```

Step 7:   **Verify connectivity.**

a.   Each PC should be able to ping the other PCs in the topology.

b.   Telnet to R1 from all PCs in the Topology.

c.   SSH to R1 from all PCs in the Topology.

d.   Telnet to S1 from all PCs in the Topology.

e.   SSH to S1 from all PCs in the Topology.

f.   Troubleshoot connectivity issues now because the ACLs that you create in Part 3 of this lab will restrict access to some areas of the network.

Note: Tera Term requires the target IPv6 address to be enclosed in brackets. Enter the IPv6 address as shown, click **OK** and then click **Continue** to accept the security warning and connect to the router.

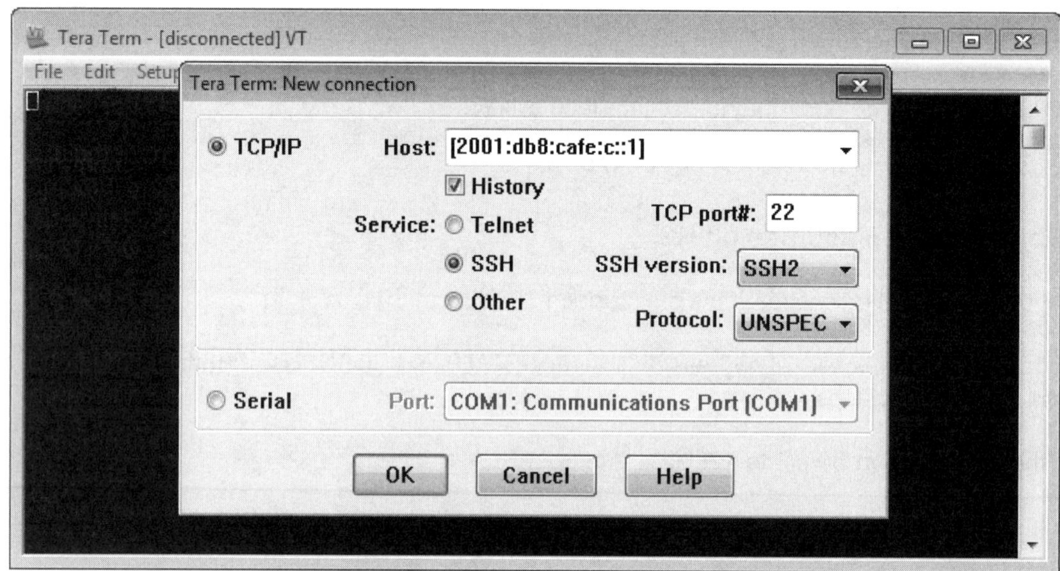

Input the user credentials configured (username **admin** and password **classadm**) and select the **Use plain password to log in** in the SSH Authentication dialogue box. Click **OK** to continue.

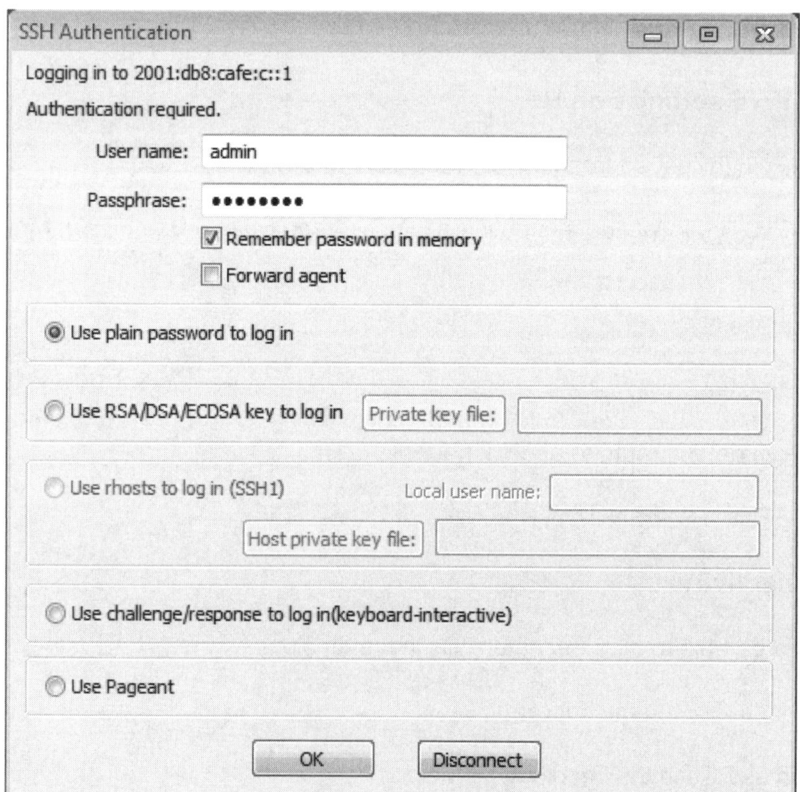

Part 3: **Configure and Verify IPv6 ACLs**

Step 1: **Configure and verify VTY restrictions on R1.**

a. Create an ACL to only allow hosts from the 2001:db8:acad:a::/64 network to telnet to R1. All hosts should only be able to ssh to R1.

```
R1(config)# ipv6 access-list RESTRICT-VTY
R1(config-ipv6-acl)# permit tcp 2001:db8:acad:a::/64 any
R1(config-ipv6-acl)# permit tcp any any eq 22
```

b. Apply the RESTRICT-VTY ACL to R1's VTY lines.

```
R1(config-ipv6-acl)# line vty 0 4
R1(config-line)# ipv6 access-class RESTRICT-VTY in
R1(config-line)# end
R1#
```

c. Show the new ACL.

```
R1# show access-lists
IPv6 access list RESTRICT-VTY
    permit tcp 2001:DB8:ACAD:A::/64 any sequence 10
    permit tcp any any eq 22 sequence 20
```

d. Verify that the RESTRICT-VTY ACL is only allowing Telnet traffic from the 2001:db8:acad:a::/64 network.

How does the RESTRICT-VTY ACL only allow hosts from the 2001:db8:acad:a::/64 network to telnet to R1?

____

____

____

____

What does the second permit statement in the RESTRICT-VTY ACL do?

____

Step 2: **Restrict Telnet access to the 2001:db8:acad:a::/64 network.**

a. Create an ACL called RESTRICTED-LAN that will block Telnet access to the 2001:db8:acad:a::/64 network.

```
R1(config)# ipv6 access-list RESTRICTED-LAN
R1(config-ipv6-acl)# remark Block Telnet from outside
R1(config-ipv6-acl)# deny tcp any 2001:db8:acad:a::/64 eq telnet
R1(config-ipv6-acl)# permit ipv6 any any
```

b. Apply the RESTRICTED-LAN ACL to interface G0/1 for all outbound traffic.

```
R1(config-ipv6-acl)# int g0/1
R1(config-if)# ipv6 traffic-filter RESTRICTED-LAN out
R1(config-if)# end
```

c.   Telnet to S1 from PC-B and PC-C to verify that Telnet has been restricted. SSH to S1 from PC-B to verify that it can still be reached using SSH. Troubleshoot if necessary.

d.   Use the **show ipv6 access-list** command to view the RESTRICTED-LAN ACL.

```
R1# show ipv6 access-lists RESTRICTED-LAN
IPv6 access list RESTRICTED-LAN
    deny tcp any 2001:DB8:ACAD:A::/64 eq telnet (6 matches) sequence 20
    permit ipv6 any any (45 matches) sequence 30
```

Notice that each statement identifies the number of hits or matches that have occurred since the ACL was applied to the interface.

e.   Use the **clear ipv6 access-list** to reset the match counters for the RESRICTED-LAN ACL.

```
R1# clear ipv6 access-list RESTRICTED-LAN
```

f.   Redisplay the ACL with the **show access-lists** command to confirm that the counters were cleared.

```
R1# show access-lists RESTRICTED-LAN
IPv6 access list RESTRICTED-LAN
    deny tcp any 2001:DB8:ACAD:A::/64 eq telnet sequence 20
    permit ipv6 any any sequence 30
```

Part 4:   Edit IPv6 ACLs

In Part 4, you will edit the RESTRICTED-LAN ACL that you created in Part 3. It is always a good idea to remove the ACL from the interface to which it is applied before editing it. After you complete your edits, then reapply the ACL to the interface.

Note: Many network administrators will make a copy of the ACL and edit the copy. When editing is complete, the administrator will remove the old ACL and apply the newly edited ACL to the interface. This method keeps the ACL in place until you are ready to apply the edited copy of the ACL.

Step 1:   Remove the ACL from the interface.

```
R1(config)# int g0/1
R1(config-if)# no ipv6 traffic-filter RESTRICTED-LAN out
R1(config-if)# end
```

Step 2:   Use the show access-lists command to view the ACL.

```
R1# show access-lists
IPv6 access list RESTRICT-VTY
    permit tcp 2001:DB8:ACAD:A::/64 any (4 matches) sequence 10
    permit tcp any any eq 22 (6 matches) sequence 20
IPv6 access list RESTRICTED-LAN
    deny tcp any 2001:DB8:ACAD:A::/64 eq telnet sequence 20
    permit ipv6 any any (36 matches) sequence 30
```

Step 3:   Insert a new ACL statement using sequence numbering.

```
R1(config)# ipv6 access-list RESTRICTED-LAN
R1(config-ipv6-acl)# permit tcp 2001:db8:acad:b::/64 host 2001:db8:acad:a::a eq
23 sequence 15
```

What does this new permit statement do?

____

Step 4:   Insert a new ACL statement at the end of the ACL.

```
R1(config-ipv6-acl)# permit tcp any host 2001:db8:acad:a::3 eq www
```

Note: This permit statement is only used to show how to add a statement to the end of an ACL. This ACL line would never be matched because the previous permit statement is matching on everything.

Step 5:   Use the do show access-lists command to view the ACL change.

```
R1(config-ipv6-acl)# do show access-list
IPv6 access list RESTRICT-VTY
    permit tcp 2001:DB8:ACAD:A::/64 any (2 matches) sequence 10
    permit tcp any any eq 22 (6 matches) sequence 20
IPv6 access list RESTRICTED-LAN
    permit tcp 2001:DB8:ACAD:B::/64 host 2001:DB8:ACAD:A::A eq telnet sequence 15
    deny tcp any 2001:DB8:ACAD:A::/64 eq telnet sequence 20
    permit ipv6 any any (124 matches) sequence 30
    permit tcp any host 2001:DB8:ACAD:A::3 eq www sequence 40
```

Note: The **do** command can be used to execute any privileged EXEC command while in global configuration mode or a submode.

Step 6:   Delete an ACL statement.

Use the **no** command to delete the permit statement that you just added.

```
R1(config-ipv6-acl)# no permit tcp any host 2001:DB8:ACAD:A::3 eq www
```

Step 7:   Use the do show access-list RESTRICTED-LAN command to view the ACL.

```
R1(config-ipv6-acl)# do show access-list RESTRICTED-LAN
IPv6 access list RESTRICTED-LAN
    permit tcp 2001:DB8:ACAD:B::/64 host 2001:DB8:ACAD:A::A eq telnet sequence 15
    deny tcp any 2001:DB8:ACAD:A::/64 eq telnet sequence 20
    permit ipv6 any any (214 matches) sequence 30
```

Step 8:   Re-apply the RESTRICTED-LAN ACL to the interface G0/1.

```
R1(config-ipv6-acl)# int g0/1
R1(config-if)# ipv6 traffic-filter RESTRICTED-LAN out
R1(config-if)# end
```

Step 9:   **Test ACL changes.**

Telnet to S1 from PC-B. Troubleshoot if necessary.

Reflection

1. What is causing the match count on the RESTRICTED-LAN **permit ipv6 any any** statement to continue to increase?

\
\
\
\

2. What command would you use to reset the counters for the ACL on the VTY lines?

\

Router Interface Summary Table

Router Interface Summary				
Router Model	**Ethernet Interface #1**	**Ethernet Interface #2**	**Serial Interface #1**	**Serial Interface #2**
1800	Fast Ethernet 0/0 (F0/0)	Fast Ethernet 0/1 (F0/1)	Serial 0/0/0 (S0/0/0)	Serial 0/0/1 (S0/0/1)
1900	Gigabit Ethernet 0/0 (G0/0)	Gigabit Ethernet 0/1 (G0/1)	Serial 0/0/0 (S0/0/0)	Serial 0/0/1 (S0/0/1)
2801	Fast Ethernet 0/0 (F0/0)	Fast Ethernet 0/1 (F0/1)	Serial 0/1/0 (S0/1/0)	Serial 0/1/1 (S0/1/1)
2811	Fast Ethernet 0/0 (F0/0)	Fast Ethernet 0/1 (F0/1)	Serial 0/0/0 (S0/0/0)	Serial 0/0/1 (S0/0/1)
2900	Gigabit Ethernet 0/0 (G0/0)	Gigabit Ethernet 0/1 (G0/1)	Serial 0/0/0 (S0/0/0)	Serial 0/0/1 (S0/0/1)

Note: To find out how the router is configured, look at the interfaces to identify the type of router and how many interfaces the router has. There is no way to effectively list all the combinations of configurations for each router class. This table includes identifiers for the possible combinations of Ethernet and Serial interfaces in the device. The table does not include any other type of interface, even though a specific router may contain one. An example of this might be an ISDN BRI interface. The string in parenthesis is the legal abbreviation that can be used in Cisco IOS commands to represent the interface.

9.6.1.1 Class Activity – FTP Denied

Objective

Implement packet filtering using extended IPv4 ACLs according to networking requirements (to include named and numbered ACLs).

Scenario

It was recently reported that viruses are on the rise within your small- to medium-sized business network. Your network administrator has been tracking network performance and has determined that one particular host is constantly downloading files from a remote FTP server. This host just may be the virus source perpetuating throughout the network!

Use Packet Tracer to complete this activity. Write a <u>named</u> ACL to deny the host access to the FTP server. Apply the ACL to the most effective interface on the router.

To complete the physical topology, you must use:

- One PC host station
- Two switches
- One Cisco 1941 series Integrated Services Router
- One server

Using the Packet Tracer text tool, record the ACL you prepared. Validate that the ACL works to deny access to the FTP server by trying to access the FTP server's address. Observe what happens while in simulation mode.

Save your file and be prepared to share it with another student, or with the entire class.

Reflection

1. What was the most difficult part of completing this modeling activity?

2. How often do you think network administrators need to change their ACLs on their networks?

3. Why would you consider using a named extended ACL instead of a regular extended ACL?

Chapter 10 — IOS Images and Licensing

10.0.1.2 Class Activity – IOS Detection

Objective

Manage IOS system image files to increase network reliability in a small- to medium-sized business network.

Scenario

Your school or university has just received a donation of Cisco routers and switches. You transport them from your shipping and receiving department to your Cisco networking lab and start sorting them into switch and router groups.

After all the equipment has been sorted, you cannot wait to turn them on to see if they really work. Once you do power them up, you find out that all of the equipment operating systems have been erased! Because computers use different operating systems, you think that routers and switches also use different internetworking operating systems (or IOS) as well.

One good thing you notice is that most of the routers are either models 1941 or 2911. The switch models are either 2960 or 3560. You have worked with this type of equipment in the past and know you can research which IOS is appropriate to purchase for each model. You also know that documenting hardware features, serial numbers, and MAC addresses is very important to do whenever you add networking equipment to any network topology.

Refer to the accompanying PDF for directions on how to proceed with this modeling activity. Save your work and share the data you found with another group or the entire class.

Resources

- Packet Tracer software
- Internet connectivity

Directions

Step 1:   **Create a switch and router matrix for documenting hardware and software information.**

    a. Design a matrix to record information about your two router models, 1941 and 2911. Both models are included in your Packet Tracer software. Record the following information in your matrix:

        1) The system serial numbers of the equipment

        2) The Cisco IOS type and version shown for each model

        3) The name of the preferred system image file

        4) How much NVRAM is present on the routers

        5) How many and which types of interfaces are built in to the routers

    b. Design a matrix to record information about your two switch models, 2960 and 3560, from Packet Tracer. Record the following information in your matrix:

        1) The system serial number for this type of equipment

        2) The Cisco IOS type and version shown for these models

        3) The name of the preferred SW image

        4) How much NVRAM is present on the models

        5) How many and which types of interfaces are built in to the switches

Step 2:   **Open Packet Tracer.**

a.   Place one router and switch for each router and switch model you will research on the desktop.

b.   Open the router or switch models on Packet Tracer and use the **show version** command to display operating system and other information about your equipment.

c.   Read and record the information found in Step 2b to your matrix designs.

Step 3:   **Visit http://www.cisco.com for further model research content.**

a.   Sign in to your account at cisco.com. If you do not have an account, create one.

b.   Research your router and switch models for additional feature sets available for the models.

c.   Note the physical hardware designs of the devices. Check if additional network cards can be installed; if so, record what types of cards can be installed for your router and switch models.

d.   Mention some of these facts below in your two matrix designs.

Step 4:   **Document the information you found to share with the class or another group of students.**

10.3.1.1 Class Activity – Powerful Protocols

Objective

A review of EIGRP and OSPF routing protocol configuration and verification commands.

Scenario

At the end of this course, you are asked to complete two Capstone Projects where you will create, configure, and verify two network topologies using the two main routing protocols taught in this course, EIGRP and OSPF.

To make things easier, you decide to create a chart of configuration and verification commands to use for these two design projects. To help devise the protocol charts, ask another student in the class to help you.

Refer to the PDF for this chapter for directions on how to create a design for this modeling project. When complete, share your work with another group or with the class. You may also want to save the files created for this project in a network portfolio for future reference.

Resources

- Previous curriculum chapter content for EIGRP and OSPF
- Word processing software

Directions

Step 1:   **Create a matrix for each routing protocol (EIGRP and OSPF).**

   a.   Within each routing protocol matrix, design two sections.

      1)   one section for configuration commands

      2)   one section for verification or **show** commands

   b.   Use a word processing program to save your matrix designs, one for EIGRP and one for OSPF.

Step 2:   **Review the chapters in this curriculum.**

   a.   Refer to the different sections and activities presented in the curriculum.

      1)   Content

      2)   Labs

      3)   Packet Tracer Activities

   b.   Record configuration commands for each protocol on their respective matrix. **Note**: Some commands are universal, and some are used only for IPv4 or IPv6.

   c.   Record verification commands used for each protocol on their respective matrix. **Note**: Some of these commands are universal, and some are used only with IPv4or IPv6.

   d.   Leave extra, blank rows for the group or classroom portion of this activity.

Step 3:   **Meet as a class or with another group.**

a. Compare configuration commands.

b. Compare verification commands.

c. Add any commands to each matrix mentioned in the full- or group-setting that you did not record in your own group.

d. Save your work for use with the two Capstone projects which summarize this entire course.

10.3.1.2 – EIGRP Capstone Project

Objectives

In this Capstone Project activity, you will demonstrate your ability to:

- Design, configure, verify, and secure EIGRP, IPv4 or IPv6 on a network
- Design a VLSM addressing scheme for the devices connected to the LANs
- Present your design using network documentation from your Capstone Project network

Scenario

You are a network engineer for your small- to medium-sized business. You and your team have been asked to design an IPv4 or IPv6 network that uses the EIGRP routing protocol.

The network consists of four branches that is connected to a headquarters router. The headquarters then connects to an ISP router.

Your job is to create an EIGRP-based, VLSM addressed network scheme using IPv4 or IPv6 to accommodate the number of hosts requested for this Capstone Project.

Required Resources

- Packet Tracer software
- Word processing or presentation software

Step 1:   **Design the network topology.**

a.   Network equipment:

1)   Six routers

(a) Four branch routers

(b) One headquarters router

(c) One ISP router

Switches to support the LANS

b.   LANs:

1)   Two LANs per branch router

(a) Two LANs with 500 hosts

(b) One LAN serving 120 hosts

(c) One LAN with 200 hosts

(d) Two LANS with 80 hosts

(e) One LAN with 60 hosts

(f) One LAN with 30 hosts

2)   One, three-host LAN assigned to the ISP router for server connectivity (DNS, Web, and TFTP).

Step 2: Devise the network addressing scheme.

    a. Use any RFC 1918 Class B address that will accommodate the specifications listed in Step 1.

    b. ISPs LAN connection will use a different IPv4 network number to indicate Internet or telecommunications connectivity to the servers.

    c. Use VLSM efficiently to conserve addresses and allow for scalability.

    d. Apply the network address scheme to hosts and LAN and WAN interfaces.

Step 3: Implement the EIGRP routing protocol on your network

    a. Requirements:

        1) Advertise directly connected networks using the wildcard mask.

        2) Disable automatic summarization.

        3) Disable routing updates from being sent across the LAN interfaces.

        4) Implement one, named extended ACL on the network.

    b. Recommendations (choose two):

        1) Selectively implement EIGRP summary routes.

        2) Modify the EIGRP hello-timers.

        3) Modify the bandwidth of the interfaces.

Step 4: Configure basic security

    a. Restrict access to the console connection.

    b. Configure encrypted passwords.

    c. Restrict access to the VTY connections.

    d. Configure a banner warning.

Step 5: Backup the configurations of each router to the TFTP server.

Step 6: Verify the network.

    a. Validate connectivity by pinging all devices.

    b. Use five **show** commands to verify EIGRP configuration.

Step 7: Present your Capstone Project to the class and be able to answer questions from your peers and Instructor.

10.3.1.3 – OSPF Capstone Project

Objectives

- Configure basic OSPFv2 to enable internetwork communications in a small- to medium-sized IPv4 business network.

- Implement advanced OSPF features to enhance operation in a small- to medium-sized business network.

- Implement multiarea OSPF for IPv4 to enable internetwork communications in a small- to medium-sized business network.

- Configure basic OSPFv3 to enable internetwork communications in a small- to medium-sized IPv6 business network.

Scenario

Your company has made the decision to implement the OSPF routing protocol on its network. You have decided that you need to review the concepts related to OSPF in order to make a smooth transition to this protocol.

Create a network using Packet Tracer. Configure the network with these OSPF routing protocol options:

- Multiarea OSPFv2
- Single-area OSPFv3
- Bandwidth
- Cost
- Authentication
- Default routes
- DR and BDR elections for segments

Required Resources

- Packet Tracer
- Student/group-created rubric for assessment of the assignment

Step 1:   Design and build a network from scratch.

a. Your design must include three routers connected to a multi-access network in area 0 for use with IPv4.

1) Enable authentication.

2) Establish the DR and BDR using the `router id` command.

Step 2:   **Add one additional router with two connections to area 0, representing another OSPF area.**

Step 3:   **Configure the bandwidth or cost to favor one route.**

Step 4:   **Add a network containing end devices and a passive OSPF interface.**

Step 5:   **Add a route to a default network such as the Internet.**

Step 6:   **Add an IPv6 addressing scheme on the routers and configure OSPFv3.**

    a.   Enable IPv6 unicast routing.

    b.   Establish the DR and BDR using the `router id` command.

    c.   Do not configure timers, bandwidth, cost, default routes, or authentication.

Appendix A — Supplemental Labs

0.0.0.1 Lab - Initializing and Reloading a Router and Switch

Topology

Objectives

Part 1: Set Up Devices in the Network as Shown in the Topology

Part 2: Initialize the Router and Reload

Part 3: Initialize the Switch and Reload

Background / Scenario

Before starting a CCNA hands-on lab that makes use of either a Cisco router or switch, ensure that the devices in use have been erased and have no startup configurations present. Otherwise, the results of your lab may be unpredictable. This lab provides a detail procedure for initializing and reloading a Cisco router and a Cisco switch.

Note: The routers used with CCNA hands-on labs are Cisco 1941 Integrated Services Routers (ISRs) with Cisco IOS Release 15.2(4)M3 (universalk9 image). The switches used are Cisco Catalyst 2960s with Cisco IOS Release 15.0(2) (lanbasek9 image). Other routers, switches, and Cisco IOS versions can be used. Depending on the model and Cisco IOS version, the commands available and output produced might vary from what is shown in the labs.

Required Resources

- 1 Router (Cisco 1941 with Cisco IOS software, Release 15.2(4)M3 universal image or comparable)
- 1 Switch (Cisco 2960 with Cisco IOS Release 15.0(2) lanbasek9 image or comparable)
- 2 PCs (Windows 7, Vista, or XP with terminal emulation program, such as Tera Term)
- Console cables to configure the Cisco IOS devices via the console ports

Part 1:   Set Up Devices in the Network as Shown in the Topology

Step 1:   Cable the network as shown in the topology.

Attach console cables to the devices shown in the topology diagram.

Step 2:   Power on all the devices in the topology.

Wait for all devices to finish the software load process before moving to Part 2.

Part 2:   Initialize the Router and Reload

Step 1:   Connect to the router.

Console into the router and enter privileged EXEC mode using the **enable** command.

```
Router> enable
Router#
```

Step 2:   Erase the startup configuration file from NVRAM.

Type the **erase startup-config** command to remove the startup configuration from nonvolatile random-access memory (NVRAM).

```
Router# erase startup-config
Erasing the nvram filesystem will remove all configuration files! Continue? [confirm]
[OK]
Erase of nvram: complete
Router#
```

Step 3:   Reload the router.

Issue the **reload** command to remove an old configuration from memory. When prompted to Proceed with reload, press Enter to confirm the reload. Pressing any other key will abort the reload.

```
Router# reload
Proceed with reload? [confirm]


*Nov 29 18:28:09.923: %SYS-5-RELOAD: Reload requested by console. Reload Reason: Re-
load Command.
```

Note: You may receive a prompt to save the running configuration prior to reloading the router. Respond by typing **no** and press Enter.

```
System configuration has been modified. Save? [yes/no]: no
```

Step 4:   Bypass the initial configuration dialog.

After the router reloads, you are prompted to enter the initial configuration dialog. Enter **no** and press Enter.

```
Would you like to enter the initial configuration dialog? [yes/no]: no
```

Step 5:   **Terminate the autoinstall program.**

You will be prompted to terminate the autoinstall program. Respond **yes** and then press Enter.

```
Would you like to terminate autoinstall? [yes]: yes
Router>
```

Part 3:   **Initialize the Switch and Reload**

Step 1:   **Connect to the switch.**

Console into the switch and enter privileged EXEC mode.

```
Switch> enable
Switch#
```

Step 2:   **Determine if there have been any virtual local-area networks (VLANs) created.**

Use the **show flash** command to determine if any VLANs have been created on the switch.

```
Switch# show flash


Directory of flash:/

    2  -rwx        1919   Mar 1 1993 00:06:33 +00:00   private-config.text
    3  -rwx        1632   Mar 1 1993 00:06:33 +00:00   config.text
    4  -rwx       13336   Mar 1 1993 00:06:33 +00:00   multiple-fs
    5  -rwx    11607161   Mar 1 1993 02:37:06 +00:00   c2960-lanbasek9-mz.150-2.SE.bin
    6  -rwx         616   Mar 1 1993 00:07:13 +00:00   vlan.dat


32514048 bytes total (20886528 bytes free)
Switch#
```

Step 3:   **Delete the VLAN file.**

a.   If the **vlan.dat** file was found in flash, then delete this file.

```
Switch# delete vlan.dat
Delete filename [vlan.dat]?
```

You will be prompted to verify the file name. At this point, you can change the file name or just press Enter if you have entered the name correctly.

b.   When you are prompted to delete this file, press Enter to confirm the deletion. (Pressing any other key will abort the deletion.)

```
Delete flash:/vlan.dat? [confirm]
Switch#
```

Step 4:   Erase the startup configuration file.

Use the **erase startup-config** command to erase the startup configuration file from NVRAM. When you are prompted to remove the configuration file, press Enter to confirm the erase. (Pressing any other key will abort the operation.)

```
Switch# erase startup-config
Erasing the nvram filesystem will remove all configuration files! Continue? [confirm]
[OK]
Erase of nvram: complete
Switch#
```

Step 5:   Reload the switch.

Reload the switch to remove any old configuration information from memory. When you are prompted to reload the switch, press Enter to proceed with the reload. (Pressing any other key will abort the reload.)

```
Switch# reload
Proceed with reload? [confirm]
```

Note: You may receive a prompt to save the running configuration prior to reloading the switch. Type **no** and press Enter.

```
System configuration has been modified. Save? [yes/no]: no
```

Step 6:   Bypass the initial configuration dialog.

After the switch reloads, you should see a prompt to enter the initial configuration dialog. Type **no** at the prompt and press Enter.

```
Would you like to enter the initial configuration dialog? [yes/no]: no
Switch>
```

Reflection

1. Why is it necessary to erase the startup configuration before reloading the router?

____

2. You find a couple configurations issues after saving the running configuration to the startup configuration, so you make the necessary changes to fix those issues. If you were to reload the device now, what configuration would be restored to the device after the reload?

____

0.0.0.2 Lab - Installing the IPv6 Protocol and Assigning Host Addresses with Windows XP

Objectives

Part 1: Install the IPv6 Protocol on a Windows XP PC

- Install the IPv6 protocol.
- Examine IPv6 address information.

Part 2: Use the Network Shell (netsh) Utility

- Work inside the **netsh** utility.
- Configure a static IPv6 address on the local-area network (LAN) interface.
- Exit the **netsh** utility.
- Display IPv6 address information using **netsh**.
- Issue **netsh** instructions from the command prompt.

Background / Scenario

The Internet Protocol Version 6 (IPv6) is not enabled by default in Windows XP. Windows XP includes IPv6 implementation, but the IPv6 protocol must be installed. XP does not provide a way to configure IPv6 static addresses from the Graphical User Interface (GUI), so all IPv6 static address assignments must be done using the Network Shell (**netsh**) utility.

In this lab, you will install the IPv6 protocol on a Windows XP PC. You will then assign a static IPv6 address to the LAN interface.

Required Resources

1 Windows XP PC

Part 1: Install the IPv6 Protocol on a Windows XP PC

In Part 1, you will install the IPv6 protocol on a PC running Windows XP. You will also use two commands to view the IPv6 addresses assigned to the PC.

Step 1: Install the IPv6 protocol.

From the command prompt window, type **ipv6 install** to install the IPv6 protocol.

Step 2: **Examine IPv6 Address Information.**

Use the **ipconfig /all** command to view IPv6 address information.

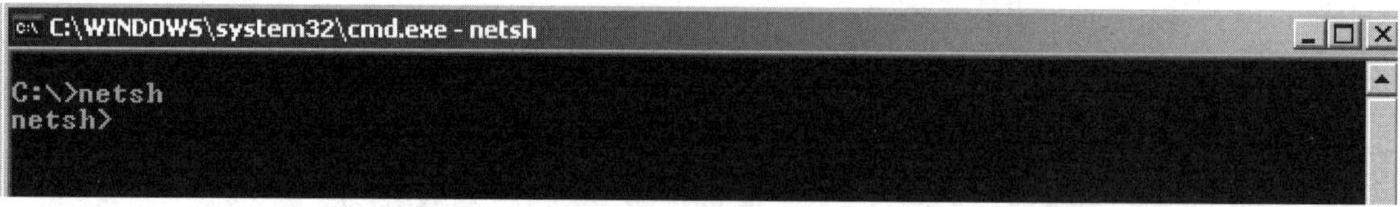

Part 2: **Use the Network Shell (netsh) Utility**

Network Shell (**netsh**) is a command-line utility included with Windows XP and newer Windows operating systems, such as Vista and Windows 7. It allows you to configure the IPv6 address information on your LAN. In Part 2, you will use the **netsh** utility to configure static IPv6 address information on a Windows XP PC LAN interface. You will also use the **netsh** utility to display the PC LAN interface IPv6 address information.

Step 1: **Work inside the Network Shell utility.**

a. From the command prompt window, type **netsh** and press Enter to start the **netsh** utility. The command prompt changes from **C:\\>** to **netsh>**.

b. At the prompt, enter a question mark (**?**) and press Enter to provide the list of available parameters.

```
netsh>?

The following commands are available:

Commands in this context:
..              - Goes up one context level.
?               - Displays a list of commands.
abort           - Discards changes made while in offline mode.
add             - Adds a configuration entry to a list of entries.
alias           - Adds an alias.
bridge          - Changes to the `netsh bridge' context.
bye             - Exits the program.
commit          - Commits changes made while in offline mode.
delete          - Deletes a configuration entry from a list of entries.
diag            - Changes to the `netsh diag' context.
dump            - Displays a configuration script.
exec            - Runs a script file.
exit            - Exits the program.
firewall        - Changes to the `netsh firewall' context.
help            - Displays a list of commands.
interface       - Changes to the `netsh interface' context.
lan             - Changes to the `netsh lan' context.
nap             - Changes to the `netsh nap' context.
offline         - Sets the current mode to offline.
online          - Sets the current mode to online.
popd            - Pops a context from the stack.
pushd           - Pushes current context on stack.
quit            - Exits the program.
ras             - Changes to the `netsh ras' context.
routing         - Changes to the `netsh routing' context.
set             - Updates configuration settings.
show            - Displays information.
unalias         - Deletes an alias.
winsock         - Changes to the `netsh winsock' context.

The following sub-contexts are available:
 bridge diag firewall interface lan nap ras routing winsock

To view help for a command, type the command, followed by a space, and then
 type ?.

netsh>
```

c.   Type **interface ?** and press Enter to provide the list of interface commands.

```
netsh>interface ?

The following commands are available:

Commands in this context:
?               - Displays a list of commands.
add             - Adds a configuration entry to a table.
delete          - Deletes a configuration entry from a table.
dump            - Displays a configuration script.
help            - Displays a list of commands.
ip              - Changes to the `netsh interface ip' context.
ipv6            - Changes to the `netsh interface ipv6' context.
portproxy       - Changes to the `netsh interface portproxy' context.
reset           - Resets information.
set             - Sets configuration information.
show            - Displays information.

The following sub-contexts are available:
 ip ipv6 portproxy

To view help for a command, type the command, followed by a space, and then
 type ?.

netsh>
```

Note: You can use the question mark (**?**) at any level in the **netsh** utility to list the available options. The up arrow can be used to scroll through previous **netsh** commands. The **netsh** utility also allows you to abbreviate commands, as long as the abbreviation is unique.

Step 2:   **Configure a static IPv6 address on the LAN interface.**

To add a static IPv6 address to the LAN interface, issue the **interface ipv6 add address** command from inside the **netsh** utility.

```
netsh>interface ipv6 add address "Local Area Connection" 2001:db8:acad:a::3
Ok.

netsh>
```

Step 3:   **Display IPv6 address information using the netsh utility.**

You can display IPv6 address information using the **interface ipv6 show address** command.

```
netsh>interface ipv6 show address
Querying active state...

Interface 5: Local Area Connection

Addr Type   DAD State   Valid Life    Pref. Life    Address
---------   ---------   ----------    ----------    -------
Manual      Preferred     infinite      infinite  2001:db8:acad:a::3
Link        Preferred     infinite      infinite  fe80::250:56ff:febe:2587

Interface 4: Teredo Tunneling Pseudo-Interface

Addr Type   DAD State   Valid Life    Pref. Life    Address
---------   ---------   ----------    ----------    -------
Link        Preferred     infinite      infinite  fe80::ffff:ffff:fffd

Interface 2: Automatic Tunneling Pseudo-Interface

Addr Type   DAD State   Valid Life    Pref. Life    Address
---------   ---------   ----------    ----------    -------
Link        Preferred     infinite      infinite  fe80::5efe:169.254.39.128

Interface 1: Loopback Pseudo-Interface

Addr Type   DAD State   Valid Life    Pref. Life    Address
---------   ---------   ----------    ----------    -------
Loopback    Preferred     infinite      infinite  ::1
Link        Preferred     infinite      infinite  fe80::1

netsh>
```

Step 4:   **Exit the netsh utility.**

Use the **exit** command to exit from the **netsh** utility.

```
netsh>exit

C:\>
```

Step 5:   **Issue netsh instructions from the command prompt.**

All **netsh** instructions can be entered from the command prompt, outside the **netsh** utility, by preceding the instruction with the **netsh** command.

```
C:\>netsh interface ipv6 show address
Querying active state...

Interface 5: Local Area Connection

Addr Type   DAD State   Valid Life   Pref. Life   Address
--------    ---------   ----------   ----------   -------------------------
Manual      Preferred      infinite     infinite 2001:db8:acad:a::3
Link        Preferred      infinite     infinite fe80::250:56ff:febe:2587

Interface 4: Teredo Tunneling Pseudo-Interface

Addr Type   DAD State   Valid Life   Pref. Life   Address
--------    ---------   ----------   ----------   -------------------------
Link        Preferred      infinite     infinite fe80::ffff:ffff:fffd

Interface 2: Automatic Tunneling Pseudo-Interface

Addr Type   DAD State   Valid Life   Pref. Life   Address
--------    ---------   ----------   ----------   -------------------------
Link        Preferred      infinite     infinite fe80::5efe:169.254.39.128

Interface 1: Loopback Pseudo-Interface

Addr Type   DAD State   Valid Life   Pref. Life   Address
--------    ---------   ----------   ----------   -------------------------
Loopback    Preferred      infinite     infinite ::1
Link        Preferred      infinite     infinite fe80::1

C:\>
```

Reflection

1. How would you renew your LAN interface address information from the **netsh** utility?

    Hint: Use the question mark (**?**) for help in obtaining the parameter sequence.

____

____